Nomads of the Mediterranean: Trade and Contact in the Bronze and Iron Ages

Culture and History of the Ancient Near East

Founding Editor

M.H.E. Weippert

Editor-in-Chief

Jonathan Stökl

Editors

Eckart Frahm
W. Randall Garr
B. Halpern
Theo P.J. van den Hout
Leslie Anne Warden
Irene J. Winter

VOLUME 112

The titles published in this series are listed at *brill.com/chan*

Michal Artzy during the Liman Tepe Excavations, Turkey
PHOTOGRAPH: AMIR YURMAN

Nomads of the Mediterranean: Trade and Contact in the Bronze and Iron Ages

Studies in Honor of Michal Artzy

Edited by

Ayelet Gilboa
Assaf Yasur-Landau

BRILL

LEIDEN | BOSTON

The Library of Congress Cataloging-in-Publication Data is available online at http://catalog.loc.gov
LC record available at http://lccn.loc.gov/2020019177

Typeface for the Latin, Greek, and Cyrillic scripts: "Brill". See and download: brill.com/brill-typeface.

ISSN 1566-2055
ISBN 978-90-04-43010-5 (hardback)
ISBN 978-90-04-43011-2 (e-book)

Copyright 2020 by Koninklijke Brill NV, Leiden, The Netherlands.
Koninklijke Brill NV incorporates the imprints Brill, Brill Hes & De Graaf, Brill Nijhoff, Brill Rodopi, Brill Sense, Hotei Publishing, mentis Verlag, Verlag Ferdinand Schöningh and Wilhelm Fink Verlag.
All rights reserved. No part of this publication may be reproduced, translated, stored in a retrieval system, or transmitted in any form or by any means, electronic, mechanical, photocopying, recording or otherwise without prior written permission from the publisher.
Authorization to photocopy items for internal or personal use is granted by Koninklijke Brill NV provided that the appropriate fees are paid directly to The Copyright Clearance Center, 222 Rosewood Drive, Suite 910, Danvers, MA 01923, USA. Fees are subject to change.

This book is printed on acid-free paper and produced in a sustainable manner.

Contents

Notes on Contributors x

Introduction: Professor Michal Artzy: A Scholarly Life by the Mediterranean 1
   Assaf Yasur-Landau and Ayelet Gilboa

Professor Michal Artzy, Curriculum Vitae 4

1 Tyre before Tyre: The Early Bronze Age Foundation 14
   María Eugenia Aubet

2 Two Imported Pottery Vessels from the Middle Euphrates to the Southern Levant and Their Contribution to the Chronology of the End of Early Bronze I and the Beginning of Early Bronze II 31
   Vladimir Wolff Avrutis and Eli Yannai

3 Burials of Domesticated Animals in the Middle Bronze Age Rampart at Tel 'Akko in Light of Archaeological Finds in the Levant and Ceremonies from the Ancient Near East 54
   Ron Beeri, Hadas Motro, Noa Gerstel-Raban, and Michal Artzy

4 "For the Wealth of the Sea Will Pass on to You": Changes in Patterns of Trade from Southern Phoenicia to Northern Judah in the Late Iron Age and Persian Periods 69
   Aaron Brody

5 Cypriot Pottery from the Second Millennium BCE at Tell Keisan in the Lower Galilee (Israel) 81
   Mariusz Burdajewicz

6 Contextualization and Typology of Ancient Island Harbors in the Mediterranean: From Natural Hazards to Anthropogenic Imprints 105
   Matthieu Giaime, Christophe Morhange, and Nick Marriner

7   The Plain of Akko Regional Survey (PARS): An Integrated Use of GIS, Photogrammetry, and LiDAR to Reconstruct Akko's Hinterland   128
    Ann E. Killebrew, Jane C. Skinner, Jamie Quartermaine, and Ragna Stidsing

8   Piracy in the Late Bronze Age Eastern Mediterranean? A Cautionary Tale   142
    A. Bernard Knapp

9   Oxhides, Buns, Bits, and Pieces: Analyzing the Ingot Cargo of the Cape Gelidonya Shipwreck   161
    Joseph W. Lehner, Emre Kuruçayırlı, and Nicolle Hirschfeld

10 The Presence of the Past: Ruin Mounds and Social Memory in Bronze and Early Iron Age Israel and Greece   177
    Joseph Maran

11 In the Footsteps of the Phoenicians in Paphos   199
    Jolanta Młynarczyk

12 Informed or at Sea: On the Maritime and Mundane in Ugaritic Tablet RS 94.2406   205
    Chris Monroe

13 A Fragmentary Small Copper Oxhide Ingot from Tell Beit Mirsim at the James L. Kelso Bible Lands Museum, Pittsburgh-Xenia Theological Seminary   221
    Cemal Pulak

14 Lévi-Strauss and the Royal Ancestor Cult in the Bronze Age Levant   247
    Marísa Ruiz-Gálvez

15 Phoenicians and Corinth   262
    Susan Sherratt

16 The Aegean-Type Pottery from Tel Nami   278
    Philipp W. Stockhammer

17 The Rag-and-Bone Trade at Enkomi: Late Cypriot Scrap Metal and the Bronze Industry   300
    Stuart Swiny

18 Sea Peoples from the Aegean: Identity, Sociopolitical Context, and Antecedents   318
    Aleydis Van de Moortel

    Archaeological Periods   337
    Index   340

Notes on Contributors

Authors

Michal Artzy
University of Haifa, Israel

María Eugenia Aubet
Pompeu Fabra University, Barcelona, Spain

Vladimir Wolff Avrutis
University of Haifa, Israel

Ron Beeri
Israel Antiquities Authority

Aaron Brody
Pacific School of Religion, Berkeley, California, USA

Mariusz Burdajewicz
University of Warsaw, Poland

Matthieu Giaime
Durham University, UK

Nicolle Hirschfeld
Trinity University, San Antonio, Texas, USA

Ann E. Killebrew
Pennsylvania State University, University Park, Pennsylvania, USA

A. Bernard Knapp
University of Glasgow, UK

Emre Kuruçayırlı
Boğaziçi University, Istanbul, Turkey

Joseph W. Lehner
The University of Sydney, Australia

Joseph Maran
University of Heidelberg, Germany

Nick Marriner
French National Centre for Scientific Research, Paris, France

Jolanta Młynarczyk
University of Warsaw, Poland

Chris Monroe
Cornell University, Ithaca, New York, USA

Christophe Morhange
Aix-Marseille University, Aix-en-Provence, France

Hadas Motro
The Hebrew University of Jerusalem, Israel

Cemal Pulak
Texas A&M University, College Station, Texas, USA

Jamie Quartermaine
Oxford University, UK

Noa Gerstel-Raban
University of Haifa, Israel

Marísa Ruiz-Gálvez
Complutense University of Madrid, Spain

Susan Sherratt
The University of Sheffield, UK

Jane C. Skinner
Pennsylvania State University, University Park, Pennsylvania, USA

Ragna Stidsing
University of Haifa, Israel

Philipp W. Stockhammer
Ludwig-Maximilians-University of Munich, Germany

Stuart Swiny
University at Albany, New York, USA

Aleydis Van de Moortel
University of Tennessee, Knoxville, Tennessee, USA

Eli Yannai
Israel Antiquities Authority

Editors

Ayelet Gilboa
University of Haifa, Israel

Assaf Yasur-Landau
University of Haifa, Israel

Manuscript Editor and Indexer

Inbal Samet
University of Haifa, Israel

INTRODUCTION

Professor Michal Artzy: A Scholarly Life by the Mediterranean

Assaf Yasur-Landau and Ayelet Gilboa

This book celebrates the long and fruitful archaeological career of Prof. Michal Artzy.

Michal's long-term research interests center on the coastal communities of the eastern Mediterranean and international trade and contact between these communities from the Bronze Age to the Persian period. Using network theory analogue, Michal's work on links and interactions has created numerous connections between scholars in Israel, Cyprus, Turkey, Greece, Europe, and the United States, to the extent that a small world has emerged: a small scholarly world looking toward the sea and the study of maritime civilizations and coastal cultures with fascination. The respect Michal has earned in this scientific community and beyond it is amply reflected in the contributions to this volume.

While it is impossible within the scope of this short introduction to summarize the many achievements of Michal in more than 50 years of academic career, we will note some landmarks:

Michal's academic career began with a BA in Rutgers University (1965), followed by an MA (1966) and Ph.D. (1972) in Brandeis University. Her dissertation research, dealing with the origin of the Bichrome pottery of the Middle and Late Bronze Ages using neutron activation analysis, was groundbreaking. She continued working on ceramic provenance during her postdoctoral research in the Lawrence Berkeley Laboratory at UC Berkeley (1975–1977).

In 1978, Michal joined the University of Haifa and taught in the Departments of Maritime Civilization and of Archaeology for more than 40 years, starting as a senior lecturer and then moving up to full professor, serving also as the head of the Leon Recanati Institute for Maritime Studies from 2011 to 2016. As a teacher, Michal supervised dozens of dissertations and theses in both departments. Currently holding a rank as Professor Emerita, Michal remains extremely active in both research and mentoring graduate students.

During the remarkable career of Michal as director of archaeological excavations, she directed or codirected excavations of no less than eight sites, both underwater and on land. The excavations of Tel Nami (1985–1997) have revealed a coastal site active in the Middle and Late Bronze Ages, with intricate international connections with Cyprus and even the Aegean area. It is a crucial site for understanding the final days of the Late Bronze Age world and its demise. The excavations at Tell Abu Hawam in the Haifa bay in 1985–1986 (directed with Jaqueline Balensi and María Dolores Herrera) and in 2001–2002 (with Shalom Yankelevitz and Uzi Ad) led to significant discoveries regarding the seafront of the site and its international connections in the Late Bronze Age and Persian period. Undoubtedly, the final publication of these pivotal excavations will become a cornerstone in the study of Bronze Age and later interactions in the eastern Mediterranean. The long-term collaboration with Ann E. Killebrew in the excavations of Tel ʿAkko, which began in 1999, extended also to innovative projects of remote sensing and geoarchaeology, exploring together with a team led by Christophe Morhange the development of the coastal landscape as well as the anchorages of ʿAkko beginning in the Bronze Age. Other land excavations codirected by Michal also demonstrate her interest in coastal landscapes, both of the Mediterranean and of the Sea of Galilee. These include Tell Keisan (2006, with Amani Abu Hamid), Tel Regev (2012 and on, with Carolina Aznar and Shalom Yankelevitz), and Kursi (2016 on, with Haim Cohen).

Michal's interest in Mediterranean archaeology did not stop at the coastline, but continued into the Mediterranean itself, with several projects of underwater archaeology. Perhaps the most significant is a decade-long (2000–2010) and very fruitful scientific collaboration with the late Hayat Erkanal of the University of Ankara in the underwater excavations at Liman Tepe/Klazomenai in Turkey. Other underwater excavations are the study of the Iron Age harbor at ʿAtlit (2006–2007, with Arad Haggi) and exploration of the ʿAkko harbor (2012, with Avner Hilman).

Michal's extremely rich scientific output is presented in the list of books and articles encompassing more than 46 years of academic hard work.

The chapters in this book relate to Michal's fields of interest:

The Near East in the Bronze Age is addressed in four papers: Vladimir Wolff Avrutis and Eli Yannai discuss two Mesopotamian vessels found in the southern Levant and their implications for Early Bronze Age chronology, and Maria Eugenia Aubet focuses on the beginning of the settlement on the island of Tyre in the Early Bronze Age. More theoretical stances are taken by Maria Ruiz-Gálvez, who examines the applicability of Lévi-Strauss's House Society Model to Mesopotamian and Levantine kingdoms in the Early–Middle Bronze Age time span; and by Joseph Maran, who explores how certain ruins in Greece and Israel may have acted as agents of collective memory as late as the Iron Age.

The Mediterranean and Mediterranean interconnections till the end of the Late Bronze Age are the focus of five papers: Matthieu Giaime, Christophe

Morhange, and Nick Marriner offer their view of environmental and anthropogenic features of Mediterranean insular harbors and anchorages. A. Bernard Knapp asks what the term "piracy" may mean in a Late Bronze Age context, if it means anything at all; and Chris Monroe, based on an Ugaritic tablet, comments on the power embedded in literacy in the Ugaritic milieu and explores the possibility that "letters could have been sent and received while at sea." Philipp W. Stockhammer studies the significance of Aegean-type ceramics at Tel Nami, excavated by Michal, in the late thirteenth/early twelfth century, and their significance for this transformative period. Aleydis Van de Moortel returns to bird-headed figureheads, feathered headdresses, and horned helmets at Medinet Habu to trace ichnographically the Aegean origins of the Sea Peoples.

Three papers discuss *Bronze Age production and trade in metals*. Cemal Pulak presents and analyzes—inert alia technologically and compositionally—a MB IIC miniature ingot from Tell Beit Mirsim, and its significance for tracing the development of copper trade in the Mediterranean. Two papers revisit different aspects of the Cape Gelidonya metal cargo. Joseph W. Lehner, Emre Kuruçayırlı, and Nicolle Hirschfeld offer their view of the ship's copper ingots, from production to consumption, while employing various analytical methods; Stuart Swiny updates his discussion of the dynamics of Late Cypriot metal scrap intended for export.

Phoenicians in the Iron Age and later periods are dealt with in three articles. Aaron Brody's point of departure is a Persian-period Phoenician mask found at Tell en-Naṣbeh in the Judean Hills, which he uses to reconstruct trade routes leading from the southern Levantine coast inland in his period. Jolanta Młynarczyk comments on several indications for a "Phoenician connection" of Paphos on western Cyprus, from the Iron Age to the Hellenistic period—commercial, religious and others. Susan Sherratt considers evidence for Phoenicians sailing through the Isthmus of Corinth and operating in the city in the Iron Age.

Finally, three papers relate to *the 'Akko Plain and 'Akko itself*. Ann E. Killebrew, Jane C. Skinner, Jamie Quartermaine, and Ragna Stidsing introduce their new survey in the 'Akko Plain, mainly from methodological and technological aspects. Ron Beeri, Hadas Motro, Noa Gerstel-Raban, and Michal Artzy present Syro-Mesopotamian ritual habits as reflected in Middle Bronze Age animal burials at 'Akko; and Mariusz Burdajewicz presents Late Cypriot ceramics at Tell Keisan, which allow insights regarding the settlement history and commercial contacts of this site in the Late Bronze Age, a period currently hardly known there.

We wish Michal many more years of joy in archaeology by the Mediterranean.

Professor Michal Artzy, Curriculum Vitae

Publications

Ph.D. Dissertation

Artzy, M.. 1972. *The Origin of the "Palestinian" Bichrome Ware*. Brandeis University, Waltham, MA. Supervisor: Ian Todd.

Authored Books

Artzy, M. 2006. *The Jatt Metal Hoard in Northern Canaanite/Phoenician and Cypriote Context* (Cuadernos de Arquelogía Mediterranean 14). Barcelona.

Artzy, M. 2007. *Los nómadas del mar* (Bellaterra Arqueologia). Barcelona (Spanish).

Ben Zeev, A., Kahanov, Y., Tresman, J., and Artzy, M. 2009. *The Ma'agan Mikhael Ship*, Vol. III: *A Reconstruction of the Hull*. Jerusalem.

Edited Book

Raban, A. 2009. *The Harbour of Sebastia (Caesarea Maritima) in Its Roman Mediterranean Context* (edited by Artzy, M., Goodman, B., and Gal, Z.) (BAR International Series 1930). Oxford.

Edited Publications of the Hatter Laboratory

Artzy, M. 2005. *Contract Archaeology Reports I* (Hatter Laboratory, Reports and Studies of the Leon Recanati Institute for Maritime Studies). Haifa.

Artzy, M. 2007. *Contract Archaeology Reports II* (Hatter Laboratory, Reports and Studies of the Leon Recanati Institute for Maritime Studies). Haifa.

Artzy, M. 2008. *Contract Archaeology Reports III* (Hatter Laboratory, Reports and Studies of the Leon Recanati Institute for Maritime Studies). Haifa.

Artzy, M. 2013. *Contract Archaeology Report IV* (Hatter Laboratory, Reports and Studies of the Leon Recanati Institute for Maritime Studies). Haifa.

Artzy, M. 2015. *Contract Archaeology Report V* (Hatter Laboratory, Reports and Studies of the Leon Recanati Institute for Maritime Studies). Haifa.

Artzy, M. 2016. *Contract Archaeology Report VI* (Hatter Laboratory, Reports and Studies of the Leon Recanati Institute for Maritime Studies). Haifa.

Articles in Refereed Journals

Artzy, M. 1976. Wheel-Made Pottery of the MC III and LC I Periods of Cyprus. *Report of the Department of Antiquities of Cyprus* 1976: 20–29.

Artzy, M. 1980. The Utilitarian Persian Storage Jar Handles. *Bulletin of the American Schools of Oriental Research* 338: 69–73.

Artzy, M. 1982. Vessel Stabilizing Stones. *Report of the Department of Antiquities of Cyprus* 1982: 37–40.

Artzy, M. 1983. Arethusa of the Tin Ingot. *Bulletin of the American Schools of Oriental Research* 251: 59–64.

Artzy, M. 1984. Unusual Late Bronze Ship Representations from Tel Akko. *Mariner's Mirror* 70: 59–64.

Artzy, M. 1987. On Boats and Sea Peoples. *Bulletin of the American Schools of Oriental Research* 266: 75–84.

Artzy, M. 1988. War/Fighting Boats in the Second Millennium BC in the Eastern Mediterranean. *Report of the Department of Antiquities of Cyprus* 1988: 181–186.

Artzy, M. 1990. Nami, Land and Sea Project. *Israel Exploration Journal* 40: .73–76.

Artzy, M. 1991. Nami Land and Sea Project, 1989. *Israel Exploration Journal* 41: 194–197.

Artzy, M. 1992. Nami, un grand port à l'âge du Bronze. *Le Monde de la Bible* 76: 42–46.

Artzy, M. 1994. Incense, Camels and Collar Rim Jars: Desert Trade Routes and Maritime Outlets in the 2nd Millennium. *Oxford Journal of Archaeology* 13: 121–147.

Artzy, M. 2003. Mariners and Their Boats at the End of the Late Bronze and the Beginning of the Iron Age Eastern Mediterranean. *Tel Aviv* 30: 232–246.

Artzy, M. 2006. The Carmel Coast during the 2nd part of the Late Bronze Age: A Center for Eastern Mediterranean Transshipping. *Bulletin of the American Schools of Oriental Research* 343: 45–64.

Artzy, M. 2013. The Importance of Anchorages of the Carmel Coast in the Trade Networks during the Late Bronze period. *Michmanim* 24: 7–24.

Artzy, M. 2015. What Is in a Name? 'Akko—Ptolemais—'Akka—Acre. *Complutum* 26: 201–212.

Artzy, M. 2018. From Akko/Acco to Beit She'an/Beth Shan in the Late Bronze Age. *Egypt and the Levant* 28: 85–98.

Artzy, M. and Asaro, F. 1979. The Origin of the Tell el-Yahudiyah Ware in Cyprus. *Report of the Department of Antiquities of Cyprus* 1979: 135–150.

Artzy, M. and Hillel, D. 1988. On Soil Salinity in Southern Mesopotamia: A Defense of the Theory of Progressive Salinization. *Geoarchaeology* 3: 235–238.

Artzy, M. and Marcus, E, 1991. The MBIIA Coastal Settlement at Tel Nami. *Michmanim* 5: 5*–16*.

Artzy, M. and Schiøler, T. 1984–1986. Daemningen ved Kibbuttzen Ma'agan Michael i Israel. *Klassisk Arkaeologiske Studier, Museum Tusculanum* 56: 331–336 (Danish).

Artzy, M. and Sheizaf, N. 2019. Clay Figurines Caches Found Underwater: A Phoenician ex voto Practice? *Complutum* 30(1): 155–163.

Artzy, M., Perlman, I., and Asaro, F. 1973. The Origin of the "Palestinian" Bichrome Ware. *Journal of the American Oriental Society* 93: 446–461.

Artzy, M., Perlman, I., and Asaro, F. 1975. The Tel Nagila Krater as a Cypriote Product. *Israel Exploration Journal* 25: 129–134.

Artzy, M., Perlman, I., and Asaro, F. 1976. Alasiya of the Amarna Letters. *Journal of Near Eastern Studies* 35: 129–134.

Artzy, M., Perlman, I., and Asaro, F. 1978. Imported and Local Bichrome Ware in Megiddo. *Levant* 10: 99–111.

Artzy, M., Perlman, I., and Asaro, F. 1981. Cypriote Imports at Ras Shamra. *Israel Exploration Journal* 31: 37–47.

Aznar Sánchez, C.A., López Rosendo, E., Aguilera Romojaro, M.J., Martin Garcia, J.M., Carrillo Pineda, A.P., Yankelevitz, S., and Artzy, M. 2017. El Periodo persa en la Ilanura sur de Akko. *Aula Orientalis* 35(1): 5–41.

Galili, E., Artzy, M., and Shavit, J. 1994. Reconsidering Byblian and Egyptian Stone Anchors Using Numeral Methods: New Finds from the Israeli Coast. *International Journal of Nautical Archaeology* 23: 93–107.

Galili, E., Shmueli, N., and Artzy, M. 1986. Bronze Age Ship's Cargo of Copper and Tin. *International Journal of Nautical Archaeology* 15: 25–37.

Giaime, M., Morhange, C., Marriner, N., Lopez-Cadavid, G.I., and Artzy, M. 2018. Geoarchaeological Investigations at Akko, Israel: New Insights into Landscape Changes and Related Anchorage Locations since the Bronze Age. *Journal of Archaeological Science Reports* 7: 71–81.

Goodman, B.E., Reinhardt, E., Dey, H.W., Boyce, J., Schwarcz, M., Sahoglu, V., Erkanal, H., and Artzy, M. 2009. A Multi-proxy Geoarchaeological Study Redefines Understanding of the Paleocoastlines and Ancient Harbors of Liman Tepe (Iskele, Turkey) *Terra Nova* 29: 97–104.

Goodman, B.E., Reinhardt, E., Dey, H.W., Boyce, J., Schwarcz, M., Sahoglu, V., Erkanal, H., and Artzy, M. 2008. Evidence for Holocene Marine Transgression and Shoreline Progradation due to Barrier Development in Iskele, Bay of Izmir, Turkey. *Journal of Coastal Research* 24(5): 1269–1280.

Hadad, E. and Artzy, M. 2011. Ship Graffiti in Burial Cave 557 at Maresha. *Near Eastern Archaeology* 74(4): 236–240.

Haddad, E., Stern, I., and Artzy, M. 2018. Ship Graffiti in Maresha Subterranean Complex 89. *Near Eastern Archaeology* 81(2): 120–127.

Haggi, A. and Artzy, M. 2007. The Atlit Harbor in Northern Canaanite/Phoenician Context. *Near Eastern Archaeology* 70(2): 75–85.

Haggi, A. and Artzy, M. 2009. On the Origin of Marine "Pier and Rubble" Building Technique. *Eretz-Israel* 29: 176–183 (Hebrew).

Kaniewski, D., Van Campo, E., Morhange, C., Guiot, J., Zviely, D., Le Burel, S., Otto, S., and Artzy, M. 2014. Vulnerability of Mediterranean Ecosystems to Long-Term Changes along the Coast of Israel. *PLOS One* 9(7): 1–9.

Kaniewski, D., Van Campo, E., Morhange, C., Guiot, J., Zviely, D., Shaked, I., and Artzy, M. 2013. Urban Impact on Mediterranean Coastal Environments. *Nature Scientific Reports* 3(3540): 1–5.

Kislev, M., Artzy, M., and Marcus, E. 1993. Import of an Aegean Food Plant to a Middle Bronze IIA Coastal Site in Israel. *Levant* 26: 145–154.

Lev-Yadun, S., Artzy, M., Marcus, E., and Stidsing, R. 1996. Wood Remains from Tel Nami, a Middle Bronze IIA and Late Bronze IIB Port, Local Exploitation of Trees and Levantine Cedar Trade. *Economic Botany* 50: 310–317.

Marcus, E. and Artzy, M. 1995. An MB IIA Scarab-Seal Impressed "Loomweight" from Tel Nami. *Israel Exploration Journal* 45: 136–149.

Misgav, H., Artzy, M., and Cohen, H. 2016. The Synagogue Inscriptions from Kursi. *Journal of Jesus Movement in Jewish Settings* 3: 167–169.

Morhange, C., Giaime, M., Marriner, N., Abu Hamid, A., Honnorat, A., Kaniewski, D., Magnin, F., Portov, A.V., Wente, J., Zviely D., and Artzy, M. 2016. Geoarchaeological Evolution of Tel Akko's Ancient Harbor. *Journal of Archaeological Science: Reports* 7: 71–81.

Raban, A. and Artzy, M. 1982. Dor Yam, (Sea and Coastal Dor). *Israel Exploration Journal* 32: 145–147.

Sharp, C. and Artzy, M. 2017. Nami's Middle Bronze Age Suburb: The Coastal Settlement at Site 104–106. *Palestine Exploration Quarterly* 149: 254–273.

Votruba, G.F. and Artzy, M. 2016. An Archaic Anchor Arm from Liman Tepe/Klazomenai, Turkey. *International Journal of Nautical Archaeology* 45(2): 1–7.

Votruba, G.F., Artzy, M., and Erkanal, H. 2016. A Set Archaic Anchor Arm Exposed within *P. Oceanica* Matte at Klazomenai/Liman Tepe, Turkey: A Contribution for Understanding Marine Stratigraphy. *Journal of Field Archaeology* 41(6): 1–13.

Articles or Chapters in Refereed Books

Artzy, M. 1973. The Late Bronze "Palestinian" Bichrome Ware in Its Cypriote Context. In: Hoffner, H.A. Jr., ed. *Orient and Occident: Essays Presented to Cyrus H. Gordon on the Occasion of His Sixty-Fifth Birthday* (Alter Orient und Altes Testament 22); Kevelaer–Neukirchen-Vluyn: 9–16.

Artzy, M. 1984. Havfolkene og deres Skibe. In: Frandsen P.J. and Læssøe, J., eds. *Mellem Nilen og Tigris*. Copenhagen: 29–39.

Artzy, M. 1985. Supply and Demand: A Study of Second Millennium Trade of Cypriote Ceramics in the Levant. In: Knapp, A.B. and Stech, T., eds. *Prehistoric Production and Exchange* (UCLA Institute of Archaeology Monograph XXV). Los Angeles: 93–99.

Artzy, M. 1987. On the Storage and Shipment of Olive Oil in Antiquity In: Hetzer, M. and Eitam, D., eds. *Olive Oil in Antiquity*. Haifa: 45–48.

Artzy, M. 1991. Conical Cups and Pumice, Aegean Cult at Tel Nami, Israel. In: Laffineur, R. and Basch, L., eds. *Thalassa. L'Égée préhistorique et la mer* (Aegaeum 7) Liège: 203–206.

Artzy, M. 1992. Akko and the Ships of the "Sea Peoples." In: Helzer, M., Segal, A., and Kaufman, D. eds. *Studies in the Archaeology and History of Ancient Israel in Honour of M. Dothan*. Haifa: 133–140 (Hebrew).

Artzy, M. 1992. The "Sea Peoples" in Egypt and Israel. In: Qashtan, N., ed. *Maritime Holy Land: Mediterranean Civilizations in Ancient Israel from the Bronze Age to the Crusaders*. Haifa: 33–38.

Artzy, M. 1994. Late Bronze Burial Practices at Tel Nami. In: Singer, I., ed. *Graves and Burial Practices in Israel in the Ancient Period*. Jerusalem: 91–96 (Hebrew).

Artzy, M. 1995. Nami: A Second Millennium International Maritime Trading Center in the Mediterranean. In: Gitin, S., ed. *Recent Discoveries in Israel: A View to the West* (American Institute of Archaeology Series, Colloquia and Papers 1). New York: 17–39.

Artzy, M. 1997. Nomads of the Sea In: Swiny, S., Hohlfelder, R.L., and Swiny, H.W., eds. *Res Maritimae: Cyprus and the Eastern Mediterranean, from Prehistory to Late Antiquity* (American Schools of Oriental Research Archaeological Reports, CAARI Monograph Series). Atlanta: 1–15.

Artzy, M. 1998. Routes Trade, Boats, and "Nomads of the Sea." In: Stern, E., Mazar, A., and Gitin, S., eds. *Mediterranean Peoples in Transition: Papers Dedicated to Trude Dothan*. Jerusalem: 439–448.

Artzy, M. 2000. Cult and Recycling of Metal at the End of the Late Bronze. In: Åstöm, P. and Sürenhagen, D., eds. *Festschrift in Honour of Prof. H-G. Buchholz*. Jonsered: 27–32.

Artzy, M. 2001. A Study of the Cypriot Bichrome Ware: Past, Present and Future. In: Åström, P., ed. *The Chronologies of Basering and Bichrome Wares*. Stockholm: 157–174.

Artzy, M. 2001. The Aegean, Cyprus, Levant and the Bichrome Ware: Eastern Mediterranean Middle Bronze Age *Koine*? In: Oren, E. and Ahituv, S., eds. *Aharon Kempinski Memorial Volume* (Be'er Sheva 15). Be'er Sheva: 1–20.

Artzy, M. 2001. White Slip Ware for Export? The Economics of Production. In: Karageorghis, V., ed. *The White Slip Ware of Late Bronze Age Cyprus*. Vienna: 107–116.

Artzy, M. 2003. Bronze Trade in the Late Bronze–Early Iron Period: Tel Masos and Tel Kinrot in Eastern Mediterranean Context. Hertog, C. den, Hübner, U., Münger, S., eds *Studien zur Archaologie Paläastinas/Israels, Festschrift fur Volkmar Fritz zum 65 Geburtstag* (Alter Orient altes Testament 302). Münster: 15–23.

Artzy, M. 2004. Results of Neutron Activation Analysis of Selected Amarna Tablets. In: Goren, Y., Finklelstein, Y., and Na'aman, N. *Inscribed in Clay: Provenance Studies of the Amarna Tablets and Other Ancient Near Eastern Texts* (Monograph Series of the Sonia and Marco Nadler Institute of Archaeology 23). Tel Aviv: 332–333.

Artzy, M. 2006. "Filling in" the Void: Observations on Habitation Pattern at the End of the Late Bronze at Tel Akko. In: Miroschedji, P. de and Maeir, A., eds. *I Will Tell Secret Things from Long Ago" (Abiah Chidot Minei-Kedem—Ps 78:2b): Archaeological and Historical Studies in Honor of Amihai Mazar on the Occasion of His Sixtieth Birthday* Winona Lake, IN: 115–122.

Artzy, M. 2007. On the Origin(s) of the Red and White Lustrous Wheel-Made Wares. In: Hein, I., ed. *The Lustrous Wares of the Late Bronze Cyprus and the Eastern Mediterranean*. Vienna: 11–18.

Artzy, M. 2007. Tell Abu Hawam: News from the Late Bronze Age. In: Bietak, M. and Czerny, E., eds. *The Synchronisation of Civilisations in the Eastern Mediterranean in the Second Millennium B.C. III*. Vienna: 357–366.

Artzy, M. 2008. Die Küste des Karmelgebirges, Zypern und die Ägäis: Internationaler Handel in der Späten Bronzezeit (14.–frühes 12 Jh. v. Chr). In: (no editor) *Austausch von Gütern, Ideen und Technologien in der Ägäis und im östlichen Mittelmeer. ; 19.–21.05.2006 in Ohlstadt/Obb. Deutschland*. Weilheim i. OB: 131–144.

Artzy, M. 2012. Continuation and Change in the 13th–10th Centuries BCE: Bronze Working *Koine*? In: Galil, G., Gilboa, A., Maeir, A.M., and Kahn, D., eds. *The Ancient Near East in the 12th–10th Centuries BCE* (Alter Orient und Altes Testament Band 392) Münster: 27–42.

Artzy, M. 2013. On the Other "Sea Peoples." In: Killebrew, A.E. and Lehmann, G., eds. *The Philistines and Other "Sea Peoples" in Text and Archaeology*. Atlanta: 329–344.

Artzy, M. 2016. Distributers and Shippers: Cyprus and the Late Bronze II Tell Abu Hawam Anchorage. In: Demeticha, S. and Knapp, A.B., eds. *Maritime Transport Containers in the Bronze–Iron Age Aegean and Eastern Mediterranean*. Uppsala: 97–110.

Artzy, M. and Beeri, R. 2006. Mended Storage Jars and Colored Plaster: A Middle Bronze IIA Practice? In: Czerny, E., Hein, I., Hunger, H., Melman, D., and Schwab, A., eds. *Timelines Studies in Honour of Manfred Bietak* (Orientalia Lovaniensia Analecta 149). Leuven: 325–330.

Artzy, M. and Lyon, J. 2003. The Ceramics from the Ma'agan Mikhael Shipwreck. In: Linder, E., Kahanov, Y., and Black, E., eds. *The Ma'agan Mikhael Ship: The Recovery of a 2400-Year Old Merchantman*, Vol. I. Jerusalem: 183–202.

Artzy, M. and Marcus, E. 1992. Stratified Cypriote Pottery in MBIIA Context at Tel Nami. In: Ioannides, G.C., ed. *Essays in Honour of Vassos Karageorghis*. Nicosia: 103–110.

Artzy, M. and Quartermaine, J. 2014. How and When Did Tel Akko Get Its Unusual Banana Shape? In: Galanakis, Y., Wilkinson, T., and Bennet, J., eds. *ΑΘΥΡΜΑΤΑ: Critical*

Essays on the Archaeology of the Eastern Mediterranean in Honour of E. Susan Sherratt. Oxford: 11–22.

Artzy, M. and Zagorski, S. 2012. Cypriot "Mycenaean" IIB Imported to the Levant. In: Ahituv, S., Gruber, M., Lehmann, G., and Talshir, Z., eds. *All the Wisdom of the East: Studies in Near Eastern Archaeology and History in Honor of Eliezer D. Oren*, Göttingen: 1–12.

Artzy, M., Mommsen, H., and Asaro, F. 2004. Arzawa, Neutron Activation Analysis of EA 3. In: Goren, Y., Finkelstein, Y., and Na'aman, N. *Inscribed in Clay: Provenance Studies of the Amarna Tablets and Other Ancient Near Eastern Texts* (Monograph Series of the Sonia and Marco Nadler Institute of Archaeology 23). Tel Aviv: 45–47.

Artzy, M., Stidsing, R., and Salmon, Y. 2013. Market Strategy—Cypriot Bichrome Wheel-Made Ware for Export. In: Knapp, A.B., Webb, J.M., and McCarthy, A., eds. *J.R.B. Stewart: An Archaeological Legacy* (Studies in Mediterranean Archaeology 139). Uppsala: 175–184.

Basch, L. and Artzy, M. 1986. The Kition Ship Graffiti. In: Karageorghis, V. and Demas, M., eds. *Kition V*: 322–336.

Martin Garcia, J.M. and Artzy, M. 2018. Cultural Transformations Shaping the End of the Late Bronze Age in the Levant. In: Horejs, B., Schwall, D., Müller, V., Luciani, M., Ritter, M., Guidetti, M., Salisbury, R.B., Höflmayer, F., and Bürge, T., eds. *Proceedings of the 10th International Congress on the Archaeology of the Ancient Near East*, Vol 1. Vienna: 97–106.

Westerdahl, C. and Artzy, M. 2002. The Fire of Tjelvar: Gutnic Symbols on Picture-Stones. In: Gheorghiu, D., ed. *Fire in Archaeology* (BAR International Series 1089). Oxford: 147–154.

Yellin, J. and Artzy, M. 2004. Provenience Study of Selected Pottery from the Ma'agan Mikha'el Shipwreck. In: Tresman, J., ed. *The Ma'agan Mikhael Ship: The Recovery of a 2400-Year Old Merchantman*, Vol. II. Jerusalem: 221–238.

Conference Proceedings

Artzy, M. 1974. Neutron Activation Analysis and the Cypriote Potter, or: Who Said the Canaanites Had an Advanced Ceramic Tradition? In: (no editor) *Proceedings of the International Workshop*. Hirschegg: 446–461.

Artzy, M. 1976. An Archaeologist Looks at X-Ray Fluorescence vs. Neutron Activation Analysis. *Proceedings of the Meeting on Application of Science to Medieval Ceramics 1975* (Lawrence Berkeley Laboratory Lab Report 5017). Berkeley. https://inis.iaea.org/collection/NCLCollectionStore/_Public/08/289/8289109.pdf?r=1&r=1.

Artzy, M. 1985. Merchandize and Merchantmen: On ships and Shipping in the Late Bronze Age. In: Papadopoulos, T. and Chatzestylly, S., eds. *Acts of the 2nd International Congress of Cypriote Studies*. Nicosia: 135–140.

Artzy, M. 1986. Fortress and Settlement: Anchorage System during the 2nd Millennium Tel Nami? In: Raban, A. and Linder, E., eds. *Cities in the Sea, Past and Present: 1st International Symposium on Harbours and Coastal Topography*. Haifa: 14-17.

Artzy, M. 1993. Anchorage Systems of the Second Millennium BC at Tel Nami. In: Tzalas, H.E., ed. *3rd International Symposium on Ship Construction in Antiquity 1989* (TROPIS III). Athens: 23-30.

Artzy, M. 1993. The International Bronze Age Anchorage Site at Tel Nami. *Proceedings of the Second International Congress on Biblical Archaeology, 1991*. Jerusalem: 632-639.

Artzy, M. 1999. Carved Ship Graffiti—an Ancient Ritual? In: Tzalas, H.E., ed. *5th International Symposium on Ship Construction in Antiquity* (TROPIS V). Athens: 21-30.

Artzy, M. 2000. The Continuation of Cypriote "Sea-Desert" Trade Involvement in the 12th Century BC. In: Ioannide, G.K. and Chatzestylle, S.A., eds. *Proceedings of the 3rd International Congress of Cypriot Studies, April 16-20, 1996*. Nicosia: 445-453.

Artzy, M. 2001. The Medinet Habu Boat Depictions: Can We Trust Ramses III? In: Tzalas, H.E., ed. *6th International Symposium on Ship Construction in Antiquity* (TROPIS VI). Athens: 35-44.

Artzy, M. 2002. Third Millennium Boat Graffito from Megiddo? In: Tzalas, H.E., ed. *7th International Symposium on Ship Construction in Antiquity* (TROPIS VII). Athens: 21-28.

Artzy, M. 2005. *Emporia* on the Carmel Coast? Tel Akko, Tell Abu Hawam and Tel Nami of the Late Bronze Age. In: Laffineur, R. and Greco, E., eds. *EMPORIA: Aegeans in the Eastern Mediterranean* (Aegaeum 25, Vol. I). Liège: 355-362.

Erkanal, H. and Artzy, M. 2001. 2000 Yili Liman Tepe Kazi Calismalari. In: (no editor) *Kazi Sonuclari Toplantisi*, Vol. 1. Ankara: 375-388.

Erkanal, H., Artzy, M., and Kouka, O. 2002. 2001 Yılı Liman Tepe Kazilari. 24. In: (no editor) *Kazi Sonuclari Toplntisi*, Vol. 1. Ankara: 423-436.

Erkanal, H., Artzy, M., and Kouka, O. 2003. 2002 Yılı Liman Tepe Kazilari. 24. In: (no editor) *Kazi Sonuclari Toplntisi*, Vol. 2. Ankara: 165-178.

Galili, E. and Artzy, M. 1996. Reconsidering Byblian and Egyptian Stone Anchors: New Finds from the Israeli Coast. In: Tzalas, H.E., ed. *4th International Symposium on Ship Construction in Antiquity 1991* (TROPIS IV). Athens: 199-211.

Other Scientific Publications

Artzy, M. 1973. Review of K.M. Kenyon's "Palestine in the Time of the Eighteenth Dynasty." *Journal of the American Oriental Society* 93: 173.

Artzy, M. 1986. Akko In: Hachlili, R. *Mound and Sea, Akko and Caesarea Trading Centers* (exhibition catalogue, Hecht Museum). Haifa.

Artzy, M. 1989. Tel Nami. *Hadashot Arkheologiyot* 94: 17–20.
Artzy, M. 1990. Pomegranate Scepters and Incense Stand with Pomegranates Found in Priest's Grave. *Biblical Archaeology Review* 16(1): 73–76.
Artzy, M. 1991. The Bronze Age Anchorage Site of Tel Nami. *Qadmoniyot* 24: 31–38 (Hebrew).
Artzy, M. 1993. Nami 1989–1991. *Hadashot Arkheologiyot* 99: 21–24 (Hebrew).
Artzy, M. and Beeri, R., 2010. Tel Akko. In: Killebrew, A. and Raz-Romeo, V., eds. *One Thousand Nights and Days Akko through the Ages* (exhibition catalog, Hecht Museum, University of Haifa). Haifa: 15–14.
Artzy, M., Cohen, H., Meir, E., and Misgav, H. 2019. The Kursi Beach Excavations: The Synagogue and the Inscription Found in It *Qadmoniyot* 157: 51–57 (Hebrew).
Khalilieh, H.S. and Artzy, M. 2007. Ramla's Urban Plan as Reflected in Primary Arabic Sources. *Contract Archaeology Reports* 11 (Institute for Maritime Studies, University of Haifa). Haifa: 5–11.
Zemer, A., Cohen, O., and Artzy, M. 2012. *A Treasure of Cultic Vessels—Tel Qashish, 13th Century BCE* (exhibition catalog, National Maritime Museum). Haifa.

Entries in Encyclopedias and Dictionaries

Artzy, M. 1993. Tel Nami. In: Stern, E., ed. *The New Encyclopedia of Archaeological Excavations in the Holy Land*. New York: 1095–1098.
Artzy, M. 2008. Tel Nami 1992/97 Excavations. In: Stern, E., Geva, H., and Paris, A., eds. *The New Encyclopedia of Archaeological Excavations in the Holy Land*, Vol. 5 (Supplementary volume). Jerusalem: 1971–1972.
Artzy, M. 2008. Tell Abu Hawam 2001/2 Excavations. In: Stern, E., Geva, H., and Paris, A., eds. *The New Encyclopedia of Archaeological Excavations in the Holy Land*, Vol. 5 (Supplementary volume). Jerusalem: 1553–1554.
Balensi, J., Artzy, M., and Herrera, M.D. 1993. Tell Abu Hawam. In: Stern, E., ed. *The New Encyclopedia of Archaeological Excavations in the Holy Land*. New York: 7–14.

Newsletter Articles

Artzy, M. 1989. Tel Nami, Land and Sea Regional Project, 1988. *CMS News* 1989: 9–10.
Artzy, M. 1990. Tel Nami, Land and Sea Regional Project, 1989. *CMS News* 1990: 1–2.
Artzy, M. 1991. Nami, Regional Project, 1990. *CMS News* 1991: 10–12.
Artzy, M. 1991. Nami: Eight Years Later. *CMS News* 1991: 9–12.
Artzy, M. 1992. Tel Nami Regional Project, 1991. *CMS News* 1992: 1–2.
Artzy, M. 1994. On Boats, on Rocks and on "Nomads of the Sea." *CMS News* 1994: 1–2.

Artzy, M. 1998. 1998 Study Tour to Turkey. *CMS News* 1998: 23–24.
Artzy, M. 1998. On Going Research Projects: Tel Nami Tell Abu Hawam, Tel Akko and Recycling, Hoarding and Trade in Bronze in the 13th–11th Centuries BCE. *CMS News* 1998: 25–26.
Artzy, M. 1999. Tel Akko. *CMS News* 1999: 3–4.
Artzy, M. 2000. Ankara-Haifa Joint University Project at Liman Tepe, 2000. *RIMS News* 2000: 3–5.
Artzy, M. 2001. Liman Tepe 2001. *RIMS News* 2001: 3–4.
Artzy, M. 2003. Tell Abu Hawam. *RIMS News* 2002–2003: 19–21.
Artzy, M. 2003. Liman Tepe 2002. *RIMS News* 2002–2003: 21–25.
Artzy, M. 2004. The Underwater Project at Liman Tepe, Summer 2003. *RIMS News* 2004: 17–21.
Artzy, M. 2006. On Birds and the Sea. *RIMS News* 2006: 10–13.
Artzy, M. 2009. Liman Tepe Underwater Excavations: A Retrospective. *RIMS News* 2009: 11–15.
Artzy, M. 2011. Return to Tel Akko, Its Anchorages, Harbor and Surroundings. *RIMS News* 2011: 5–14.
Artzy, M. 2012. Akko Underwater Excavations Report of the 2012 Season: Looking for the Phoenician Harbor *RIMS News* 2012: 10–13.

CHAPTER 1

Tyre before Tyre: The Early Bronze Age Foundation

María Eugenia Aubet

I would like to express herewith my friendship as well as my personal and scientific admiration for Michal Artzy.

1   The Origins of the Settlement in the Archaeological Record

1.1   *Introduction*

Until 2010 the Tyre Project had focused exclusively on the excavation of the Iron Age Phoenician necropolis at al-Bass (Aubet 2010; Aubet, Núñez, and Trellisó 2014, 2016). In 2014, the Direction Générale des Antiquités du Liban (DGA) charged us with opening a new excavation area in the central part of the ancient island (Fig. 1.1a), with the goal of exposing a significant segment of the Phoenician city.[1]

Within the boundaries of Tyre's archaeological park, located in the middle of the ancient island, the density of monumental remains from Ottoman,

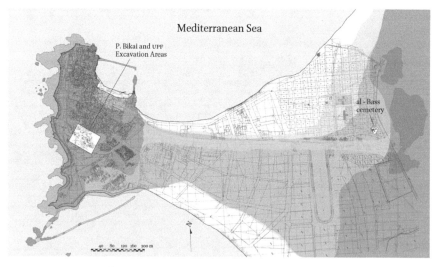

FIGURE 1.1A   Map of Tyre with location of the excavation areas

---

1   The excavations were directed by Francisco J. Núñez, Ali Badawi, and the present author.

medieval, Byzantine, Roman, and Hellenistic times make it extraordinarily difficult to access the pre-Roman occupational strata. For this reason, in 2014 we decided to open a large excavation area of 30 × 10 m (Area A) (Figs. 1.1b and 1.2) in the vicinity of the deep sounding that Patricia Bikai made in 1973–1974, adjacent to a modern road that rings the island. Area A was situated in one of the few places where the archaeological remains uncovered by Bikai all but guaranteed the presence of Iron Age occupational levels close to the surface. We followed the same north–south oriented grid used during the 1973–1974 excavations and, although the density of structures from various periods made it difficult to identify the exact location of the earlier excavations, the area we selected turned out to be close to the mark. During the 2016 campaign, upon enlarging Area A to the north into Areas 1–4, we encountered an area briefly excavated by Maurice Chéhab, in which the original 4 × 4 m squares grid system was still visible (Figs. 1.1b and 1.2).

The 2014 excavations in Area A were located in one of the central and most elevated parts of the ancient island—at 5.92 m above sea level—which we called the Acropolis. Area A is also about 100 m to the west of the medieval enclosure of the Crusader Cathedral. Among the structures identified in 2014, of particular interest were the remains of an Ottoman house (still inhabited in the eighteenth and nineteenth centuries) and a partly-preserved monumental ashlar structure of Persian or Hellenistic date.

1.2   Chéhab's Sounding (Area 1)

During the months of May and June in 2014, the limits of Area A were expanded to the north of the Ottoman structure mentioned above, in keeping with the goal of obtaining wide exposure. Upon clearing away the brush from the area, however, we found the remains of a large stratigraphic sounding measuring 8 × 8 m, which is not mentioned in the literature (Fig. 1.2: Chéhab's sounding). Signs of it can be seen in aerial photographs taken in the 1960s by Emir Maurice Chéhab (Jidejian 1969; Chéhab 1972), indicating that the sounding was carried out before Bikai's excavations. Some witnesses suggest the possibility

FIGURE 1.1B   The excavation areas in 2014–2016

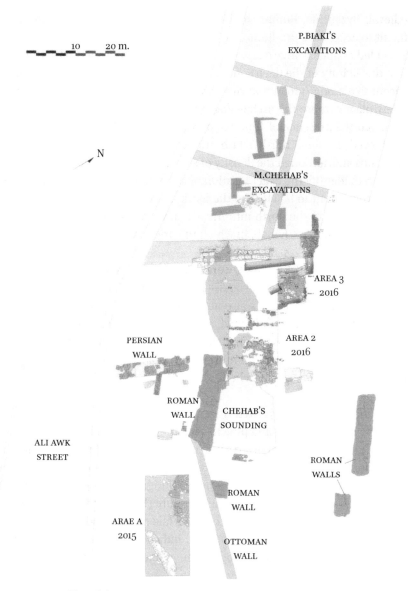

FIGURE 1.2   Plan of the excavation areas in 2014–2016

that this sounding was made in 1967–68 by Chéhab himself or by Michel Chami, Chéhab's assistant at the DGA. Either way, it is clear that the findings from this sounding served as a reference when, in 1972, Chéhab entrusted Bikai with the nearby excavations.

Despite the fact that the sounding was very poorly preserved and obstructed by collapses and recent disturbances—it had served as a dump and weapons cache during the civil war (1975–1990)—it was possible to reconstruct its outer limits and original north–south orientation. Given the sounding's characteristics, which clearly indicate the supervision of a professional archaeologist, it seemed judicious, in the context of our first campaign of excavations on the island, to obtain a partial record of the sounding's stratigraphic sequence from the surface (4.98 m above sea level), taking advantage of the window opened by a preceding excavation.[2]

A careful cleaning of the sounding's western section revealed interesting vertical stratigraphy, some 3.23 m high, which spans occupational layers dating from the origins of the city all the way to the late Iron Age (Fig. 1.3). In other words, the western section of the Chéhab sounding reveals the complete stratigraphy for pre-classical Tyre. A small quantity of ceramic and organic

FIGURE 1.3   Chéhab's sounding, 2014; western section

---

2 The team members in the 2014 season were Antonio Esteban, Michal Krueger, Isabel Muntalt, Mohamed El Mhassani, Barbara Mura, and Ida Oggiano.

samples was collected from each stratum during cleaning, revealing a very complex occupational sequence. The following comments focus exclusively on the deepest levels of the old sounding from the 1960s and on a preliminary interpretation of the finds mentioned above. These observations are limited, of course, by the fact that they are based on a small archaeological sample that was not obtained through systematic excavation.

Overall, the structure and features of Chéhab's sounding provide yet another confirmation of the rigor and clarity of Bikai's assessment of Tyre's stratigraphy.

1.3 The First Tyre

Given the limitations of space and the risk of collapse, the cleaning of the sounding's section did not proceed all the way to bedrock, although it did reach a depth of 1.75 m above sea level. The deepest stratum exposed, about half a meter in thickness, contained abundant ashes, charcoal bits, and large, loose stones, in addition to a fine layer of sand. These features suggest an identification as Bikai's Stratum XX (1978: 6–7), which is a destruction horizon following the important occupational horizon of Stratum XXI. Over this lay a thicker layer (0.5–0.7 m) consisting of a collapse of large stones, wall fragments, ashes, and charcoal, which yielded comb-incised ware as well as abundant stone tools (Fig. 1.4). Given the morphology of the artifacts and the features of the layer itself, this level can be confidently identified as Bikai's Stratum XIX.

Immediately above these alternating unequal early layers attesting human frequentation, destruction, and abandonment, there is a substantial accumulation of sterile sand of eolic origin nearly 1 m thick—spanning 3.39 to 2.63 m above sea level (= Bikai's Stratum XVIII). It corresponds to an extended period of abandonment of the island, which appears to span the totality of the Middle Bronze Age (ca. 2000–1600 BCE). Over this we find the first Late Bronze Age levels (Strata XVII–XVI), which represent the first permanent settlement of the island (Bikai 1978: 64–65).

The lowest levels identified in the western section of Chéhab's sounding thus correspond to Strata XX and XIX in the 1973–1974 sequence, dated to the Early Bronze Age IV (ca. 2500–2000 BCE) (Bikai 1978: 6–7). These deposits are significant because the same levels were discovered also in the 1970s excavations, lying over a considerable ash destruction layer (Strata XXII–XXI), some 0.15 m thick, which sealed the remains of a large rectangular structure, of which one corner was exposed (Fig. 1.4). This structure was built very close to bedrock on the highest point of the reef, and was found to have thick stone walls nearly 1 m wide, a plaster floor, and, as in Byblos, stone pillar bases presumably meant to support wooden columns. Bikai estimated that this exceptional building,

FIGURE 1.4 Early Bronze Age building, 1973–1974
PHOTO COURTESY OF P.M. BIKAI

which she dated to the end of the Early Bronze Age III, a little before the midthird millennium BCE, might have reached a length of 15 m (Bikai 1978: 5; 1992: 67; Bikai and Bikai 1987: 74–75).

Based on stratigraphic and architectural evidence, Bikai subdivided the Early Bronze Age strata in Tyre into three subphases: (a) a first occupational phase just above bedrock (Strata XXVII–XXIII); (b) the aforementioned structure (Strata XXII–XXI); and (c) a period following the abandonment of the structure (Strata XX–XIX). Following this, the second major period at the site is the occupational break attested by the sterile sand layer of Stratum XVIII (Middle Bronze Age) (Bikai 1978: 14).

Clearly, our section in Chéhab's sounding only reaches the third subphase of the Early Bronze Age, in which the large Strata XXII–XXI building was abandoned, as well as the upper part of the levels associated with the structure's construction.

As expected from a superficial section cleaning, the archaeological materials collected were not abundant, although they are significant. Among the finds, the lithic finds stand out—including a number of very fine blanks and a flint core (Fig. 1.5e)—as do bowls (Fig. 1.5d), juglets and a stone vessel of Egyptian origin (Fig. 1.5c). Of chronological relevance are large two-handled jars with combed incised decoration (Fig. 1.5a, b), typical of Tyre's Strata

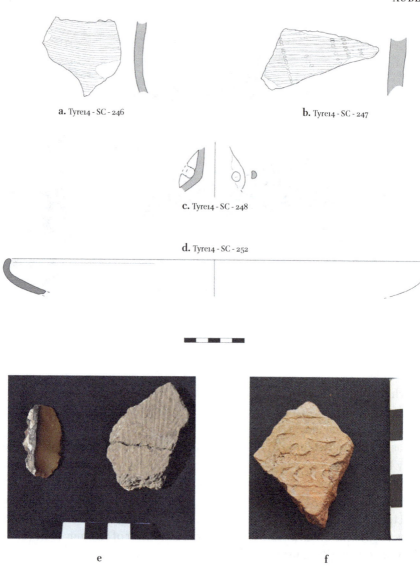

FIGURE 1.5 Early Bronze Age pottery and flint from the 2014 excavations

XXVII–XXI (Bikai 1978: 69, pls. LVI.22, LVII.69), and also attested at Sidon (Doumet-Serhal 2006a: 40–41; 2006b: 10, pl. 14) and in Levels 17–16 at Tell Arqa ("céramique peignée"), belonging to the late EB III (Phase R) and EB IV (Phase P), c. 2700–2000 BCE (Thalmann 2006: 17–28, pl. 46, 50–53). At Tell Arqa this pottery style is found in association with a lithic assemblage very similar to ours. In general, the combed wares at Tyre are slightly later than those at

Byblos or Tell Arqa, where they are especially abundant in the earliest Level 17 (2700–2500/2450 cal BCE). One exceptional find associated with these materials is a sherd with a partially preserved impressed frieze featuring an animal, probably a lion (Fig. 1.5f). The piece belongs to a category of vessels characteristic of the EB III and IV, called cylinder-seal-impressed ware and represented, for example, by large jars in the Early Bronze levels at Ebla (Palace G), Hama, Tell Fadous-Kfarabida, and Sidon (Genz 2014: 300, fig. 21.4; 2015: 102, fig. 9; 2017: 77, fig. 4.3; Doumet-Serhal 2006a: 259–270). In large urban centers of this period, this ware appears associated with public structures or administrative activities, like commercial transactions and record keeping.

The first human occupation on the island of Tyre occurred during a period in which urban centers with public structures and fortifications were thriving on the northern Lebanese coast at Tell Arqa, Byblos, and Tell Fadous-Kfarabida (Dunand 1952; Saghieh 1983; Thalmann 2006; Genz 2014). In contrast to these centers on the northern coast, however, the Early Bronze Age has usually been understood to be a period of marked decline on the southern coast, a process reaching its peak with the occupational break at Tyre during the Middle Bronze Age. Compared with the great northern centers, understood to be incipient territorial states, the only EB IV site known in the south—the island of Tyre—would constitute little more than an "ephemeral campsite" (Genz 2015: 105; 2017: 76).

The great building of Strata XXII–XXI, dating to the mid-third millennium at Tyre, however, suggests a deliberate choice toward permanence on a small rocky islet, probably related to the construction of a temple—what we might understand as a symbolic appropriation of coastal reefs to serve as an outpost for a nearby center on the mainland. The discovery of cylinder-seal-impressed pottery implies that a range of commercial and administrative activities was taking place in the vicinity of the Tyre stone structure, since this ceramic style is associated with similar activities and notably with the use of weight systems in the northern urban centers. The discovery in 1973–1974 of an Early Dynastic Egyptian inscribed quartz cylinder seal in Stratum XIX (Ward 1978: 84) carries with it the additional implication of incipient interregional trade. The number of combed sherds—some handmade—related to large storage jars also suggests transport and trade activities in this period.

It is reasonable to assume that the population that first occupied the Tyre reef came from the nearby mainland. In my opinion, there is only one possible candidate: given its characteristics, the amplitude of its stratified deposits, and its location in a fertile plain, all signs point to the tell at Al Rashidiyeh, located on the coast just 4 km southeast of the island of Tyre, close to the important freshwater springs at Ras el-ʿAyn. It has not yet been possible to carry out excavations on Tell Al Rashidiya, due to the presence of a dense Palestinian refugee camp at the site; however, future research at this site may well yield surprises, especially as concerns the periodization of the Bronze Age on the southern Lebanese coast.

Without more details concerning this coastal tell, situated in an area bearing evidence of human occupation stretching back to the Neolithic, it is premature to speak of periods of decline, occupation, and abandonment on the southern Lebanese coast, based exclusively on the stratigraphy at Tyre, which was a settlement of little relevance before the Late Bronze and Iron Ages. We are informed about this by a reference to a "ruler (king) of Tyre" in an Egyptian Execration Text (ca. 1880 BCE), during the Middle Bronze Age, when the island of Tyre was deserted (Katzenstein 1973: 19; cf. Bikai 1978: 72). It seems clear that the Egyptian text is referring to a different Tyre, the "continental" one.

Later documentary sources also refer to this continental Tyre, calling it *Ushu*. In the Amarna period (fourteenth century BCE), Ushu supplied water to the island, was a faithful ally to Egypt, and was the capital of a monarchy. Much later, the Assyrian Annals mention that Ushu was the bridgehead for the assault on the island, and in the time of Alexander the Great, it was still the site of an old temple to the god Melqart (Katzenstein 1973: 14, 29). The classical geographers knew Ushu by the names *Palaityros* or *Palaetyros* (Old Tyre)—a late appellation that is first attested in Strabo (16.224)—as well as *Tirus vetus* (Just. *Epit.* 11.10–11).

1.4 Tyre, "The Rock"

As a whole, the remains discovered in 2014 and especially those from 1973–1974 reveal that the island of Tyre was occupied for the first time around 2700 BCE by small groups from the mainland, perhaps fishermen. Rather than "occupation," perhaps it would be more accurate to speak of the occasional or seasonal presence on the reef of a community otherwise residing at a nearby mainland center.

The reef could not have been very attractive for its first occupants. It was probably made up of two parallel sandstone islets, the largest of which did not rise much higher than 1 m above sea level (Fig. 1.6), offering only minimal space poorly suited to the establishment of a long-term settlement.[3] The original name of the islet was *Ṣur*, meaning "rock" or "outcrop"—a name that the city

---

3 Recent geophysical research suggests that from 6000 to 4000 BCE, that is, during the Neolithic and Chalcolithic periods, sea level was lower than it is currently, such that the exposed

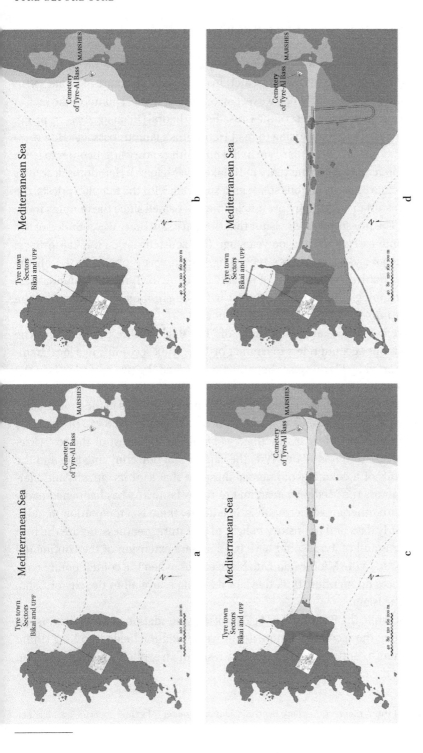

FIGURE 1.6   Reconstruction of the evolution of Tyre
BASED ON P.M. BIKAI 1992

has kept to this day, and from which the Greek transcription *Tyros* derives (Katzenstein 1973: 9).

The first evidence for deliberate, permanent occupation on the islet—a proper "foundation"—is the construction of the large structure of Strata XXII–XXI, ca. 2700/2500 BCE, which was set on one of the highest points of the reef, at a short distance to the west of the Crusader Cathedral (Bikai 1992: 74–75, pl. 13).

It is nevertheless surprising to read Herodotus's famous passage (Hdt. 2.44) describing his visit to insular Tyre in the mid-fifth century BCE in order to learn more about its famous sanctuary to Herakles (= Melqart). Herodotus describes the sanctuary and its famous stelae and, speaking with the temple's priests, the Greek historian asks them how much time has passed since the temple's foundation. The priests tell their visitor that the god's sanctuary was founded at the same time as Tyre itself, 2300 years ago (Katzenstein 1973: 18; Bikai 1978: 72; Bondì 1990: 258). Herodotus's reckoning, which was probably based on the temple's archives, yields a date of roughly 2750 BCE for Tyre's first "foundation." This reckoning is in broad agreement with the chronology attributed to the Early Bronze Age materials described above.

There are hardly any descriptions of "The Rock" before the Iron Age. The most famous account refers to Hiram I of Tyre, who, according to a local tradition reported by Flavius Josephus (*Ap.* 1.113), united the two reef islands in the tenth century BCE in order to found a new capital. In the tenth and ninth centuries, the city is already represented with impressive walls in the bronze gates of Balawat, and referred to as "the fortress" (2 Samuel 24:6–7). In the early sixth century BCE, Tyre is described as being "in the midst of the sea" (Ezekiel 27:32). But that is a later Tyre, the capital of a powerful kingdom and the metropolis of a colonial-commercial diaspora that sent its citizens and merchants across the Mediterranean and to the Atlantic. As has happened many times with other great metropoleis, like Rome, there is a temptation to judge Tyre's early days and prehistory in light of its future greatness. Before the Iron Age, the island of Tyre would have been a mere extension of the continental Tyre, Ushu. In the Middle and Late Bronze Ages, when the contemporary written sources do mention Tyre, they are referring above all to the city of Ushu, not to the island.

Thus, while the Early Bronze Age marks the foundation of Tyre's first insular settlement, the second and more definitive foundation belongs to King Hiram I in the tenth century BCE, this time the result of an explicitly political decision marking the creation of a great capital.

---

area of the Tyrian reef may have been considerably greater (Marriner 2008: 68–99; Marriner, Morhange, and Carayon 2008).

2 The Legends about Tyre's Origins

A discussion of the earliest Tyre attested archeologically is also an opportunity to review the textual data at hand regarding the site's beginnings. In the absence of direct written sources relating to Tyre's history, which are now lost, we are left with the translations of Phoenician works—for example, those of Menander of Ephesus (via Flavius Josephus) and Sanchuniathon (via Philo of Byblos)—as well as with various, often quite late, pseudo-historical sources that tend to conflate myth and real history.

As a starting point, a noteworthy source is the work of Flavius Josephus (37–100 CE), who states in *Contra Apionem* (1.107) and *Antiquitates Judaicae* (8.55) that he transcribed entire passages from the Hellenistic writers Menander of Ephesus (*The History of Tyre*, third–second centuries BCE) and Dius (*The History of the Phoenicians*), a Hellenistic historian cited by Josephus (*Ap.* 1.116). These, in turn, claimed to have translated into Greek the *Annals of Tyre* that were kept among the city's archives and official records (Katzenstein 1973: 77–79).

Josephus says (*Ap.* 1.113) that Tyre was originally formed from two islands, one larger than the other, and that in the tenth century BCE, King Hiram I united them in order to increase the city's size and erect the capital's primary public and religious structures.

Another description of Tyre's origins is related by Philo of Byblos, a grammarian from the time of Nero and the author of an eight-volume *Phoenician History*, part of which was transcribed in Eusebius of Caesarea's *Praeparatio evangelica* (1.10.9–11) in the third–fourth centuries CE. Philo's work was, in turn, a translation into Greek of the writings of a certain Sanchuniathon, who claimed to have lived at the time of the Trojan War. Philo prided himself in recovering ancient Phoenician traditions, and interpreted myths as memories of ancient events that actually occurred (Attridge and Oden 1981: 43; Baumgarten 1981: 159–165; Ribichini 1985: 20–22). According to this legend, Tyre's origins are connected with two rival, founding brothers: Samemrumos, also called Hypsuranios, and Ousoos. Hypsuranios lived in Tyre and clashed with his brother Ousoos, the first human sailor. One day, as a storm hit the coast and started forest fires near Tyre, Ousoos, a great hunter who wore animal skins, built a canoe and set out to sea. Then he consecrated two stelae to the fire and the wind—the divine forces that had helped him—founded the city, and offered sacrifices to these stelae in the form of blood libations from the animals he had hunted. For the first time the symbol of the two stelae or columns appears connected to a foundation myth, an allegory of the "twin cities"—the insular and continental Tyre (Ousoos, Usoos = Ushu?)—which is also communicated through the two eponymous heroes or mythical ancestors (Grotanelli 1972: 52–53).

Classical mythology preserves another foundation myth, although this time we are dealing with very late sources. In this one, Tyre was founded on two rocks connected by the roots of a sacred olive tree (Nonnus, *Dion.* 40.468). The *Dionysiaca* is a text in verse by Nonnus of Panopolis, written in the fifth century CE, which describes the visit of Dionysus or Bacchus to the city of Tyre (*Dion.* 40.300–500). Fascinated as he beholds the temple of Herakles Astrochiton, he pays homage to the Tyrian god, who then invites Dionysus to his table, where they share a banquet of ambrosia—the elixir of immortality and drink of the gods—nectar, and wine (line 420). Later Dionysus asks Herakles about the origin of the city and who set the "rocks" in the sea. Herakles tells him that he himself did, using an oracle of dreams to instruct the first inhabitants of the region—the first men on earth or "sons of the earth"—in the art of navigation, of shipbuilding, and to set out at sea until they reached the appointed location. There they found two rocks drifting in the sea—the floating islands—that were named "Ambrosians" or immortals (lines 467–469). Herakles proceeds with the description: On one of these rocks a sacred olive tree was growing, as old as the islands themselves, permanently enveloped in flames without burning up. On the tree were a bird and a cup, and a snake was wrapped around its trunk. The men who were sent to the island had to capture the eagle and sacrifice it to Zeus, making a libation of its blood, which they were to pour over the Ambrosian Rocks in order to cement them together, fix them to the ocean floor, and found the two islands (lines 499–505). The eagle offered itself as a sacrifice, and, through this self-immolation and the blood sacrifice, the islands stopped wandering. Then the god ordered the construction of the city "by the sea of Tyre." "The place of the eagle sacrifice indicates where Tyre should be founded and the image of the island that emerges from the sea from two wandering rocks will remain as a metaphor for creation, the sacred birth, and the etymology of the original Phoenician name of the city" (Katzenstein 1973: 9; see Naster 1986: 361–363). Throughout this story, the protagonist is clearly Herakles-Melqart, the principal god of Tyre—the *Baal Ṣur*, "Lord of Tyre"—who, in turn, would also immolate himself in fire in order to achieve immortality.[4]

It is difficult to date the origin of these legends, which seem to have been set down in writing quite late, since they do not appear before the fourth or fifth

---

[4] The bibliography on Melqart and his Greek and Latin equivalents (Herakles and Hercules) is infinite, particularly regarding foundation myths and the well-known sanctuaries in Tyre and Gadir.

century CE.[5] The two versions of the myth, the one of Philo of Byblos and the one of Nonnus, contain early features that are clearly oriental and probably emerged from the same original tradition. Indeed, despite their differences, the myths encapsulate a number of common elements: the flaming olive tree, the blood sacrifice, the two rocks, the close relationship between the fire and the olive tree, etc.[6]

Earlier, in the third century CE, the legends passed on by Nonnus and Philo of Byblos had enjoyed tremendous popularity in the city of Tyre. Indeed, the motif of the Ambrosian Rocks and the flaming olive tree appear on bronze coins from the Tyrian mint even before they show up in Nonnus's erudite writings. Between the reigns of Elagabalus (218–222) and Gallienus (253–268) the Ambrosian Rocks appear on Tyrian coins accompanied by the Greek or Latin legend AMBROSIE PETRE or PETRAI (Cook 1940: 975–1015; Naster 1986: 364–368; Bijovsky 2005). The rocks are depicted as round objects on a joint pedestal, flanking a flaming olive tree (Fig. 1.7) and are sometimes accompanied by other motifs connected to Tyrian legends, such as the dog and the murex. Indeed, alongside the symbols explicitly related to the foundation myths, other legendary Tyrian figures are common on Roman coins from Tyre— the hero Cadmus, the bull representing Zeus in the myth of the abduction of

FIGURE 1.7
Bronze coin of Elagabalus (218–222 CE)
PHOTO COURTESY OF G. BIJOVSKY

---

5   Another author from this period, Achilles Tatius (fourth century CE), alludes to the same symbols: in his *Leucippe and Clitophon* (2.14), Tatius mentions the sacred precinct of Herakles in Tyre, where there was a burning olive tree.

6   Evidence dating to the beginning of the Roman Empire gives us an even earlier attestation of the myth. A small limestone relief, found in Tyre and now housed at the Museum of the American University of Beirut, depicts a strange scene, featuring a large tree with burning branches, an eagle sitting on it, a serpent wrapped around its trunk, and a deer (Will 1950–1951; Zanovello 1981). The Beirut relief is presently the earliest known representation of the legend about Tyre's origins.

Europa, the eagle, the murex, dolphins, Herakles-Melqart, Pygmalion, the two stelae, the palm tree, and a flaming altar. On the coins of Gordian III (238–244) there also appear two brief legends in Phoenician script (*lṣr*, "of Tyre") (Naster 1986: 364; Bijovsky 2000: 326).

Of course, there is some confusion surrounding the symbolic significance of these Tyrian coinages and regarding the possibility that the Ambrosian Rocks depicted on them represent the two islands, mountains, stelae, betyls, or even the famous Pillars of Herakles (Bijovsky 2005: 831; Butcher 2016: 236).

Whatever the case, in my opinion, the crucial question is not whether the iconography of the coins or the late texts of Philo of Byblos, Nonnus, or Achilles Tatius demonstrate the persistence into Roman times of a remote and ancient myth—one whose origin cannot even be dated today. Rather, the question is why such a remote past is being invoked—and with it the ancient Tyrian heritage, its foundation myths, and its heroes—in coinages and erudite texts within the heavily Hellenized context of the Eastern Roman Empire, in a sort of "renaissance" of early Tyrian heritage, a glorification of the past, with the goal of underscoring the unique nature of the cults and traditions of Roman Tyre (Bijovsky 2000: 326; Butcher 2016: 236, 252). The idea of using the remote, albeit reinvented, past as a means of promoting present greatness would seem to be typical of the elite culture of the second–third-centuries Eastern Roman Empire, which would have found in the supposed, or probable, antiquity of its foundational myths a measure of legitimacy for its political ambitions.

Thus, there were several versions of a legend surrounding the origins of Tyre, which was deformed and adapted to suit to present interests and circumstances. Poets and thinkers told myths designed to create a unifying referent that would cement the community around the idea that the foundation of a city is always a unique event, auspiciously ordained by the gods. Out of all these legends, collective memory latched onto the image of two islands, the flaming olive tree, and the "king of the city" in the divine origins of Tyre.

Acknowledgments

I would like to thank Patricia Bikai for her goodwill and collaboration throughout all our years working in Tyre, since the late 1990s. Likewise, I am grateful to her for the authorization to reproduce images from her excavations. Moreover, I would like to express my thanks to the various colleagues who have contributed their advice and assistance to the production of this article: Manuel Alvarez, Ali Badawi, Amelie Beyhum, Gabriela Bijovsky, Philip Johnston, Francisco Núñez and José M. López-Garí.

References

Attridge, H.W. and Oden, R.A. 1981. *Philo of Byblos: The Phoenician History* (The Catholic Biblical Quarterly Monograph Series 9). Washington, DC.

Aubet, M.E. 2010. The Phoenician Cemetery of Tyre. *Near Eastern Archaeology* 73: 144–155.

Aubet, M.E., Nuñez, F.J., and Trelliso, L., eds. 2014. *The Phoenician Cemetery of Tyre-Al Bass II. Archaeological Seasons 2002–2005*. 2 vols. Beirut.

Aubet, M.E., Nuñez, F.J., and Trelliso, L. 2016. Excavations in Tyre 1997–2015: Results and Perspectives. *Berytus* 56: 3–14.

Baumgarten, A.I. 1981. *The Phoenician History of Philo of Byblos: A Commentary* (Études préliminaires aux religions orientales dans l'Empire romain t. 89). Leiden.

Bijovsky, G. 2000. More about Pygmalion from Tyre. *Quaderni Ticinesi di Numismatica e Antichità Classiche* 29: 319–332.

Bijovsky, G. 2005. The Ambrosial Rocks and the Sacred Precinct of Melqart in Tyre. In: Alfaro, C., Marcos, C., and Otero, P., eds. *Actas del XIII Congreso Internacional de Numismática, Madrid, 2003*, Vol. 1. Madrid: 829–834.

Bikai, P.M. 1978. *The Pottery of Tyre*. Warminster.

Bikai, P.M. 1992. The Site. In: (no editor) *Actes des symposiums: Tyr et la formation des civilisations méditerranéennes*. Paris: 67–85.

Bikai, P.M. and Bikai, P. 1987. Tyre at the End of the Twentieth Century. *Berytus* 35: 67–96.

Bondì, S.F. 1990. I fenici in Erodoto. *Hérodote et les peuples non grecs* (Entretiens sur l'Antiquité Classique, tome 35). Vandoeuvres: 255–286.

Butcher, K. 2016. Coinage and Communal Memory in the Roman East. *Berytus* 56: 235–255.

Chéhab, M. 1972. *Tyr. Histoire, topographie, fouilles*. Beyrouth.

Cook, A.B. 1940. *Zeus: A Study in Ancient Religion*, Vol. 3, Part 2. Cambridge.

Doumet-Serhal, C. 2006a. *The Early Bronze Age in Sidon: "College Site" Excavations (1998–2001)* (Bibliothèque archéologique et historique 178). Beirut.

Doumet-Serhal, C. 2006b. Sidon: A Mud Brick Building at the Close of the Third Millennium BC. *Archaeology and History in Lebanon* 24: 4–17.

Dunand, M. 1952. Byblos au temps du Bronze Ancien et la conquête amorite. *Revue Biblique* 59: 82–90.

Genz, H. 2014. The Northern Levant (Lebanon) during the Early Bronze Age. In: Steiner, M.L. and Killebrew, A.E., eds. *The Oxford Handbook of the Archaeology of the Levant, c. 8000–332 BCE*. Oxford: 292–306.

Genz, H. 2015. Beware of Environmental Determinism: The Transition from the Early to the Middle Bronze Age on the Lebanese Coast and the 4.2 ka BP Event. *Tagungen des Landesmuseums für Vorgeschichte Halle* 12: 97–111.

Genz, H. 2017. The Transition from the Third to the Second Millennium B.C. in the Coastal Plain of Lebanon: Continuity or Break? In: Höflmayer, F., ed. *The Late Third Millennium in the Ancient Near East: Chronology, C14, and Climate Change.* Chicago (Oriental Institute Seminars 11): 73–85.

Grotanelli, C. 1972. Il mito delle origini di Tiro: due "versioni" duali. *Oriens antiquus* 9: 49–63.

Jidejian, N. 1969. *Tyre through the Ages.* Beirut.

Katzenstein, H.J. 1973. *The History of Tyre: From the Beginning of the Second Millennium BCE until the Fall of the Neo-Babylonian Empire in 538 BCE.* Jerusalem.

Marriner, N. 2008. Paléo-environnements des ports antiques de Tyr, Sidon et Beyrouth. *Archaeology and History in Lebanon* 28: 66–138.

Marriner, P., Morhange, C., and Carayon, N. 2008. Ancient Tyre and Its Harbours: 5000 Years of Human-Environment Interactions. *Journal of Archaeological Science* 35: 1281–1310.

Naster, P. 1986. Ambrosiai petrai dans les textes et sur les monnaies de Tyr. In : Bonnet, C., Lipinski, E., and Marchetti, P., eds. *Religio Phoenicia* (Studia Phoenicia 4). Namur: 361–371.

Ribichini, S. 1985. *Poenus advena. Gli dei fenici e l'interpretazione classica* (Collezione di Studi Fenici 19). Roma.

Saghieh, M. 1983. *Byblos in the Third Millennium B.C.: A Reconstruction of the Stratigraphy and a Study of the Cultural Connections.* Warminster.

Thalmann, J.-P. 2006. *Tell Arqa—I. Les niveaux de l'âge du Bronze* (Bibliothèque archéologique et historique 177). Beirut.

Ward, W.A. 1978. The Egyptian Objects. In: P.M. Bikai, *The Pottery of Tyre.* Warminster: 83–86.

Will, E. 1950–1951. Au sanctuaire d'Héraklès à Tyr: L'olivier enflammé, les stèles et les roches ambrosiennes. *Berytus* 10: 1–12.

Zanovello, P. 1981. I due "betili" di Malta e le Ambrosiai Petrai di Tiro. *Rivista di Archeologia* 5: 16–29.

CHAPTER 2

Two Imported Pottery Vessels from the Middle Euphrates to the Southern Levant and Their Contribution to the Chronology of the End of Early Bronze I and the Beginning of Early Bronze II

Vladimir Wolff Avrutis and Eli Yannai

1   Introduction

The dating of the transition from the end of Early Bronze (EB) I to EB II has been under debate for many years. Two ceramic vessels imported from the Middle Euphrates Basin were found in archaeological excavations in two late EB I cemeteries in Israel: a spouted jar was found at el-Khirbe, in the Nesher-Ramla quarry and a goblet was found at 'Ein Asawir. This paper will present the two vessels, their dates and the significance of their chronological correlation with vessels imported from Egypt. In addition, a hypothesis will be made as to how the two vessels were brought to the southern Levant from such a great distance.

2   The Burial Grounds

The site of el-Khirbe is located in the Lod Valley, bordering the Judean foothills (Shephelah) (Fig. 2.1). It is situated within the Nesher-Ramla cement quarry, 5 km southeast of the modern-day cities of Lod and Ramla. During the excavations, nine late EB I burial caves, hewn in chalky marl, were discovered (Fig. 2.2). Stone, flint, and copper tools were found alongside ceramic vessels, all of which are dated strictly to the late phases of EB I (Fig. 2.3a, b; Avrutis 2012: 101–199, 213–220). The 'Ein Asawir necropolis is located at the outlet of Wadi 'Ara to the Coastal Plain, east of the settlement site (Yannai 2006) (Fig. 2.1). Tomb 20 was found in a cave hewn in the chalky marl (Yannai and Grosinger 2000: 153–154; Yannai 2016). Among the many finds unearthed in this tomb were a few ceramic vessels imported from the Amuq Valley, as well as imports from Egypt (Yannai and Braun 2001: figs. 3: 3, 4; 4: 1, 2; Yannai 2006: 223–224).

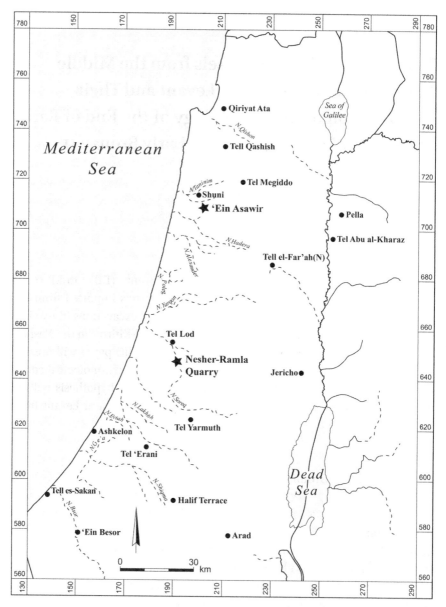

FIGURE 2.1   Location map of Nesher-Ramla Quarry, 'Ein Asawir, and other EB I sites

3   The Vessels

The two vessels imported from the Middle Euphrates Basin, found at Nesher-Ramla Burial Cave F-662 and Tomb 20 at 'Ein Asawir belong to different ceramic groups. The Nesher-Ramla jar is characterized by a globular body, high neck, and out-turned, thickened rim (Fig. 2.4: 1). Its surface was finished with

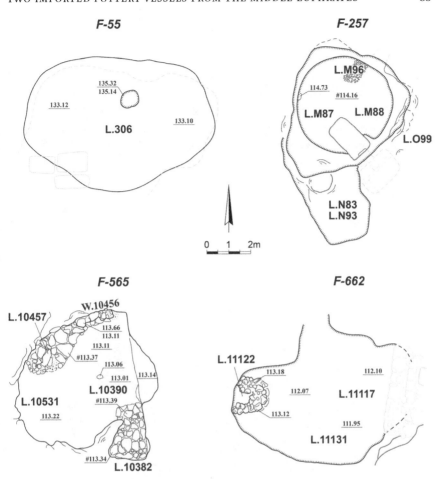

FIGURE 2.2   Plans of four of nine EB I burial caves unearthed at Nesher-Ramla Quarry

oblique burnish on the upper part of the body and horizontal burnish on its lower part. Both the neck and the spout, which was set on the vessel's shoulder, were made as separate segments and attached to the body when the vessel was in leather-hard condition. The jar's morphology can be related to Late Reserve Slip Ware (LRSW; Jamieson 2013), although it differs from LRSW in its surface finishing (see below). The'Ein Asawir goblet (Fig. 2.4: 2) belongs to the Vertically-Pierced Lugged-Handle goblet family (VPLH; Sconzo 2015: 96). These two ware groups are representative of pottery production common in the Middle Euphrates Basin during Early Middle Euphrates 0.[1]

---

[1] The Early Middle Euphrates periodization scheme and terminology, now accepted by AR-CANE (= Associated Regional Chronologies of the Ancient Near East and the Eastern Mediterranean; Lebeau and de Miroschedji 2013), will be used henceforth.

FIGURE 2.3   EB I ceramic vessels and flint and copper tools from EB I Nesher-Ramla Quarry burials

The spouted and spoutless globular jars are especially characteristic of the Mesopotamian ceramic repertoire. Parallels for the Nesher-Ramla jar were recorded at Tepe Gawra (Fig. 2.5: 2, 8; Speiser 1935: 47–48, pls. LXV: 63, LXVI: 80), Mohammed 'Arab (Fig. 2.5: 3; Rova 2013: 7, pl. 2: 1), Tell Brak (Fig. 2.5: 9; Felli 2003: 67, figs. 4.16, 4.25: 20), and Khafajah (Fig. 2.5: 4; Delougaz 1952: pl. 187: C. 655.222). Parallels found among LRSW vessels are similar only in form, as mentioned above (e.g., Fig. 2.5: 5–7; Braidwood and Braidwood 1960: fig. 219: 1, 3; Frangipane 2007: fig. 8.17: 13). This group is well known in the Euphrates and Amuq Valleys (Jamieson 2013) and the majority of its vessels is dated to Early Middle Euphrates 1–2, corresponding with southern Levantine EB IA to the early phases of EB II.

TWO IMPORTED POTTERY VESSELS FROM THE MIDDLE EUPHRATES

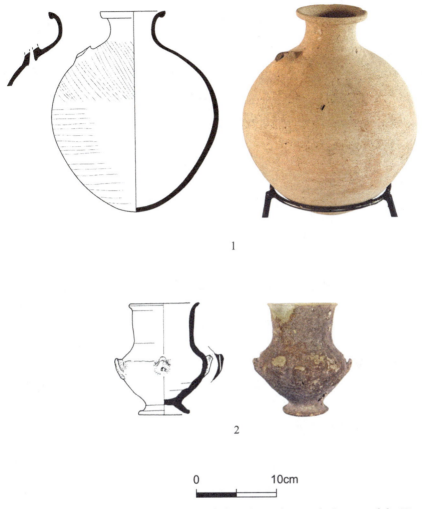

FIGURE 2.4   Imported Mesopotamian vessels from the Nesher-Ramla Quarry and the ʿEin Asawir burials

The LRSW family was first defined in Phase G of the Amuq excavations during the 1950s (Braidwood and Braidwood 1960: 276, figs. 218, 219). It is widespread in the Middle Euphrates Basin, east of the Balih and west of the Habur Basin. Outside the Middle Euphrates Basin, vessels of this group were found also in the northern Levant and at Tell Judaidah and Tell Afis in the Amuq Valley and its vicinity (Jamieson 2013: fig. 1). This family is dated to Early Middle Euphrates 1–2, parallel to early Ninevite 5, ca. 3100/2900–2700/2600 BCE. Middle Euphrates 1–2 and the Early Upper Euphrates are included in early Mesopotamian 1–2 and include Early Jezirah (EJ) 0–1 and Northern Levant 1–2 ARCANE periods (ibid.: 101).

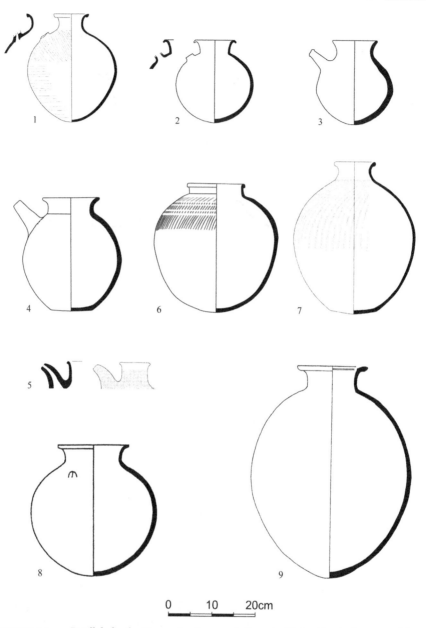

FIGURE 2.5   Parallels for the Mesopotamian vessels from the Nesher-Ramla Quarry and the 'Ein Asawir burials

VPLH goblets were found in the Middle Euphrates Basin and, according to the accepted terminology of this region's pottery, they are dated to EB IA (Rova 2013: 8). They are a part of vessel groups typical of the fourth millennium BCE, characterized mainly by bowls with cut rims (Helwing 2013). According to

P. Sconzo's classification, the VPLH goblets are common mostly in graves and date to the second half of Middle Euphrates 2 (Sconzo 2015: 96, Type 29, pl. 5: 58). LRSW jars and VPLH goblets were found together in graves at Hassek Höyük (Beham-Blancke 2003: figs. 14: 2, 15: 3).

4 Chronological Data from Egypt

Three pottery vessels imported from Egypt were found in graves at Nesher-Ramla. Two jugs were found in two different burial caves, F-355 and F-565 (Fig. 2.6: 1, 2); both were made of Nile clay (Golding-Meir and Isirlis 2012: Samples 75, 117). Similar jugs were found at sites in northern Sinai in the south and up to 'Ein Asawir (Tombs 3, 20) in the north, all in assemblages dating to late EB I (Amiran and van den Brink 2001: fig. 3.10). In the Egyptian Nile Delta similar vessels appear in Naqada IIIA-B contexts (e.g., van den Brink 1992: fig. 7: 2, l. 18: 2; Köhler 1992: fig. 7). The third Egyptian vessel, a jar found in Burial Cave F-55 (Fig. 2.6: 3), is made of Egyptian mud and was fired at a high temperature (Tsatskin 2010: 55–56, fig. 4.25). Most of the parallels to this type of jar in Egypt are dated to Naqada II-IIIA or Naqada IIIB-C (Avrutis 2012: 117–118, table 4.2.1). Based on its archaeological context, the jar from Nesher-Ramla belongs to Naqada IIIC.

Egyptian chronology from the end of Dynasty 0 down to the beginning of the First Dynasty was traditionally based mainly on archaeological finds that were traded between Egypt and Canaan (Hornung, Krauss, and Warburton 2006; Braun 2011a, 2011b; Braun and van den Brink 2008: 659–670). The accepted terminology for cultures of these periods, such as "Naqada II-IIIA" and "Naqada IIIB-C," is based on seriation of pottery vessels from tombs, rather than on pottery assemblages from dated settlement strata. Some of the vessel types are found in more than one group, so it is difficult to base an exact chronology on them. Radiocarbon dating before the 1990s was rare and frequently based on samples from assemblages originating in unclear contexts. New excavations at Tel es-Shuna (Philip 2001, 2008), Tel Yarmuth (Regev, Miroschedji, and Boaretto 2012), Pella (Bourke et al. 2009), and Jericho (Bruins and van den Plicht 2001) provided clean samples and clearer data (Regev et al. 2012), but the samples were gathered from sites with no Egyptian artifacts. Only four sites yielded ^{14}C samples with in situ Egyptian artifacts: at Tell Abu al-Kharaz (Stadler and Fischer 2008) and Tel Halif (van den Brink 2002; Braun 2011a, 2011b, 2014) only a few samples were found. Most of the ^{14}C samples were found at Tell es-Sakan (Miroschedji et al. 2001; Miroschedji 2009; Dee et al. 2013; Dee et al. 2014) and at Ashkelon (Golani 2013). These two sites provided a large number of clean ^{14}C samples (from grain seeds) from clean contexts. The archaeological

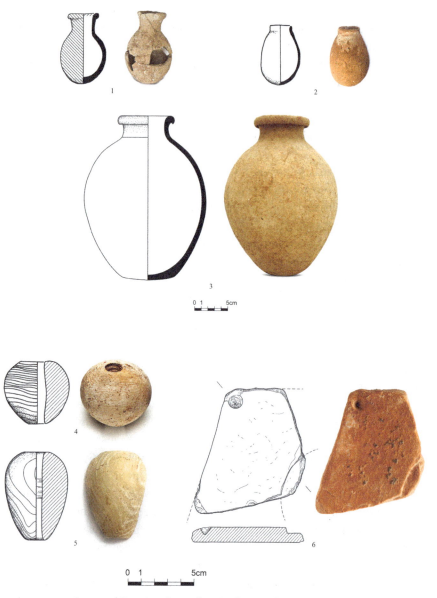

FIGURE 2.6　　Imported Egyptian objects from Nesher-Ramla Quarry burials

context of some of the artifacts, mainly Strata 7–6 at Tell es-Sakan, is associated with Naqada IIIB–C, dated to Dynasty 0, and includes imported jugs from Egypt of types identical to those found in Tombs 3 and 20 at 'Ein Asawir (Yannai and Braun 2001: figs. 3: 3, 4; 4: 1, 2: Yannai 2016: figs. 2.16: 18; 2.30: 9) and in

Burial Caves F-355 and F-565 at Nesher-Ramla (Avrutis 2012: figs. 4.29, 4.30; Table 2.1 herein). Excavations at Tell el-Farkha (Chlodnicki, Cialowicz, and Mączyńska 2012) provided additional ^{14}C samples (Dee et al. 2013; Dee et al. 2014). On the basis of these new tests, the Naqada II and Naqada III cultures were more exactly dated, and the continuity between the two periods and their internal subdivisions were redetermined. Based on the updated data and the renewed subdivisions of the Naqada cultures (Czarnowicz 2012: 264, pl. 1; 2014: 97, table 1), the Egyptian vessels from Nesher-Ramla and 'Ein Asawir belong to Naqada IIIC. Over 99% of pottery vessels found in the tombs with the Egyptian jugs belong to late EB I. A majority of the vessels, mainly platters and oval-shaped body (OSB) juglets, are fashioned in shapes similar to vessels from the beginning of EB II, but no metallic-ware technology or Abydos-style vessels were found in any of the tombs. According to the Upper Egyptian Chronology and the vessels found in the tombs, the vessels from Naqada IIIC are dated to late EB I. Burial within the tombs ceased before the earliest stage of EB II.

5   Chronological Data from the Middle Euphrates Basin (Northern Mesopotamia)

Goblets similar to that from 'Ein Asawir arrived in the Malatia-Elaziğ region, in the Middle Euphrates, influenced by the Ninevite 5 culture, which developed in the Jezirah area and the northern Tigris (Grossman 2013: 92). Their dates may be based on dateable finds from the same contexts in stratified archaeological sites in the area (Table 2.2).

Five ^{14}C samples from Period 2 in Area D at Tell Shiukh Fawqani were tested. Though there was only a small amount of carbon, the date range of the sample could be limited to EB IA in the Middle Euphrates (Morandi Bonacossi 2005: 124–128). According to the samples, EB IA at Tell Shiukh Fawqani is dated to 3390–3080 BCE, which correlates well with dates from Strata VIB2–VIA at Arslantepe (Frangipane and Palmieri 1983: fig. 18: 4–5; Helwing 2001), the EB I stratum at Norşuntepe, and the Late Uruk Stratum EB IA at Hessek Höyük (di Nocera 2000: pls. 1–3; figs. 2a–b, 3a–b). These data match the ^{14}C samples from Stage G at Tell Judaidah, and from Acarköy in the Amuq Valley (Yener et al. 1996: 69, pl. 2; Yener and Wilkinson 1996–1997: 3; Yener, Edens, and Harrison 2000: 197, table 1; Yener 2009).

A small number of goblets were found in a Ninevite 5 layer at Telul eth-Thalathat in the Jezirah area (Fukai, Horiuchi, and Matsutani 1974: fig. 51: 6, 17, 18; Hiroyuki 2003: pl. 14: 3, 4). These artifacts are dated to the transitional

TABLE 2.1 Synchronization of the EB I–II chronologies at Nesher-Ramla and 'Ein Asawir with other sites in the southern Levant and with Egypt, based on finds from the tombs

Period	Nesher-Ramla tomb no.				'Ein Asawir tomb no.			Southern Levant	Egypt
	55	355	565	662	3	1, 20, 45	40		
EB II							Local vessels; Egyptian calcite vase; palette	NCMW; Arad Str. II	First Dynasty
Terminal EB I / early EB II					Proto-Abydos and OSB vessels	OSB vessels		Arad St. III	Naqada IIIC2–D

TABLE 2.1 Synchronization of the EB I–II chronologies at Nesher-Ramla and 'Ein Asawir with other sites in the southern Levant and with Egypt, based on finds from the tombs (*cont.*)

Period	Nesher-Ramla tomb no.				'Ein Asawir tomb no.			Southern Levant	Egypt
	55	355	565	662	3	1, 20, 45	40		
Late EB I	Local vessels; proto-Abydos; Egyptian jar (Naqada IIIC)	Local vessels; Egyptian bottle (Naqada IIIC)	Local vessels; Egyptian bottle (Naqada IIIC); alabaster mace-head	Local vessels; ME spouted jar; palette	Local vessels; Egyptian bottle (Naqada IIIC)	Local vessels; Egyptian bottle (Naqada IIIC); ME goblet (Ninevite 5)		Arad St. IV	Naqada IIIB–C1
Middle EB I			Erani C vessels			Local vessels	Local vessels	Erani Phase C	Naqada IID2–IIIB

TABLE 2.2 Synchronization of traditional southern Levant Late Chalcolithic–EB II terminology and dates with chronological sequences from the Middle Euphrates, northern Levant (Inland/northern Syria), Upper Euphrates, and Jezirah (based on data from Algaze 1990; Frangipane 2000; Gerber 2000, 2005; Marro and Hauptmann 2000; Pearce 2000; Helwing 2002; Rothman 2002; Akkermans and Schwartz 2003; fig. 4; Rova 2013; Fischer 2014; Finkbeiner and Novák 2015; Finkbeiner et al. 2015)

Southern Levant traditional terminology	ARCANE terminology	cal BC	Middle Euphrates (ARCANE ME)			Northern Levant (ARCANE NL)	Upper Euphrates (ARCANE UE)	Jezirah (ARCANE JZ)
EB II	ESL 4	2900–3000 3000–3050 3100–3150	Arslantepe	Hassek Höyük (ME)	Kurban Höyük	Tell Brak, Tell Leilan	Painted and incised Ninevite 5	Phase EJ 1
Late EB IB Middle EB I Early EB I	ESL 3b ESL 3a		Period VI B2 Period VI B1	Phases 1–2 Phases 3–4	Period VB	TW 2–8 TW 9–10 Brak Phase H	Transitional Ninevite 5 End Uruk Late Uruk	Phase EJ 0 Jemdet Naṣr
Late Chalcolithic			Period VIA					

period from EJ 0 to EJ 1, a phase parallel to the beginning of Ninevite 5 (Rova 2011: 68, pl. 3: 8–12), which enables dating VPLH goblets and LRSW jars to these horizons as well. In the Jezirah and in the Middle Euphrates, the transitional EJ 0–EJ 1 is dated to 2900 BCE, contemporaneous with the transitional phase from the end of EB I to the beginning of EB II in the southern Levant.

During new excavations at Arslantepe, numerous ^{14}C samples were taken, enabling exact dating of many well-stratified stages. As a result of the ^{14}C dating, Period VIA at Arslantepe is classified as parallel to the Late Uruk culture (3300–3100 BCE) and Period VIB as parallel to the Jemdet Nasr culture (3100–2800 BCE) (Conti and Persiani 1993: 366; Frangipane 1998, 2000). Conti and Persiani concluded that Period VIB1 is later than the Late Uruk culture and parallel to the Jemdet Nasr culture (ibid.: 368).

According to Stager (1992: 38), vessels identical to Abydos Ware vessels were found in Amuq Phase G contexts. In his opinion, combined marine and overland trade between the northern Levant (Amuq) and the Middle Euphrates and the Nile Delta began during EB I. The proposed synchronicity is not based on imported Egyptian items found in the Middle Euphrates Basin and the Amuq, but on shape resemblance and technological changes that appear contemporaneously in the Nile Valley and the northern Levant. Stager's suggestion is reflected in the artifacts from Tomb 20 at ʿEin Asawir. The VPLH goblet from the Middle Euphrates found at ʿEin Asawir and the spouted jar from Nesher-Ramla enable to solidly synchronize between Naqada in Egypt and parallel cultures (Ninevite 5 and Jemdet Nasr) in Mesopotamia. While we do not wish to reduce Stager's suggestion, today we have convincing evidence of marine trade between Egypt and the southern Levant (Gophna and Liphschitz 1996; Sharvit et al. 2002) and northward to the Lebanese littoral (Prag 1986) as early as EB I. The spouted jar from Nesher-Ramla and the goblet from ʿEin Asawir indicate that merchandise traveled the opposite way as well—from the Middle Euphrates Basin to the southern Levant. This course probably passed through the Amuq Valley, the Orontes Valley, the Lebanon Valley, and the northern part of the southern Levant.

6   Discussion and Conclusions

Tombs 1, 3, 45, and 20 at ʿEin Asawir and Burial Caves F-55, F-257, F-355, F-380, F-565, F-662, F-715, F-732, and F-832 at Nesher-Ramla were established as burial sites during late EB I. Burial activity at both the burial grounds began contemporaneously with the end of the Uruk culture and the transitional period between Jezirah 0 and Ninevite 5 and. This is also contemporary with

Naqada III in Egypt, ca. 3300 BCE. Dating the final usage of Tomb 20 at 'Ein Asawir and the Tombs at Nesher-Ramla is based on the Egyptian ceramic vessels of Naqada IIIC origin, with the VPLH goblet and the LRSW jar imported to 'Ein Asawir and Nehser-Ramla, respectively, from the Middle Euphrates Basin (Rova 2013: 8). Based on parallels to the items imported from the Middle Euphrates Basin that were carbon-dated, the final use of Tomb 20 was in the latest stage of EB I, before the appearance of vessels produced using "metallic technology" and of Abydos Ware vessels, meaning before EB II. This phase is contemporary with to Ninevite 5 and Jemdet Nasr and to the First Dynasty in Egypt (3100–3000 BCE), and is represented also in Stratum V at Buto, Stratum III at Arad, and Stratum II at 'En Besor (Czarnowicz 2012: 264, table 1; 2014: table 1; Table 2.2 herein).

Rova has pointed out the difficulties of correlating between Anatolian and Mesopotamian chronology and the accepted dates for the end of EB I and the beginning of EB II, the latest stage of the southern Levant Period 3 (in ARCANE terminology). In her article on this topic, Rova writes: "If one accepts the traditional synchronization with the Anatolian and Mesopotamian chronologies, this would appear too early not only for the ME but also for the TG examples; the question is, therefore, still open for discussion" (Rova 2013: 8). This lack of chronological correlation between the Middle Euphrates and the southern Levant is significant for the dating of the final use of Tomb 20 at 'Ein Asawir and the burial caves at Nesher-Ramla. OSB juglets and amphoriskoi were found in the final burial stage in Tomb 3 (Yannai and Grosinger 2000: fig. 9.1: 8; Yannai 2016: 31) and Tomb 20 at 'Ein Asawir. Vessels of this group were found in Tomb 14 at Tell el-Far'ah (North) (de Vaux 1952: fig. 11: 18–20) and in all strata and stages of late EB I at Tell Abu al-Kharaz (Fischer 2014: figs. 2: 8–10; 3: 7; 4: 3; 6: 5; 7: 1–4). Based on the large number found at Tell Abu al-Kharaz, it is likely that the OSB jugs and amphoriskoi were made at Tell Abu al-Kharaz or in the surrounding area. A fragment of an Egyptian Naqada III cylindrical vessel was found in a Phase IB context at Tell Abu al-Kharaz (ibid.: fig. 3: 8). Accordingly, Fischer concluded that the OSB vessels are from the latest stage of EB I (Fischer 2008: 368; 2014: 23). His conclusion agrees with the vessel's Naqada III origin. OSB vessels from the group found at sites with EB II strata, such as 'Ein Asawir, Tell el-Far'ah (North), and Tell Abu al-Kharaz, suggest that this group dates to EB II, parallel to Naqada III. Several OSB vessels were discovered at Megiddo, where there are no EB II strata (Esse 1991; Greenberg 2002; Finkelstein, Ussishkin, and Halperin 2006), proving, therefore, that these first appear during the final stage of late EB I. This evidence, however, does not preclude the possibility that they appear also in assemblages from the beginning of EB II. The imported Naqada jars, the spouted jar from Nesher-Ramla Burial Cave

F-662 and the goblet from Tomb 20 at 'Ein Asawir were found in graveyards with no EB II finds. OSB vessels are absent in EB II strata at Tel Qashish (Zuckerman 2003) and Qiryat Ata (Golani 2003). Based on these finds, we may accept Fischer's conclusion and posit that OSB vessels debuted not in EB II but already in late EB I.

Late EB I can be divided into three chronological stages, the earliest of which is called "Middle Early Bronze I," and also known as "Erani C" (Braun and van den Brink 1998; Yekutieli 2000, 2006; Czarnowicz 2014). This stage predates the abovementioned burials and is not discussed here. The two later stages are included under the name "Late Early Bronze IB" or "post-Erani C." The first of these two stages is characterized by immigration and settlement of Egyptians in the southern part of Israel (Braun 2014; van den Brink 2015: 159). During this time, a large amount of Egyptian pottery arrived in Canaan, including bottles found at the burial grounds at Nesher-Ramla and 'Ein Asawir (see Table 2.1) and the cylindrical vessel at Tell Abu al-Kharaz. Some of these vessels were brought from Egyptian settlements in southern Canaan (Gophna 1992: figs. 4: 7; 6: 4). No Egyptian artifacts were found in contexts attributed to the second of these two stages, such as Stratum III at Arad and Stratum IVA at Lod. Judging by the lack of Egyptian artifacts in these strata, it seems that the Egyptian settlers left at the final stage of late EB I (van den Brink 2015: 159). By this time, Egyptian trade dwindled and was limited to a few luxury objects (Yannai and Grosinger 2000: 160–161). We may assume that it was at this late stage that the OSB vessels known from Tell Abu al-Kharaz arrived at the tombs at 'Ein Asawir, Tell el-Far'ah (North), and Tel Megiddo. The definition of this late stage as the beginning of EB II or the end of EB I is still debated. The division of the two later stages of late EB I strengthens the supposition that the assemblages in Israel in which the imported vessels from the Middle Euphrates Basin were found date to late EB I rather than to the transition into EB II.

In the two latest stages of late EB I, great changes in the economy and society of the southern Levant took place. During this period of time, the first fortified settlements appeared (Paz 2002) and commerce between centers along central trade routes developed greatly (Adams 2006; Milevski 2009, 2011). It seems that these changes and the local trade in OSB vessels occurred in the background of the long-distance trade that developed between the southern Levant and its neighboring countries. Among the numerous Egyptian artifacts in the southern Levant, jars were found with the incised *serekh* signs of the last kings of Dynasty 0 and the first three kings of the First Dynasty, especially those of (Horus) Narmer (Levy et al. 2001: 430–437, figs. 22.13–22.15; van den Brink and Braun 2002). We may assume that the favorable trade conditions, which were created as a result of the Egyptian kingdom's intervention, increased commercial traffic between the different areas (Anđelković 2012); however, the finding of only two vessels from the Middle Euphrates in the southern Levant—the spouted jar from Nesher-Ramla and the goblet from 'Ein Asawir—may indicate that relations between these regions were indirect. The commercial relations represented by these two "elite" vessels may reflect the exchange of goods between the Middle Euphrates and the southern Levant. They may also reflect mutual cultural influence between societies of commercial centers in the southern Levant—like 'Ein Asawir and Lod—and the Middle Euphrates.

It is safe to say that the two vessels were not traded for their contents, as neither are storage vessels. The spouted jar from Nesher-Ramla and the goblet from 'Ein Asawir are typical pouring and drinking vessels. It seems that the trade in pouring vessels (spouted jar) and serving/drinking vessels (goblet) may have been connected to ceremonial drinking and was an expression of social elites participating in activities in which drinking played a role (Bloch and Parry 1982; Alfredo 2012). It is likely that these were luxury goods that were placed in tombs among other prestige items.

References

Adams, R.B. 2006. Copper Trading Networks across the Arabah during the Later Early Bronze Age. In: Bienkowski, P. and Galor, K., eds. *Crossing the Rift: Resources Routes, Settlement Patterns and Interaction in the Wadi Arabah* (LSS 3). London: 135–142.

Algaze, G., ed. 1990. *Town and Country in Southeastern Anatolia: The Stratigraphic Sequence at Kurban Höyük* (Oriental Institute Publications 110). Chicago.

Akkermans, P.M.M. and Schwartz, G. 2003. *The Archaeology of Syria: from Complex Hunter-Gatherers to Early Urban Societies (c. 16.000–3000 B.C.)*. Cambridge.

Alfredo, A. 2012. Cult of the Ancestors and Funerary Practices at Ebla. In: Pfälzner, P., Niehr, H., Pernicka, E., and Wissing, A., eds. *(Re-)Constructing Funerary Rituals in the Ancient Near East. Proceedings of the First International Symposium of the Tübingen Post-Graduate School "Symbols of the Dead" in May 2009*. Wiesbaden: 5–32.

Amiran, R. and Brink, E.C.M. van den 2001. A Comparative Study of Egyptian Pottery from Tel Ma'ahaz, Stratum I. In: Wolff S., ed. *Studies in Archaeology of Israel and Neighboring Lands in Memory of Douglas L. Esse* (SAOC 59/AASOR 5). Chicago: 29–58.

Anđelković, B. 2012. Hegemony for Beginners: Egyptian Activity in the Southern Levant during the Second Half of the Fourth Millennium B.C. *Issues in Ethnology and Anthropology* 7(3): 789–808.

Avrutis, W.V. 2012. *Late Chalcolithic and Early Bronze Age I Remains at Nesher-Ramla Quarry*. Haifa.

Beham-Blancke, M.R. 2003. Northern Frontiers: Early Ninevite 5 Contacts with Southern Anatolia. In: Rova, E. and Weiss, H., eds. *The Origin of North Mesopotamian Civilization: Ninevite V Chronology, Economy, Society* (Subartu 9). Turnhout: 481–492.

Bloch, M. and Parry, J. 1982. *Death and the Regeneration of Life.* Cambridge.

Bourke, S., Zoppi, U., Hua, O., Meadows, J., and Gibbins, S. 2009. The Beginning of the Early Bronze Age in the North Jordan Valley: New [14]C Determinations from Pella in Jordan. *Radiocarbon* 51: 905–913.

Braidwood, R. and Braidwood, L. 1960. *Excavations in the Plain of Antioch I: The Earlier Assemblages Phases A–J* (Oriental Institute Publications 61). Chicago.

Braun, E. 2011a. Early Interaction between Peoples of the Nile Valley and the Southern Levant. In: Teeter, E., ed. *Egypt before the Pyramids: The Origins of Egyptian Civilization.* Chicago: 106–122.

Braun, E. 2011b. South Levantine Early Bronze Age Chronological Correlations with Egypt in Light of the Narmer Serekhs from Tel Erani and Arad: New Interpretation. In: Braun, E. with contributions by Ilan, D., Marder, O., Braun, Y., and Shalev, S. 2013. *Early Megiddo on the East Slope (the "Megiddo Stages"): A Report on the Early Occupation of the East Slope of Megiddo (Results of the Oriental Institute's Excavations, 1925–1933)* (Oriental Institute Publications 139). Chicago: 106–122.

Braun, E. 2014. Reflections on the Context of a Late Dynasty 0 Egyptian Colony in the Southern Levant: Interpreting Some Evidence of Nilotic Material Culture at Select Sites in the Southern Levant (ca. 3150 BCE–ca. 2950 BCE). In: Mączyńska, A., ed. *The Nile Delta as a Centre of Cultural Interactions between Upper Egypt and the Southern Levant in the 4th Millennium BC.* Poznań: 37–55.

Braun, E. and Brink, E.C.M. van den 1998. Some Comments on the Late EB I Sequence of Canaan and the Relative Dating of Tomb Uj at Umm el Ga'ab and Graves 313 and 787 from Minshat Abu Omar with Imported Ware: Views from Egypt and Canaan. *Egypt and the Levant* 7: 71–94.

Braun, E. and Brink, E.C.M. van den. 2008. Appraising South Levantine-Egyptian Interaction: Recent Discoveries from Israel and Egypt. In: Midant-Reynes, B., Tristant, Y., Rowland, J., and Hendrix, S., eds. *Egypt at Its Origins* 2 (Orientalia Lovaniensia Analecta 172). Leuven: 643–688.

Brink, E.C.M. van den 1992. Preliminary Report on the Excavations at Tell Ibrahim Awad, Seasons 1988–1990. In: Brink, E.C.M. van den, ed. *The Nile Delta in Transition: 4th–3rd Millennium B.C. Proceedings of the Seminar Held in Cairo, 21.–24. October 1990, at the Netherlands Institute of Archaeology and Arabic Studies.* Tel Aviv: 43–68.

Brink, E.C.M. van den. 2002. An Egyptian Presence at the End of the Late Early Bronze Age I at Tel Lod, Central Coastal Plain, Israel. In: Brink, E.C.M. van den and Levy, T.E., eds. *Egypt and the Levant: Interrelations from the 4th through the Early 3rd Millennium B.C.E.* New York: 286–305.

Brink, E.C.M. van den. 2015. Excavations at Tel Lod: Remains from the Pottery Neolithic A, Chalcolithic, Early Bronze Age I, Middle Bronze Age I and Byzantine Periods. *'Atiqot* 82: 141–177.

Brink, E.C.M. van den and Braun, E. 2002. Wine Jars with Serekhs from Early Bronze Lod: Application Vallée Du Nil Contrôlée, but for Whom? In: Brink, E.C.M. van den and Yannai, E., eds. *In Quest of Ancient Settlements and Landscapes: Archaeological Studies in Honor of Ram Gophna*. Tel Aviv: 167–192.

Bruins, H. and Plicht, J. van den 2001. Radiocarbon Challenges Archaeo-Historical Time Frameworks in the Near East: The Early Bronze Age of Jericho in Relation to Egypt. *Radiocarbon* 43(3): 1321–1332.

Chlodnicki, M., Cialowicz, K.M., and Mączyńska, A., eds. 2012. *Tell el-Farkha* I: *Excavations 1998–2011*. Poznań.

Conti, A.M. and Persiani, C. 1993. Chronology of the Malatya-Elaziğ Area. In: Frangipane, M., Hauptmann, H., Liverani, M., Matthiae, P., and Mellink, M., eds. *Between the Rivers and over the Mountains* (AAM, Alba Palmieri Dedicata). Rome: 362–369.

Czarnowicz, M. 2012. Southern Levantine Imports and Imitations. In: Chlodnicki, M., Cialowicz, K.M., and Mączyńska, A., eds. *Tell el-Farkha* I: *Excavations 1998–2011*. Poznań: 245–267.

Czarnowicz, M. 2014. Erani C Pottery in Egypt. In: Mączyńska, A., ed. *The Nile Delta as a Centre of Cultural Interactions between Upper Egypt and the Southern Levant in the 4th Millennium BC*. Poznań: 95–104.

Dee, M., Wengrow, D., Shortland, A., Stevenson, A., Brock, F., Girdland, Fink, L., and Bronk Ramsey, C. 2013. An Absolute Chronology for Early Egypt Using Radiocarbon Dating and Bayesian Statistical Modelling. *Proceeding of the Royal Society A*. https://royalsocietypublishing.org/doi/full/10.1098/rspa.2013.0395 (accessed 21 August 2019).

Dee, M.W., Wengrow, D., Shortland, A.J., Stevenson, A., Brock, F., and Bronk Ramsey, C. 2014. Radiocarbon Dating and the Naqada Relative Chronology. *Journal of Archaeological Science* 46: 319–323.

Delougaz, P. 1952. *Pottery from the Diyala Region* (Oriental Institute Publications 63). Chicago.

Esse, D. 1991. *Subsistence, Trade, and Social Change in Early Bronze Age Palestine* (Studies in Ancient Oriental Civilization 50). Chicago.

Felli, C. 2003. Developing Complexity: Early to Mid Fourth-Millennium Investigations: The Northern Middle Uruk Period. In: Matthews, R., ed. *Excavations at Tell Brak* 4: *Exploring an Upper Mesopotamian Regional Center, 1994–1996*. London: 53–95.

Finkbeiner, U. and Novák, M. 2015. Introduction. In: Finkbeiner, U., Novák, M., Sakal, F., and Sconzo, P., eds. *Middle Euphrates* (ARCANE IV). Turnhout: 1–16.

Finkbeiner, U., Novák, M., Sakal, F., and Sconzo, P. 2015. Conclusion. In: Finkbeiner, U., Novák, M., Sakal, F., and Sconzo, P., eds. *Middle Euphrates* (ARCANE IV). Turnhout: 431–487.

Finkelstein, I., Ussishkin, D., and Halpern, B. 2006. *Megiddo* IV: *The 1998–2002 Seasons* (Monograph Series of the Institute of Archaeology of Tel Aviv University 24). 2 vols. Tel Aviv.

Fischer, M.P. 2008. *Tell Abu al-Kharaz in the Jordan Valley* I: *The Early Bronze Age* (OAW 48). Vienna.

Fischer, M.P. 2014. Primary Early Bronze Age Contexts from Tell Abu al-Kharaz, Jordan Valley. In: Höflmayer, F. and Eichmann, R., eds. *Egypt and the Southern Levant in the Early Bronze Age*. Rahden: 19–56.

Frangipane, M. 1998. Changes in Upper Mesopotamian/Anatolian Relations at the Beginning of the 3rd Millennium B.C. In: Lebeau, M., ed. *About Subartu: Studies Devoted to Upper Mesopotamia*, I: *Landscape, Archaeology, Settlement;* II: *Culture, Society, Image* (Subartu 4: 1). Turnhout: 195–205.

Frangipane, M. 2000. The Late Chalcolithic/EB I Sequence at Arslantepe: Chronological and Cultural Remarks from a Frontier Site. In: Marro, C. and Hauptmann, H., eds. *Chronologie des pays du Caucase et de l'Euphrate aux IVe–IIIe millénaires. Acts du colloque international, Istanbul 16–19.12.1998* (Varia Anatolica 11). Paris: 439–471.

Frangipane, M. 2007. Establishment of a Middle/Upper Euphrates Early Bronze I Culture from the Fragment of the Uruk World: New Data from Zeytini Bahçe Höyük (Urfa, Turkey). In: Peltenberg, E., ed. *Euphrates River Valley Settlement: The Carchemish Sector in the Third Millennium BC* (Levant Supplementary Series 5). Oxford: 122–141.

Frangipane, M. and Palmieri, A. 1983. Cultural Developments at Arslantepe at the Beginning of the Third Millennium. In: Frangipane, M. and Palmieri, A., eds. *Perspectives and Protourbanization in Eastern Anatolia: Arslantepe (Malatya): An Interim Report on 1975–1983 Campaigns* (Origini 12). Rome: 287–454.

Fukai, S., Horiuchi, K., and Matsutani, T. 1974. *Telul eth Thalathat: The Excavation of Tell* V: *The Fourth Season (1965)* (The Tokyo University Iraq-Iran Archaeological Expedition Report 15). Tokyo.

Gerber, J.C. 2000. Die Keramic der Frühen Bronzezeit im Karababa Becken. In: Marro, C. and Hauptmann, H., eds. *Chronologies des pays du Caucase et de l'Euphrate aux IVe–IIIe millénaires. Actes du colloque d'Istanbul* (Varia Anatolica 11). Paris: 213–229.

Gerber, J.C. 2005. *Hassek Höyük* III. *Die Frübronzezeilische Keramik* (Istanbuler Forschungen 47). Tübingen.

Golani, A. 2003. *Salvage Excavations at the Early Bronze Age Site of Qiryat Ata* (IAA Reports 18). Jerusalem.

Golani, A. 2013. The Transition from the Late Chalcolithic to the Early Bronze I in Southwestern Canaan–Ashqelon as a Case for Continuity. *Paléorient* 39: 95–110.

Golding-Meir, N. and Isirlis, M. 2012. Petrographic Examination of Ceramics. In: Avrutis, W.V. *Late Chalcolithic and Early Bronze Age I Remains at Nesher-Ramla Quarry*. Haifa: 255–268.

Gophna, R. 1992. The Contacts between 'En Besor Oasis, Southern Canaan, and Egypt during the Late Predynastic and the Threshold of the First Dynasty: A Further Assessment. In: Brink, E.C.M. van den, ed. *The Nile Delta in Transition: 4th–3rd Millennium B.C. Proceedings of the Seminar Held in Cairo, 21.–24. October 1990, at the Netherlands Institute of Archaeology and Arabic Studies.* Tel Aviv: 385–394.

Gophna, R. and Liphschitz, N. 1996. The Ashkelon Trough Settlements in the Early Bronze Age I: New Evidence of Maritime Trade. *Tel Aviv* 23: 143–153.

Greenberg, R. 2002. *Early Urbanization in the Levant: A Regional Narrative.* London.

Grossman, K. 2013. Ninevite 5 Ceramics. In: Lebeau, M., ed. *Ceramics* (ARCANE Interregional I). Turnhout: 83–94.

Helwing, B. 2001. Vieröenpokale vom Mittleren Euphrat. Anmerkungen zom Kulturkontakt im frühen dritten Jartausend v. Chr. In: Boehmer, R.M. and Maran, J., eds. *Lux Orientis. Archäologie zwischen Asien und Europa: Festschrift für Harald Hauptmann zum 65 Geburtstag* (Internationale Archäologie. Studia honoraria 12). Rahden: 187–195.

Helwing, B. 2002. *Hassek Höyük II. Die Spätchalkolitische Keramik* (Istanbuler Forschungen 45). Tübingen.

Helwing, B. 2013. Late Reserved Slip Ware. In: Lebeau, M., ed. *Ceramics* (ARCANE Interregional I). Turnhout: 25–32.

Hiroyuki, L. 2003. Tell Jigan and the Relationship between the Ninevite V and Scarlet Ware. In: Weiss, H. and Rova, E., eds. *The Origins of North Mesopotamian Civilization: Ninevite V Chronology, Economy, Society* (Subartu 9, PAS 6). Berlin: 1–10.

Hornung, E.R., Krauss, R., and Warburton, D.A., eds. 2006. *Ancient Egyptian Chronology: Handbook of Oriental Studies, Section One: The Near and Middle East.* Boston.

Jamieson, A. 2013. Late Reserved Slip Ware. In: Lebeau, M., ed. *Ceramics* (ARCANE Interregional I). Turnhout: 101–113.

Köhler, C.E. 1992. The Pre- and Early Dynastic Pottery of Tell el-Fara'in/Buto. In: Brink, E.C.M. van den, ed. *The Nile Delta in Transition: 4th–3rd Millennium B.C. Proceedings of the Seminar Held in Cairo, 21.–24. October 1990, at the Netherlands Institute of Archaeology and Arabic Studies* Tel Aviv: 11–22.

Lebeau, M. and Miroschedji, P. de 2013. Foreword. In: Lebeau, M., ed. *Ceramics* (ARCANE Interregional I). Turnhout: IX–X.

Levy, T.E., Alon, D., Brink, E.C.M. van den, Kansa, E.C., and Yekutiely, Y. 2001. The Protodynastic/Dynasty 1 Egyptian Presence in Southern Canaan: A Preliminary Report on the 1994 Excavations at Naḥal Tillah, Israel. In: Wolff, R., ed. *Studies in the Archaeology of Israel and Neighboring Lands in Memory of Douglas L. Esse.* Chicago: 407–438.

Marro, C. and Hauptmann, H., eds. 2000. *Chronologies des pays du Caucase et de l'Euphrate aux IVe–IIIe millénaire. Actes du colloque d'Istanbul* (Varia Anatolica 11). Paris.

Milevski, I. 2009. Local Exchange in the Southern Levant during the Early Bronze Age: A Political Economy Viewpoint. *Antiguo Oriente* 7: 125–159.

Milevski, I. 2011. *Early Bronze Age Goods Exchange in the Southern Levant: A Marxist Perspective.* London.

Miroschedji, P. de 2009. Rise and Collapse in the Southern Levant in the Early Bronze Age. *Scienze dell'antichità storia archeologia antropologia* 15: 101–129.

Miroschedji, P. de, Sadek, M., Faltings, D., Boulez, V., Naggiar-Moliner, L., Sykes, N., and Tengberg, M. 2001. Les fouilles de Tell es-Sakan (Gaza): nouvelles données sur les contacts égypto-cananéens aux IVe–IIIe millénaires. *Paléorient* 27: 75–104.

Morandi Bonacossi, D. 2005. The Late Chalcolithic and Early Bronze Age I Sequences of Area D. In: Bachelot, L. and Fales, F.M., eds. *Tell Shiukh Fawqani 1994–1998.* Padua: 21–248.

Nocera, G.M. di 2000. Radiocarbon Datings from Arslantepe and Norşuntepe: The Fourth–Third Millennium Absolute Chronology in the Upper Euphrates and Transcaucasian Region. In: Marro, C. and Hauptmann, H., eds. *Chronologies des pays du Caucase et de l'Euphrate aux IVe–IIIe millénaires. Actes du colloque d'Istanbul* (Varia Anatolica 11). Paris: 73–93.

Paz, I. 2002. Fortified Settlements of the EB IB and the Emergence of the First Urban System. *Tel Aviv* 29: 238–261.

Pearce, J. 2000. The Late Chalcolithic at Hacinebi Tepe. In: Marro, C. and Hauptmann, H., eds. *Chronologies des pays du Caucase et de l'Euphrate aux IVe–IIIe millénaires. Actes du colloque d'Istanbul* (Varia Anatolica 11). Paris: 115–143.

Philip, G. 2001. The Early Bronze I–III Ages. In: MacDonald, B., Adams, R., and Bienkowski, P., eds. *The Archaeology of Jordan.* Sheffield: 163–232.

Philip, G. 2008. The Early Bronze I–III. In: Adams, R., ed. *Jordan: An Archaeological Reader.* London: 161–226.

Prag, K. 1986. Byblos and Egypt in the Fourth Millennium BC. *Levant* 18: 59–74.

Regev, J., Miroschedji, P. de, and Boaretto, E. 2012. Early Bronze Age Chronology: Radiocarbon Dates and Chronological Models from Tel Yarmuth (Israel). *Radiocarbon* 54: 505–524.

Regev, J., Miroschedji, P. de, Greenberg, R., Braun, E., and Greenhut, Z. 2012. Chronology of the Early Bronze Age in the Southern Levant: New Analysis for a High Chronology. *Radiocarbon* 54: 525–556.

Rothman, M.S. 2002. Tepe Gawra: Chronology and Socio-Economic Change in the Foothills of Northern Iraq in the Era of State Formation. In: Postgate, J.N., ed. *Artefacts of Complexity: Tracking the Uruk in the Near East* (British School of Archaeology in Iraq 5). Warminster: 49–78.

Rova, E. 2011. Ceramics. In: Lebeau, M., ed. *Jezirah* (ARCANE Interrgional 1). Turnhout: 49–68.

Rova, E. 2013. Post-LC 5 North Mesopotamian Developments. In: Lebeau, M., ed. *Ceramics* (ARCANE Interregional I). Turnhout: 1–23.
Sconzo, P. 2015. Ceramics. In: Finkbeiner, U. and Buoso, M., eds. *Middle Euphrates* (ARCANE IV). Turnhout: 85–202.
Sharvit, J., Galili, E., Rosen B., and Brink, E.C.M. van den 2002. Predynastic Maritime Traffic along the Carmel Coast of Israel: A Submerged Find from North 'Atlit Bay. In: Brink, E.C.M. van den and Yannai, E., eds. *In Quest of Ancient Settlements and Landscapes: Archaeological Studies in Honor of Ram Gophna*. Tel Aviv: 159–166.
Speiser, E.A. 1935. *Excavations at Tepe Gawra* I: *Levels I–VII*. Philadelphia.
Stadler P. and Fischer P.M. 2008. Radiocarbon Datings. In: Fischer, P.M. *Tell Abu al-Kharaz in the Jordan Valley*, Vol. 1: *The Early Bronze Age*. Vienna: 323–326.
Stager, L. 1992. The Periodization of Palestine from the Neolithic through Early Bronze Times. In: Ehrich, R.W., ed. *Chronologies in Old World Archaeology* (3rd ed.). Chicago: 22–41.
Tsatskin, A. 2010. Petrographic Examination of Ceramics from Burial Cave F-355 and Burial F-257. In: Kol-Ya'aqov, S. *Salvage Excavations at Nesher-Ramla Quarry* I. Haifa: 43–57.
Vaux, R. de 1952 La Quatrième campagne de fouilles à Tell el-Far'ah près Naplouse. *Revue Biblique* 59: 551–583.
Yannai, E. 2006. *'En Esur ('Ein Asawir)* I: *Excavations at a Protohistoric Site in the Coastal Plain, Israel* (IAA Reports 31). Jerusalem.
Yannai, E. 2016. *'En Esur ('Ein Asawir)* II: *Excavations at the Cemeteries* (IAA Reports 31/2). Jerusalem
Yannai, E. and Braun, E. 2001. Anatolian and Egyptian Imports from Late EB I at Ain Asawir, Israel. *Bulletin of the American Schools of Oriental Research* 321: 41–56.
Yannai, E. and Grosinger, Z. 2000. Preliminary Summary of Early Bronze Age Strata and Burials at 'Ein Assawir, Israel. In: Philip, G. and Baird, D., eds. *Ceramics and Change in the Early Bronze Age of the Southern Levant* (Levantine Archaeology 2). Sheffield: 153–164.
Yekutieli, Y. 2000. Early Bronze Age I Pottery in Southern Canaan. In Adams, R. and Goren, Y., eds. *Ceramics and Change in the Early Bronze Age of the Southern Levant* (Levantine Archaeology 2). Sheffield: 129–153.
Yekutieli, Y. 2006. The Ceramics of the Tel Erani, Layer C. *Glassink* 22: 225–242.
Yener, K.A., ed. 2009. *The Amuq Valley Regional Project* 1: *Surveys in the Plain of Antioch and Orontes Delta, Turkey 1995–2002* (Oriental Institute Publications 131). Chicago.
Yener, K.A. and Wilkinson, T. 1996–1997. *Amuq Valley Regional Project* (Oriental Institute Annual Report 11–12). Chicago.
Yener, K.A., Edens, C., and Harrison, T.P., 2000. The Amuq Valley Regional Project, 1995–1998. *American Journal of Archaeology* 104: 163–220.

Yener, K.A., Wilkinson, T.G., Branting, S., Friedman, E.S., Lyon, J.D., and Reichel, C.D. 1996. The 1995 Oriental Institute Amuq Regional Projects. *Anatolica* 22: 49–84.

Zuckerman, S. 2003. The Early Bronze Age I. In: Ben-Tor, A., Bonfil, R., and Zuckerman, S. *Tel Qashish: A Village in the Jezreel Valley. Final Report of the Archaeological Excavations (1978–1987)* (Qedem Reports 5). Jerusalem: 35–48.

CHAPTER 3

Burials of Domesticated Animals in the Middle Bronze Age Rampart at Tel 'Akko in Light of Archaeological Finds in the Levant and Ceremonies from the Ancient Near East

Ron Beeri, Hadas Motro, Noa Gerstel-Raban, and Michal Artzy

1   Introduction

A burial of several animals was exposed at Tel 'Akko, on the inner slope of a rampart (L911 and L920). It was ascribed to the end of the Middle Bronze (MB) IIA (Fig. 3.1; Beeri 2008: 132–135, 384–390).[1] The burial included the skeletons of a donkey (Fig. 3.2; L916) and a dog (L921) and part of the upper jawbone of a pig that were interred together.[2] The fact that two of the three skeleton remains that were found were almost intact and next to each other indicates that in all likelihood these are indeed burials (below).

Several of the donkey bones were found burnt, and a layer of ash was discovered beneath the animal's cervical vertebrae and its head. The donkey was a 4.5 year old female (withers height [WH]) estimation in cm, based on the metapodials is 118.80 cm [Motro 2014: 27-33]). It was placed on an inclined floor of black mud bricks (L911) and beneath the skeleton, a small fishing weight[3] and a number of beach rocks with marine fossils on them were found. Two fragments of a thick red-slipped ceramic disc were also found nearby (Fig. 3.3).[4]

The skeleton of the dog (Fig. 3.4), like that of the donkey, underwent special treatment at the time of the burial or thereafter. Below it were a number of beach

---

1   Area AB, Phase 3, Rampart 920.
2   The pig's jaw was not articulated and therefore not drawn.
3   The fishing weight was made of a small pebble through which a hole was drilled. The surface of the pebble is perforated with tiny orifices of marine origin, indicating that it was in the water for a prolonged period of time. Other similar weights were also found in Area AB in an infant jar-burial (L1045) that is attributed to Phase 4 and in a built burial chamber (L691) ascribed to Phase 2A (Beeri 2008: 124, 157).
4   This is a thick ceramic disc-like object. Its upper part is arched and its bottom is concave to flat. It is 53 cm in diameter with a maximum thickness of 5.3 cm (of the part that is preserved) and its center is slightly thicker than its edges. The surface of the object is treated with a thick rough red slip. On the edge and the bottom part of the object are concentric wear marks indicating the item was spun around a central axis.

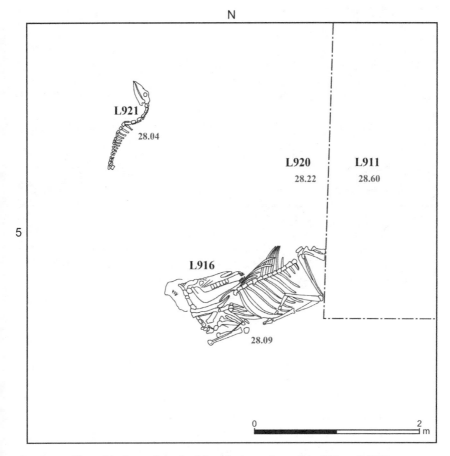

FIGURE 3.1 Plan of donkey and dog burial on the inner slope of the MB IIA Tel 'Akko rampart

rocks with marine fossils, similar to those that were discovered beneath the skeleton of the donkey. The head and the entire spine of the dog were found in full anatomical articulation, whereas the other parts of the skeleton were missing.

The following analysis of this unique 'Akko burial is significant, since there seems to be no evidence of a dog, donkey, and pig buried in a common grave from Mesopotamia, the Levant, or Egypt in the Middle and Late Bronze Ages.

2   General Background about Tel 'Akko

Tel 'Akko is located on a *kurkar* hill situated at the end of a *kurkar* ridge, ca. 700 m east of the Mediterranean Sea.[5] The tell was founded in a fertile agricultural

---

5 Tel 'Akko was not systematically excavated until the 1970s. The first scientific excavation on the tell took place in 1973, and from that year until 1989 twelve seasons of excavation were

FIGURE 3.2 Donkey skeleton from the donkey and dog burial in the Tel 'Akko rampart

region and next to one of the most protected natural anchorages along the coast of the Land of Israel. Numerous abundant springs are located next to Tel 'Akko, the largest of which, 'Ain el Baqar, was used until the end of the Ottoman period. During its ancient past, Tel 'Akko was surrounded by water on the northwest, west, and south (Inbar and Sivan 1984; Raban 1991; Artzy 2006: 116; 2012; Zviely et al. 2006; Beeri 2008; Artzy and Beeri 2010; Artzy and Quartermaine 2014). These conditions made it possible to approach the city by sailing from the south and west and facilitated the establishment of the anchorage that was built south of the tell (Raban 1991; Artzy 2012, 2018; Artzy and Quartermaine 2014; Morhange et al. 2016; Giaime et al. 2018).

'Akko was situated on a continental crossroads where the Via Maris met the roads that ran east and passed through relatively moderate terrain toward eastern Transjordan and the Jordan Valley. The combination of fertile ground, abundant and stable springs, control of a natural harbor, and a main intersection attracted settlers and merchants to 'Akko. These factors resulted in the city's prosperity that lasted from the MB II until the end of the Ottoman period. During these periods, the city served, almost without interruption, as an

conducted under the direction of Moshe Dothan, as part of what was then called the Center for Maritime Studies at the University of Haifa. In 1999, a study excavation of the Departments of Archaeology and Maritime Civilizations at the University of Haifa was conducted in Area G under the direction of Michal Artzy and Ann Killebrew. The tell is presently being excavated as part of the "Total Archaeology Project" directed by Ann Killebrew of Pennsylvania State University and Michal Artzy of the University of Haifa.

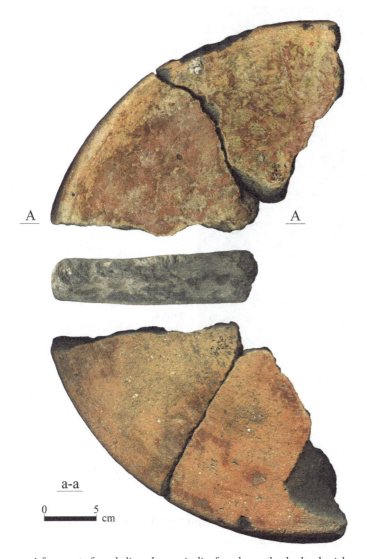

FIGURE 3.3 A fragment of a red-slipped ceramic disc found near the donkey burial

important administrative and economic center in the geographic-cultural domain of southern Syria, Phoenicia, and the Land of Israel (Beeri 2008; Artzy and Beeri 2010).

3 The Location of the Burials

The dog (L921) and donkey burials (L916) were discovered in Phase 3 at ʿAkko, which is ascribed to the second half of the eighteenth century BCE (Beeri 2008: 132–135, 384–390). The burials were exposed in Area AB (Square N/4), slightly

FIGURE 3.4
Dog skeleton from the donkey and dog burial in the Tel 'Akko rampart

below the northernmost and highest point on the mound. They were sealed by one of a number of inner sand ramparts (L920) that were part of the northern fortifications of 'Akko in Phase 3 in Area AB (Beeri 2008: 127–150). These inner ramparts were used for burials in Phases 4–1, (MB IIA–Late Bronze [LB] I) and yielded a number of tombs with infants, adolescents, and adults situated a few meters from animal burials (e.g., Fig. 3.5; Beeri 2003, 2008).

4 Burials of Donkeys, Dogs, and Pigs during the Second Millennium BCE

Burials of a donkey and a dog not accompanying human interment were found at Tell Brak (northern Syria, Akkadian period, 2580–2455 cal BCE) and Tel Haror (Middle Bronze Age) in the southern Levant. At Tell Brak six donkey skeletons and one canine skeleton were found below a temple courtyard (Clutton-Brock 1989; Clutton-Brock and Davis 1993). Sacrifices of a dog and a pig were found in a temple courtyard at Tel Haror (Oren 1997; Bar-Oz et al. 2013), and funerary offerings of donkeys were also found in the courtyards of Middle Bronze Age temples at Tell el-Dab'a (van den Brink 1982: 74–77; Oren 1997: 265–266).

BURIALS OF DOMESTICATED ANIMALS IN MIDDLE BRONZE AGE RAMPART 59

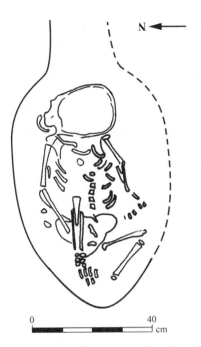

FIGURE 3.5 Jar burial of an infant (Burial 868, Phase 4) in the MB IIA rampart at Tel 'Akko
BEERI 2008: 127

A "horse's skull"[6] was reportedly buried outside a burial chamber (691) at the top of the northern fortress of Tel 'Akko, Phase 2 (Beeri 2008: 137, MB IIC). Another horse skull was found in a tomb at Tel Shiqmona, not far from Tel 'Akko (Elgavish 1994: 29). Bones of donkeys and horses were also found in tombs at Tell el-'Ajjul (MB IIB), sometimes at an elevation that was slightly higher than that of human burials in the same levels (Petrie 1931: 4–5). Some researchers believe that parts of animals, such as those from Tel 'Akko, Tel Shiqmona, and Tell el-'Ajjul, were used in a ceremonial meal held in honor of the dead during their interment (Stiebing 1971: 116; Wapnish 1997: 359).

In the southern Levant, donkey burials were documented at the following sites: Tell el-'Ajjul (buried donkeys and horses), Tombs 101, 210, 411, 441, 1417 (MB IIB); Tell Jemmeh (MB IIB); Jericho, Tombs B48, B50, B51, D9, D22, J3, J37, M11, P22 (MB IIB); and Tel Hazor (MB IIB) (Clutton-Brock 1979; Wapnish 1997 and references threin; Nahshoni 2015 and references therein).

Donkey burials were also common in Egypt (in the Second Intermediate Period). They were found at Tell el-Dab'a Strata E, F, and G (Tombs L/12, 2; L12,

---

6 This is how it was registered in the daily log. The "horse's skull" was lost and cannot therefore be identified.

5; M/12, 9; N/11; N/13, 8), Tell el-Maskhuta, and Inshas (van den Brink 1982: 74–77; Wapnish 1997: 353–355). At these sites these animals were slaughtered and subsequently parts of them were eaten in funerary ceremonies; the remaining parts of the donkey would be buried along with the deceased (Ziffer 1990: 86, based on Bietak 1979: 246; Van Beek 1984: 688–689).

In Syria, equid burials were found at Tell Ababra[7] and at Tell Brak, as mentioned above. Most of the donkeys were interred alongside human burials. With the exception of the burial in Tomb 916 at Tel 'Akko and Tomb 1417 at Tell el-'Ajjul, most of the animal skeletons were incomplete.

Canine burials of two dogs without human remains or any funerary offerings were found at 'Ezbet Helmi C/3–2 (Bietak 2006: 123–136, fig. 8; LB I–II). These are attributed to nomads who lived in the area in the fifteenth century BCE (Bietak 2006). In Mesopotamia canine burials were associated with the cult of Gu-la and burials of dogs and puppies were uncovered at Isin (Oren 1997). Pig burial is attested at Sidon, where pig parts were found in the tomb of a woman, attributed to the MB IIA (Vila and Chahoud 2006).

5   Evidence of a Dog, Pig, and Donkey Cult in Mesopotamia, Syria, and Anatolia and Their Religious Significance

In Mesopotamia and Anatolia positive characteristics are ascribed to dogs and donkeys: images of guard dogs adorned the gates of cities in Mesopotamia, denoting the strength of the gate. Figurines of guard dogs that were placed in the entrances of houses and bedrooms were meant "to chase away the daughter of Anu" and "to stand watch over (the house) during the night," as was written on some of them (Wiggermann 2000: 239). In Mesopotamia dogs were associated with Gu-la, the goddess of healing, and the burials of dogs and puppies were uncovered in the excavation of a temple of Gu-la at Isin (Oren 1997 and references therein).

At Uruk evidence of the cult of Gu-la was found beginning with the Third Dynasty of Ur (Sallaberger 1993: 191). We learn about the worship and offerings made to the goddess in the Neo-Babylonian period from the inscriptions that were found in the Eanna archive in Uruk, and there was a place for the Gu-la cult in the Eanna temple (Beaulieu 2003: 274–282, 315–316). A city named "Bīt-Gulu," which is mentioned in the archive, was probably close to Uruk (Beaulieu 2003: 315). In a Neo-Babylonian text from the archive, Gu-la is explicitly

---

7   Four graves ascribed to the Early Babylonian period were found with donkey burials (Zarins 1986).

mentioned as the one who attacks Lamaštu and protects infants (Dunham 1993: 247 n. 45).

Apart from its association with Lamaštu (see below), the Mesopotamian donkey is also associated with the god of fertility, Shakkan/Sumuqan, who is also identified with deer, sheep, and gazelle (Tallqvist 1938: 450–451; Wapnish 1997: 357 n. 20).

In Mesopotamia sacrificed donkeys were interred in Sumerian burials as part of a religious practice (Black and Green 1992: 32). An Amorite practice was to "kill a donkey to make peace" and in Akkadian the sacrificial donkey is called "hara qatalu; ha-a-ri-m qa-ta-li-im," which means "to sacrifice a young ass" and also "to form an alliance" (Dossin 1938: 109; Firmage 1992: 1137; Wapnish 1997: 364, n. 25–26). The similarity of these two acts is attested in the Mari letters. Donkey sacrifices were considered, therefore, sacred and binding (Ziffer 1990: 80, based on Jean 1950: 82–83 n. 37).

In a letter from Mari dating to the thirteenth year of the reign of Zimri-Lim (XRM XXXVI.410.4'–25'), Yasim-El, the commander of the Mari garrison at Andarig, tells of messengers (apparently of Zimri-Lim) who were dispatched to Atamrum king of Andarig, in order to ensure peace between him and Hammu-Rabi king of Kurda. Atamrum agreed to make peace by conducting a sacrificial ceremony of a young ass (Anbar 2007: 118).

In other letters from Mari (LAPO 16.284–285) Ibal-El, in charge of the royal pasturelands, reports to his king, Zimri-Lim, about making peace between the Hana pastoralist tribes, who were a West Semitic group of seminomads, and the people of Idamaraṣ. Both groups agreed on sacrificing a puppy and a goat; however, Ibal-El objected because it was not Zimri-Lim's custom to use such animals; instead, Zimri-Lim would offer a donkey foal, and therefore a donkey foal of a she-ass was sacrificed and peace prevailed between the adversaries (Jean 1950: 82–83, Letter 37; Stiebing 1971: 116; Oren 1997: 264; Anbar 2007: 188, 193–192).

A sacrifice involving a she-asses is also mentioned in an Ugaritic document (Gordon 1965: 177, Text 62, line 28; Tarragon 1980: 37–39).[8] In the Bible, the donkey is the only impure animal that is included in a ritual: the Torah commands that the firstborn donkey be redeemed with a lamb or that its head be cut off (Exodus 13:13).

Sacrifices of dogs and pigs were common in Anatolia. The Hittites sacrificed young dogs and pigs in ceremonies intended to eradicate impurity or disease

---

8 S. Rin and S. Rin (1996), who translated the text (pl. 33 = 62, line 28, p. 311), are of the opinion that fallow-deer rather than donkeys were sacrificed, because all the other animals that are mentioned in the text have horns.

(Firmage 1992: 1132, 1143). According to Firmage, the dog and pig were almost always sacrificed together with another animal (ibid.). Young pigs were sacrificed in order to restore harmony and reconciliation in the family, to banish an epidemic from an agricultural field and to rehabilitate an army after defeat (Firmage 1992: 1131, 1143, based on Friedrich 1925; Masson 1950; Rost 1953; Gurney 1954: 151). In the case of a military defeat, a pig, dog, goat, and person were sacrificed; they were cut in two and their cleaved parts were placed some distance apart from each other. Afterwards, a gate was built near them and the vanquished army would pass through it and march between the butchered pieces of the sacrifices (Firmage 1992: 1144).

6   Dog, Pig, and Donkey Burials in the Context of Rituals against Lamaštu

A common burial of a dog, pig, and donkey may be linked to the Mesopotamian ritual against the demon Lamaštu (corresponding to the Sumerian Dimme), who is identified with the daughter of Anu, god of the heavens. The abovementioned ceramic disc found at 'Akko may have symbolized the sun. Amulets inscribed with sun discs were used in Mesopotamia as talismans against Lamaštu (Wiggermann 2000: 239, 246), who is usually identified as having a human body with body members of a donkey, dog, and lion and sometimes of other animals as well (Figs. 3.6, 3.7). Often, the demon is presented together with a puppy and a piglet nursing at her breasts. Her image was described many times in the Sumerian, Akkadian, Early Babylonian, Early Assyrian, Neo-Assyrian, and Neo-Babylonian mythologies (Wiggermann 2000). Evidence of the Lamaštu cult was also found at Ugarit (Nougayrol 1969) and in Israel (Cogan 1995; Ornan 2006). In a text from the Early Babylonian period (BIN 2 72: 1f) Lamaštu is described as one who "was born to Anu, was raised by Ea and was given the face of a dog by Enlil" (Wiggermann 2000: 232 n. 118).

Beginning in the Akkadian period it is explicitly written that the principal "victims" of Lamaštu were premature babies and newborns "whose blood she would drink and flesh she would eat" (Thureau-Dangin 1921: 169, 194; Black and Green 1992: 115–116; Firmage 1992: 1144; Farber 1995: 1897; Cunningham 1997: 108–109; Green 1997: 142–143; Wiggermann 2000: 231–232). The demon is described as causing sickness and death, killing babies in their mother's wombs, murdering infants during their birth, and snatching them when they nurse. For these reasons she has been identified with abortions and the death of infants

FIGURE 3.6 Seventh–ninth-centuries BCE Neo-Assyrian Lamaštu amulet
AFTER WIGGERMANN 2000: FIG. 6

and of young mothers, as well as of adults (Thureau-Dangin 1921: 169, 194; Firmage 1992, 1144; Black and Green 1992: 115–116; Farber 1995: 1897; Green 1997, 142–143; Cunningham 1997: 108–109; Wiggermann 2000: 231–232).

In Mesopotamia, children and adults were protected with Lamaštu amulets that were incorporated in necklaces, armlets and anklets. Many archaeological finds from the Sumerian and Akkadian civilizations attest to these characteristics of the goddess and her cult (Strommenger 1957–1971: 603; Tonietti 1979: 305; Dunham 1993; Cunningham 1997: 108–109, 140, 148, 152–153, 155, Texts 187, 188, 189, 306, 347, 359, 362, 394, 396; Green 1997: 152, figs. 19–20; Wiggermann 2000: 229 n. 76). The goddess is portrayed as a donkey with puppies and piglets at her feet on Mesopotamian amulets dating to the Bronze Age (Wiggermann 2000: 220–221, 239, fig. 1, Amulet no. 85; fig. 4).

A figurine of a dog that is thought to be a Lamaštu amulet was found in a child burial at Tell al-Raqā'i (in the central Habur Valley), dating to MB IIA (Dunham 1993: 246). On a Neo-Assyrian amulet from the ninth–seventh centuries BCE, Lamaštu is portrayed with a head that combines the features of a lion and a donkey (the face of a lion and the teeth and ears of a donkey), with the

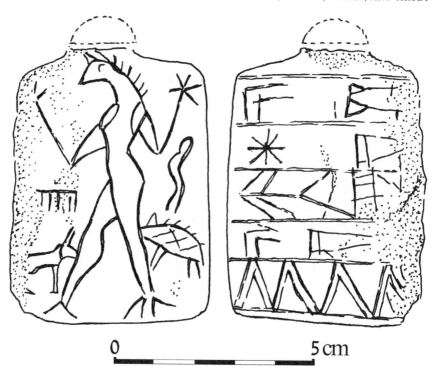

FIGURE 3.7 Mesopotamian amulet presenting Lamaštu as a donkey accompanied by a dog and pig
AFTER WIGGERMANN 2000: FIG. 1

hairy body of a donkey and the talons of a bird of prey (Pritchard 1954: nos. 657, 658, 660). She is nursing a puppy and a piglet, her long arms are holding snakes, and she is kneeling over a donkey that allows her to cross deserts and mountains. The goddess and the donkey are portrayed on a boat sailing on the river of the underworld (Pritchard 1954: nos. 657, 658; Black and Green 1992: 65, 70–71, 115–116, 181; Wiggermann 2000: 243–246, fig. 6). A talisman plaque against Lamaštu was found ex situ near Tel Burnat in Israel (Cogan 1995: 156–161, figs. 1–2). Only the lower part of the amulet, which dates to the Neo-Assyrian period, has survived (Cogan 1995: 156–161). The lower part of the body of Lamaštu, who is standing on an animal, is engraved on it. A snake and a pig, which she is nursing, are seen to her left. On her right the leg of another animal can be seen—probably that of a dog (ibid.). On the obverse of the plaque there is an incantation in cuneiform, in which the names of the gods Enlil and Marduk are mentioned (Cogan 1995: 158).

Presently, no actual sacrifices have been found that are identified with the Lamaštu cult, but the donkey, canine, and pig sacrifices from 'Akko may be have been offered to the demon in return for human life.

7 Summary

This paper presents a group burial of a donkey, dog, and pig that were buried near human burials inside the Middle Bronze Age rampart at Tel 'Akko. Separate burials of each of these animals are found at sites dating from the third millennium to the first millennium BCE in the ancient Near East. However, so far, no burial has been discovered in which these three animals were entombed together. This unique burial inside the Tel 'Akko rampart reflects a cultural phenomenon that is yet unknown in the Canaanite culture. It may be assumed that it emulates customs from the Syrian-Mesopotamian cultural sphere that influenced Canaanite society and its religious practices.

References

Anbar, M. 2007. *Prophecy, Treaty-Making and Tribes in the Mari Documents during the Period of the Amorite Kings (From the End of the 19th Century B.C.E.)*. Jerusalem (Hebrew).

Artzy, M. 2006. "Filling in" the Void: Observations on the Habitation Pattern at Tel Akko at the End of the Late Bronze Age. In: Maeir, A.M. and Miroschedji, P. de, eds. *"I Will Speak the Riddles of Ancient Times": Archaeological and Historical Studies in Honor of Amihai Mazar*, Vol. 1. Winona Lake, IN: 115–122.

Artzy, M. 2012. Return to Tel Akko, Its Anchorages, Harbor, and Surroundings. *Recanati Institute for Maritime Studies News*: 5–14.

Artzy, M. 2018. From Akko/Acco to Beit She'an/Beth Shan. *Egypt and the Levant* 18: 85–98.

Artzy, M and Beeri, R. 2010. Tel Akko. In: Killebrew, A. and Raz-Romeo, V., eds. *One Thousand Nights and Days: Akko through the Ages*. Haifa: 15–14.

Artzy, M. and Quartermaine, J. 2014. How and When Did Tel Akko Get Its Unusual Banana Shape? In: Galanakis, Y., Wilkinson, T., and Bennet, J., eds. *Critical Essays on the Archaeology of the Eastern Mediterranean in Honour of E. Susan Sherratt*. Oxford: 11–22.

Beeri, R. 2003. *Middle and Late Bronze Age Tombs from Tel Akko (Area AB)*. M.A. thesis. University of Haifa. Haifa.

Beeri, R. 2008. *Tel Akko and the Urbanization of the Akko Plain in the First Half of the Second Millennium BCE*. Ph.D. dissertation. University of Haifa. Haifa.

Bar-Oz, G., Nahshoni, P., Motro, H., and Oren, E.D. 2013. Symbolic Metal Bit and Saddle-bag Fastening in a Middle Bronze Age Donkey Burial. *PLOS ONE* 8(3): 1–7.

Beaulieu, P.-A. 2003. *The Pantheon of Uruk during the Neo-Babylonian Period*. Leiden.

Bietak, M. 2006. Nomads or mnmn.t-Shepherds in the Eastern Nile Delta in The New Kingdom. In: Maeir, A.M. and Miroschedji, P. de, ed. *"I Will Speak the Riddles of*

Ancient Times": Archaeological and Historical Studies in Honor of Amihai Mazar, Vol. 1. Winona Lake, IN.: 123–136.

Black, J. and Green, A. 1992. *God, Demons and Symbols of Ancient Mesopotamia: An Illustrated Dictionary*. London.

Bietak, M. 1979. *Avaris and Piramese: Archaeological Exploration in the Eastern Nile Delta*. London.

Brink, E.C.M., van den. 1982. Tombs and Burial Custom at Tell el Dab'a and Their Cultural Relationship to Syria-Palestine during the Second Intermediate Period (Beiträge zur Ägyptologie 4), Vienna.

Clutton-Brock, J. 1979. The Mammalian Remains from the Jericho Tell. *Proceeding of the Prehistoric Society* 45: 35–157.

Clutton-Brock, J. 1989. A Donkey and Dog Excavated at Tell Brak. *Iraq* 51: 217–224.

Clutton-Brock, J. and Davis, S. 1993. More Donkeys from Tell Brak. *Iraq* 55: 209–221.

Cogan, M. 1995. A Lamashtu Plaque from the Judaean Shephelah. *Israel Exploration Journal* 45: 155–161.

Cunningham, G. 1997. *Deliver Me from Evil: Mesopotamian Incantations 2500–1500 BC*. Rome.

Dossin, G. 1938. Les archives épistolaires du palais de Mari, *Syria* 19 : 105–126.

Dunham, S. 1993. Beads for Babies, *Zeitschrift für Assyriologie und Vorderasiatische Archäologie* 83: 237–257.

Elgavish, Y. 1994. *Shiqmona, on the Carmel Coast*. Tel Aviv (Hebrew).

Farber, W. 1995. Witchcraft, Magic, and Divination in Ancient Mesopotamia. In: Sasson, J., Baines, J., Beckman, G., and Rubinson, K.S., M., eds. *Civilizations of the Ancient Near East* III. New York: 1895–1909.

Firmage, E. 1992. Zoology. In: Herion, G.A., Graf, D.F., and Pleins, J.D., eds. *The Anchor Bible Dictionary* 6. New York: 1109–1167.

Friedrich, J. 1925. Zwei Bwschwörungen gegen Seuchen in Land und Herr. In: Friedrich, J. *Aus dem hethitischen Schrifttum. Übersetzungen von Keilschrifttexten aus dem Archiv von Boghazköi*. Leipzig : 10–16.

Giaime, M., Morhange, C., Marriner, N., López-Cadavid, G.I., and Artzy, M. 2018 Geoarchaeological Investigations at Akko, Israel: New Insights into Landscape Changes and Related Anchorage Locations since the Bronze Age, *Geoarchaeology* 33: 641–660.

Gordon, C. 1965. *Ugaritic Textbook*. Rome.

Green, A. 1997. Myths in Mesopotamian Art. In: Finkel, I.L. and Geller, M.J., eds. *Sumerian Gods and Their Representation* (Cuneiform Monographs 7). Groningen: 135–158.

Gurney, O. 1954. *The Hittites* (2nd ed.) Harmondsworth.

Inbar, M., and Sivan, D. 1984. Paleo-Urban Development and Late Quaternary Environmental Change in the Akko Area, *Paléorient* 9(2): 85–91.

Jean, C-F. 1950. *Archives royales de Mari* II. *Lettres diverses*, Paris.

Masson, O. 1950. A propos d'un rituel pour la lustration d'une armée, *Revue de l'histoire des religions* 127 : 5–25.

Morhange, C., Giaime, M., Marriner, N., abu Hamid, A., Honnorat, A., Kaniewski, D., Magnin, F., Portov, A.V., Wente, J., Zviely, D., and Artzy, M. 2016. Geoarchaeological Evolution of Tel Akko's Ancient Harbor. *Journal of Archaeological Science: Reports* 7: 71–81.

Motro, H. 2014. *Medieval Equids in the Southern Levant: Methods for Characterizing Species and Breed*. PhD diss.The Hebrew University, Jerusalem.

Nahshoni, P. 2015. *Ritual Practice and Feasting in the Middle Bronze II–III Temples in Canaan in Light of the Finds from the Sacred Precinct at Tel Haror*. MA thesis. Ben-Gurion University. Beer-Sheva (Hebrew).

Nougayrol, J. 1969. La Lamaštu à Ugarit, *Ugaritica* VI: 393–408.

Oren, E.D. 1997. The "Kingdom of Sharuhen" and the Hyksos Kingdom. In: Oren, E.D., ed. *The Hyksos: New Historical and Archaeological Perspectives* (University of Pennsylvania Museum Monographs 8). Philadelphia: 253–284.

Ornan, T. 2006. An Amulet of the Demon Pazuzu. In: Mazar, A., ed. *Excavations at Tel Beth-Shean 1989–1996*, Vol. 1: *From the Late Bronze Age IIB to the Medieval Period*. Jerusalem: 517–519.

Petrie, W.M.F. 1931. *Ancient Gaza* I. London.

Pritchard, J.B., ed. 1954. *The Ancient Near East in Pictures Relating to the Old Testament*. Princeton.

Rost, L. 1953. Ein hethitisches Ritual gegen Familienzwist. *Mitteilungen des Instituts für Orientforschung* 1: 345–379.

Raban, A. 1991. The Port City of Akko in the MB II, *Michmanim* 5: 17–34.

Rin, S. and Rin S. 1996. *Acts of the Gods: The Ugaritic Epic Poetry*. Philadelphia.

Sallaberger, W. 1993. *Der kultische Kalender der Ur III-Zeit*, Vol. 2 (Untersuchungen zur Assyriologie und Vorderasiatischen Archäologie 7), Berlin.

Stiebing, H.W. 1971. Hyksos Burials in Palestine: A Review of the Evidence. *Journal of Near Eastern Studies* 30: 110–117,

Strommenger, E. 1957–1971. Grab, Grabbeigabe, *Reallexikon der Assyriologie* 3: 581–608.

Tallqvist, K. 1938. *Akkadische Götterepitheta* (Studia Orientalia 7). Helsinki.

Tarragon, J-M. 1980. *Le culte à Ugarit*, Paris.

Thureau-Dangin, F. 1921. Rituel et amulettes contre Labartu, *Revue d'Assyriologie* 18 : 161–198.

Tonietti, M.V. 1979. Un Incantesimo sumerico contro la Lamaštu, *Orientalia NS* 48: 301–323.

Van Beek, G.W. 1984. Archaeological Investigations at Tell Jemmeh, Israel. *National Geographic Research Reports* 16: 675–696.

Vila, E. and Chahoud, J. 2006. Remains of the Fauna from the Middle Bronze Age Burials of Sidon: Burials 28 to 50, *Archaeology and History in the Lebanon* 24: 96–105.

Wapnish, P. 1997. Middle Bronze Equid Burials at Tell Jemmeh and Reexamination of a Purportedly "Hyksos" Practice. In: Oren, E.D., ed. *The Hyksos: New Historical and Archaeological Perspectives*. Philadelphia: 335–367.

Wiggermann, F.A.M. 2000. Lamaštu, Daughter of Anu: A Profile. In: Stol, M. *Birth in Babylonia and the Bible: Its Mediterranean Setting* (Cuneiform Monographs 14). Groningen: 217–252.

Zarins, J. 1986. Equids Associated with Human Burial in Third Millennium B.C. Mesopotamia: Two Complementary Facets. In: Meadow, R.H. and Uerpmann, P., eds. *Equids in the Ancient World* (Beihefte zum Tübinger Atlas des Vorderen Orients, Series A). Wiesbaden: 164–193.

Ziffer, I. 1990. *At That Time the Canaanites Were in the Land: Daily Life in Canaan in the Middle Bronze Age 2 2000–1550 B.C.E*. Tel Aviv.

Zviely, D., Sivan, D., Ecker, A., Bakler, N., Rohrlich, V., Galili, E., Boaretto, M., Klein, M., and Kit. E. 2006. Holocene Evolution of the Haifa Bay Area, Israel, and Its Influence on Ancient Tell Settlements. *The Holocene*, 16(6): 849–861.

CHAPTER 4

"For the Wealth of the Sea Will Pass on to You": Changes in Patterns of Trade from Southern Phoenicia to Northern Judah in the Late Iron Age and Persian Periods

Aaron Brody

It is an honor to dedicate the following study to Michal Artzy, esteemed friend, colleague, and mentor. Michal was my first dig director on the Tel Nami project in 1987. I joined the project after a year affiliation with the Department of Maritime Civilizations at the University of Haifa, which Michal helped to shape over her distinguished career. I had gone to Israel to study and participate in underwater archaeology, but under Michal's guidance gained a deep appreciation for harbor sites and the interaction between the land and the sea, a maritime focus which has had a profound effect on my research interests and career. After graduate school, it was Michal who offered me access to her excavation materials from Moshe Dothan's 'Akko project to work on as a postdoctoral project. It has been a pleasure to spend additional seasons in the field with Michal, on her and Ann Killebrew's codirected Total Archaeology Project at Tel 'Akko.

Interregional interconnections are coming into their own as a focus of study in the Iron II and Persian period southern Levant (Master 2003; Brody and Friedman 2007; Zukerman and Ben-Shlomo 2011; Brody 2014a, 2014b; Faust et al. 2014; Ariel 2016; Freud 2016; Cohen-Weinberger, Szanton, and Uziel 2017; Gilboa et al. 2017). In past research I have focused on ceramics and bronze bangles as items exchanged westward from Transjordan to Tell en-Naṣbeh in northern Judah (Brody and Friedman 2007; Brody 2014a). I have also investigated the Iron II evidence from Naṣbeh for a small repertoire of Phoenician ceramics, which were brought from the eastern Mediterranean coastal region to the site in the Judean Highlands (Brody 2014b). The identification of an artifact from Naṣbeh as a fragment of a Phoenician mask (Figs. 4.1, 4.2) helps us to reconsider connections from the coast to the province of Yehud in the Persian period, long evinced by the presence of a limited number of Greek fine ware ceramics uncovered at the site and elsewhere in the Judean Highlands (von Bothmer 1947; Stern 1982: 137–141; Nunn 2014). Drawing on evidence for

FIGURE 4.1 Mask fragment; field registration no. Rm 478 I x15
PHOTO BY NATALIE GLEASON AND BROOKE NORTON

interregional networks, commerce, and connections helps to fill in the gaps between international trade and regional studies of local economies and administration of the province of Yehud (Stern 1982; van Alfen 2002; Chirpanlieva 2013; Nunn 2014; Lipschits 2015; Ariel 2016; Gilboa et al. 2017). Considering interregional interconnections along with the international and local levels of exchange and economies helps us to frame the interconnected world of the southern Levant better and to identify changes in commercial links from the coast to the Judean Highlands in the late Iron Age and the Persian period.

The object that I identify as a fragment of a Persian period Phoenician mask was not recognized as such in its original publication. Joseph Wampler, the ceramicist for the Tell en-Naṣbeh project, includes the piece in a photograph of decorated wares grouped together with other "examples of ribbing, rouletting, and miscellaneous impressions" (Wampler 1947: pl. 89: 2), but does not discuss it further. Wampler identifies the fragment in his unpublished object notes as "1 fragment of [a] curious object of clay; medium hard; surfaces medium red orange over core of blue grey containing occasional fine white grits. Finish: wet-smoothed; incised decorations on two sides and a peculiar spout-like depression on one surface."[1] The sketch he provides in these notes is upside down,

---

1 These object notes, or millimeter cards, are in the collection of the Badè Museum of Biblical Archaeology at Pacific School of Religion in Berkeley, California. The information is quoted from the card for Room 478, Square X/18, Level I, April 16–18, 1935. The ceramic object was

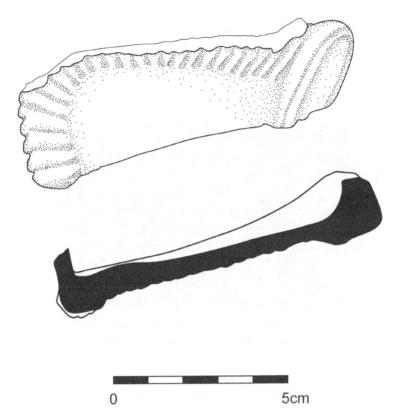

FIGURE 4.2 Mask fragment
DRAWING BY NATALIE GLEASON

which likely explains his identification of a type of spout, as this feature on the piece is pointing downwards. The proper stance, however, is represented in the photo in the final report. The artifact is neither treated further nor identified in publication or object notes. What Wampler describes as a spout-like depression in his unpublished records, I identify as a left ear; the incised decorative lines on the piece form the arch and suggest the hairs of a left eyebrow. The eyebrow is especially clear when the piece is reconstructed by sorting out its proper stance and flipping the image to simulate the mirrored right side of the mask. The reconstruction suggests two thick eyebrows, which have good parallels in representations of eyebrows on Bes images (Fig. 4.3). The thick eyebrow and animal ear are nicely paralleled on a Phoenician scarab from the western Mediterranean that depicts a satyr in profile, represented on a janiform helmet

---

registered with the field number: Rm 478 I x15; which is an abbreviation for Room 478, Level I, fifteenth object recorded for the locus (= x15).

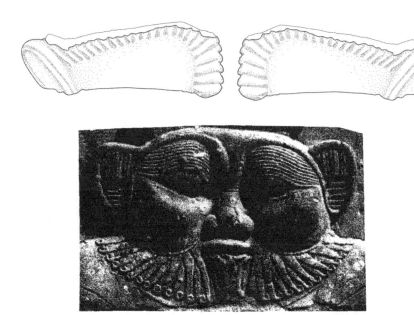

FIGURE 4.3   Reconstruction with left side of mask flipped to represent the missing right side, in comparison with Bes image for aid in understanding eyebrow(s)
IMAGE BY AARON BRODY

(Fig. 4.4). When positioned correctly, one can also make out the curve of the eyelid between the eyebrow and ear. Given the distinguishable features of the ear, eyebrow, and eyelid, I identify this fragment as a clear portion of a mask or protome,[2] a common artifact type found at Phoenician sites along the Levantine coast and throughout the Mediterranean in the late Iron Age and Persian period. To my knowledge, however, it is the first Phoenician mask identified in Persian period Judah.[3]

---

2   Technically, masks have eye holes and often mouth and nostril holes, and were worn by an individual to disguise, but also transform, the wearer. Protomes are clay plaques that represent a divinity or divine being but lack any eye/mouth/nostril holes and are presumed to have been displayed rather than worn. The fragment from Naṣbeh is not big enough to preserve any remaining indications of an eye, mouth, or nostril hole, so it might have been either a mask or a protome. Given the more common use of the term "mask" to refer to both masks and protomes, I will use mask in the article, but admit that one cannot determine whether the full object was a wearable mask or a protome for display, given its highly fragmentary nature.

3   Raz Kletter (2007) has identified two locally made masks in Iron II Judah, one of which was discovered at a site in the hill country north of Jerusalem. These two examples predate the mask from Naṣbeh, whose fabric does not appear to be local to the Judean hill country region.

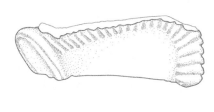

FIGURE 4.4 Comparison of flipped drawing of mask with satyr eyebrow and ear, represented on a janiform helmet depicted on a Phoenician scarab
AFTER HTTP://WWW.BEAZLEY.OX.AC.UK/GEMS/SCARABS/IMAGES/ROBS%20
IMAGES%2008/37.05M.JPG; IMAGE BY AARON BRODY AND NATALIE GLEASON

The mask fragment can be dated to the Persian period by its fabric, context, and type. The piece's ware is salmon pink in color[4] and is well fired (Fig. 4.1), two qualities known from ceramics and pottery masks from the coast of the southern Levant in the Persian period. Context is always tricky when dealing with the legacy excavations at Tell en-Naṣbeh, because of excavation and recording methods typical of the 1920s–1930s. That said, Wampler dates the architectural context in which the mask was found, Room 478 in Squares X/17 and X/18, to between 600 and 450 BCE, based on its ceramics (Wampler 1947: 122; Fig. 4.5 herein). He does note, however, that the finds in Room 478 were mixed and his dating is not certain. All other associated rooms in the vicinity of Room 478 are dated by their ceramics to 600–450 BCE, with a similar level of mixing and uncertainty noted (Wampler 1947: 122). Having checked the unpublished object records, or millimeter cards, for all of these contexts, I can say that there are no ceramics that date later than the Persian period, and many are either from the Iron IIC or are seventh-century types that carry forward the late Iron Age potting traditions into the sixth–fifth centuries BCE (Zorn 2003). These

---

4 Here I disagree with Wampler's view on the color of the surface of the mask fragment, which he described in his unpublished notes as "red orange." Having handled numerous similar wares from the Persian period levels in the field at the Ashkelon and Tel 'Akko excavations, I would describe the surface of this similar ware as salmon pink in color.

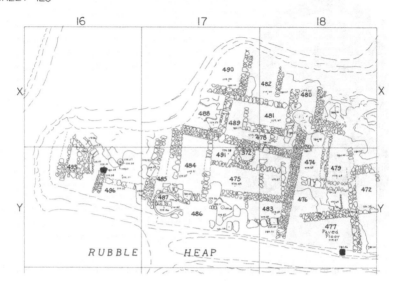

FIGURE 4.5 Architectural context of mask fragment: Room 478 with surrounding architectural features. Each excavation square is 10 × 10 m; the grid is oriented to the cardinal directions.
DETAIL FROM UNPUBLISHED 1:100 ARCHITECTURAL DRAWING BY LABIB SORIAL, WITH PERMISSION FROM THE BADÈ MUSEUM, PACIFIC SCHOOL OF RELIGION

ceramics reflect the vague nature of hill country typologies and overwhelming continuities in the pottery transitions from the Iron IIC to the Babylonian/early Persian periods in Judah, yet certain lamp and cooking pot forms from these rooms are firmly in the Persian period tradition.

Jeffrey Zorn's analysis of the architectural features in the vicinity of Room 478 summarizes some of the frustrations of working on these legacy materials: "Rm 478, Rm 480, Rm 481, Rm 482, Rm 488, Rm 489, and Rm 490 are a series of "rooms" in [Squares] X17–18 which cannot be grouped into coherent building plans. Nor can they be assigned to specific strata since walls of different types are used to mark off these areas. They belong to Strata 3 and 2, but that is all that can be said," (Zorn 1993: 584; see Fig. 4.5 herein). This lack of coherent context was the reason the mask fragment was not included in José Balcells Gallarreta's recent treatment of household and family religion at Tell en-Naṣbeh in the Persian period (2017: 49–79). Despite lacking a good architectural context, the mask fragment can elucidate elements of interregional interconnections between northern Judah and the coastal region in the early Achaemenid period.

In the Persian period, masks, specifically Phoenician types, are known primarily from sites along the coast of the southern Levant, as far south as Tel Dor and further south and inland at Tell es-Safi (Stern 1995; Dayagi-Mendels 2002: 156–160; Martin 2007, 2014).[5] Masks are also prevalent at contemporary Phoenician sites along the central and northern Levantine littoral, in modern Lebanon and Syria, and are found in various locations throughout the Phoenician diaspora across the Mediterranean and Atlantic coasts (Ciasca 1999; Dayagi-Mendels 2002: 159–160; Morstadt 2010; Averett 2015; Orsingher 2017).[6]

The mask fragment uncovered at Tell en-Naṣbeh likely had its origins somewhere in the northern coastal regions of modern Israel or southern Lebanon,[7] and was transported up to the hill country of northern Judah, perhaps together with a variety of other trade goods. Coastal goods that were transshipped in small but significant numbers east into Judah include a group of Greek fine wares from Naṣbeh and elsewhere in the region (von Bothmer 1947; Stern 1982: 137–141; Nunn 2014), an Athenian coin (McCown 1947: 275, plate 102.1), and newly identified imported "Greek style," or East Greek, amphorae, table amphorae, and an askos, which are among the finds from Tell en-Naṣbeh in the collection in the Badè Museum at Pacific School of Religion in Berkeley, California.[8]

The Phoenician mask deposited at Tell en-Naṣbeh likely represents a satyr, as is indicated by its faun-like ear.[9] Phoenician satyr, or silenic masks do not

---

5   Along with the well-known comparanda from the Akhziv tombs and Tel Dor, I gathered data on numerous mask fragments from Persian period contexts at Tel 'Akko, as a coroplastic specialist affiliated with the Total Archaeology Project. I would like to thank the codirectors, Michal Artzy and Ann Killebrew, for entrusting me with this material. These data, however, are still being processed and remain unpublished. I would also like to thank S. Rebecca Martin for sharing her research and her expertise in the archaeology of the Persian period with me throughout this project.
6   I would like to thank Erin Averett for sharing her research on masks from Cyprus prior to its publication and to thank Adriano Orsingher for sharing his article with me before it was in print and for providing valuable insights based on an early draft of this paper.
7   Petrographic testing of a Gorgon mask from Tel Dor indicates its origins in coastal Lebanon. I would like to thank Ayelet Gilboa for the personal communication of this unpublished result from the Tel Dor Project.
8   The possible "Greek style" or East Greek amphorae and table amphorae from Naṣbeh were not identified as imports by Wampler in his publication of the ceramics from the site (1947). I believe I have "discovered" sherds from imported amphorae, table amphorae, and an askos in the Naṣbeh collection in storage in the Badè Museum at Pacific School of Religion, but this identification requires confirmation by an expert in Greek utilitarian imports to the region and further research and publication.
9   I would like to thank S. Rebecca Martin for pointing out the details of the satyr-style ear to me, while I was fixated on the Bes-like eyebrow.

resemble the fragment from Naṣbeh stylistically (Ciasca 1999: 415; Morstadt 2010; Orsingher 2017: 282–285). Images on Phoenician stamp seals, however, suggest a representative style of satyr paralleled in the Naṣbeh mask (Fig. 4.4).[10] Given the established presence of Greek fine ware drinking sets[11] at Naṣbeh and the possible presence at the site of "Greek style," or East Greek, amphorae, table amphorae, and an askos, we may posit a grouping related to the importation, serving, and celebratory drinking of Greek wine. Since satyrs are known to have been affiliated with symposia, which have a Northwest Semitic counterpart in the *marzēaḥ* (Dvorjetski 2016), it is not too far of an interpretive stretch to suggest a link between the Phoenician mask and wine-drinking festivities. These celebrations garnered further prestige because the drinking cups, serving vessels, and perhaps even the wines were valued foreign luxury goods brought in over the Mediterranean from Greece, Crete, and Ionia and transshipped over land routes from harbors on the southern Levantine coast (Gilboa et al. 2017).

One possible exchange route could have brought the mask and other items from the coast to Tell es-Safi and then up into the hill country. Safi and other Shephelah sites would have acted as regional hubs for goods from the Mediterranean, some of which were then redistributed into the Judean Hills (Faust et al. 2014). Donald Ariel has already demonstrated the interconnectivity of the southern coastal region or Philistia, the Shephelah, and Judah through his study of the interregional circulation and distribution of primarily late Persian period coins minted at a variety of local mints (Ariel 2016).[12] I would suggest that imported ceramics, such as Greek and East Greek wares and Phoenician masks, were exchanged within similar spheres of interregional interaction.

This Persian period west to east movement of goods originating along and transshipped from the Mediterranean coast, likely through the Shephelah and up to the Judean hill country, marks a shift in connectivity from the earlier Iron II period. My prior research has suggested that while there was Iron II contact with the coast, marked by Phoenician imported pottery and eye beads, this commerce was directed from the 'Akko Plain through the Jezreel Valley and

---

10   For comparative representations of satyrs on Phoenician stamp seals see http://www.beazley.ox.ac.uk/gems/scarab/ scarab31.htm, and http://www.beazley.ox.ac.uk/gems/scarab/ scarab37.htm where a satyr image is depicted on a janiform helmet that is worn, perhaps, as an aspect of ritual transformation (Fig. 44; Averett 2015). Raz Kletter observed that Iron Age masks were individually made (2007: 194–195), which may partially explain the lack of good stylistic parallels for the Naṣbeh mask.

11   For the interpretation of imported Greek fine wares as drinking sets, see Stewart and Martin 2005.

12   I would like to thank Donald Ariel for sharing his important article with me, and for reading and commenting on an early draft of this paper.

then up into northern Judah (Brody 2014b). This Iron II trade may have gone along the trunk road to Tell en-Naṣbeh and then on to Jerusalem (Freud 2016), although it is possible that Phoenician goods went to Jerusalem first and then back to Naṣbeh. These late Iron Age coastal connections were quite limited in absolute numbers, while larger quantities of imported ceramics were being brought in to Naṣbeh from the region of Ammon, indicating a favored east-to-west interregional movement of goods from Transjordan to northern Judah (Brody 2014a). So, the focus of interregional commerce to Naṣbeh shifts toward the coastal region in the Persian period, which should not come as a surprise given the robust nature of eastern Mediterranean trade in this period (Stern 1982; van Alfen 2002; Chirpanlieva 2013; Nunn 2014; Gilboa et al. 2017). The transshipment of goods from the coast to the highlands is represented proportionally by the absolute numbers of imported Greek fine wares uncovered at sites along the southern Levantine coast and at Shephelah sites, numbers that drop off exponentially at sites further east in Judah and Transjordan (Faust et al. 2014; Nunn 2014; Ray 2016).

The identification of an unusually decorated ceramic from Tell en-Naṣbeh as a Phoenician mask fragment from the early Persian period has allowed for further elucidation of contacts of the site to the Mediterranean coast, long suggested by the presence of Greek fine wares.[13] The mask also metaphorically links to our historiographical sources, which specify Tyrian trade of fish and other goods to Jerusalem in the late Persian period (Nehemiah 13:16; Noonan 2011).[14] A slightly earlier historiographical text details the interregional and international trade to Tyre in the early sixth century BCE and suggests the return exchange of Judean agricultural products to the Phoenician coast (Ezekiel 27:12–24). Perhaps it was Phoenician merchants that carried the mask and Greek ceramics to Tell en-Naṣbeh along with other goods, just as later in the same period they brought fish and other products to a revitalized Jerusalem. These Phoenician merchants likely returned to the coast with Judean

---

13   Tell en-Naṣbeh is unfortunately missing from Oren Tal's important map of suggested routes in Persian period Palestine (Tal 2005: fig. 1). Naṣbeh was most likely the settlement of Mizpah of Benjamin, which was the provincial capital of the Babylonian province of Judah, a status that continued into the early Persian period. The revitalization of Jerusalem in the late sixth–fifth centuries BCE and the reconstitution of the city as the capital of late Persian period Yehud likely caused the eclipse of Tell en-Naṣbeh, whose Persian period settlement ends around 450–420 BCE.

14   Egon Lass's remarkable recent discovery of the otoliths, or ear bones, from Atlantic species of fish in Persian period remains at Ashkelon are direct evidence of wide-ranging Phoenician piscine trade, likely exchanged as a dried commodity (Lass 2016). These fish otolith data demonstrate that goods were traded from the Atlantic literally across the entire length of the Mediterranean to a harbor site on the Sea's southeastern coast.

agricultural goods. Conceptualizing interregional exchange between the coastal region and the hill country of Judah helps to bridge the gap between international and local commerce in the Persian period southern Levant and suggests differences in routes of contact with the Phoenician coast from those of the late Iron Age. Analogously, an anonymous Judean prophet metaphorically described commerce coming to the Persian province of Yehud: "For the wealth of the sea will pass on to you, the riches of nations will flow to you" (Isaiah 60:5b). Given the imperial geopolitical, regional political, and local social shifts between the Iron II, Babylonian, and early Persian periods in the southern Levant, it is not surprising to find dynamic changes in all levels of exchange from the southern Phoenician coast to Tell en-Naṣbeh in the northern hill country of Judah over the seventh–fifth centuries BCE.

References

Alfen, P.G. van 2002. *PANT'AGATHA: Commodities in Levantine-Aegean Trade during the Persian Period, 6–4th c. BC*. Ph.D. dissertation. The University of Texas at Austin. Austin.

Ariel, D.T. 2016. The Circulation of Locally Minted Persian-Period Coins in the Southern Levant. *Notae Numismaticae* 11: 13–62.

Averett, E.W. 2015. Masks and Ritual Performance on the Island of Cyprus. *American Journal of Archaeology* 199(1): 3–45.

Balcells Gallarreta, J.E. 2017. *Household and Family Religion in Persian-Period Judah: An Archaeological Approach* (Ancient Near East Monographs 18.) Atlanta.

Bothmer, D. von 1947. Greek Pottery. In: McCown, C.C., ed. *Tell en-Naṣbeh*, Vol. 1: *Archaeological and Historical Results*. Berkeley: 175–178, 304.

Brody, A.J. 2014a. Transjordanian Commerce with Northern Judah in the Iron II–Persian Period: Ceramic Indicators, Interregional Interaction, and Modes of Exchange at Tell en-Nasbeh. In: Zorn, J.R. and Brody, A., eds. *"As for Me, I Will Dwell at Mizpah...": The Tell en-Nasbeh Excavations after 85 Years*. Piscataway, NJ: 59–93.

Brody, A.J. 2014b. Interregional Interaction in the Late Iron Age: Phoenician and Other Foreign Goods from Tell en-Nasbeh. In: Spencer, J., Mullins, B., and Brody, A., eds. *Material Culture Matters: Essays on the Archaeology of the Southern Levant in Honor of Seymour Gitin*. Winona Lake, IN: 55–69.

Brody, A.J. and Friedman, E.S. 2007. Bronze Bangles from Tell en-Nasbeh: Cultural and Economic Observations on an Artifact Type from the Time of the Prophets. In: Coote, R.B. and Gottwald, N.K., eds. *To Break Every Yoke: Essays in Honor of Marvin L. Chaney* (The Social World of Biblical Antiquity, Second Series 3). Sheffield: 97–114.

Chirpanlieva, I. 2013. *Grecs et phéniciens en Méditerranée orientale. Les céramiques grecques, témoins des échanges entre la Grèce, Chypre et la côte levantine (XE–IVE s. av. JC.)*. Ph.D. dissertation. Aix-Marseille University. Aix-en-Provence and Marseille.

Ciasca, A. 1999. Masks and Protomes. In: Moscati, S., ed. *The Phoenicians*. New York: 406–417.

Cohen-Weinberger, A., Szanton, N., and Uziel, J. 2017. Ethnofabrics: Petrographic Analysis as a Tool for Illuminating Cultural Interactions and Trade Relations between Judah and Philistia during the Iron Age II. *Bulletin of the American Schools of Oriental Research* 377(1): 1–20.

Dayagi-Mendels, M. 2002. *The Akhziv Cemeteries: The Ben-Dor Excavations, 1941–1944* (IAA Reports 15). Jerusalem.

Dvorjetski, E. 2016. From Ugarit to Madaba: Philological and Historical Functions of the *Marzēaḥ*. *Journal of Semitic Studies* 61(1): 17–39.

Faust, A., Katz, H., Ben-Shlomo, D., Sapir, Y., and Eyall, P. 2014. Tel 'Eton/Tell 'Etun and Its Interregional Contacts from the Late Bronze Age to the Persian-Hellenistic Period: Between Highlands and Lowlands. *Zeitschrift des Deutschen Palästina-Vereins* 130(1): 43–76.

Freud, L. 2016. A Note on Sixth-Century BCE Phoenician Chalice-Shaped Vessels from Judah. *Israel Exploration Journal* 66(2): 177–187.

Gilboa, A., Shalev, Y., Lehmann, G., Mommsen, H., Erickson, B., Nodarou, E., and Ben-Shlomo, D. 2017. Cretan Pottery in the Levant in the Fifth and Fourth Centuries B.C.E. and Its Historical Implications. *American Journal of Archaeology* 121(4): 559–593.

Kletter, R. 2007. To Cast an Image: Masks from Iron Age Judah and the Biblical *Masekah*. In: White Crawford, S., Ben-Tor, A., Dessel, J.P., Dever, W.G., Mazar, A, and Aviram, J., eds. *"Up to the Gates of Ekron": Essays on the Archaeology and History of the Eastern Mediterranean in Honor of Seymour Gitin*. Jerusalem: 189–208.

Lass, H.E. 2016. Soil Flotation from the Persian Period at Ashkelon, Israel. *STRATA: Bulletin of the Anglo-Israel Archaeological Society* 34: 73–90.

Lipschits, O. 2015. The Rural Economy of Judah during the Persian Period and the Settlement History of the District System. In: Miller, M.L., Ben Zvi, E., and Knoppers, G.N., eds. *The Economy of Ancient Judah in Its Historical Context*. Winona Lake, IN: 237–264.

Martin, S.R. 2007. *"Hellenization" and Southern Phoenicia: Reconsidering the Impact of Greece before Alexander*. Ph.D. dissertation. University of California, Berkeley. Berkeley.

Martin, S.R. 2014. From the East to Greece and Back Again: Terracotta Gorgon Masks in a Phoenician Context. In: Lemaire, A., Dufour, B., and Pfitzmann, F., eds. *Phéniciens d'Orient et d'Occident. Mélanges Josette Elayi*, Vol. 2. Paris: 289–299.

Master, D.M. 2003. Trade and Politics: Ashkelon's Balancing Act in the Seventh Century BCE. *Bulletin of the American Schools of Oriental Research* 330: 47–64.

McCown, C.C., ed. 1947. *Tell en-Naṣbeh*, Vol. 1: *Archaeological and Historical Results*. Berkeley.

Morstadt, B. 2010. Phönizische Masken—zwischen Abbild und Abschreckung. *Tagungen des Landesmuseums für Vorgeschichte Halle* 4: 203–211.

Noonan, B.T. 2011. Did Nehemiah Own Tyrian Goods? Trade between Judea and Phoenicia during the Achaemenid Period. *Journal of Biblical Literature* 130(2): 281–298.

Nunn, A. 2014. Attic Pottery Imports and Their Impact on "Identity Discourses": A Reassessment. In: Frevel, C., Pyschny, K., and Cornelius, I., eds. *A "Religious Revolution" in Yehûd? The Material Culture of the Persian Period as a Test Case* (Orbis Biblicus et Orientalis 267). Fribourg: 391–429.

Orsingher, A. 2017. Ritualized Faces: The Masks of the Phoenicians. In: Berlejung, A. and Filitz, J.E., eds. *The Physicality of the Other: Masks from the Ancient Near East and the Eastern Mediterranean*. Tübingen: 265–305.

Ray, P.J. 2016. Connectivity: Transjordan during the Persian Period. In: LaBianca, O.S. and Scham, S.A., eds. *Connectivity in Antiquity: Globalization as a Long-Term Historical Process*. London: 75–92.

Stern, E. 1982. *Material Culture of the Land of the Bible in the Persian Period 538–332 B.C.* Warminster, UK.

Stern, E. 1995. Clay Figurines, Popular Cult Objects, and Sculpture. In: Stern, E., ed. *Excavations at Dor: Final Report* (Qedem Reports 2). Jerusalem: 435–454.

Stewart, A. and Martin, S.R. 2005. Attic Imported Pottery at Tel Dor, Israel: An Overview. *Bulletin of the American Schools of Oriental Research* 337: 79–94.

Tal, O. 2005. Some Remarks on the Coastal Plain of Palestine under Achaemenid Rule—an Archaeological Synopsis. In: Briant, P. and Boucharlat, R., eds. *L'Archéologie de l'empire achéménide: nouvelles recherches. Actes du colloque organisé au Collège de France par le "Réseau international d'études et de recherches achéménides" (GDR 2538 CNRS), 21–22 novembre 2003*. Paris: 71–96.

Wampler, J.C. 1947. *Tell en-Naṣbeh, Vol. 2: The Pottery*. Berkeley.

Zorn, J.R. 1993. *Tell en Nasbeh: A Re-evaluation of the Architecture and Stratigraphy of the Early Bronze Age, Iron Age and Later Periods*. Ph.D. dissertation, University of California, Berkeley. Berkeley.

Zorn, J.R. 2003. Tell en-Naṣbeh and the Problem of the Material Culture of the Sixth Century. In: Lipschits, O. and Blenkinsopp, J., eds. *Judah and the Judeans in the Neo-Babylonian Period*. Winona Lake, IN: 413–447.

Zukerman, A. and Ben-Shlomo, D. 2011. Mortaria as a Foreign Element in the Material Culture of the Southern Levant during the 8th–7th Centuries BCE. *Palestine Exploration Quarterly* 143(2): 87–105.

CHAPTER 5

Cypriot Pottery from the Second Millennium BCE at Tell Keisan in the Lower Galilee (Israel)

Mariusz Burdajewicz

Tell Keisan, situated about 8 km to the southeast of the mound of ʿAkko, is one of the largest tells in northern Israel.[1] Excavations at the site, conducted by a team from the École biblique et archéologique française in Jerusalem, have yielded rich pottery material from the Iron Age and the Hellenistic and Byzantine periods. The very fast publication of the excavation results (Briend and Humbert 1980) was pioneering in all scientific respects, focusing not only on the Lower Galilee but on the broader region of the southern Levant. Iron Age and later pottery (from the eleventh–second centuries BCE and the Byzantine period) was presented and discussed in the final publication, which soon became a standard reference work for studies on the pottery found in southern Phoenicia, including present-day northern Israel. This publication also provided a better understanding of cultural relations and trade patterns between the Levantine coast and Cyprus, one of the subjects to which Michal Artzy is deeply devoted in her scholarly activity.

TABLE 5.1   Cypriot Wares at Tell Keisan

Ware/Area	Area B	Area D	Area A	Surface	Total
Bichrome	1	1	–	–	2
Base Ring	17	15	4	2	37
Bucchero	2	–	–	–	2
Composite	1	–	–	–	1
Monochrome	3	3	–	–	6
Red-on-Black	1	–	–	1	2
White Painted	14	6	2	1	23
White Slip	49	29	1	2	81
Total	88	54	7	6	155

---

1   It is a great pleasure to mention that I owe my first visit to Tell Keisan in 1992 to the kindness of Michal Artzy, who not only arranged my trip but also accompanied me on the tell.

TABLE 5.2 Distribution of Cypriot pottery in Area B (chronological/stratigraphic dating of levels after Humbert 1980: 5)

Ware	13	13/12	12	11	11–10	10	10–9	9	8	11–7	Other	Total
Bichrome											1	1
Base Ring	1		5					3		1	7	17
Bucchero	1	1										2
Composite						1						1
Monochrome						2					1	3
RoB								1				1
White Painted			3				2	1	1		5	14
White Slip	5	2	5	1	4	9		5	1		13	49
Total	7	3	13	1	4	12	2	10	2	1	27	88

In the present paper I offer some preliminary information about Cypriot pottery of the second millennium BCE at Tell Keisan before its final publication.[2] During the 1971–1976, 1979, and 1980 excavation seasons at the site, 155 potsherds of Cypriot origin were found in the main excavated areas and on the surface (Table 5.1). Most of them (around 63%) were unearthed in Areas B and D during the last two seasons conducted under the direction of J.-B. Humbert (Humbert 1980, 1981, 1993). In Area B, the Cypriot pottery originates, with a few exceptions, from Levels 13–9, dated generally to the Iron Age I (twelfth–eleventh centuries BCE) (Table 5.2). In the more recently opened Area D, on the northeastern edge of the tell, Cypriot finds originated, similarly, in Iron I contexts (local Levels 9' and 8'). Additionally, Level 10' was reached in this latter area and preliminarily dated to the final stage of the Late Bronze Age (Table 5.3) (Humbert 1980: 5, 12–13).[3]

Not a single complete vessel has been preserved; the excavated material is very fragmentary and consists exclusively of body sherds, rims, bases, and handles. However, in some cases we estimated the minimum number of vessels based on the number of rims that must have each belonged to a different vessel.

TABLE 5.3   Distribution of Cypriot pottery in Area D (chronological/stratigraphic dating of levels after Humbert 1980: 5)

Ware	10'	9'	9'-8'	8'	Other	Total
Bichrome					1	1
Base Ring	1	6		4	4	15
Monochrome					3	3
White Painted	2		1	1	2	6
White Slip	3	9	2	2	13	29
Total	6	15	3	7	23	54

---

2 I have studied the Cypriot pottery of Tell Keisan previously (Burdajewicz 1992: 19–32) and I am reevaluating it here within the aims of a project concerning the unpublished Late Bronze and Iron Age pottery from the 1979 and 1980 seasons of excavation, supported by a grant from the Polish National Science Centre (No. DEC UMO-2016/23/B/HS3/01879).

3 Level designations are local, per area. Numerals followed by a diacritic relate to levels in Area D and those without to Area B. The exact correlation between the levels in these two areas still remains to be established.

1   White Slip Ware

White Slip Ware (81 sherds) accounts for slightly more than half of the total Cypriot assemblage. Two sherds probably represent White Slip I, while the rest of the finds are of the White Slip II regular style (Figs. 5.1, 5.2) and four sherds are possibly White Slip II late. If one excludes body sherds and handles,

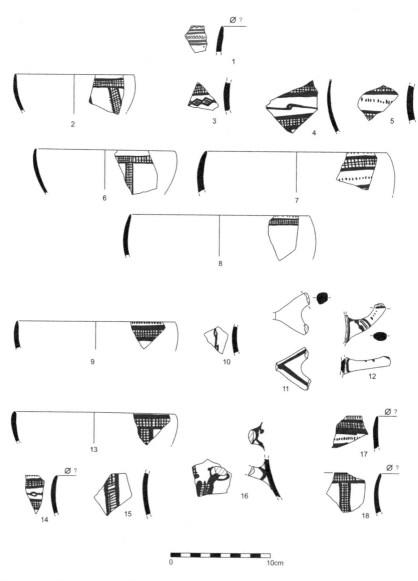

FIGURE 5.1   White Slip Ware from Area B
DRAWINGS BY MARIUSZ BURDAJEWICZ

FIGURE 5.1

No.	Inventory no.	Area	Level	Ware
1	8.009	B	Non stratified	White Slip I
2	8.429	B	13	White Slip II
3	8.430	B	12b/13	White Slip II
4	8.432b	B	12	White Slip II
5	8.430a	B	12	White Slip II
6	7.261j	B	12	White Slip II
7	8.432c	B	12	White Slip II
8	8.432g	B	10/11	White Slip II
9	7.261	B	10	White Slip II
10	7.261f	B	10	White Slip II
11	7.262	B	10	White Slip II
12	7.261b	B	10	White Slip II
13	8.433	B	9	White Slip II
14	7.261h	B	9	White Slip II
15	8.432a	B	9	White Slip II
16	8.433b	B	9	White Slip II
17	75.426	B	Non stratified	White Slip II
18	76.957b	B		White Slip II

the minimum number of White Slip vessels is 20, all of which belong to a hemispherical bowl type, the so-called milk bowl.

1.1   *White Slip I*

Figure 5.1: 1 is one of two sherds that can be tentatively identified as White Slip I (the other is not illustrated). It is decorated with a reddish wavy line just below the edge of the rim; below it is a crisscross lattice pattern with two horizontal lines below it and two above it. There is a small dot on the vessel's outer wall, which has a whitish, shiny slip. The fabric and most of the decorative elements seem typical of White Slip I, apart from the crisscross lattice pattern, which is rather rare in this ware. Parallels can be found at Ayia Irini Tombs 3 and 20 (Pecorella 1977: figs. 114: 127; 315: 112), Myrtou-Pigadhes (du Plat Taylor et al. 1957: fig. 19: F.179), Tomb 12 at Kourion-Bamboula (Benson 1961: 64, pl. VII; figs. 3–6, "lozenge in cursive design"), and Tomb 105 at Palaepaphos-Teratsoudhia (Karageorghis 1990: pl. VII). Two additional parallels are housed at the Cyprus Museum in Nicosia (late and regional White Slip I; Åström 1972b: fig. LXXXII: 4, 5) and there are also three from Enkomi (Dikaios 1969–1971: pl. 63: 3;

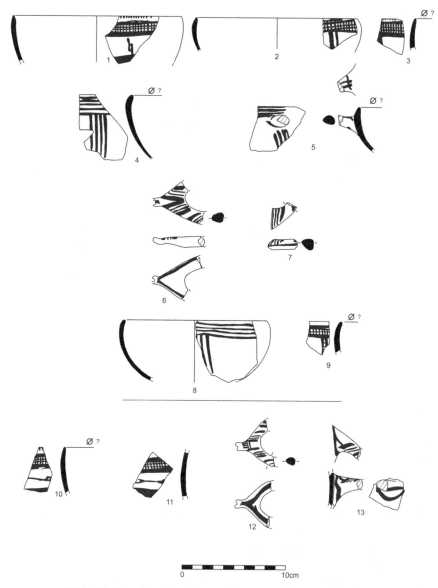

FIGURE 5.2 White Slip Ware from Area D
DRAWING BY MARIUSZ BURDAJEWICZ

Courtois 1981: fig. 131) and one from Hala Sultan Tekke (Åström, Bailey, and Karageorghis 1976: pl. XL: 44).

The same pattern also occurs on a White Slip IIA bowl from Tomb 104 at Palaepaphos-Teratsoudhia (Karageorghis 1990: pl. XV: E.6) and on three White

FIGURE 5.2

No.	Inventory no.	Area	Level	Ware
1	8.435	D	10'	White Slip II
2	8.435b	D	10'	White Slip II
3	7.261e	D	10'	White Slip II
4	8.435h	D	9'	White Slip II late
5	8.436	D	9'	White Slip II late
6	8.435f	D	9'	White Slip II
7	8.436a	D	9'	White Slip II
8	8.436e	D	8'	White Slip II late
9	8.436d	D	8'	White Slip II
10	8.434a	D		White Slip II
11	7.262c	D	Non stratified	White Slip II
12	8.437c	D		White Slip II
13	8.434b	D		White Slip II

Slip IIA bowls found during the old British excavations at Palaepaphos (Åström 1972b: fig. 51: 1, 2, 5). Disintegration of lozenges into a crisscross lattice pattern has been considered a characteristic of the final phase of White Slip I, and is perhaps a testimony of local production in northwestern Cyprus (Åström 1972b: 442–443; Courtois 1981: 158). According to Kromholtz, such style "shows some association with the western Mesaoria" (1978: 18).

White Slip I Ware dates to Late Cypriot (LC) IA2 and LC IB (White Slip I late) (Eriksson 2007: 13, table 1B). Some close parallels to Figure 5.1: 1 can be cited from Canaan: one, classified as White Slip I, comes from the Late Bronze (LB) I temple at Tel Mevorakh. It is decorated with "a diagonal criss-cross lattice of thin reddish line..." (Kromholtz 1984: 18, fig. 10: 25, pl. 39: 5). Two other examples come from Tell Abu Hawam (Balensi 1980: 259, pl. 27: 6, classified as White Slip IIA), and Hazor (Yadin et al. 1961: pl. CCLXIX: 38). Other than at Tell el-'Ajjul, White Slip I is fairly rare among Cypriot imports in Canaan (Bergoffen 2002: 27).

1.2   *White Slip II*

The decoration on other potsherds from Tell Keisan is characteristic of White Slip II production and includes a lattice pattern frieze and a pendent lattice pattern (Fig. 5.1: 2); a hooked chain between two lattice pattern friezes (Fig. 5.1: 4); a dotted row surrounding the rim and below it another between two lattice pattern friezes (Fig. 5.1: 7); and a dotted line on a rim edge and a lattice pattern frieze below it (Fig. 5.1: 9). Fragments of wishbone handles are decorated with various combinations of lines, dots, and circles (Figs. 5.1: 11, 12, 16; 5.2: 6, 7, 12, 13). The fabric of this ware is either light gray, light reddish-gray or gray; the slip is creamy white to light gray and mostly matt; and the painted decoration ranges in color from dark brown to dark gray.

Parallels for White Slip II from Cyprus and elsewhere are too numerous to be cited here. It is sufficient to refer to the finds from Tell Abu Hawam (Balensi 1980: pls. 27–29; Artzy 2001a: fig. 2) and ʿAkko (Dothan 1976: fig. 18: 3, 7, 9–12; Artzy 2001a: figs. 4, 5).

One of the items from Keisan is, however, worthy of a more detailed discussion. The bowl in Figure 5.2: 1 is distinguished by an unusual decoration: two lattice pattern friezes enclose a single vertical lozenge. It corresponds to Kromholtz's "J-pattern," which appears to be rather uncommon (Kromholtz 1978: 125, fig. 26). Usually, lozenges between two lattice pattern friezes surrounding the walls of the vessel are drawn horizontally. A few parallels can be cited from Enkomi (Murray, Smith, and Walters [1900] 1969: fig. 64: 1030; Dikaios 1969–1971: pl. 68: 9; Kromholtz 1978: 125, fig. 26), Hala Sultan Tekke (Åström et al. 1983: fig. 71d), and Arpera (Kromholtz 1978: 128), and one on a jar in the Cyprus Museum in Nicosia (Åström 1972b: fig. 54: 10, pl. LXXXIV: 8). From outside Cyprus, a possible parallel can be found at Tell Beit Mirsim Stratum C (Albright 1932: pl. 18: 24; see, also, Gittlen 1978: 459–460).

1.3   *White Slip II Late (or White Slip III)*
Three bowl fragments from this group (Fig. 5.2: 4, 5, 8) bear a simple decoration consisting of a frieze of four to five parallel lines below the rim and four parallel pendent lines on the body and below the handle. Such simple decoration is characteristic of White Slip II late (Åström 1972b: 445, 465; Gittlen 1978: 471; Steel 2010: 110–111, fig. 13.2: 4), which occurred as late as the second half of LC IIC (till the beginning of the twelfth century BCE). In Canaan, examples of White Slip II late bowls are known from thirteenth-century contexts at Aphek, Tell er-Ridan, Tell el-Farʿah (S), and Tell Jemmeh (Bergoffen 2014: 664 with references, fig. 11.8j). White Slip II is generally dated to LC IB–IIC2, while White Slip II late (or III) falls within LC IIC1–2 (Eriksson 2007: table 1B). At Tell Keisan all three sherds were found in Area D, Levels 9' and 8', dated to Iron I.

2 Base Ring Ware

Base Ring Ware is the most common among Cypriot imports found at Tell Keisan, apart from White Slip Ware. The material assigned to this group is too fragmentary to enable the precise classification into I, II, and Proto-Base Ring,[4] especially since the fabrics of Base Ring I and II are almost identical (Artzy, Perlman, and Asaro 1981: 40–44, 46–47); however, a short commentary on selected and illustrated examples is offered below.

A few body sherds retained decoration in white paint on the dark brown and/or dark gray surface (Fig. 5.3: 3, 4, 18, 20). One of these sherds (Fig. 5.3: 4) probably belonged to a jug with a truncated neck, a rare type known, for example, from Enkomi (Dikaios 1969–1971: pl. 206; 21, Tomb 10, dated to 1300–1200 BCE; Courtois 1981: 152, fig. 83: 51, Tomb 110, from LC IA to LC IIC, 1575–1200 BCE). Another fragment of a shoulder and the bottom of a neck shows a relief decoration characteristic especially of Base Ring I (Fig. 5.3: 6). It is probably part of a Type VI jug, with a high cylindrical neck, ovoid body, and ring base (Åström 1972b: figs. XLIX: 9, 10; L: 2). A similar jug type is represented in Figure 5.3: 21 (Åström 1972b: fig. LIII: 1).

Three illustrated potsherds (Fig. 5.3: 13–15) belong to a type very common in Cyprus: bowl Type IF of Base Ring II, with a conical body and annular base (Åström 1972b: 175–177, fig. LII: 2–4). Parallels are to be found, among other places, at Enkomi (Courtois 1981: fig. 93: 1, 3–6). Bowls are also represented by some rims still attached to fragmentary wishbone handles (Fig. 5.3: 8, 11, 12).

A base of an open vessel shown in Figure 5.3: 10 can be identified as belonging to bowl Type IB of Base Ring I (Åström 1972b: fig. XLVII: 7–9). Figure 5.3: 22 is one of two bases found at Tell Keisan that represent Type IX Base Ring spindle bottles (Åström 1972b: 166–167, fig. LI: 10–14).

Figure 5.3: 5, 7, 9, 16, 19 shows fragments of bases and necks belonging to common Base Ring I and II types.

A fragment of a bowl with slightly concave walls and a narrow flat base comes from Level 13 in Area B (Fig. 5.3: 1). Though it falls within the general Type Y of Base Ring I–II bowls, it seems to belong also to the wheel-made category of Base Ring (Dikaios 1969–1971: 829–830; Åström 1972b: 197–198). Parallels come mostly from Enkomi, where 276 similar vessels were found in the Sanctuary of the Horned God, dated to the second half of the twelfth century BCE, and classified by Dikaios as Plain Wheel-made Base Ring II bowls

---

4 For an alternative typology of Base Ring fabrics, instead of the traditional and prevailing Swedish classification (Åström 1972b: 126–198), see Vaughan 1991.

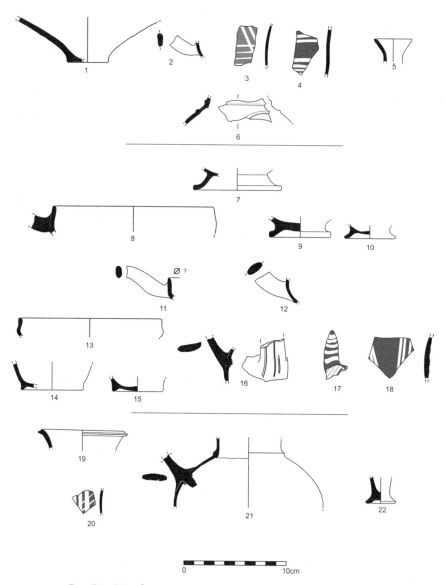

FIGURE 5.3 Base Ring Ware from Areas B, D, and A
DRAWINGS BY MARIUSZ BURDAJEWICZ

(1969–1971: 316, 595, 616, pls. 77: 6; 83: 30, 36; 95: 4 [nos. 338, 486, 527, 392]). Other examples from Kouklia-Mantissa are dated to the end of the thirteenth century BCE (Karageorghis 1965: fig. 45: 27). In Cyprus wheel-made Base Ring Ware is dated to LC IIC–IIIB (Åström and Åström 1972: 700).

A fragment of a ceramic horn decorated with white paint (Fig. 5.3: 17) belongs to a bull-shaped zoomorphic vessel corresponding to Base Ring II Type XVI b (and c?), denoting an Animal-Shaped Vase (Åström 1972b: 191–194, 197,

FIGURE 5.3

No.	Inventory no.	Area	Level	Ware
1	8.440c	B	13	Base Ring
2	8.440	B	12	Base Ring
3	8.441c	B	9	Base Ring
4	8.441b	B	9	Base Ring
5	8.441a	B	Non stratified	Base Ring
6	8.439a	B		Base Ring I
7	8.442	D	10'	Base Ring
8	8.442e	D	9'	Base Ring
9	8.442a	D	9'	Base Ring
10	8.442f	D	9'	Base Ring I
11	8.442b	D	9'	Base Ring
12	8.442d	D	9'	Base Ring
13	8.442h	D	8'	Base Ring II
14	8.442l	D	8'	Base Ring II
15	8.442g	D	8'	Base Ring II
16	8.442j	D	8'	Base Ring
17	7.047	D		Base Ring II
18	8.443b	D	Non stratified	Base Ring
19	72.772	A		Base Ring
20	75.427a	A		Base Ring
21	8.050		Surface	Base Ring
22	8.274			Base Ring

fig. LIII: 12, 15). Such bull figurines were found at many sites in Cyprus, especially as part of tomb assemblages, for example, at Enkomi (see, e.g., Dikaios 1969–1971: pls. 209: 14; 227: 16, Tomb 10; Åström, Bailey, and Karageorghis 1976: 51, fig. 50) and Kazaphani (Nicolaou and Nicolaou 1989: 102, pls. XII, XXXIII, XXXIV).

In the Levant, animal-shaped Base Ring vessels are known both from domestic contexts and tombs (Gittlen 1978: 100). Another horn fragment of a zoomorphic Base Ring vessel had already been found at Tell Keisan (Briend and Humbert 1980: 345–346, pl. 106: 70). Additional examples can be found in the LB I/II tomb at Ugarit (Schaeffer 1978: 290–291, fig. 32), the area of Temple 50 at Tell Abu Hawam (Balensi 1980: pl. 47: 1, 2, 10), Timnah (Steel 2006: pl. 45: 11; photo 73); Gezer, Lachish, Megiddo, Tel Mor, and Tell Zakariya (Azekah; after Gittlen 1978: 235–237).

3 Possible Monochrome Ware

Two potsherds (Fig. 5.4: 1, 2) belong to hemispherical and slightly carinated bowls. Although their hard, metallic fabric and brown/red matt slip

FIGURE 5.4 Various Cypriot wares from Areas B, D, and A
DRAWINGS BY MARIUSZ BURDAJEWICZ

FIGURE 5.4

No.	Inventory no.	Area	Level	Ware
1	7.263a	B	10b	Monochrome
2	8.458a	D		Monochrome
3	76.683	B	Non stratified	Bichrome
4	8.445	D		Bichrome
5	8.449	B	10a	Composite
6	8.444	B	13	Bucchero
7	8.444a	B	12b/13	Bucchero
8	8.446	B	Non stratified	Black-on-Red
9	8.447c	B	12/13	White Painted V
10	8.447a	B	10	White Painted VI
11	8.447h	B	11	White Painted V–VI
12	6.70.25	B	Non stratified	White Painted V
13	8.448c	D	10'	White Painted III–IV
14	8.447e	D	10'/9'	White Painted V
15	8.447f	D	10'/9'	White Painted V–VI
16	8.448d	D	9'–8'	White Painted III–IV
17	8.448e	D	8'	White Painted V–VI
18	6.71.38	D	8'	White Painted IV–VI
19	71.362	A	Non stratified	White Painted V–VI
20	5.05.13	A	Non stratified	White Painted V–VI

indicate no doubt their Cypriot origin, it is difficult to propose a more precise classification. They can represent either Base Ring Ware or Monochrome Ware. The two can be confused, especially when the sherds are small and devoid of characteristic decoration (Artzy, Perlman, and Asaro 1981: 40–41). Nonetheless, the profiles of the examples from Tell Keisan seem to be characteristic of Type IIB–C Monochrome bowls rather than of regular Base Ring bowls (Åström 1972b: 94–95, fig. XLV: 7, 8; Lagarce and Lagarce 1985: fig. 27: 129, 130, 134, 156, etc.).

Monochrome Ware bowls were found at several Levantine sites such as Sarepta (Koehl 1985: 34; Anderson 1988: 262–263), Tyre (Bikai 1978: 54–55), Tell Abu Hawam (Balensi 1980: 384–385), Hazor, Megiddo (Åström and Åström 1972: 720–721), and Timnah (Steel 2006: 157, pls. 10: 20, 21; 19: 16). According to the Swedish chronology, Monochrome Ware is characteristic of LC IA1–IA2 (Åström and Åström 1972: 700, 758, 765). In the Levant, Monochrome vessels appear in transitional Middle Bronze (MB) IIC–LB I contexts (Oren 1969: 140–142) and continue into LB II.

4 Bucchero Ware

Handmade Bucchero Ware is represented by two ribbed body sherds from Area B. The first comes from Level 13 and the second from Level 13/12b (Fig. 5.4: 6, 7). They may belong to the same closed vessel, probably a jug. The ribs are pinched, which suggests that this is the later style of this ware (Bergoffen 2014: 664).

In Cyprus, Bucchero Ware (I and II) occurs mainly in tomb assemblages, e.g., at Stephania, Kition, Lapithos-Ayia Anastasia, and Kourion-Bamboula and in large numbers in the tombs at Enkomi (references in Åström 1972b: 425–427; Courtois 1981: 261). Handmade Bucchero Ware is characteristic of LC IIA–IIIB1, that is, 1425/1415–1100/1075 BCE (Åström and Åström 1972: 701, 770). Outside Cyprus, in Canaan, this ware is fairly rare. A similar body sherd of a jug was found at Deir el-Balah (Merrillees 2010: fig. 8.1: 4) and two other Bucchero items have been recently published from Tell Jemmeh (Bergoffen 2014: 664, fig. 11.4 c, f; for other examples from Canaan, see Gittlen 1978: 291–303).

5 Bichrome Wheel-Made and Handmade Wares

Two body sherds have been identified as belonging to the Bichrome Ware family.[5] Bichrome Wheel-made Ware is represented by a single body sherd decorated with a circle and possibly a Maltese cross or a spoked wheel motif (Fig. 5.4: 3). Such motifs are well attested in Bichrome-style pottery in Canaan (see, e.g., Epstein 1966: fig. 5).

According to Maguire, Bichrome Ware comprises three separate groups derived from Cypriot, southern Palestinian, and Egyptian sources (Maguire 1990: 130). At present, we are unable to state in a satisfactory way which of these three sources should be linked with the example from Tell Keisan. This being said, considering the geographic location of the site, a Cypriot source seems much more probable than the other two. In Cyprus, the Bichrome Wheel-made Ware was produced in the eastern part of the island and, to a smaller extent, in

---

5 I am very grateful to A. Mazar who helped me identify these sherds.

its northern part (Artzy, Asaro, and Perlman 1973, 1978; Artzy 2001b; Charaf 2013: 154).

Apart from findings in Egypt and Canaan (Maguire 1990, 1995) Cypriot Bichrome Wheel-made Ware is known also from sites in Phoenicia: Tell 'Arqa, Beirut, and Tell el-Ghassil (Charaf 2013: 154–155).

Bichrome Handmade Ware is represented by a fragment of a wide, tapering neck decorated with reddish-brown and dark gray matt horizontal bands (Fig. 5.4: 4). It was probably part of a tankard, a popular type of vessel during LC I–II (see, e.g., Åström 1972b: fig. XLIV: 2).

Handmade Bichrome Ware is fairly rare in Cyprus (Åström 1966: 59–60; 1972b: 112–113). It originated in its east and some examples can be cited from Kalopsidha, Akaki (Åström 1966: 59), and Stephania (Stewart 1965: pl. IV).

As for the date, Bichrome Ware, both wheel- and handmade, is characteristic of the Late Bronze Age in Canaan.

6 Handmade Red-on-Black Ware

This ware is represented at Tell Keisan by two sherds, of which one is illustrated (Fig. 5.4: 8). Red-on-Black ware is characteristic of MC III–LC I, but it also appears in LC II contexts (Åström 1972a: 199). It occurs mainly in northeastern Cyprus, especially the Karpass Peninsula, where it was probably produced (Åström 1966: 77; 1972a: 108–118).

In the Levant, Black-on-Red Ware was identified at Tell el-'Ajjul, Megiddo, Tell el-Far'ah (S), Gezer, Lachish (after Åström 1972a: 226s), Ashkelon (Bergoffen 1988: 161, 167), Tel Mevorakh (Salz 1984: 59, pl. 44: 6), Tell Abu Hawam (Balensi 1980: 383–384), Sarepta (Koehl 1985: 32; Anderson 1988: 266–267); Tyre (Bikai 1978: 55–56), and Ugarit (Schaeffer 1978: 210, fig. 5: 12).

7 White Painted Ware

The excavations at Tell Keisan yielded 23 White Painted sherds found in Late Bronze (Area D) and Iron Age contexts (Areas B, D), which are therefore no doubt residual material. Since the sherds are very small, some of the proposed identifications of particular styles should be treated with caution. White Painted Ware appeared at the end of Early Cypriot III and is characteristic of the Middle Cypriot and beginning of the Late Cypriot period (Campbell Gagné 2012: 4). Neutron activation analyses have demonstrated that the vessels of the White Painted family were produced in eastern Cyprus, mainly in the region of Kalopsidha and Enkomi (Artzy, Perlman, and Asaro 1981: 38, 46–47).

7.1 Alternating Broad Bands and Wavy Lines

Figure 5.4: 13 is a body sherd of a White Painted III–IV jar or jug decorated in Alternating Broad Bands and Wavy Lines Style. According to Åström, this style is dated to Middle Cypriot (MC) II and III (1966: 82; see, also, Bergoffen 1988: 166). It is characteristic of pottery production of eastern Cyprus: at Kalopsidha (Åström 1966: 81–82, figs. 81: row 2: 2–7, row 3; 83: rows 2, 3; 84: row 2: 2; Åström 1972a: fig. IA: 23, 28, 38), Arpera-Mosphilos, Stavroti-Alaminos, Politiko, Bey Keuy, Kythera, and Galinoporni (after Åström 1966: 81).

In the Levant this style is rarely found among Cypriot imports. Examples come from Ugarit (Schaeffer 1978: 210, fig. 5: 5), Tell 'Arqa (Charaf 2013: 151, fig. 9), Sarepta (Koehl 1985: fig. 1: 1), Tyre (Bikai 1978: pl. XVIIIA: 21), Tel Kabri (Kempinski, Gershuny, and Scheftelowitz 2002: 117, figs. 5: 17, 5: 18), Dhahrat el-Humraiya (Ory 1948: pl. XXXIII: 24), and Ashkelon (Bergoffen 1988: 161, 166, fig. 1: 1).

7.2 Pendent Line Style

Figure 5.4: 16 presents a body sherd of a White Painted III–IV jug(?) decorated in the Pendent Line Style: two groups of straight, parallel and vertical lines and two wavy lines between them (Motifs 3 + 10 according to Frankel's classification [1974: 20, 21, fig. 4a]).

This style probably originated in the western part of the island and is characteristic of MC III and LC IA (Merrillees 2002: 6). It is known, among other places, from Kalopsidha, Enkomi, Alambra, Yeri, Ayia Paraskevi, Dhiorios, Politiko-Lambertis, and Kythera in the Karpass Peninsula (for references, see Courtois 1981: 16).

Vessels representing the White Painted Pendent Line Style are well attested outside Cyprus: at Tell el-Dab'a in Egypt (Merrillees 2002: 3) and in the Levant, at sites such as Tell 'Arqa (Charaf 2013: 149–150, fig. 4), Sidon (Doumet-Serhal 2008: 16, fig. 16), Sarepta (Koehl 1985: fig. 1: 3, 4; Anderson 1988: pls. 21: 5, 7; 29: 1), Dhahrat el-Humraiya (Ory 1948: pl. XXXII: 6, 8, 9, 19–21), Tel Kabri (Kempinski, Gershuny, and Scheftelowitz 2002: 118), Tel Megadim (Wolff and Bergoffen 2012: fig. 3: 1–7), 'Atlit (Mazar and Ilan 2014: 122, fig. 10: 4–5), Megiddo (Loud 1948: pls. 26 :16; 46 : 11), and Gezer (Macalister 1912: 172).

The body sherd of a closed White Painted V vessel (Fig. 5.4: 9) is another example of Pendent Line Style decoration. It presents two horizontal bands below which run at least five vertical lines, one wavy and thin and the others straight (Frankel 1974: 22, fig. 4a; Motif 12). A similar pattern can be found on an amphora from Stephania (Åström 1972a: fig. XVIII: 9) and on vessels from Enkomi (Dikaios 1969–1971: pls. 54: 14; 64: 4), Politiko, and Galinoporni (Frankel 1974: 22). Outside Cyprus, the same motif occurs on a White Painted V jug at Ugarit (Schaeffer 1949: fig. 104: 27). The Pendent Line Style is also represented by body sherds in Figure 5.4: 12, 14.

7.3 Cross Line Style

The Cross Line Style is characteristic of MC III and the beginning of LC I, at Enkomi, Arpera, Milia, Alambra, and, first and foremost, at Kalopsidha (Åström 1966: 83–87; 1972a: 63–66, fig. IX: 10–14; see, also, Courtois 1981: 16–18, with references to other sites). At Tell Keisan this style is represented by only one body sherd (Fig. 5.4: 18), decorated possibly in the Close Net Style (Åström 1966: 84, fig. 91).

Examples of the White Painted IV–VI Cross Line Style from the Levant are known from Tell 'Arqa, Sidon (Charaf 2013: 150–151, fig. 8), Dhahrat el-Humraiya (Ory 1948: pl. XXXII: 14), Megiddo (Loud 1948: pls. 26: 15; 34: 4, 8, 9), 'Akko (Dothan 1976: 9, figs. 8: 13, 16), Tel Mevorakh (Salz 1984: 59, pl. 44: 5), Ashkelon (Bergoffen 1988: 161, 166, fig. 1: 2), Tell Beit Mirsim (Albright 1932: 70, pl. 22: 7), and Gezer (Macalister 1912: pl. LXII: 51).

7.4 Tangent Line Style

One body sherd (Fig. 5.4: 19) is decorated in a manner close to the Tangent Line Style, which is characteristic of White Painted V and V–VI. Vessels with such decoration are known mainly from Kalopsidha (Åström 1966: 89–90, fig. 102: 3, 4; 1972a: figs. IIB: 30; XVI: 17), and Enkomi (Courtois 1981: 17, fig. 5: 5–7, 9). Some examples from outside Cyprus come from Ugarit (Schaeffer 1949: figs. 105: 37; 108: 23; 131: 13, 14, 15, 17), Tell 'Arqa (Charaf 2013: 152), Sarepta (Anderson 1988: fig. 18), Hazor (Yadin et al. 1958: pl. C: 2), Tel Megadim (Wolff and Bergoffen 2012: fig. 3: 12), Megiddo (Loud 1948: pls. 34: 13; 42: 1), and Gezer (Macalister 1912: pl. CLVII: 4).

7.5 Framed Band Style

The decoration of two body sherds of closed vessels (Fig. 5.4: 11, 17) consists of a broad band between thin parallel lines (Frankel's Motif 4; Frankel 1974: 20, fig. 4a). Such a pattern, the Framed Band Style, occurs on White Painted V and V–VI vessels, primarily at Kalopsidha and Enkomi (Åström 1966: 45, no. 1073, fig. 30; 1972a: 77; Dikaios 1969–1971: pls. 52: 4531/3; 53: 16, 30).

The Framed Band Style is characteristic of closed vessels like jugs and amphorae (Åström 1972a: figs. XVI: 17; XVIII: 10; Frankel 1974: 20; Courtois 1981: fig. 15: 1–2 [White Painted IV–VI]; Lagarce and Lagarce 1985: fig. 12).

In Canaan, a complete White Painted V amphora and a body sherd of another one, decorated in the Framed Band Style, were found in a MB IIB context at Tel Mevorakh XIII (Salz 1984: 58, fig. 17: 4, pl. 44: 1) and a jar from Megiddo XI (MB IIB) is decorated similarly (Loud 1948: pls. 36: 3, 126: 5).

7.6 Other White Painted Wares

In the case of the body sherds shown in Figure 5.4: 10, 15, 20 (and several others not illustrated here) it is not easy to present a convincing stylistic analysis. They are decorated with horizontal lines or bands surrounding the base of the neck and/or the neck and shoulders, generally of White Painted Handmade Style, possibly V and/or VI. The neck in Figure 5.4: 10 possibly comes from a Type VD2C White Painted VI juglet (Åström 1972b: fig. XLI: 2, 3). Its surface is slightly knife trimmed or shaved vertically, which is characteristic of some forms in this class (ibid.: 54).

Such juglets were found in Cyprus in LC IA–B contexts at such sites as Enkomi, Hala Sultan Tekke, Athienou, and Kalopsidha (Åström 1972b: 58; Courtois 1981: 115 and references there). White Painted VI is considered characteristic of LC I. Some finds, however, date to the beginning of LC IIIB (Åström and Åström 1972: 700).

Examples of this ware were found at numerous sites off the island: Ugarit, Sarepta, Hazor, Tell Abu Hawam, Megiddo, Gezer, Tell el-Far'ah (S), Tell el-Hesi, Lachish, etc. (Åström and Åström 1972: 710–715).

8 Composite Ware

The body sherd in Figure 5.4: 5 probably came from a large Type III bowl, according to the Swedish classification (Åström 1972a: 124, fig. XXXVII: 8); its exterior is slipped and parallel white lines are painted on its interior. It represents the so-called Composite Ware, which combines two styles: Black Slip II and White Painted III–IV. Composite Ware appeared during MC II and continued in MC III (Åström 1972a: 199, 276). It was produced in the eastern part of Cyprus, at such sites as Kalopsidha, Ayios Iakovos (Åström 1966: 68–69, 145; 1972a: 125, 229), and Enkomi (Dikaios 1969–1971: pls. 54: 21; 76: 19).

Composite ware is rarely found outside Cyprus. Examples of this ware in the Levant come from Tell 'Arqa, Sidon (Charaf 2013: 154, fig. 18), 'Akko (Dothan

1976: 9, fig. 8: 12[6]), Megiddo (Loud 1948: pl. 19: 5), and Tel Michal (Negbi 1989: 50, fig. 5.4: 4).

9 Summary

The beginning of trade between Tell Keisan and Cyprus—most probably via one of the coastal harbor sites such as 'Akko (the nearest to our site)—started as early as MB II with such imports as White Painted III–IV and Composite Wares. The presence of Red-on-Black, White Painted IV–VI, V, V–VI, VI, and Bichrome Wares confirms an uninterrupted influx of Cypriot pottery in MB III and LB I. A continuum of trade throughout the end of the Late Bronze Age is well attested at the site by the arrival of White Slip, Base Ring, Monochrome, and Bucchero Wares.

The significance of Cypriot pottery found at Tell Keisan is rather limited. Most of the material found at the site, especially the Middle Cypriot wares, comprises residual sherds in Iron Age contexts—a result of various post-depositional processes.[7] Therefore, it cannot help in resolving questions related to the absolute and/or relative chronology of Cypriot imports to the Levant, nor can it contribute to the understanding of second-millennium BCE Levantine chronology. Nevertheless, these finds shed new light on interconnections between Cyprus and Canaan, and allow to update the map of quantitative and geographical distribution of Cypriot Bronze Age pottery outside the island, specifically in northern Canaan/southern Phoenicia. However, it should be emphasized that quantitative data may change after the entire ceramic material from the 1979 and 1980 excavations will be thoroughly investigated. This work is still in progress.

Acknowledgments

I would like to thank Father Jean-Baptiste Humbert, OP, for entrusting me with the pottery from Tell Keisan for study and publication.

---

6 Maguire classified this sherd as White Painted Cross Line Style (Maguire 1990, Vol. 2: 62).
7 Three possible exceptions are White Slip II late (or III) sherds of the LC IIC1–2 period (Fig. 5.2: 4–5, 8), found in Late Bronze/Iron Age I contexts.

References

Albright, W.F. 1932. *The Excavations of Tell Beit Mirsim* 1: *The Pottery of the First Three Campaigns* (Annual of the American Schools of Oriental Research 12). New Haven.

Anderson, W.P. 1988. *Sarepta* 1: *The Late Bronze and Iron Age Strata of Area II, Y* (Publications de l'Université libanaise. Section des études archéologiques 2). Beirut.

Artzy, M. 2001a. The White Slip Ware for Export? The Economics of Production. In: Karageorghis, V., ed. *The White Slip Ware of Late Bronze Age Cyprus: Proceedings of an International Conference Organized by the Anastasios G. Leventis Foundation, Nicosia, in Honour of Malcolm Wiener, Nicosia, 29th–30th October 1998* (Österreichischen Akademie der Wissenschaften, Denkschriften der Gesamtakademie20; Contributions to the Chronology of the Eastern Mediterranean2). Vienna: 101–115.

Artzy, M. 2001b. A Study of the Cypriote Bichrome Ware: Past, Present and Future. In: Åström, P., ed. *The Chronology of Base-Ring Ware and Bichrome Wheel-Made Ware: Proceedings of a Colloquium Held at the Royal Academy of Letters, History and Antiquities, Stockholm, May 18–19, 2000*. Stockholm: 157–174.

Artzy, M., Asaro, F., and Perlman, I. 1973. The Origin of the "Palestinian" Bichrome Ware. *Journal of the American Oriental Society* 93: 446–461.

Artzy, M., Asaro, F., and Perlman, I. 1978. Imported and Local Bichrome Ware in Megiddo. *Levant* 10: 99–111.

Artzy, M., Perlman, I., and Asaro, F. 1981. Cypriote Pottery Imports at Ras Shamra. *Israel Exploration Journal* 31: 37–47.

Åström, P. 1966. *Excavations at Kalopsidha and Ayios Iakovos in Cyprus* (Studies in Mediterranean Archaeology 2). Lund.

Åström, P. 1972a. *The Middle Cypriote Bronze Age* (The Swedish Cyprus Expedition 4 [1B]). Lund.

Åström, P. 1972b. *The Late Cypriote Bronze Age: Architecture and Pottery* (The Swedish Cyprus Expedition 4 [1C]). Lund.

Åström, L. and Åström, P. 1972. *The Late Cypriote Bronze Age: Other Arts and Crafts. Relative and Absolute Chronology, Foreign Relations, Historical Conclusions* (The Swedish Cyprus Expedition 4 [1D]). Lund.

Åström, P., Bailey, D.M., and Karageorghis, V. 1976. *Hala Sultan Tekke* 1: *Excavations 1897–1971* (Studies in Mediterranean Archaeology 45/1). Gothenburg.

Åström, P., Åström, E., Hatzianoniou, A., Niklasson, K., and Öbrink, U. 1983. *Hala Sultan Tekke* 8: *Excavations 1971–79* (Studies in Mediterranean Archaeology 45/8). Gothenburg.

Balensi, J. 1980. *Les Fouilles de R.W. Hamilton à Tell Abu Hawam, niveaux IV et V (1650-950 environs av. J.C.)*. Ph.D. dissertation. Université des Sciences Humaines. Strasbourg.

Benson, J.L. 1961. The White Slip Sequence at Bamboula, Kourion. *Palestinian Exploration Quarterly* 93: 61-69.

Bergoffen, C.J. 1988. Pottery from Ashkelon. *Levant* 20: 161-168.

Bergoffen, C.J. 2002. Early Late Cypriot Ceramic Exports to Canaan: White Slip I. In: Ehrenberg, E., ed. *Leaving No Stones Unturned: Essays on the Ancient Near East and Egypt in Honor of Donald P. Hansen*. Winona Lake, IN: 23-41.

Bergoffen, C.J. 2014. Bronze and Iron Age Cypriote and Aegean Imports. In: Ben-Shlomo, D. and Beek, G.W. van, eds. *The Smithsonian Institution Excavation at Tell Jemmeh, Israel, 1970-1990*. Washington, DC: 657-720.

Bikai, P.M. 1978. *The Pottery of Tyre*. Warminster.

Briend, J. and Humbert, J. 1980. *Tell Keisan (1971-1976): une cité phénicienne en Galilée* (Orbis Biblicus et Orientalis. Series Archaeologica 1). Fribourg.

Burdajewicz, M. 1992. *Contribution au corpus céramique de Tell Keisan. Le niveau 13 augmenté du catalogue des importations chypriotes, mycéniennes, chypro-phéniciennes et de la céramique philistine* (Mémoire de l'École biblique et archéologique française de Jérusalem). Jerusalem.

Campbell Gagné, L.A. 2012. *Middle Cypriot White Painted Ware: A Study of Pottery Production and Distribution in Middle Bronze Age Cyprus*. Ph.D. dissertation. University of Toronto. Toronto.

Charaf, H. 2013. Cypriot Imported Pottery from the Middle Bronze Age in Lebanon. *Berytus* 53-54: 147-165.

Courtois, J.C. 1981. *Alasia 2: les tombes d' Enkomi: le mobilier funéraire (fouilles C.F.-A. Schaeffer 1947-1965)*. Paris.

Dikaios, P. 1969-1971. *Enkomi: Excavations 1948-1958*. 3 vols. Mainz am Rhein.

Dothan, M. 1976. Akko: Interim Excavation Report. First Season, 1973/4. *Bulletin of the American Schools of Oriental Research* 224: 1-48.

Doumet-Serhal, C. 2008. The Kingdom of Sidon and Its Mediterranean Connections. In: Doumet-Serhal, C., ed. *Networking Patterns of the Bronze and Iron Age Levant: The Lebanon and Its Mediterranean Connections*. Beirut: 1-70.

Epstein, C.M. 1966. *Palestinian Bichrome Ware*. Leiden.

Eriksson, K.O. 2007. *The Creative Independence of Late Bronze Age Cyprus: An Account of the Archaeological Importance of White Slip Ware* (Denkschriften der Gesamtakademie Band 38; Contributions to the Chronology of the Eastern Mediterranean 10). Vienna.

Frankel, D. 1974. *Middle Cypriot White Painted Pottery: An Analytical Study of the Decoration* (Studies in Mediterranean Archaeology 42). Gothenburg.

Gittlen, B.M. 1978. *Studies in the Late Cypriote Pottery Found in Palestine*. Ph.D. dissertation. University of Pennsylvania. Philadelphia.

Humbert, J.-B. 1980. *Tell Keisan 1980. Sommaire* (unpublished manuscript of the École biblique et archéologique française). Jerusalem.

Humbert, J.-B. 1981. Récents travaux à Tell Keisan. *Revue Biblique* 88: 374–398.

Humbert, J.-B. 1993. Keisan, Tell. In: Stern, E., ed. *The New Encyclopedia of Archaeological Excavations in the Holy Land*, Vol. 3. Jerusalem: 862–867.

Karageorghis, V. 1965. *Nouveaux documents pour l'étude du Bronze récent à Chypre* (Etudes Chypriotes III). Paris.

Karageorghis, V. 1990. *Tombs at Palaepaphos*, Vol. 1: *Teratsoudhia*; Vol. 2: *Eliomylia*. Nicosia.

Kempinski, A., Gershuny, L., and Scheftelowitz, N. 2002. Middle Bronze Age. In: Kempinski, A. *Tel Kabri: The 1986–1993 Excavation Seasons* (edited by Scheftelowitz, N. and Oren, R.) (Monograph Series of the Institute of Archaeology of Tel Aviv University 20). Tel Aviv: 109–175.

Koehl, R.B. 1985. *Sarepta 3: The Imported Bronze and Iron Age Wares from Area II, X* (Publications de l'Université libanaise. Section des études archéologiques 2). Beirut.

Kromholtz, S. 1978. *Cypriote White Slip II Hemispherical Bowls*. Ann Arbor.

Kromholtz, S. 1984. Imported Cypriot Pottery. In: Stern, E., ed. *Excavations at Tel Mevorakh (1973–1976)*, Part 2: *The Bronze Age* (Qedem 18). Jerusalem: 16–20.

Lagarce, J. and Lagarce, E. 1985. *Deux tombes du Chypriote récent d'Enkomi (Chypre): tombes 1851 et 1907* (Mémoire 51). Paris.

Loud, G. 1948. *Megiddo 2: Seasons of 1925–1939* (Oriental Institute Publications 62). Chicago.

Macalister, R.A.S. 1912. *Excavations of Gezer 1902–1905*. 2 vols. London.

Maguire, L.C. 1990. *The Circulation of Cypriot Pottery in the Middle Bronze Age*. Ph.D. dissertation. University of Edinburgh. Edinburgh.

Maguire, L.C. 1995. Tell el-Dab'a: The Cypriot Connection. In: Davies, W.V. and Schofield, L., eds. *Egypt, the Aegean and the Levant: Interconnections in the Second Millennium BC*. London: 54–65.

Mazar, E. and Ilan, D. 2014. A Middle Bronze Age Tomb at 'Atlit. *'Atiqot* 79: 111–130.

Merrillees, R.S. 2002. The Relative and Absolute Chronology of the Cypriote White Painted Pendent Line Style. *Bulletin of the American Schools of Oriental Research* 326: 1–9.

Merrillees, R.S. 2010. Cypriot Pottery. In: Dothan, T. and Brandl, B., eds. *Deir el-Balah: Excavations in 1977–1982 in the Cemetery and Settlement*, Vol. 2: *The Finds* (Qedem 50). Jerusalem: 137–143.

Murray, A.S., Smith, A.H., and Walters, H.B. (1900) 1969. *Excavations in Cyprus*. London. Reprint, Oxford.

Negbi, O. 1989. Bronze Age Pottery (Strata XVII–XV). In: Herzog, Z., Rapp, G., Jr., and Negbi, O., eds. *Excavations at Tel Michal, Israel* (Monograph Series of the Institute of Archaeology of Tel Aviv University 8). Minneapolis–Tel Aviv: 43–63.

Nicolaou, I. and Nicolaou, K. 1989. *Kazaphani: A Middle/Late Cypriot Tomb at Kazaphani-Ayios Andronikos: T. 2A, B*. Nicosia.

Oren, E. 1969. Cypriot Imports in the Palestinian Late Bronze I Context. *OpusculaAtheniensia* 9: 127–150.

Ory, J. 1948. A Bronze Age Cemetery at Dhahrat el Humraiya. *The Quarterly of the Department of Antiquities in Palestine* 13: 75–92.

Pecorella, P.E. 1977. *Le tombe dell'Eta del Bronzo Tardo della Necropoli a mare di Ayia Irini "Palaeokastro"* (Biblioteca di antichita cipriote 4/1). Rome.

Plat Taylor, J. du, Birmingham, J.M., Catling, H.W., and Gray, D.H.F. 1957. *Myrtou-Pigadhes: A Late Bronze Age Sanctuary in Cyprus*. Oxford.

Salz, D.L. 1984. The Pottery of the Middle Bronze Age: Imported Cypriot Pottery. In: Stern, E., ed. *Excavations at Tel Mevorakh (1973–1976)*, Part 2: *The Bronze Age* (Qedem 18). Jerusalem: 58–59.

Schaeffer, C.F.A. 1949. *Ugaritica II. Mission de Ras Shamra* (Tome V). Paris.

Schaeffer, C.F.A. 1978. *Ugaritica VII. Mission archéologique de Ras Shamra* (Tome XVIII; Institut Français d'Archéologie de Beyrouth, Bibliothèque archéologique et historique, tome XCIX). Paris.

Steel, L. 2006. Cypriot and Mycenaean Pottery. In: Panitz-Cohen, N. and Mazar, A., eds. *Timnah (Tel Batash) 3: The Finds from the Second Millennium BCE* (Qedem 45). Jerusalem: 151–172.

Steel, L. 2010. Late Cypriot Ceramic Production: Heterarchy or Hierarchy? In: Bolger, D. and Maguire, L.C., eds. *Development of Pre-state Communities in the Ancient Near East*. Oxford: 106–116.

Stewart, J. 1965. Notes on Cyprus. *Opuscula Atheniensia* 6: 157–164.

Vaughan, S.J. 1991. Material and Technical Characterization of Base Ring Ware: A New Fabric Typology. In: Barlow, J.A., Bolger, D., and Kling, B., eds. *Cypriot Ceramics: Reading the Prehistoric Record* (University Museum Monograph 74). Philadelphia: 119–130.

Wolff, S.R. and Bergoffen, C.J. 2012. Cypriot Pottery from MB IIA Loci at Tel Megadim. In: Gruber, M., Ahituv, S., Lehmann, G., and Talshir, Z., eds. *All the Wisdom of the East: Studies in Near Eastern Archaeology and History in Honor of Eliezer D. Oren*. Fribourg–Göttingen: 419–430.

Yadin, Y., Aharoni, Y., Amiran, R., Dothan, T., Dunayevsky, M., and Perrot, J. 1958. *Hazor* 1: *An Account of the First Season of Excavations, 1955*. Jerusalem.

Yadin, Y., Aharoni, Y., Amiran, R., Dothan, T., Dothan, M., Dunayevsky, M., and Perrot, J. 1961. Hazor 3–4: *An Account of the Third and Fourth Seasons of Excavations, 1957–1958*. Jerusalem.

CHAPTER 6

Contextualization and Typology of Ancient Island Harbors in the Mediterranean: From Natural Hazards to Anthropogenic Imprints

Matthieu Giaime, Christophe Morhange, and Nick Marriner

1   Introduction

For several decades, archaeological studies undertaken on Mediterranean islands have showed that these have been, since prehistoric times, attractive areas for human societies. The islands played an important role in the improvement of navigation technics (Ferentinos et al. 2012; Vigne et al. 2014). If Late Pleistocene occupation seems to be a phenomenon restricted to members of the "Big Five" (Sardinia and Corsica [united at times of glacial maxima as "Corsardinia"], Sicily, Crete, and Cyprus; Cherry and Leppard 2018), Epipaleolithic presence has been attested on the majority of Mediterranean islands. This fixes an earlier settlement date of 9000 BCE for most of them (Guilaine 2012; Papoulia 2016). Populations in search of new territories were attracted to islands. They settled and flourished on islands such as Cyprus (Bar-Yosef Mayer et al. 2015) or Malta (Marinner et al. 2019; Gambin 2020), maintaining contacts with their own home settlement on the mainland (Simmons 2012). This phenomenon is particularly perceptible in Cyprus. Vigne et al. (2014) demonstrated an increase of large ruminants transported by boats from the Levant and the coast of Turkey between the twelfth and tenth centuries BCE. Crete is also one of the first islands where the presence of "agricultural villages" is attested. It is one of the oldest pieces of evidence for successful "maritime transfer" of a full agricultural economy (Broodbank and Strasser 1991). This phenomenon would not only be related to major enhancement of naval engineering technics, but could also be associated with a better control of sailing by Upper Paleolithic and Neolithic peoples thanks to knowledge transfer from generation to generation (Vigne et al. 2014). Although islands are regarded as key steps in the colonization process of the Mediterranean (Howitt-Marshall and Runnels 2016; Marriner et al. 2019), the importance of the island in human-environment relations of island harbors has never been clarified or classified.

It seems therefore appropriate to specify changing landscapes and the plurality of ancient island harbors, insofar as the islands played a crucial role in the development and the shaping of ancient coastal societies (Gras 1995; Broodbank 2013; Walsh 2013; Dawson 2014; Fitzpatrick, Rick, and Erlandson 2015). For example, islands were preferred areas for the establishment of Phoenician-Punic and Greek settlements in the first millennium BCE (Carayon 2008). Among the cities of the Levantine coastline, Tyre and Arwad reflect a two-party social organizational model in which the city, located on an island situated a few tens or hundreds of meters from the mainland, enjoys privileged relations with the hinterland, maintaining a favorable defensive position (Carayon 2011). Arwad, for example, had close ties with the cities of Tartous, Tell Ghamqe, and Amrit, located on the continent (Rey-Coquais 1974). Tyre also controlled a coastal strip along the mainland, which granted her access to freshwater (Ras al-'Ayn spring) and forest resources and to an area to bury the dead (Sauvage 2012). The main advantage of this insularity is obviously defensive. This is particularly the case of the cities of Phoenicia. Arwad, for example, was never taken; however, in order to preserve its independence, the city submitted itself to the conquerors in antiquity. Tyre was only definitively breached by Alexander the Great in 332 BCE, following the construction of a causeway connecting artificially the island to the mainland (Katzenstein 1997; Marriner, Morhange and Meulé 2007). In medieval times, the construction of Venice is also a good example of the defensive advantage of islands. In fact, Venice was founded during the sixth century CE, due to the resettlement of the Roman city of Altinum, threatened by Lombard invasions.

In this paper, we turn our attention to several small Mediterranean islands and islets with an area smaller than a few tens or hundreds of square kilometers (Fig. 6.1: A). These islands are associated with ancient settlements and their harbor(s) and have been affected mostly by environmental changes through time. In this study, we focus on the recognition of geomorphological features and of the hydro-sedimentary processes along the shoreline of the islands. We have chosen to study relatively small islands in order to affirm that they have (or had) a clear island nature, by contrast with larger Mediterranean islands (e.g., Cyprus, Sardinia, Sicily), which have a more "continental" nature that may enable the inhabitants to live self-sufficiently. In this sense, their small size, the ratio between their estimated shoreline and their estimated emerged land area in antiquity ("*indice côtier*" as described by Doumenge 1987),[1] the presence of a single harbor city, and the distance between the island

---

1 Due to the modification of the island shoreline and emerged area since ancient times, it is difficult to obtain a reliable estimation of this ratio. Nevertheless, we mention that, for

FROM NATURAL HAZARDS TO ANTHROPOGENIC IMPRINTS 107

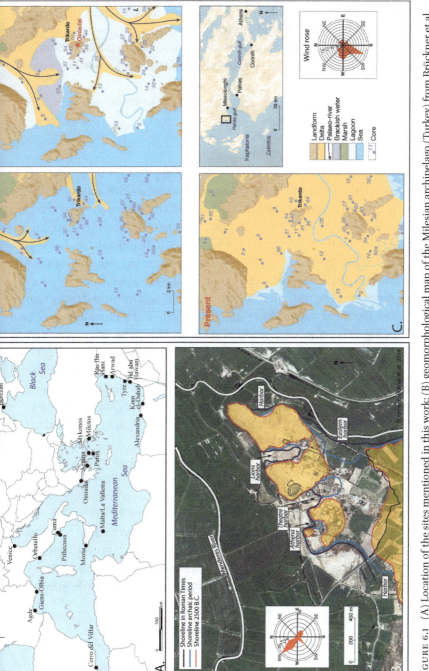

FIGURE 6.1 (A) Location of the sites mentioned in this work; (B) geomorphological map of the Milesian archipelago (Turkey) from Brückner et al. 2014; wind rose, Patmos weather station (in knots, windfinder.com); (C) geomorphological evolution of the Acheloos River delta and landlocking of Oiniadai's ancient harbors (from Vött 2007; Vött et al., 2007); wind rose, Aitoliko weather station IN KNOTS, WWW.WINDFINDER.COM

and the continent explain our choice. Though the assessment of a territory by a single indicator (size, in this case) is reductive, these characteristics are essential in the choice of our studied sites, allowing a non-exhaustive synthesis of the islands. Nevertheless, since these sites are small, their island nature can be limited because they are dependent on the continent for resources on raw materials.

2 Methods

In this work, we identified four geomorphological processes or anthropogenic impacts underlying major changes of island landscape since antiquity. We distinguish (i) the sedimentary budget at base level; (ii) relative sea level changes; (iii) the distance between the island and the mainland; and (iv) human impacts on the coastline. We propose a semiquantitative database that is supported by the attribution of a percentage according to the influence of the role played by each particular process or characteristic (example given in Fig. 6.2: A). The distance between the island and the mainland was measured using Google Earth. The sediment budget was estimated based on the proximity to coastal rivers. In a context of relative sea level stability, with some exceptions such as in Alexandria, the rapid sedimentary inputs at base level led to important constraints in the use and management of ancient harbor basins (Morhange and Marriner 2010; Morhange, Marriner, and Carayon 2015; Giaime Marriner and Morhange 2019). The artificialization of the coastline highlights the variable density of harbor works or the building of a causeway linking the island to the continent.

According to this estimation, we created a heat map to represent the data visually (Fig. 6.2: D). We chose to apply multivariate statistical techniques because they facilitate the investigation of large datasets, while taking into consideration the effects of all variables on the responses. In this study, cluster analysis (algorithm: paired group; similarity measure: correlation) was used to group data according to the estimated importance of each pressure identified on the harbor (Fig. 6.2: D). Finally, a principal component analysis (PCA) allowed us to highlight the main processes that have affected each island over time (Fig. 6.2: B, C).

---

example, an elongated island (such as Tyre) will have a higher ratio than a more circular island (such as Mozia). Thus, according to the "*indice côtier*" (Doumenge 1987), the higher the ratio is, the more the insular nature of the island is significant.

FROM NATURAL HAZARDS TO ANTHROPOGENIC IMPRINTS 109

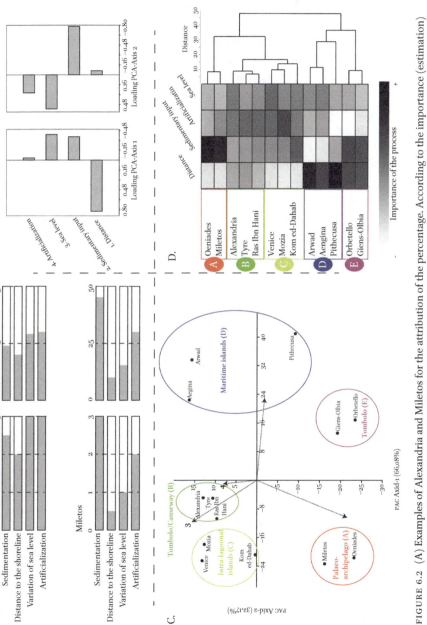

FIGURE 6.2 (A) Examples of Alexandria and Miletos for the attribution of the percentage. According to the importance (estimation) of the pressure, we attributed a certain degree of importance (from 0 to 3) to the role played by each particular process or characteristic that will allow us to calculate a percentage; (B) loading for the two PCA axes; (C) PCA of the harbor presented; (D) heat map showing the estimated importance of each pressure identified and cluster analysis associated

3 Results

The cluster analysis highlights five main groups of sites, each characterized by the most significant variables that led to the modification of the island landscape (Fig. 6.2: D). Group A comprises paleoislands located near the shoreline. For these islands, the sedimentary input was very important and explains their landlocking by shoreline progradation (e.g., Miletos). Group B includes islands that underwent an important artificialization in antiquity, mainly because of the construction of an artificial causeway linking the island to the mainland (e.g., Tyre). Group C comprises intra-lagoonal islands, protected from the sea (e.g., Venice). Group D is composed of islands lying far from the continental shoreline and the importance of sea level on the evolution of its ancient harbors (e.g., Aegina). Finally, group E incorporates islands linked to the mainland by tombolos (e.g., Giens-Olbia).

The PCA undertaken on the same database allowed us to prioritize these five groups according to the main variable that played an important role in their geomorphological evolution (Fig. 6.2: B, C). PCA Axis-1 contrasts maritime islands (negative figures) far from the mainland and not significantly affected by base-level sediment supply, with landlocked paleoislands (positive figures) subject to important sedimentary inputs. This axis illustrates the "insularity level" of the islands, as discussed earlier in this chapter. The more "insular" islands are opposed to the lagoonal and paleoisland on either side of the axis. PCA Axis-2 is marked by the important management of the coastal zone. Positives figures are related to a significant artificialization of the shoreline in antiquity, while the island with a less reduced artificialization was characterized by negative figures.

Thanks to these results, we have built a typology based on five distinct geomorphological types:

Type 1: maritime islands, such as Arwad (Syria), Pithecusa (Ischia in Italy), or Aegina (Greece), that are distant enough from the continent to be protected from the sedimentary processes and the coastal smoothing. This distance, as well as the depth of the water channel between the island and the continental shoreline, is associated with a very low accommodation space on the shoreline of the island.

Type 2: paleoislands, nowadays infilled and landlocked by deltaic progradation, such as Miletos on the Büyük-Menderes Delta (Turkey) or Oiniadai on the Acheloos delta plain (Greece).

Type 3: islands linked to the mainland by a tombolo, such as Orbetello (Tuscany, Italy) or Giens-Olbia (Var, France).

Type 4: islands linked to the mainland by a tombolo and an artificial causeway, such as Tyre on the southern margin of the Awali delta (Lebanon),

Alexandria on the Nile Delta, or Ras Ibn Hani (Syria). Unlike the infilled paleo-archipelagos in deltaic contexts, these islands still present a maritime façade.

Type 5: intra-lagoonal islands, such as Venice (Italy), Mozia (Italy), or Kom ed-Dahab (Egypt).

4 The Typology

4.1 Type 1: Maritime Islands

A number of islands in the Aegean Sea, for example, are situated far from the continent. Nonetheless, these islands, situated close to each other, might have contributed to the development of maritime activities since the Middle Pleistocene (Howitt-Marshall and Runnels 2016). Relative sea level variation is the predominant forcing for these islands, such as for Mykonos (Dalongeville et al. 2007), Paros (Karkani et al. 2018; Karkani et al. 2019), or Aegina in the Saronic Gulf (Mourtzas and Kolaiti 2013). It is also the case of the islands that marked the first step of the Greek colonization in the Mediterranean and the Black Sea. At the time of the Greek expansion, during the Archaic period (750–550 BCE), coastal islets had often been privileged emplacements for the foundation of settlements, like Berezan, located in present-day Ukraine, in the Black Sea (Fig. 6.1: A). In the western Mediterranean, Greek colonists coming from Chalcis in Euboea (Greece) founded the first settlement of Magna Graecia on the island of Ischia. Pithecusa was, during the eighth century BCE, an emporium where the Greeks traded with local people (Ridgway 1992). Some years later, colonists founded Cumae close to Pithecusa to control trade routes to the north (Pasqualini 2000). The reduced size of the watersheds of these small maritime islands explains the low sediment budget and limited accumulation at base level. The main forcing agent is relative sea level rise that could have led to a flooding of some ancient harbor structures (e.g., Poulos, Ghionis, and Maroukian 2009; for Paros, see Papathanassopoulos and Schilardi 1981; Evelpidou, Tziligkaki, and Karkani 2018; for Aegina, see Mourtzas and Kolaiti 2013), as well as a reduction of the islands' surface area since the Bronze Age (Karkani et al. 2017). For example, some islands, such as Malta (Marriner et al. 2012), show limited coastal progradation even in reduced rias. La Valletta is still one of the best insular harbors in the Mediterranean (Bernardie-Tahir 2000).

4.2 Type 2: Paleoislands Infilled and Landlocked in Deltaic Contexts

Because of general sea level stabilization (Vacchi et al. 2016), sustained sediment supply beginning around 6,000 years ago led to shoreline regularization (Anthony, Marriner, and Morhange 2014). This led to a relocation of the harbors due to island landlocking and the infilling of harbor basins (Marriner and

Morhange 2007; Morhange et al. 2015; Brückner et al. 2017; Giaime, Marriner, and Morhange 2019). This "race to the sea" has been clearly identified for a number of river mouths. It shows strong modifications in the human occupation of the catchments in the long term (Brückner et al. 2005). We propose to synthesize two examples: the Milesian archipelago of the Latmian Gulf (now virtually closed) is nowadays landlocked in the Büyük-Menderes deltaic plain (Turkey), 8 km east from the present shoreline (Fig. 6.1: B). This paleo-ria, was an important sink for sediments eroded in the watershed because of intense land cultivation. Thus, in the course of the Bronze Age (ca. 1900–1100 BCE), the increasing erosion of soils led to the transformation of the archipelago into a peninsula (Brückner et al. 2006). Gradually, the progradation of the delta during Roman imperial times led to a progradation of the coastline through the west and the infilling of the harbor basins (Brückner et al. 2014). The Lion harbor in Miletos, partly infilled as early as the Byzantine period (seventh–fifth centuries CE), is a good example of the geomorphological changes induced by a high sediment supply. The apparent sedimentation rate rose from 6.3 mm/year between 510 and 390 BCE to more than 12 mm/year between 75 BCE and 400 CE (Brückner et al. 2014).

In the same vein, geomorphological research on the Acheloos River delta in Greece has highlighted the effect of deltaic progradation on shoreline changes (Fouache et al. 2005; Vött 2007; Vött et al. 2007). The paleoisland of Trikardo, where the city of Oiniadai was located, was washed by the sea 6,000 years ago because of the rise in sea level (Fig. 6.1: C). Thereafter, the progradation of the Acheloos River delta disconnected the island from the sea. The ancient harbors remained connected to the sea through the utilization of fluvial arms as communication channels. By Roman and Byzantine times, the island was permanently landlocked and integrated into the deltaic plain. This limitation was overcome by the establishment of a fluvial harbor, on the bank of a meander of the Acheloos, on the southern part of the island. This relocation of the harbor is typical of the "race to the sea" induced by the environmental changes at this time.

4.3   Type 3: Islands Linked to the Mainland by a Tombolo

If the island is located close to the continent and the sedimentary input is substantial, a tombolo forms. A tombolo is a sand spit, perpendicular to the shore, linking an island to the mainland coast. These isthmuses form because of significant sedimentary inputs and wave action that, linked to the wave diffraction induced by the island, lead to the deposition of sediments. The scales of these landforms can vary considerably from a few tens of meters behind small obstacles up to 15 km, as in the case of Orbetello on the Italian coast (Gosseaume 1973). We emphasize two main factors in the formation of tombolos: the distance to the shoreline (d) and the length of the island (l). Sunamura and

Mizuzo (1987) suggest that a ratio (d/l) lower than or equal to 1.5 led to the natural formation of a tombolo. A salient would form with a ratio of between 1.5 and 3.5. Beyond this value, there can be no spit formation because the island is too far from the continental shoreline (Fig. 6.3: C). On a much larger scale, Van Rijn (2013), using the same parameters but a different formula (l/d), suggests that a ratio higher than or equal to 1 would be necessary for the development of a tombolo between the shoreline and the breakwater. With a ratio of between 0.5 and 1, a salient would form. Beyond this value, there would be no effect on the shoreline. These two parameters have a major role to play in the formation of a tombolo whose morphogenesis differs depending on the context and the coastal processes, including the sedimentary inputs, the orientation of the island with respect to the waves, and weather and marine environments of each site. We present the data regarding the length of the island, the distance between the island and the coast, and the associated ratios for each tombolo studied in this paper (Table 6.1). In the Mediterranean, a number of ancient islands have been connected to the mainland by a tombolo. The majority of tombolos are formed by a single ridge, though there are good examples of tombolo pairs (Giens; Courtaud 2000) and even triplets (Orbetello; Gosseaume 1973). Multiple tombolo formation is attributed to waves

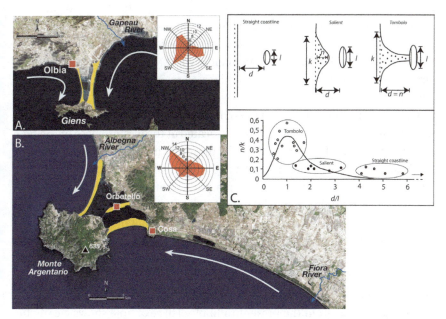

FIGURE 6.3 (A) Triplet tombolo of Orbetello; (B) twin tombolo of Giens-Olbia, (images Google Earth); wind roses, Monte Argentario (Orbetello) and Giens airport (Olbia) weather stations (in knots, windfinder.com); (C) key parameters of tombolo formation
FROM SUNAMURA AND MIZUZO 1987

TABLE 6.1 Measurements of length and distance from the coast of the different tombolos presented in this work and associated ratios

	Distance from the continent (m)	Length of the island (m)	Ratio (d/l) (Sunamura and Mizuzo 1987)	Ratio (l/d) (Van Rijn 2013)
Alexandria	1,300	2,100	0.62	1.62
Giens-Olbia	4,000	6,000	0.67	1.50
Orbetello	4,500	11,000	0.41	2.44
Ras Ibn Hani	900	2,500	0.36	2.78
Tyre	1,000	2,500	0.40	2.50

approaching the island flanks at different angles of incidence, with lagoons developing in the sheltered area between the salients (Blanc 1959). The island of Monte Argentario is connected to the mainland by the triple tombolo of Orbetello (Fig. 6.3: B). The first permanent occupation is attested from the fifth millennium BCE onward, on the Punta degli Stretti promontory, located on the eastern façade of the island in an area protected from the dominant wave direction, close to the only still-navigable inlet between the sea and the lagoon (Dolci 2014). This may suggest that an inlet was present in this sector in ancient times. Thereafter, during the seventh century BCE, the Etruscan settlement of Orbetello was founded on a sand spit located in the center of the current lagoon (central salient). Its harbors enjoyed calm lagoonal waters.

Olbia de Provence, a Massalian colony founded in the late fourth century BCE (Ugolini, Arcelin, and Bats 2010), is located at the western base of the twin tombolo of Giens (Fig. 6.3: A). A mole, presently underwater, appears as the single ancient harbor structure identified (Long and Cibecchini 1996). The discovery of a fragment of an amphora incorporated into the mortar suggests that this mole was built during the late first century BCE. This construction would be linked to the relocation of the "primitive" harbor, potentially located in the lagoon, because of its infilling (Long and Vella 2005). Vella et al. (2000) argued the ancient tombolo was 30 m wider in its western part, compared with the present tombolo, and a lagoonal environment is attested behind the sand spit since the Neolithic. At present, underwater remains of this spit are still visible around 30 m away from the present tombolo. This example shows clearly the protective role of the island for the mainland. Nevertheless, in the present context of diminished sedimentary inputs, the protective role of the islands does not facilitate the accretion of the tombolo and the salients of Giens' tombolo are eroding.

4.4 Type 4: Islands Linked to the Mainland by a Tombolo and an Artificial Causeway

The formation of the tombolos detailed in this part is linked to a twofold influence, natural and anthropogenic. We would like to highlight three sites with similar geomorphological traits: the tombolos of Ras Ibn Hani (Fig. 6.4: A) and Tyre (Fig. 6.4: C) and that of Alexandria, linking the island of Pharos to the Nile Delta shoreline (Fig. 6.4: B). The formation of the tombolos of Tyre and Alexandria is clearly linked to the construction of an artificial causeway under the reign of Alexander the Great. At Tyre the causeway was built in 332 BCE (Marriner, Morhange, and Meulé 2007). At Alexandria it was built soon after the foundation of the city in 331 BCE. At Ras Ibn Hani, the causeway predates the Hellenistic period (Sanlaville 1978; Dalongeville et al. 1993). At these three sites the formation of the tombolo is divided into three main steps (Marriner, Goiran, and Morhange 2008; Marriner et al. 2012; Fig. 6.4). First, because of sea level stabilization over the last 6,000 years and the hydrodynamic processes, the development of an underwater salient engendered the formation of a proto-tombolo. Research undertaken in Tyre and Ras Ibn Hani demonstrates that a rapid accretion phase started around 3500 BCE because of significant sedimentary input following the intense cultivation of the watersheds (Marriner et al. 2012). It was upon these amphibious sandbanks (proto-tombolos) that the causeways were built. In Alexandria, for example, the tombolo/causeway divided the bay into two parts and two harbors had been installed on either side (Goiran et al. 2005). The third phase of tombolo formation consists of a widening of the spit on both sides of the causeway. In Alexandria the harbor basins were affected by intense siltation (sedimentation rates: 10 mm/year; Goiran 2001).

We could include artificial islands such as Palm Islands or The World archipelago in Dubai as a subtype. Palm Islands are three artificial islands, Palm Jumeirah, Deira Island, and Palm Jebel Ali, on the coast of Dubai (United Arab Emirates). To date, only Palm Jumeirah has been completed (in 2011), which adopts the form of a palm tree topped by a crescent. These islands are intended to host a large number of residential, leisure, and entertainment centers and will add a total of 520 km of nonpublic beaches to the city of Dubai. These totally artificial islands illustrate the extreme nature of anthropogenic impact on the coastline. The islands will probably never undergo important morphological changes, given the limited sedimentary inputs along the coast of Dubai; however, their construction has heavily modified the hydrodynamic regime of the coastline.

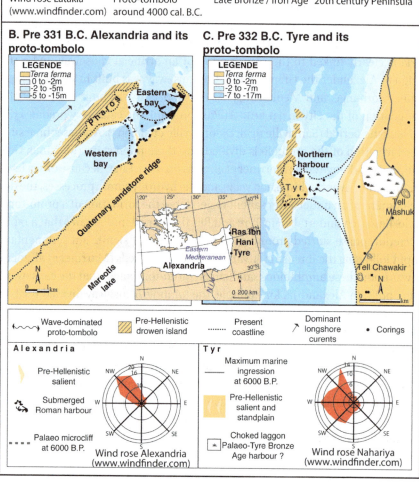

FIGURE 6.4 Morphodynamic evolution of the (A) Ras Ibn Hani, (B) Alexandria, and (C) Tyre isthmuses since antiquity, from Marriner, Goiran, and Morhange 2008 and Marriner et al. 2012; wind roses: Latakia (Ras Ibn Hani), Nahariya (Tyre), and Giens airport (Olbia) weather stations
IN KNOTS, WINDFINDER.COM

4.5 Type 5: Intra-lagoonal Islands

Lagoons are particularly attractive areas for the installation of ancient harbors (Morhange et al. 2015; Morhange et al. 2017), being naturally protected from the sea by the presence of a coastal spit. The Mediterranean's lagoons are particularly reduced in size and have almost disappeared since ancient times because they act as sedimentary traps and have been rapidly infilled by sediments. Nevertheless, some large lagoons protected from significant sedimentary inputs and/or largely open to the sea are still in water. In some of them there are small islets, such as the city of Venice in the Venetian Lagoon (Veneto, Italy), Mozia in the Stagnone Lagoon near Marsala (Sicily, Italy), or Kom ed-Dahab in Lake Manzala (Nile Delta, Egypt).

The Phoenician settlement of Mozia was founded on the islet of San Pantaleo in the large lagoon of Marsala. Though this lagoon is located downstream of the mouth of the Birgi River, the small size of the watershed has precluded its infilling (Fig. 6.5: A). The vast lagoon presented a strong environmental interest for ancient populations, such as the Phoenician colony of Mozia founded during the second half of the eighth century BCE. This large water body of 2,000 ha, with a depth of 2 m, is protected from the sea by the Isola Grande sand spit, which has acted as a natural breakwater during the last 5,000 years at least (Basso et al. 2008). During the sixth century CE, a causeway was constructed between the island and the continent, where remains of a necropolis linked to Mozia have been found near the village of Birgi (Fama and Toti 2000). A rectangular-shaped basin, located on the southern part of the island, has been interpreted as a Phoenician *cothon* harbor, with an anthropogenic modification of the natural lagoon during the sixth century BCE. Archaeological research has demonstrated that it was a freshwater basin linked to cultic activities related to the nearby temple (Nigro 2006; Spagnoli 2013). Moreover, the entire coast of the island of San Pantaleo could be used as a berthing area for small draft boats, which does not necessarily necessitate the construction of a protected harbor.

The island on which Kom ed-Dahab is situated, located in the present-day Manzala Lagoon (Fig. 6.5: B) hosted an important Roman settlement that was recently identified (Marouard 2014). The site at Kom ed-Dahab is an early Roman town and an ex nihilo foundation, established in the lagoon around the mid-first century BCE. Archaeological explorations have unearthed specific installations indicating that it was certainly a strategic harbor settlement, possibly located at the extremity of one of the Nile branches and once connected to a hinterland metropolis in the center of the Delta (Marouard 2014). A lack of paleoenvironmental reconstructions of the Early Roman period in this

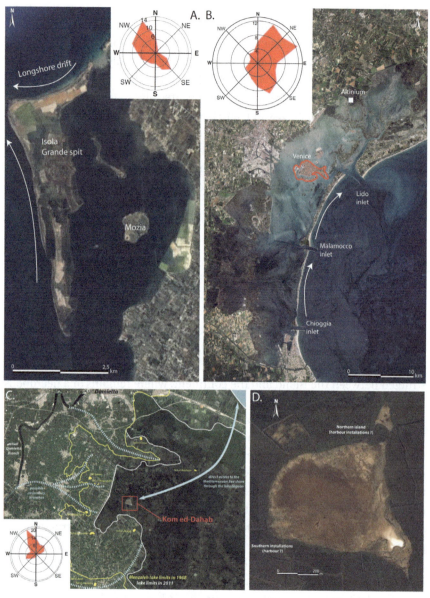

FIGURE 6.5 Geomorphological setting of the islands of (A) Mozia, (B) Venice, and (C; D) Kom ed-Dahab, from Marouard 2014. Image ESA and Google Earth; wind roses: Venezia-Lido (Venice), Trapani-Birgi Aeroporto (Mozia), and Port Said (Kom ed-Dahab) weather station
IN KNOTS, WINDFINDER.COM

region did not allow us to affirm that the present landscape was as it is today in antiquity. However, the emerged area of the island seems to be similar to its area in Roman times, because no submerged structures have been identified. The city probably had two harbors: one was in the northeast of the island; other possible harbor installations found in the southwest of the island may indicate the presence of a second harbor in that area (Fig. 6.5: D). In all likelihood, the city was founded in an estuarine-lagoon environment enjoying a water body protected from the sea and a direct connection with the hinterland. Nevertheless, the settlement was susceptible to hazards due to Nile floods, which could explain its short period of occupation, between the first and third centuries BCE (Marouard, personal communication).

Such water bodies present the uniqueness of being naturally protected from the sea; the islands located within are also particularly interesting with regard to protection against enemies. In medieval times the construction of Venice illustrates this example. In fact, the foundation of Venice in the eponymous lagoon (on the archipelago of *Rivus Altus*) during the fifth–seventh centuries CE resulted from the threat of Lombardian invasions of the Roman municipium of Altinum (Ammerman 2003; Christie 2006). Ninfo et al. (2009) described the configuration of this Roman city, located some 12 km northeast of Venice (Fig. 6.5: B). The study of aerial photographs with a digital elevation model (DEM) revealed important harbor structures with an artificial canal network linked to the transportation of goods to the lagoonal harbor. The city of Venice, due to its location on the island, was protected from enemies and enjoyed direct access to the sea. This privileged location allowed the inhabitants to build an important commercial and maritime city during the Middle Ages. Due to its size, the Venetian Lagoon is not threatened by infilling but, conversely, it is susceptible to tidal-flat erosion, which results in the long-term degradation of the lagoon morphology and its deepening (Carniello, Defina, and D'Alpaos 2009).

5   Conclusion

Earlier in the text, we mentioned another island type, that of "temporary islands." Such settlement types, located near the river or on the flood plain, were sometimes surrounded by water during flood events, giving them a temporary insular nature. These settlements enjoyed a privileged location and direct access to the sea, or were connected to it via river arms, benefiting good harbor conditions (e.g., Avaris, Egypt; Tronchère et al. 2012). In addition, they were located on fertile land, perfect for agriculture, and had a permanent freshwater supply. On the Languedoc coast (southern France), the city of Agathe (Agde), was founded on a rocky hill situated on the shoreline. It seems that the present topography of the area was already in place at the time of the Greek foundation of the city in 525 BCE. Agathe was probably surrounded by water during flood events (Devillers et al. 2015a). This ephemeral island, in a marine-lagoonal context, also raises the issue of the ancient installations of the city of Agathe.

The establishment of these attractive lagoonal environments for human societies may have facilitated the foundation of harbor area(s) (Devillers et al. 2015b). The case of Tell Abu Hawam, located in northern Israel, is particularly interesting. The site was an artificial or ephemeral island in the Bronze Age, located at the mouth of the Kishon River, and was probably a port of trade that served merchants on the Syrian-Lebanese coast, Anatolia, the Greek islands, and Cyprus (Artzy 2006). Nevertheless, the tell is a good example of environmental problems linked to its location at the mouth of the Kishon River and Wadi Selman (the paleo-mouth of the Kishon River). This artificial Egyptian-Canaanite "island" reflects the early capacity of human societies to reshape the coastal landscape more than three millennia ago (Balensi 1985, 2000; Aznar, Balensi, and Herrara 2005). On the Nile Delta, the *koms* ("turtle back" or *gezira*, 'island in Arabic) emerge from the deltaic plain. These landforms are inherited from the incision of the inundation plain during the Last Glacial Maximum (Tristan 2004). These *koms* afforded protection from the Nile floods. In Lake Maryut these spaces provided attractive areas for predynastic societies and allowed the inhabitants to be free from the seasonal variation of the water body (Flaux 2012).

We have intentionally taken a global and normative approach in seeking to determine the general rules for our typology of insular landscape harbors. Our first results demonstrate the advantage in adopting such an approach in defining the evolution of ancient insular harbors.

The transformation of harbor environments located in different insular contexts highlights the key role of the geomorphological context and marine weather conditions in shaping the evolution of the islands. The island nature of each site is important because the more distant from the shoreline the island is, the less affected it would have been by sediment supply and coastal progradation over the last 6,000 years. This fact inspired a differentiation between oceanic and coastal islands. Considering the small size of the islands studied, the sedimentary budget appears to be another important natural forcing in the transformation of the island environments located close to river mouths. More generally, while small islands and islets are affected mostly by external factors (with the exception of coastal "artificialization"), the bigger islands, with continental characteristics, are also characterized by endogenous variables; because of the presence, for example, of permanent rivers and of shoreline accommodation space. This isolation acted as an advantage with respect to the impact of continental influence.

In ancient times, the stabilization of sea level associated with a high fluvial sediment supply led to the regularization of the coastline because of the infilling of the rias and the landlocking of the islands and archipelagos located near river mouths. By contrast, rocky coasts are characterized by the relative environmental stability of their shorelines (Stanley and Warne 1994; Stewart and Morhange 2009). These ancient fluvial mouths were particularly attractive because they offered numerous opportunities for agriculture, fishing, and commerce. Rivers, such as the Rhône, were important fluvial paths into the hinterland. Fishing resources, particularly within coastal lagoons, were diversified and the freshwater input required for the development of agriculture and human settlement was constant. However, hyper-sedimentation was difficult to control and the dredging of ancient harbors was mandatory (Morhange and Marriner 2010). Ancient sites located in paleo-ria or gulfs nowadays infilled (e.g., Miletos and Oiniadai) highlight the impact of the base-level sedimentation of harbors, the latter being relocated according to the progradation of the coastline. The major tombolos are also located near important river mouths. In this way, the triple tombolo of Orbetello was formed in part by sediment inputs from the Fiora River to the south and the Albegna River to the north.

For several millennia coastal populations have adapted to environmental pressures and the transformation of the coastline due to the smoothing of the coasts and the infilling of ancient harbors and lagoons (Morhange et al. 2015). Broadly speaking, if islands located in estuarine contexts (ria) are particularly attractive for the installation of harbors in the short term (centennial timescales), such as Miletos or Oiniadai, the maritime islands, linked or not to the continent via a tombolo, can constitute long-term occupation sites, such as at Tyre. Some anthropogenic impacts, such as the construction of artificial causeways, have often modified natural sedimentation processes and entrapment.

Acknowledgements

M. Giaime acknowledges the support of the Institute of Advanced Studies and the Department of Geography at Durham University and was supported by a Durham Junior Research Fellowship, co-funded by the European Union under grant agreement number 609412. The project leading to this publication received funding from the Excellence Initiative of Aix-Marseille Université (A*MIDEX), a French "Investissements d'Avenir" project in the framework of Labex OT-Med (ANR-11-LABEX-0061). The authors warmly thank F. Bertoncello, N. Carayon, C. Flaux, A. Gilboa, and A. de Grauw for the careful revision of an earlier version of the manuscript.

References

Ammerman, A.J. 2003. Venice before the Grand Canal. *Memoirs of the American Academy in Rome* 48: 141–158.

Anthony, E.J., Marrnier, N., and Morhange, C. 2014. Human Influence and the Changing Geomorphology of Mediterranean Deltas and Coasts over the Last 6000 Years: From Progradation to Destruction Phase? *Earth-Science Reviews* 139: 336–361.

Artzy, M. 2006. The Carmel Coast during the Second Part of the Late Bronze Age: A Center for Eastern Mediterranean Transshipping. *Bulletin of the American Schools of Oriental Research* 343: 45–64.

Aznar, C., Balensi, J., and Herrara, M.D. 2005. Las excavaciones de Tell Abu Hawam en 1985–86 y la cronología de la expansión fenicia hacia Occidente. *Gerión, Revista de Historia Antigua* 23(1): 17–38.

Balensi, J. 1985. Revising Tell Abu Hawam. *Bulletin of the American Schools of Oriental Research* 257: 65–74.

Balensi, J. 2000. Une île artificielle égypto-cananéenne (Haïfa, Israël). *Le Monde de la bible* 128: 62.

Bar-Yosef Mayer, D.E., Kahanov, Y., Roskin, J., and Gildor, H. 2015. Neolithic Voyages to Cyprus: Wind Patterns, Routes, and Mechanisms. *The Journal of Island and Coastal Archaeology* 10(3): 412–435.

Basso, D., Bernasconi, M.P., Robba, E., and Marozzo, S. 2008. Environmental Evolution of the Marsala Sound, Sicily, during the Last 6000 Years. *Journal of Coastal Research* 241: 177–197.

Bernardie-Tahir, N. 2000. From the Naval Arsenal of the Knights to "Hub": The Evolution of Maltese Port Functions at the Crossroads of New Maritime Routes in the Mediterranean. *Annales de géographie* 616: 597–612.

Blanc, J.J. 1959. *Recherches sédimentologiques littorales et sous-marines en Provence occidentale.* Paris.

Broodbank, C. 2013. *The Making of the Middle Sea: A History of the Mediterranean from the Beginning to the Emergence of the Classical World.* Oxford.

Broodbank, C. and Strasser, T.F. 1991. Migrant Farmers and the Neolithic Colonization of Crete. *Antiquity* 65(247): 233–245.

Brückner, H., Herda, A., Kerschner, M., Müllenhoff, M., and Stock, F. 2017. Life Cycle of Estuarine Islands: From the Formation to the Landlocking of Former Islands in the Environs of Miletos and Ephesos in Western Asia Minor (Turkey). *Journal of Archaeological Science: Reports* 12: 876–894.

Brückner, H., Herda, A., Müllenhoff, M., Rabbel, W., and Stümpel, H. 2014. On the Lion Harbour and Other Harbours. In: Frederiksen, R. and Handberg, S., eds. *Miletos: Recent Historical, Archaeological, Sedimentological, and Geophysical Research. Proceedings of the Danish Institute at Athens* 7. Athens: 49–103.

Brückner, H., Müllenhoff, M., Vött, A., Gehrels, R., Herda, A., Knipping, M., and Gehrels, W.R. 2006. From Archipelago to Floodplain: Geographical and Ecological Changes in Miletus and Its Environs during the Past Six Millennia (Western Anatolia, Turkey). *Zeitschrift fur Geomorphologie, Supplementband* 142: 63–83.

Brückner, H., Vött, A., Schriever, A., and Handl, M. 2005. Holocene Delta Progradation in the Eastern Mediterranean: Case Studies in Their Historical Context. *Méditerranée* 104: 95–106.

Carayon, N. 2008. *Les Ports phéniciens et puniques. Géomorphologie et infrastructures*. Ph.D. dissertation. Université Marc Bloch. Strasbourg.

Carayon, N. 2011. Note sur l'organisation spatiale des agglomérations insulaires phéniciennes et puniques. *Méditerranée* 117: 111–114.

Carniello, L., Defina, A., and D'Alpaos, L. 2009. Morphological Evolution of the Venice Lagoon: Evidence from the Past and Trend for the Future. *Journal of Geophysical Research: Earth Surface* 114(F4). https://agupubs.onlinelibrary.wiley.com/doi/pdf/10.1029/2008 JF001157 (accessed September 12, 2019).

Cherry, J.F. and Leppard, T.P. 2018. Patterning and Its Causation in the Pre-Neolithic Colonization of the Mediterranean Islands (Late Pleistocene to Early Holocene). *The Journal of Island and Coastal Archaeology* 13(2): 191–205.

Christie, N. 2006. *From Constantine to Charlemagne: An Archaeology of Italy AD 300–800*. Aldershot, UK.

Courtaud, J. 2000. *Dynamiques géomorphologiques et risques littoraux. Cas du tombolo de Giens (Var, France méridionale)*. Ph.D. dissertation. Université de Provence. Marseille.

Dalongeville, R., Desruelles, S., Fouache, E., Hasenohr, C., and Pavlopoulos, K. 2007. Hausse relative du niveau marin à Délos (Cyclades, Grèce): rythme et effets sur les paysages littoraux de la ville hellénistique. *Méditerranée* 108: 17–28.

Dalongeville, R., Laborel, J., Pirazzoli, P.A., Sanlaville, P., Arnold, M., Bernier, P., Evin, J., and Montaggioni, L.F. 1993. Les Variations récentes de la ligne de rivage sur le littoral syrien. *Quaternaire* 4: 45–53.

Dawson, E. 2014. *Mediterranean Voyages: The Archaeology of Island Colonisation and Abandonment*. London.

Devillers, B., Bony, G., Degeai, J.P., Gascó, J., Oueslati, H., Bermond, I., and Yung, F. 2015a. Coastal Metamorphosis of the Herault Valley (Southern France) since the Neolithic: Environment—Human Society Interactions in Holocene Mediterranean. Poster presented in INQUA Congress, Nagoya, Japan, July 26–August 3, 2015.

Devillers, B., Bony, G., Degeai, J.P., Gascó, J., Oueslati, H., Sutra, M., and Yung, F. 2015b. Agathe, an Ephemeral Island of the Languedoc Coast? (Agde Hérault, France). Poster presented in Mediterranean Geoarchaeology Workshop Shaping the Mediterranean Basin: Island, Coastlines and Cultures across Time, Cagliari, May 14–15, 2015.

Dolci, M. 2014. Paesaggi d'Acque. Survey della laguna di Orbetello e del Monte Argentario, *Lanx* 17: 24–31.

Doumenge, J.P. 1987. Quelques contraintes du milieu insulaire. In: CRET (eds), Îles tropicales: insularité, "insularisme" 8: 9–15.

Evelpidou, N., Tziligkaki, E., and Karkani, A. 2018. Submerged Antiquities on Paros and Naxos Islands, Aegean Sea, Greece: New Evidence for the Mean Sea Level during the Late Bronze Age and the Roman Period. *Bulletin of the Geological Society of Greece* 52(1): 71–97.

Fama, M.L. and Toti, P. 2000. Materiali dalla 'Zona E'dell'abitato di Mozia. Prime considerazioni. *Terze Giornate Internazionali di Studi sull'Area Elima, Gibellina-Erice-Contessa Entellina* 1997: 451–478.

Ferentinos, G., Gkioni, M., Geraga, M., and Papatheodorou, G. 2012. Early Seafaring Activity in the Southern Ionian Islands, Mediterranean Sea. *Journal of Archaeological Science* 39(7): 2167–2176.

Fitzpatrick, S.M., Rick, T.C., and Erlandson, J.M. 2015. Recent Progress, Trends, and Developments in Island and Coastal Archaeology. *The Journal of Island and Coastal Archaeology* 10(1): 3–27.

Flaux, C. 2012. *Paléo-environnements littoraux Holocène du lac Maryut, nord-ouest du delta du Nil, Egypte*. Ph.D. dissertation. Aix-Marseille Université. Marseille.

Fouache, E., Dalongeville, R., Kunesch, S., Suc, J.P., Subally, D., Prieur, A., and Lozouet, P. 2005. The Environmental Setting of the Harbor of the Classical Site of Oeniades on the Acheloos Delta, Greece. *Geoarchaeology* 20: 285–302.

Gambin, T. 2020. Malta: Submerged Landscapes and Early Navigation. In *The Archaeology of Europe's Drowned Landscapes*: "41-346. Springer, Cham.

Giaime, M., Marriner, N., and Morhange, C. 2019. Evolution of Ancient Harbours in Deltaic Contexts: A Geoarchaeological Typology. *Earth-Science Reviews* 191: 141–167.

Goiran, J.P. 2001. *Recherche géomorphologique dans la région littorale d'Alexandrie, Egypte: mobilité des paysages à l'Holocène récent et évolution des milieux portuaires antiques*. Ph.D. dissertation. Aix-Marseille Université. Marseille.

Goiran, J.P., Marriner, N., Morhange, C., El-Maguib, A., Espic, K., Bourcier, M., and Carbonel, P. 2005. Evolution géomorphologique de la façade maritime d'Alexandrie (Egypte) au cours des six derniers millénaires. *Méditerranée* 104: 61–64.

Gosseaume, E. 1973. Le tombolo triple d'Orbetello (Toscane). *Bulletin de la Société Languedocienne de Géographie* 7: 3–11.

Guilaine, J. 2012. Les Réseaux néolithiques : quelques réflexions préalables. In: Congrés Internacional Xarxes Al Neolitic: Neolithic Networks. *Rubricatum: Revista Del Museu de Gavà* 5: 21–30.

Gras, M. 1995. *La Méditerranée archaïque*. Paris.

Howitt-Marshall, D. and Runnels, C. 2016. Middle Pleistocene Sea-Crossings in the Eastern Mediterranean? *Journal of Anthropological Archaeology* 42: 140–153.

Karkani, A., Evelpidou, N., Vacchi, M., Morhange, C., Tsukamoto, S., Frechen, M., and Maroukian, H. 2017. Tracking Shoreline Evolution in Central Cyclades (Greece) Using Beachrocks. *Marine Geology* 388: 25–37.

Karkani, A., Evelpidou, N., Giaime, M., Marriner, N., Maroukian, H., and Morhange, C. 2018. Late Holocene Palaeogeographical Evolution and Relative Sea Level Changes of Paroikia Bay (Paros Island, Greece). *Comptes-rendus Géosciences* 350(5): 202–211.

Karkani, A., Evelpidou, N., Giaime, M., Marriner, N., Morhange, C., and Spada, G. 2019. Late Holocene Sea-Level Evolution of Paros Island (Cyclades, Greece). *Quaternary International* 500: 139–146.

Katzenstein, H.J. 1997. *The History of Tyre: From the Beginning of the Second Millennium BCE until the Fall of the Neo-Babylonian Empire in 538 BCE*. Beer-Sheva.

Long, L. and Cibecchini, F. 1996. Olbia, structures antiques submergées. *Bilan scientifique du DRASSM* 1996: 91–92.

Long, L. and Vella, C. 2005. Du Nouveau sur le paysage de Giens au Néolithique et sur le port d'Olbia. Recherches sous-marines récentes devant l'Almanarre (Hyères, Var). In: Pasqualini, M., Arnaud, P., and Valardo, C., eds. *Des îles à la côte. Histoire du peuplement des îles de l'Antiquité au Moyen-âge (Provence, Alpes Maritimes, Ligurie, Toscane)*. Aix-en-Provence : 165–173.

Marouard, G. 2014. Kom el-Dahab Interpreted. *Egyptian Archaeology* 45: 25–27.

Marriner, N., Goiran, J.P., and Morhange, C. 2008. Alexander the Great's Tombolos at Tyre and Alexandria, Eastern Mediterranean. *Geomorphology* 100: 377–400.

Marriner, N., Goiran, J.P., Geyer, B., Matoïan, V., al-Maqdissi, M., Leconte, M., and Carbonel, P. 2012. Ancient Harbours and Holocene Morphogenesis of the Ras Ibn Hani Peninsula (Syria). *Quaternary Research* 78: 35–49.

Marriner, N., Kaniewski, D., Gambin, T., Gambin, B., Vannière, B., Morhange, C., Djamali, M., Kazuyo, T., Robin, V., Rius, D., Bard, E., 2019. Fire as a motor of rapid environmental degradation during the earliest peopling of Malta 7500 years ago. *Quaternary Science Reviews* 212: 199–205.

Marriner, N. and Morhange, C. 2007. Geoscience of Ancient Mediterranean Harbours, *Earth-Science Reviews* 80: 137–194.

Marriner, N., Morhange, C., and Meulé, S. 2007. Holocene Morphogenesis of Alexander the Great's Isthmus at Tyre in Lebanon. *Proceedings of the National Academy of Sciences* 104: 9218–9223.

Morhange, C. and Marriner, N. 2010. Paleo-Hazards in the Coastal Mediterranean: A Geoarchaeological Approach. In: Martini, P. and Chesworth, W., eds. *Landscapes and Societies*. Dordrecht: 223–234.

Morhange, C., Marriner, N., Baralis, A., Blot, M.L., Bony, G., Carayon, N., Carmona, P., Flaux, C., Giaime, M., Goiran, J.P., Kouka, M., Lena, A., Oueslati, A., Pasquinucci, M., and Porotov, A.V. 2015. Dynamiques géomorphologiques et typologie géoarcheologique des ports antiques en contextes lagunaires. *Quaternaire* 26(2): 117–139.

Morhange, C., Marriner, N., Bony, G., Flaux, C., Giaime, M., and Kouka, M. 2017. Geoarchaeology of Ancient Harbours in Lagoonal Contexts: An Introduction. In: Franconi, T.V., ed. *Fluvial Landscapes in the Roman World* (Journal of Roman Archaeology Supplement 104). Portsmouth: 97–110.

Morhange, C., Marriner, N., and Carayon, N. 2015. The Geoarchaeology of Ancient Mediterranean Harbours. In: Arnaud-Fassetta, G. and Carcaud, N., eds. *French Geoarchaeology in the 21st Century*. Paris: 281–289.

Mourtzas, N.D. and Kolaiti, E. 2013. Historical Coastal Evolution of the Ancient Harbor of Aegina in Relation to the Upper Holocene Relative Sea Level Changes in the Saronic Gulf, Greece. *Palaeogeography, Palaeoclimatology, Palaeoecology* 392: 411–425.

Nigro, L. 2006. Mozia e il mistero del Kothon. *Archeo* 254: 42–53.

Ninfo, A., Fontana, A., Mozzi, P., and Ferrarese, F. 2009. The Map of Altinum, Ancestor of Venice. *Science* 325(5940): 577.

Papathanassopoulos, G. and Schilardi, D. 1981. An Underwater Survey of Paros, Greece: 1979. Preliminary Report. *The International Journal of Nautical Archaeology and Underwater Exploration* 10(2): 133–144.

Papoulia, C. 2016. Late Pleistocene to Early Holocene Sea-Crossings in the Aegean: Direct, Indirect and Controversial Evidence. In: Ghilardi, M., ed. *Géoarchéologie des îles de Méditerranée*. Paris: 33–46.

Pasqualini, M. 2000. Cumes: cadre géographique et historique, avant-propos à l'étude des ports (note). *Méditerranée* 94: 69–70.

Poulos, S.E., Ghionis, G., and Maroukian, H. 2009. Sea-Level Rise Trends in the Attico–Cycladic Region (Aegean Sea) during the Last 5000 Years. *Geomorphology* 107(1): 10–17.

Rey-Coquais, J.P. 1974. *Arados et sa Pérée aux époques grecque, romaine et byzantine. Recueil des témoignages littéraires anciens, suivis de recherches sur les sites, l'histoire, la civilisation*. Paris.

Ridgway, D. 1992. *The First Western Greeks*. Cambridge.

Sanlaville, P. 1978. Notes sur la géomorphologie de la presqu'île d'Ibn Hani. *Syria* 55: 303–305.

Sauvage, C. 2012. *Routes maritimes et systèmes d'échanges internationaux au Bronze récent en Méditerranée orientale*. Lyon.

Simmons, A. 2012. Mediterranean Island Voyages. *Science* 338(6109): 895–897.

Spagnoli, F. 2013. Demetra a Mozia: evidenze dell'area sacra del kothon nel V sec. aC. *Vicino Oriente* 17: 153–164.

Stanley, D.J. and Warne, A.G. 1994. Worldwide Initiation of Holocene Marine Deltas by Deceleration of Sea-Level Rise. *Science* 265: 228–231.

Stewart, I.S. and Morhange, C. 2009. Coastal Geomorphology and Sea-Level Change. In: Woodward, J., ed. *The Physical Geography of the Mediterranean*. Oxford: 385–414.

Sunamura, T. and Mizuzo, O. 1987. A Study on Depositional Shoreline Forms behind an Island. *Annual Report of the Institute of Geosciences, the University of Tsukuba* 13: 71–73.

Tristan, Y. 2004. *L'Habitat prédynastique de la vallée du Nil: vivre sur les rives du Nil Ve et IVe millénaires* (British Archaeological Reports, International Series 1287). Oxford.

Tronchère, H., Goiran, J.P., Schmitt, L., Preusser, F., Bietak, M., Forstner-Müller, I., and Callot, Y. 2012. Geoarchaeology of an Ancient Fluvial Harbour: Avaris and the Pelusiac Branch (Nile River, Egypt). *Géomorphologie: relief, processus, environnement* 18(1): 23–36.

Ugolini, D., Arcelin, P., and Bats, M. 2010. Établissements grecs du littoral gaulois : Béziers, Agde, Arles et Hyères. In: Delestre, X. and Marchesi, H., eds. *Archéologie des rivages méditerranéens : 50 ans de recherche : actes du colloque d'Arles (Bouches-du-Rhône), 28–29–30 octobre 2009*. Paris, 149–164.

Vacchi, M., Marriner, N., Morhange, C., Spada, G., Fontana, A., and Rovere, A. 2016. Multiproxy Assessment of Holocene Relative Sea-Level Changes in the Western Mediterranean: Sea-Level Variability and Improvements in the Definition of the Isostatic Signal. *Earth-Science Reviews* 155: 172–197.

Van Rijn, L. 2013. Design of Hard Coastal Structures against Erosion. https://www.leovanrijn-sediment.com/papers/Coastalstructures2013.pdf (accessed September 12, 2019).

Vella, C., Provansal, M., Long, L., and Bourcier, M. 2000. Contexte géomorphologique de trois ports antiques provençaux : Fos, Les Laurons, Olbia. *Méditerranée* 94: 39–46.

Vigne, J.D., Zazzo, A., Cucchi, T., Carrere, I., Briois, F., and Guilaine, J. 2014. The Transportation of Mammals to Cyprus Sheds Light on Early Voyaging and Boats in the Mediterranean Sea. *Eurasian Prehistory* 10(1–2): 157–176.

Vött, A. 2007. Silting Up Oiniadai's Harbours (Acheloos River Delta, NW Greece): Geoarchaeological Implications of Late Holocene Landscape Changes. *Géomorphologie: relief, processus, environnement* 1: 19–36.

Vött, A., Schriever, A., Handl, M., and Brückner, H. 2007. Holocene Palaeogeographies of the Central Acheloos River Delta (NW Greece) in the Vicinity of the Ancient Seaport Oiniadai. *Geodinamica Acta* 20: 241–256.

Walsh, K. 2013. *The Archaeology of Mediterranean Landscapes: Human-Environment Interaction from the Neolithic to the Roman Period*. Cambridge.

CHAPTER 7

The Plain of Akko Regional Survey (PARS): An Integrated Use of GIS, Photogrammetry, and LiDAR to Reconstruct Akko's Hinterland

Ann E. Killebrew, Jane C. Skinner, Jamie Quartermaine, and Ragna Stidsing

The Plain of Akko, the southernmost of the Phoenician plains, served for millennia as the gateway linking the northern coastal regions with the southern Levant and its interior. Situated at the northern end of the Haifa-Akko Bay, the largest natural bay along the Levantine coast, the maritime center of Akko has dominated the plain during the past five millennia. As one of the few major Bronze and Iron Age Phoenician centers accessible to large-scale exploration, Tel Akko has been the focus of archaeological investigation for the past 40 years. First excavated by the late Moshe Dothan from 1973 to 1989, his findings confirmed Tel Akko's centrality as a major international maritime center and economic hub connecting the Plain of Akko with the eastern Mediterranean world (see, e.g., Dothan 1976, 1985, 1993; Artzy and Beeri 2010). Renewed excavations directed by A.E. Killebrew and M. Artzy commenced in 2010. The Tel Akko Total Archaeology Project aims to investigate the site's pivotal role in the eastern Mediterranean and reconstruct its ancient environment during the second and first millennia BCE (see, e.g., Artzy 2012; Killebrew and Olson 2014; Artzy and Quartermaine 2014; Killebrew and Quartermaine 2016; Killebrew et al. 2017 for a summary of the project's preliminary results and research goals).[1]

---

[1] The 2017 excavations were conducted on behalf of the University of Haifa, in collaboration with the Pennsylvania State University, Claremont Graduate University, Claremont McKenna College, Trinity College (Hartford, CT), Baker University, University of Warsaw, and the Israel Antiquities Authority (IAA). The excavations were directed by Ann E. Killebrew (Pennsylvania State University and Leon Recanati Institute for Maritime Studies, University of Haifa) and Michal Artzy (Leon Recanati Institute for Maritime Studies and Sir Maurice and Lady Irene Hatter Laboratory for Coastal and Harbour Archaeology, University of Haifa), with the assistance of Tammi Schneider and Gary Gilbert (coheads of the Claremont Graduate and Claremont McKenna, Claremont, California, expedition), Martha Risser (project ceramicist and head of the Trinity College, Hartford, Connecticut, expedition), Nicholaus Pumphrey (Baker University), Jolanta Młynarczyk (project ceramicist; University of Warsaw) and Lori Anne Ferrell (Claremont Graduate University). Nicholaus Pumphrey, Daniel Griswold (University at Buffalo), and Justin Batista (Independent Scholar) served as Area A field supervisors. Square supervisors included Amanda Pumphrey (Claremont Graduate University),

During the Hellenistic period, occupation shifted westward, which coincided with the receding coastline (Morhange et al. 2016). From the third century BCE onward, the area underneath the historic old town and modern Akko became the urban nucleus of this port city (Beeri 2008).

In addition to excavation, intensive tell survey, and geophysical examination of the mound, the project incorporates a regional survey.[2] The Plain of Akko Regional Survey (PARS), initiated in 2014, utilizes LiDAR,[3] 3D documentation,[4] photogrammetry, and GIS (Geographic Information System), combined with

---

Monica Genuardi (Pennsylvania State University), John T. Crawmer (Independent Scholar), Mark Van Horn (Pennsylvania State University), Darcy Calabria (Pennsylvania State University), Cas Popp (Pennsylvania State University), and Marcin Gostkowski (University of Warsaw). Justin Lev-Tov (Alexandria Archive Institute), Emily Holt (SUNY Buffalo), and Melissa Rosenzweig (Miami University, Ohio) were the project's zooarchaeologists (Lev-Tov and Holt) and archaeobotanist (Rosenzweig). Ümit Güder (Çanakkale Onsekiz Mart Üniversitesi) served as the project's archaeometallurgist. Jacek Michniewicz (Adam Mickiewicz University) served as the geologist. Omri Lernau (independent scholar) analyzed the recovered fish bones. The site GIS expert was Jane C. Skinner (Yale University). Jamie Quartermaine (Oxford Archaeology North, England) and Brett Seibert (independent scholar) codirected the intensive on-site pedestrian survey assisted by Cassidy Ross (Hampshire College). Tell survey ceramics were read by Michal Artzy. Jamie Quartermaine and A.J. Tessner Risser supervised the 3D/photogrammetry digital recording system. David Zell (conservation and 3D documentation) served as a consultant. The community outreach program was run by Evan Taylor (University of Massachusetts Amherst) and Elena Sesma (University of Massachusetts Amherst) and would not have been possible without the help of Shelley-Anne Peleg (Israel Antiquities Authority), Ornit Babani-Schnecke (Israel Antiquities Authority), and Aurora Lattarulo (Israel Antiquities Authority). Additional staff included Rachel Ben Dov (artifact registrar; Albright Institute of Oriental Research), Weronika Karpinska-Szarata (registrar; University of Warsaw), Jennifer Munro (website designer; Munro Marketing, London), Ragna Stidsing (database manager; Hatter Laboratory, University of Haifa), Rahel Merhav (camp administrator), and Jihad Abu Janam (majordomo).

2 PARS is codirected by A.E. Killebrew and J. Quartermaine. In 2017 the survey staff included R. Abu Raya (Israel Antiquities Authority), J.C. Skinner, and O. Gutfeld (Israel Archaeological Services).

3 LiDAR (Light Detection and Ranging) is a technique of collecting remote sensing data that is used to measure accurately the true topography of the earth's surface (meaning without buildings and flora). Aerial LiDAR, which is utilized by PARS, was collected from an airborne laser scanner flying over the area of interest. From these data, point clouds are created and turned into digital elevation models (DEMs).

4 In recent years, it has become possible to create quickly spatially accurate and photo-realistic 3D models of areas of archaeological interest by photographing the area from the ground or from an unmanned aerial vehicle (UAV). In 2011 the Tel Akko Total Archaeology Project developed and implemented an inexpensive, easy-to-use, and very effective documentation system that produces highly accurate 3D models using a UAV and photogrammetric processing software Agisoft Photoscan Pro (see, e.g., Olson et al. 2013; Quartermaine, Olson, and Killebrew 2014 for a detailed description). Based on these 3D models, we are able to easily manipulate and measure the landscape data and create orthophotographs. In 2014 we began to apply these methods to the regional survey.

a systematic nonintrusive pedestrian survey and the incorporation of results from previous surveys to contextualize the human and environmental history of Akko and its interaction with the surrounding hinterland (Killebrew and Quartermaine 2016: 498–500). We aim to accomplish this by means of a high-resolution documentation of the visible remains of human interaction with the landscape including settlements, tombs, industrial remains, agricultural installations, and utilization of natural resources. Among our goals is the reconstruction of Akko's interaction with local, regional, and interregional social, cultural, and economic exchange networks. In what follows, we present the preliminary results of our integrated approach to documenting settlement patterns, demography, and land use to produce a high-resolution 3D reconstruction of Akko's environs. We dedicate this essay to Professor Michal Artzy, mentor, colleague, and friend, in appreciation of her significant contribution to our understanding of Akko's cultural, maritime, and environmental past.

1 The Plain of Akko

The Plain of Akko (Fig. 7.1) is delimited in the north by Ras en-Naqurah (Hebrew: Rosh ha-Niqra, also known as the Ladder of Tyre) and the Carmel Mountain along the south. In the southeast, it is connected to the Jezreel Valley by a narrow pass where Naḥal Kishon flows between the Carmel and the hills of Lower Galilee. The Mediterranean Sea forms its western boundary while the limestone mountains of the Upper Galilee (ca. 500–1,000 m elevation) and Lower Galilee (ca. 300 m elevation) define the eastern extent of the Plain of Akko. Although Akko was the best sheltered and safest harbor along the southern Levantine coast, smaller harbors were also located at the mouths of Naḥal Kishon (Tell Abu Hawam) and Naḥal Kziv (Tel Achziv), situated at the southern and northern borders of the Plain of Akko, respectively. The Haifa-Akko Bay is one of the most prominent features of the plain. This relatively shallow bay is filled with heavy deposits of sand that also cover the southern part of the Plain of Akko extending several kilometers inland. It is the special quality and purity of these sands in the Haifa-Akko Bay, especially where Naḥal Naʿaman enters the Mediterranean Sea, which, according to first-century CE Roman historian Pliny the Elder (*NH* 36.65), led to the invention of glass. These sand dunes continue, on a smaller scale, along the coastal plain north of Akko. Historically, they have served as a barrier to the outflow of the rivers into the Mediterranean Sea. The resulting marshes discouraged habitation next to the sea, forcing roads, agricultural lands, and settlements further inland into the plain.

THE PLAIN OF AKKO REGIONAL SURVEY (PARS)

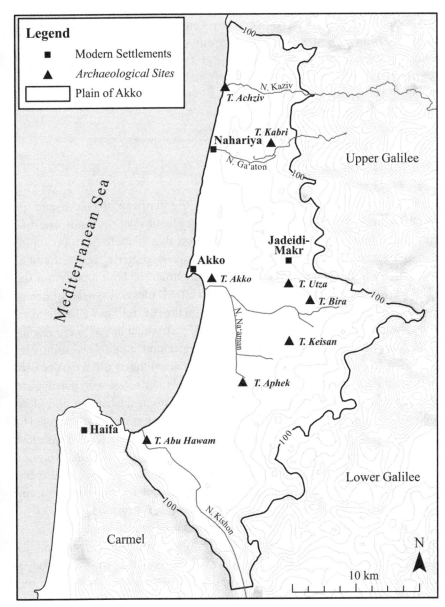

FIGURE 7.1 Map of the Plain of Akko
GRAPHICS BY J.C. SKINNER AND R. STIDSING; TEL AKKO TOTAL ARCHAEO-
LOGY PROJECT

Thus, most premodern settlements are located at the interface between the alluvial soils and lower slopes of the Galilee hills or on limestone outcrops in the plain itself, where most of the plain's tells are found. Following Pliny the Elder's account of the sand dunes and swamps surrounding Akko (classical Ptolemais), numerous travelers, pilgrims, historical geographers, and archaeologists have documented the Plain of Akko (see Lehmann 2001 for an overview and analysis of the literature). The most relevant survey for our current investigations is the *Archaeological Survey of Israel, Map of Ahihud* (20), published in 2012 by G. Lehmann and M. Peilstöcker. These previous travelers' accounts and modern-day surveys provide us with a wealth of valuable archaeological and environmental data for the Plain of Akko.

2 PARS Survey Methodology

The PARS methodological approach entails the marriage of LiDAR and 3D photogrammetry to identify and record the key features of the landscape, utilizing a GIS to collate all the pertinent data sets that relate to the topography, communication routes, agricultural fields, drainage patterns, and settlement distribution in the Plain of Akko over the millennia. The base tapestry for the survey is the incorporation of 1 m resolution LiDAR tiles across a study area of 100 sq km of the Akko coastal plain centered on the city itself as well as detailed geo-referenced aerial orthophotographs (Fig. 7.2), which are of 10 cm resolution. Although LiDAR, which can be used to generate a digital terrain model (DTM) of the ground surface by airborne laser scanning, is not a particularly new technique, it has seldom been used in Israel to investigate archaeological sites (see, e.g., Ebeling, Franklin, and Cipin 2012; Koh, Yasur-Landau, and Cline 2014: 1–3; Greenfield, Wing, and Maeir 2015) and even less frequently applied to landscapes (see Killebrew and Quartermaine 2016: 498–500). LiDAR has most successfully been applied to areas of thick flora such as in Central America (Chase et al. 2012) and North America (Johnson and Ouimet 2014). This is because of LiDAR's ability to record ground surfaces beneath the tree canopy and create a model of the earth's topography despite the ground cover.

The present project is distinctive in its combination of several survey techniques, including ground survey/ground truthing, orthophotographs, and 3D photogrammetry, which are then overlaid with the results of previous studies into the archaeology of the plain, most notably the survey by G. Lehmann and M. Peilstöcker in the Akko Plain from 1993–1995 with sporadic investigation through 2002 (see, e.g., Lehmann and Peilstöcker 2012 and bibliography there). All sites we have identified by ground truthing are described and entered into a Filemaker database. The most significant sites are also documented using 3D photogrammetry, based on several criteria: (1) whether the site is endangered or if there is evidence of looting; (2) accessibility from the ground or air; and (3) the extent of preservation and visibility of the site. To collect the data for the 3D model we utilized a camera mounted on a mast or a UAV. The photos are entered into Agisoft Photoscan Pro, a photogrammetric software program

FIGURE 7.2 Map of 100 sq km pilot survey of region surrounding Akko, utilizing DTM and key areas of investigation
GRAPHICS BY J.C. SKINNER AND R. STIDSING; ORTHOPHOTOGRAPH BY DIGITALGLOBE

that generates a point cloud from which a 3D model can be made. These models can be georectified within the program or in GIS. The process takes only minutes to implement in the field and provides a particularly effective and precise record of the archaeological landscape (for more information on our process, see Killebrew and Olson 2014). On average, five to seven features, sites, or landscapes can be modeled per day. An important benefit of our use of LiDAR and GPS has been to refine the geographic coordinates of previously surveyed sites that had been located using low-grade mapping and therefore lacked the precision of modern GPS and LiDAR.

A preliminary study to check the viability of the use of LiDAR and orthophotographic techniques in Akko's hinterland was undertaken during the 2014 season. This approach proved to be especially successful in locating archaeological features and sites across the upland areas or other regions that had not been subjected to intensive cultivation within the survey area. In the intensively cultivated lowland areas, the surface features highlighted by LiDAR tended to be modern or relatively recent, thus of lesser significance. However, based on our preliminary study in 2014, our examination of the orthophotographs noted areas of soil marks that apparently reflect subsurface sites or features that have been disturbed by the plow, resulting in soil differences on the surface. This may hold potential for the identification of new sites to be confirmed and documented by the pedestrian survey.

Our first goal was the identification of possible sites based on the digital terrain model (DTM), which was created from LiDAR data with a resolution of 1 sq m. It entailed an analysis of LiDAR data and orthophotographs to identify potential sites, of which several were examined by ground truthing. This was done by systematic examination of hillshade views of the DTM and their comparison with orthophotographs. When looking for sites, we examined the designated area with the hillshade, or artificial light source, coming from two different directions, the east and the south; features can look dramatically different when the light source is shifted. Once the whole survey area was examined, the sites were ranked based on probable site type, including paleochannels, terracing, quarries, and possible occupation sites. When trying to identify these types of sites, comparing what we were seeing on the LiDAR with the results of the Lehmann-Peilstöcker survey sometimes influenced how we categorized or prioritized the sites. Since the Lehmann-Peilstöcker survey was done before the availability of GPS as we employ it on the survey today, many of the site coordinates from these earlier surveys are inaccurate and lack the detailed documentation that the present survey has been able to generate. During the 2014 and 2015 seasons, we conducted targeted surveys on areas that appeared to be favorable based on the LiDAR and orthophotographic imagery. We identified several areas where the ancient landscape remained relatively intact based on these initial surveys. These included Giv'at Tantur, Adamun, and er-Raba'in, all of which are located on the low flanks of the Galilee foothills, at an elevation of less than 100 m situated on the eastern edges of our survey area (Fig. 7.2).

3 The Case Study of Givʻat Tantur

Based on the preliminary examination of the LiDAR imagery and ground truthing, we initiated a pedestrian survey on Givʻat Tantur (700777, 3644250; see Atrash, Mazor, and Aboud 2018 for a summary of the salvage excavations conducted at the site). This locale is especially well suited due to its proximity to Tel Akko (4.5 km east) and its undeveloped landscape. An additional consideration is that this hill is an endangered region because of plans to develop an extension of the adjoining towns of Jadeidi-Makr (see Fig. 7.1) to the north of the forest planted during the last half-century (see Khoury 2017). Our pedestrian survey, of approximately 20% of Givʻat Tantur, has revealed a plethora of archaeological sites including agricultural and industrial installations, quarries, settlements, and tombs. The two most obvious features on this hill in the DTM image are Ḥorbat Ṭurit, a Hellenistic temple or tower, which has recently been excavated (Abu Raya 2014), and a 1.5 km long trench that transects most of the hill (Fig. 7.3). During the 2014 and 2015 seasons of exploring Givʻat Tantur,

FIGURE 7.3 Givʻat Tantur: key features visible on the DTM and area of nonintrusive pedestrian survey
GRAPHICS BY J.C. SKINNER AND R. STIDSING; AND DTM BY OFEK AERIAL PHOTOGRAPHY, ISRAEL

we focused on the visible trench, using the LiDAR beneath the dense woodland canopy and the area around the Hellenistic structure. Following a detailed nonintrusive survey of the trench, it seems to be mainly modern, most likely dating to the second half of the twentieth century, but with a few areas that are weathered, cut by the modern ditch, and are seemingly ancient. Some parts of the trench have iron ore and flint veins within the limestone and may suggest earlier mineral extraction.

At Ḥorbat Ṭurit, a site that is well documented by nineteenth-century explorers (e.g., Zimmermann [1861]: Ras Tantur; Guérin [1880]: Dj, Tantour; Schumacher[1878]: Tell et-Tantur) and during the British Mandate period (Khirbet et-Tantur; see Grootkerk 2000: 160 for a summary of the sources mentioned here), surface features were clearly visible in the DTM and orthophotograph, and were subsequently confirmed by ground truthing (Fig. 7.3). During our visit to the site, we produced a 3D model of the excavated remains (Fig. 7.4).

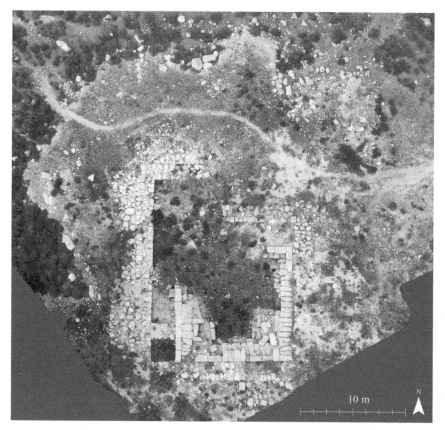

FIGURE 7.4 Orthophotograph from 3D model of Ḥorbat Ṭurit
TEL AKKO TOTAL ARCHAEOLOGY PROJECT

Beginning in 2016, we expanded our investigation to include a systematic nonintrusive pedestrian survey with the aim of documenting, in high resolution, the entirety of Giv'at Tantur. We divided this area into survey units based on geographical features of the hill to better facilitate total coverage. The DTM has been especially useful in our methodology because it reveals many of the natural features not visible on the surface of the terrain covered by vegetation, which enable us to divide the area of investigation into logical, geographically based survey units. We have ground truthed about 20% of the hill and identified 110 sites in the systematically walked area. This represents a significant increase in the number of sites from the Lehmann-Peilstöcker 1993–1995 survey that identified two sites in the same area. Among the most common types of sites that we documented were limekilns (5), tombs (11), quarries (69), and 25 additional sites including structures, winepresses, and caves (Fig. 7.5). Among the most significant sites we documented in 3D is a limestone quarry exploited to extract millstones used to crush olives in the production of olive oil (Fig. 7.6).

The overall survey of Giv'at Tantur has generated the identification of sites, field boundaries, and 3D models of significant geographical features that have

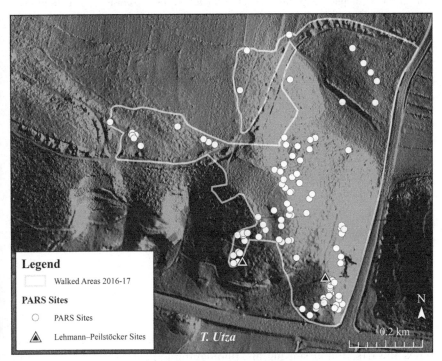

FIGURE 7.5 Detail of nonintrusive pedestrian survey with sites documented by Lehmann and Peilstöcker (indicated by black triangles) and PARS (indicated by white circles)
GRAPHICS BY J.C. SKINNER AND R. STIDSING; DTM BY OFEK AERIAL PHOTOGRAPHY, ISRAEL

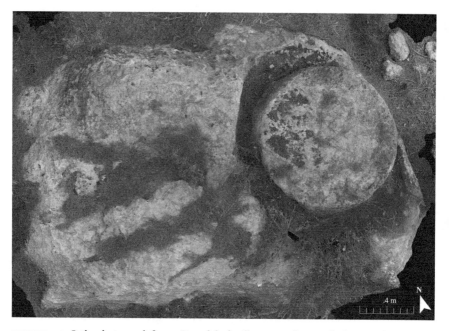

FIGURE 7.6   Orthophotograph from 3D model of millstone used to crush olives, in the process of being quarried
TEL AKKO TOTAL ARCHAEOLOGY PROJECT

been recorded within the GIS system. These include settlement remains, agricultural and industrial installations, quarries, and tombs, all of which are components of a rich multiperiod, predominantly agricultural, landscape that served as Akko's hinterland. While the survey of the entire study area has yet to be completed, this type of high-resolution documentation and analysis presents an unprecedented opportunity to assess how this landscape developed and was used over time. The detailed models of significant sites and installations provide an invaluable record of human activity on Giv'at Tantur through the ages in response to the anticipated urban development and expansion of the hillside.

4   Conclusions

The Plain of Akko Regional Survey and case study discussed in this essay illustrates how GIS, remote sensing, and photogrammetry are being applied within the Tel Akko Total Archaeology Project, both on the local and regional scales. Our survey demonstrates how these technologies allow us to reconstruct the ancient human landscape, utilizing complex data from a variety of sources to pursue our research questions within the framework of Akko and its plain. On the tell, we are applying these technologies to integrate successfully the results from the Tel Akko Total Archaeology excavations in Area A with those of the previous excavations directed by M. Dothan. Our regional survey also builds on the results of previous archaeological research and incorporates new technologies to document and interpret quickly and accurately a rapidly disappearing landscape. While PARS is still in its infancy, it demonstrates the potential of a methodological approach that integrates ground truthing, LiDAR for high-resolution terrain/topography, GIS for mapping, and photogrammetry for 3D imaging to produce a precise and hyper-detailed documentation of Akko and its hinterland through the ages.

References

Abu Raya, R. 2014. Horbat Turit (South). *Hadashot Arkheologiyot: Excavations and Surveys in Israel* 126. http://www.hadashot-esi.org.il/Report_Detail_Eng.aspx?id=11634 (accessed February 4, 2018).

Artzy, M. 2012. Return to Tel Akko, Its Anchorages, Harbor, and Surroundings. *The Leon Recanati Institute for Maritime Studies News* 2012: 5–14.

Artzy, M., and Beeri, R. 2010. Tel Akko. In: Killebrew, A.E. and Raz-Romeo, V., eds. *One Thousand Nights and Days: Akko through the Ages.* Haifa: 15*–24*.

Artzy, M., and Quartermaine, J. 2014. How and When Did Tel Akko Get Its Unusual Banana Shape? In: Galanakis, Y., Wilkinson, T., and Bennet, J., eds. *ΑΘΥΡΜΑΤΑ: Critical Essays on the Archaeology of the Eastern Mediterranean in Honour of E. Susan Sherratt.* Oxford: 11–22.

Atrash, W., Mazor, G., and Aboud, H. 2018. A Phoenician/Hellenistic Sanctuary at Horbat Turit (Kh. et-Tantur). In: Rosenthal-Heginbottom, R. and Kögler, P., eds. *Journal of Hellenistic Pottery and Material Culture* 3: 61–87.

Beeri, R. 2008. Hellenistic Akko. In: Bar, S., ed. *In the Hill-Country, and in the Shephelah, and in the Arabah (Joshua 12, 8): Studies and Researches Presented to Adam Zertal in the Thirtieth Anniversary of the Manasseh Hill-Country Survey.* Jerusalem: 195*–210*.

Chase, A.F., Chase, D.Z., Fisher, C.T., Leisz, S.J., and Weishampel, J.F. 2012. Geospatial Revolution and Remote Sensing LiDAR in Mesoamerican Archaeology. *Proceedings of the National Academy of Sciences of the United States of America* 109 (32): 12916–12921.

Dothan, M. 1976. Akko: Interim Excavation Report First Season, 1973/4. *Bulletin of the American Schools of Oriental Research* 224: 1–48.

Dothan, M. 1985. A Phoenician Inscription from Akko. *Israel Exploration Journal* 35: 81–94.

Dothan, M. 1993. Tel Akko. In: Stern, E., ed. *The New Encyclopedia of Archaeological Excavations in the Holy Land*, Vol. 1. Jerusalem: 17–23.

Ebeling, J., Franklin, N., and Cipin I. 2012. Jezreel Revealed in Laser Scans: A Preliminary Report of the 2012 Survey Season. *Near Eastern Archaeology* 75: 232–239.

Greenfield, H.J., Wing, D., and Maeir, A.M. 2015. LiDAR Technology as an Analytical Tool at Tell es-Safi/Gath, Israel. In: Crook, R., Edwards, K., and Hughes, C., eds. *Breaking Barriers: Proceedings of the 47th Annual Chacmool Archaeological Conference November 7–9, 2014, Calgary, Alberta, Canada*. Calgary: 76–85.

Grootkerk, S.E. 2000. *Ancient Sites in Galilee: A Toponymic Gazetteer* (Culture and History of the Ancient Near East 1). Leiden.

Guérin, V. 1880. *Description géographique, historique et archéologique de la Palestine*, Vols. 6–7 : *Galilée I–II*. Paris.

Johnson, K.M. and Ouimet, W.B. 2014. Rediscovering the Lost Archaeological Landscape of Southern New England Using Airborne Light Detection and Ranging (LiDAR). *Journal of Archaeological Science* 43: 9–20.

Khoury, J. 2017. Israel Promised to Build Its First Modern Arab City since 1948: Here's What Came of It. *Haaretz*, October 17, 2017. https://www.haaretz.com/israel-news/.premium.MAGAZINE-israel-vowed-to-build-its-first-modern-arab-city-since-48-then-nothing-1.5457042 (accessed February 7, 2018).

Killebrew, A.E., DePietro, D., Pangarkar, R., Peleg, S.-A., Scham, S., and Taylor, E. 2017. Archaeology, Shared Heritage, and Community at Akko, Israel. *Journal of Eastern Mediterranean Archaeology and Heritage Studies* 5: 365–392.

Killebrew, A.E. and Olson, B.R. 2014. The Tel Akko Total Archaeology Project: New Frontiers in the Excavation and 3D Documentation of the Past. In: Bieliński, P., Gawlikowski, M., Koliński, R., Ławecka, D., Sołtysiak, A., and Wygnańska, Z., eds. *Proceedings of the 8th International Congress on the Archaeology of the Ancient Near East, 30 April–4 May 2012, University of Warsaw*, Vol. 2: *Excavation and Progress Reports, Posters*. Wiesbaden: 559–574.

Killebrew, A.E. and Quartermaine, J. 2016. Total Archaeology@Tel Akko (The 2013 and 2014 Seasons): Excavation, Survey, Community Outreach and New Approaches to Landscape Archaeology in 3D. In: Stucky, R.A., Kaelin, O., and Mathys, H.-P., eds. *Proceedings of the 9th International Congress on the Archaeology of the Ancient Near East. 9–13 June 2014, Basel*, Vol. 3: *Reports*. Wiesbaden: 491–502.

Koh, A.J., Yasur-Landau, A., and Cline, E.H. 2014. Characterizing a Middle Bronze Palatial Wine Cellar from Tel Kabri, Israel. *Plos One* 9/8 https://doi.org/10.1371/journal.pone.0106406 (accessed February 7, 2018).

Lehmann, G. 2001. Phoenicians in Western Galilee: First Results of an Archaeological Survey in the Hinterland of Akko. In: Mazar, A., ed. *Studies in the Archaeology of the Iron Age in Israel and Jordan* (Journal for the Study of the Old Testament Supplement Series 331). Sheffield: 65–112.

Lehmann, G. and Peilstöcker, M. 2012. *Archaeological Survey of Israel: Map of Ahihud (20)*. Jerusalem. http://www.antiquities.org.il/survey/newmap_en.asp#zoom=8.000 0;xy:34.80852508545,31.298049926757;mapname=20 (accessed March 19, 2018).

Morhange, C., Giaime, M., Marriner, N., Abu Hamid, A., Bruneton, H., Honnorat, A., Kaniewski, D., Magnin, F., Porotov, A.V., Wante, J., Zviely, D., and Artzy, M. 2016. Geoarchaeological Evolution of Tel Akko's Ancient Harbour (Israel). *Journal of Archaeological Science: Reports* 7: 71–81.

Olson, B.R., Placchetti, R.A., Quartermaine, J., and Killebrew, A.E. 2013. The Tel Akko Total Archaeology Project (Akko, Israel): Assessing the Suitability of Multi-Scale 3D Field Recording in Archaeology. *Journal of Field Archaeology* 38: 244–262.

Quartermaine, J., Olson, B.R., and Killebrew, A.E. 2014. Image-Based Modeling Approaches to 2D and 3D Digital Drafting in Archaeology at Tel Akko and Qasrin: Two Case Studies. *Journal of Eastern Mediterranean Archaeology and Heritage Studies* 2: 110–127.

CHAPTER 8

Piracy in the Late Bronze Age Eastern Mediterranean? A Cautionary Tale

A. Bernard Knapp

1   Preface

It was intermediaries who carried out a large part of the maritime transport during the 14th and especially the 13th centuries BCE. These "Nomads of the Sea" were the employees of the established economic systems, hirelings from peripheral groups whose maritime expertise rendered them a meaningful element. While at first those economic mercenaries were dependent on polities, soon the balance of reliance slanted in their favour; their "sailors' trade" became an entrepreneurial vocation. The line distinguishing intermediaries from entrepreneurs, mercenaries and pirates was fine.

ARTZY 1998: 439

Some twenty years ago, Michal Artzy published two key articles dealing with "sailors' trade" and "Nomads of the Sea" (Artzy 1997, 1998), establishing a baseline for scholars whose research interests revolve around the mechanisms and personnel involved in maritime trade during the Late Bronze Age eastern Mediterranean. In effect, what she argued was that the maritime expertise of such people—harbor masters, entrepreneurs, and liminal agents—afforded them a level of economic adaptability that made it possible to shift from independent ventures of seaborne trade (cabotage or tramping) to state-sponsored expeditions or directed commercial ventures to piracy—as the situation demanded (see, also, Monroe 2011: 94). Indeed, it may be suggested that whether we define them as maritime nomads, sea peoples, or pirates, they surely must also have been merchants or seafaring traders at one time or another. In Artzy's view, their involvement in sailors' trade, entrepreneurial in nature, meant that they eventually came into competition or conflict with land-based powers, and as economic conditions declined at the end of the Late Bronze Age, they effectively became sea peoples. The recent resurgence of interest in piracy in the Late Bronze Age eastern Mediterranean (discussed in detail below) owes a great debt to these studies. I only want to add that, as a fledgling research student at the University of California at Berkeley in the 1970s, I took a course on the archaeology of Cyprus from Michal Artzy, who was then a visiting scholar and research assistant of Isadore Perlman and Frank Asaro at the Lawrence Berkeley National Laboratory. I hope this chapter serves both to recognize Michal Artzy's influence on my own career and, at the same time, to demonstrate the influence of her work upon the many recent studies on piracy and pirates in the Late Bronze Age Aegean and eastern Mediterranean.

2   Introduction

Piracy is likely as old as the emergence of sailing ships on the high seas, and it has been suggested that the Mediterranean was its birthplace (Backman 2014: 170). Broodbank (2013: 394) regards the sea as a lawless space and the Mediterranean as "an anarchic, free-for-all zone for anyone with the skill, daring and funds to set out upon it." Bronze Age seafaring merchants would have known that commerce always involves risks—natural and human—and may have accepted that some form of piracy was the price of doing business. After all, many of them probably engaged in similar activities themselves.

The practice of piracy required people who had some essential maritime skills, boats in which to utilize them, and some access to or knowledge of commercial networks (Artzy 1997: 7; 1998: 445). As is known better from post-Roman times, pirates often used small, swift boats and attacked merchant vessels as they were approaching a port or anchored in it. Geographic and political factors also must be considered. For example, Venetian traders sailing in the Adriatic Sea were highly vulnerable to attacks from pirates operating out of Dalmatia or any of the hundreds of small islands along the eastern shore of that sea. Intense local loyalties and political rivalries in this region meant that pirates could always find a shelter or port with a harbor master who would grant refuge—for a small share of the profits (Backman 2014: 179).

A study such as this demands at least a working definition of pirates and piracy. De Souza (1999: 1) describes Greco-Roman pirates as "armed robbers whose activities normally involve the use of ships"; he also notes that it was their enemies and their victims, not themselves, who defined them as pirates. Here I define piracy as an irregular, typically hostile, ongoing economic activity carried out for personal benefit and involving the use of ships, maritime mobility, and plundering, at sea and along coastal areas (after Leeson 2009: 195; Samaras 2015: 191). Moreover, as Braudel (1972, Vol. 2: 883–884) noted, there is a positive correlation between trade and piracy, as both are dependent on a flourishing network of maritime exchange.

Although a case has been made that Ionians (*Iaunaya/Iamnaya*) (Greeks?) were involved in piratic activities (Luraghi 2006), it is only with classical authors that we gain literary insights into piracy and people who were actually called pirates. Both the Homeric and classical word *lêistes* and the later (third-century BCE onward) word *peiratis* meant "pirate" or "bandit" but could also be translated as "plunderer." Another, less common term, *katapontistes*, refers exclusively to "pirate," not "bandit": the third-century CE author Cassius Dio (36.20.1) wrote: "The pirates [*katapontistai*] had always attacked shipping, just as the bandits [*lêisteias*] did those who live on land." Thus, following de Souza (1999: 8–11), we should understand that (1) pirates used ships and operated mainly at sea, unlike bandits whose activities are restricted to land, and (2) the use of ships meant that pirates needed access to anchorages or harbors, bases crucial for their activities. Both factors represent important distinctions in my arguments.

Ancient Greek records often refer to pirate attacks, whether at sea or on land (usually coastal areas). Homer, for example, was generally disapproving of piracy, but at times rather equivocal: Menelaus stated that it took him seven years and great hardships to amass his fortune "and bring it home in my ships" (*Od.* 4.75–85). Although Thucydides (1.5.1–3) viewed piracy (*lêisteia*) as an impediment to progress, he commented that there was "no disgrace," and "even some glory" attached to attacking and plundering small towns in the days before the Minoan thalassocracy. Plutarch's bombastic *Life of Pompey* describes how Roman commerce was harassed by a vast pirate fleet that supposedly held 400 port cities to ransom. Plutarch reports that many wealthy men in these ports hastened not only to invest in these thieving ventures but also to take part in them. Cicero, writing in the first century BCE, felt that pirates were "the common enemy of all mankind," but Saint Augustine, some four centuries later, was of the opinion that piracy was relative, as beauty is to the eye of the beholder— what we would call a social construct (Gabrielsen 2013: 133, with references).

Perhaps the most significant lesson we may take from all these examples is that piracy was very much an individual initiative, not restricted to any class, upper or lower, freeman or slave. Moreover, it seems to have offered to some seafaring people a way to enter the lucrative commercial activities of the eastern Mediterranean world.

In what follows, I examine a range of Late Bronze Age archaeological and textual evidence from the eastern Mediterranean, and conclude that (1) there is no unequivocal association between the wide sweep of material culture linked to Bronze Age piracy and what has been termed a "culture of piracy" (Hitchcock and Maeir 2016: 247), and (2) there is little correlation between sea-based encounters as known from later periods and the actions or representations called into evidence for the Bronze Age.

3 Bronze Age Piracy? The Material Evidence

The literature on piracy during the Bronze Age is relatively recent and, in general, tends to be limited in scope. Curiously, some scholars refer to the work of de Souza (1999: 241), who maintained that any form of seaborne raiding or plunder could not be distinguished from warfare in general before the fifth-fourth centuries BCE. Furthermore, he argued that "*all* evidence of piracy in the Graeco-Roman world is textual" (emphasis in original) and that "pirates did not leave any distinct trace in the archaeological record" (de Souza 1999: 2). While I do not accept such restrictions, I, too, deliberately take a skeptical approach in considering the material insignia of piracy or pirates during the Bronze Age.

Leaving to one side de Miroschedji's (2012) recent reanalysis of the Sixth Dynasty Egyptian "autobiography" of Uni (Weni), where the actions of a group called the Ḥeryu-sha are regarded as one of the earliest textual references to piracy in the eastern Mediterranean, I turn to what are primarily archaeological studies focused on the Late Bronze Age. Although Cesarano (2008) maintains there was no such thing as Mycenaean piracy, Jung (2009) suggested that the Mycenaeans engaged in piracy as well as trade, and that "the immigration of persons from Italy to Mycenaean Greece may have been part of the piracy of the so-called Sea Peoples starting in the time of Ramesses II" (Jung 2009: 78–79). Gilan (2013: 53–54) likewise discusses Mycenaean "sea raiders." For their part, Hitchcock and Maeir (2014, 2016, 2017) seek to link multiple aspects of the Mycenaean world—Linear B documents, disadvantaged workers, feasting and drinking, representations on pottery, the "Mycenaean galley," site locations, "slavery," Handmade Burnished Ware, and even "grooming and depilatory habits"—to a "culture of piracy" (Hitchcock and Maeir 2016: 247 and *passim*). They speculate, for example, that "the display of Sea Peoples' regalia ... served to maintain tribal identity within pirate cultures" (Hitchcock and Maeir 2014: 626), and that "tribes of pirates" like the sea peoples developed "a unified culture aboard their ships that coalesced around dress, weaponry and warrior culture, Mycenaean styles of drinking, and Mycenaean and Italian grooming habits" (Hitchcock and Maeir 2016: 260; Hitchcock and Maier [2017] elaborate on Mycenaean-style drinking vessels and feasting as related to pirates). Wachsmann (e.g., 1981, 1998: 172–196) has long argued that the sea peoples ships from Medinet Habu have their closest parallels in Aegean (Mycenaean) galleys depicted in representations of Late Helladic and Iron Age warships, and recently has argued that the Abu Gurob (Egypt) ship model, dated to the twelfth century BCE, represents a (Late) Helladic galley (Wachsmann 2013: 26, 28, 33, 59, 201–203). Emanuel (2016: 267–268, 277) links the ship model to the *Sherden* and suggests that piracy posed a significant threat during the Late Bronze Age;

polities like Ugarit and merchants alike may have addressed such a threat by maintaining small fleets of "combat-capable" (Emanuel 2016: 268) vessels to defend their coastal waters.

In multiple, and at times contradictory, ways these scholars view events at the end of the Bronze Age as involving Mycenaeans, sea peoples and other, mixed tribal groups made up of peasants, immigrants, and the disenfranchised from all classes. In the case of the Philistines, at least, Ben-Dor Evian (2016, 2017) has now argued forcefully that the sea peoples mentioned in the texts from Medinet Habu were of northern Levantine and Anatolian origin, and that pirates from the Aegean had nothing to do with the infamous naval battle(s) in the Nile Delta. Molloy's (2016: 367, 371) take on piracy and the sea peoples is equally compelling: he posits a "maritime movement of warriors" following the Mycenaean "collapse" that reflects the devolution of trading into raiding and involved "multi-ethnic confederations that were soluble, transient, archaeologically ephemeral but potentially sizeable in both numbers and socio-political impact."

Based on archaeological criteria such as ship representations on pottery, Samaras (2015) suggests that piracy existed also in the Postpalatial Aegean (after ca. 1150–1100 BCE) and again during the Geometric period (after 900 BCE). Indeed, a few Late Helladic (LH) III pottery vessels show weapon-wielding warriors aboard ships, e.g., from Enkomi (LH IIIB), Bademgediği Tepe in western Turkey (LH IIIB–C) (Fig. 8.1), and Kynos in East Lokris (LH IIIC) (Mountjoy 2011: 484–486, figs. 2, 3) (for all sites mentioned in the text, see Fig. 8.2). Mountjoy (2011: 487) suggests that the scenes on the Bademgediği Tepe and Kynos kraters may well portray a sea battle with warriors on deck prepared to board another ship. A small body sherd from another LH IIIC krater found at Liman Tepe depicts a figure thought to be an oarsman like the one depicted on the Bademgediği Tepe vessel (Aykurt and Erkanal 2017: 62–66, figs. 4, 5). From Çine-Tepecik, inland from Miletos, the rim of yet another krater preserves the figure of what may be a warrior standing on the deck of a ship (Günel and Herbordt 2014: 4–5, figs. 3–5). Along with the representation of a naval battle depicted on the wall reliefs of Ramesses III's temple at Medinet Habu (Wachsmann 2000a: 106, fig. 6.1), these highly schematic scenes are the closest we come in any medium to what is commonly viewed as piracy, i.e., shipborne raiders attacking another ship at sea in the attempt to plunder, loot cargo, or seize captives.

Samaras (2015: 195–196) also notes some locational features that might point to the existence of pirate bases: naturally defensible sites or features with fortifications or towers; or situation on or near the coast but invisible from the

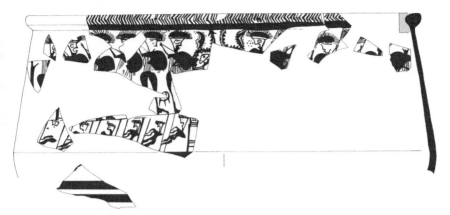

FIGURE 8.1 LH IIIC krater fragments, Bademgediği Tepe, Turkey (after Mountjoy 2011: 486, fig. 3, center, bottom)
COURTESY OF PENELOPE MOUNTJOY

sea. Like Samaras, Hitchcock and Maeir (2014: 629–630) suggest that defensible Cypriot sites like Maa-Palaeokastro and Pyla-Kokkinokremnos may be associated with piracy, the former as a refuge and the latter to protect against pirates. In some respects, this follows on from Sherratt's (1998: 300–301 n.15; 2016: 292) suggestion that Maa and Pyla may have been bypass and outflanking centers serving mercantile elites who had broken away from longer established ports (at Palaepaphos and Kition) to set up their own seaside bases. With respect to Pyla, at least, Caraher, Moore, and Pettegrew (2014: 5 fig. 1.5, 43–47) have now identified a paleo-coastline some 150 m inland from the present-day beach, and defined the area of a likely prehistoric to historic harbor; this tends to support the notion that the site served not as a defense against "pirates" but rather to facilitate the movement of traded goods from coastal ports inland (e.g., Stanley Price 1979: 80–81).

Certainly Maa and Pyla, along with many other sites in the Aegean or eastern Mediterranean, might be construed as bases for pirates or refuges to escape them. (Samaras [2015: 195–196] suggests Postpalatial Koukounaries on Paros or the islet of Modi just east of Poros in the Saronic Gulf.) Indeed, Korfmann (1986: 13) once described Troy as a "pirate fortress," an idea that finds support in Troy's location at a natural choke point, where maritime routes are constricted by capes, straits, or islands (Galvin 1999: 12; cited by Hitchcock and Maeir 2016: 255).

Beyond such generalizations, however, demonstrating the existence of pirates during the Bronze Age remains problematic. Beyond some interesting *assertions* by Hitchcock and Maeir (2014, 2016, 2017), we know little if anything

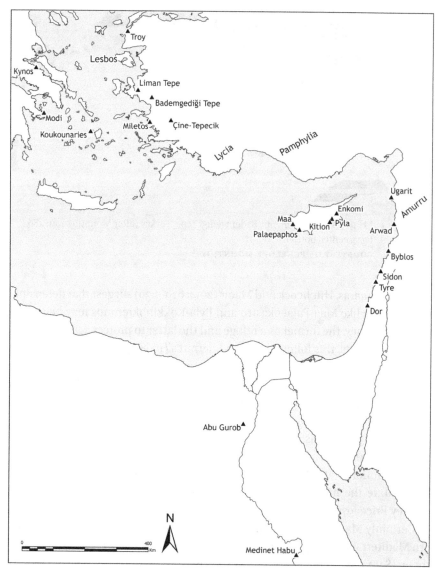

FIGURE 8.2 Map showing location of all sites mentioned in text
DRAWING BY LUKE SOLLARS

about any people or community involved in prehistoric or early historic piratic practices, about their leaders and crews, their insignia or memorabilia, their dress, or the tools of their trade. Simply stating that certain practices or symbols could be piratic in nature does not make them so.

As to the sea peoples, perhaps we might more appropriately think of them as an ephemeral group or groups of varying origins that brought together diverse material, social, and cultural practices, and whose influences, once these groups fragmented, spread far and wide in the Mediterranean (Molloy 2016: 371). In Broodbank's (2013: 466) view, characterizing the sea peoples as pirates only validates the concepts of a land-based polity that had no control over what constituted legality on the high seas.

4 Bronze Age Piracy? The Documentary Evidence

All this archaeological maneuvering does little to instill confidence in our ability to detect piratical activity or to establish the existence of pirates in the material record of the Bronze Age. Equally important to this discussion, however, is the lack of any mention in any Late Bronze Age cuneiform or Linear B document of "piracy" or "pirates" per se—or of any words translated as such. I leave aside here Hitchcock and Maeir's (2014, 2017: 148–150) suggestion that Luwian *tarwanis* and Hebrew *seren* (if not Greek *tyrannos*) might have designated a "pirate leader or warlord," which demands an entirely different level of criticism.

Nonetheless, there are several references to groups of people or the raiding and sacking of coastal towns/ports that could be construed as indicative of Bronze Age piracy: these groups include the Šikila and Lukki and the *miši*—the "enemy" noted in certain cuneiform letters from Ugarit and Alašiya and more. Twenty-four Late Bronze Age documents (in Akkadian, Hittite, and Ugaritic) refer to various individuals, groups of people, or acts and events that mention ships, sea battles, enemy raiders sacking ports or abducting captives, and the like, and that thus may point to the existence of pirates or piracy (Table 8.1).

Various Egyptian documents of Ramesses II, Merneptah, and Ramesses III (thirteenth–eleventh centuries BCE) describe seaborne raiders or battles usually linked to the sea peoples. In particular, Ramesses III's Medinet Habu inscription proclaims that certain elements of the sea peoples had devastated Hatti and Arzawa (Anatolia), Qodi and Carchemish (Syria), and Alašiya (Cyprus) (Breasted 1906.4: §64). Egyptologists and Assyriologists have long expressed skepticism about the historicity or purpose behind the Medinet Habu inscription (e.g., Lesko 1980; Liverani 1990: 121; Cifola 1994). Weeden (2013: 5–6), an Assyriologist, questions the value of assigning to specific and known ethnic or geographic names any of the ethnonym lists used in the texts of Ramesses III, as such lists simply provided the means to construct a stereotype of Egyptian enemies. One Egyptologist recently has questioned the validity of virtually all past scholarship on the sea peoples, in particular the historicity of an invasion as recorded at Medinet Habu (Roberts 2014: 359–360). More generally,

TABLE 8.1 Late Bronze and early Iron Age texts mentioning ships, sea battles, and other hostile maritime activities

No.	Text nos./ language	Findspot	Subject	References
1	RS 20.18/ Akkadian	Ugarit	Alašiya official warns Ugarit of 20 enemy ships	Nougayrol et al. 1968: 83–85 no. 22
2	RS 20.212/ Akkadian	Ugarit	Large boat and crew to ship grain to Ura in Cilicia	Nougayrol et al. 1968: 105–107, no. 33
3	RS 20.238/ Akkadian	Ugarit	Ugarit and Alašiya; navy of Ugarit in Lukka land	Nougayrol et al. 1968: 87–89, no. 24
4	RS 34.129/ Akkadian	Ugarit	"Šikila-people, who live on ships"	Bordreuil 1991: 38–39, no.12
5	RS 34.147/ Akkadian	Ugarit, une bibliothèque au sud de la ville	Fourteen Carchemish ships at Ugarit	Bordreuil 1991: 23–25, no. 5
6	RS 94.2523 + RS 94.2530/ Akkadian	Ugarit, House of Urtenu	King of Ugarit fails to send ships to Lukka	Lackenbacher and Malbran-Labat 2016: 25–30
7	RSL 1/Akkadian	Ugarit	Warning to Ugarit: enemy ships seen at sea	Nougayrol et al. 1968: 85–86 n. 1, no. 23
8	BM 1939,0613.101/ Akkadian	Alalakh	Idrimi built ships to raid Mukish	Dietrich and Loretz 1981
9	EA 38/Akkadian	Amarna, Egypt	Lukki raids on Egyptian territory and Cyprus	Moran 1992: 111
10	EA 101, 105/ Akkadian	Amarna, Egypt	Miši ships vs. Byblos	Moran 1992: 174–75, 178–179

PIRACY IN THE LATE BRONZE AGE EASTERN MEDITERRANEAN? 151

TABLE 8.1   Late Bronze and early Iron Age texts mentioning ships, sea battles, and other hostile maritime activities (cont.)

No.	Text nos./ language	Findspot	Subject	References
11	EA 114/Akkadian	Amarna, Egypt	Yapah-Hadda (Beirut?) seized ship of Byblos	Moran 1992: 188–190
12	EA 98, 101, 104, 105, 149/ Akkadian	Amarna, Egypt	Men and ships of Arwad	Moran 1992: 171, 174–175, 177–179, 236–237
13	KTU 2.42 + 2.43 = RS 18.113A + B/ Ugaritic	Ugarit, palace Room 77	Alašiyan merchant at Ugarit to buy ships	Virolleaud 1965: 14–15
14	KBo XII 38/ Hittite	Boğazköy	Hittite fleet(?) vs. Alašiya	Otten 1963; Güterbock 1967
15	KUB XIV 1 + KBo XIX 38/Hittite	Boğazköy	Madduwatta and raid on Alašiya	Beckman, Bryce, and Cline 2011: 69–100
16	KUB XIX 5 + KBo XIX 79/Hittite	Boğazköy	Piyamaradu made a raid against Lazpa (Lesbos)	Beckman, Bryce, and Cline 2011: 140–144
17	CTH 105/Hittite	Boğazköy	"Ships of Ahhiyawa" not to enter land of Amurru	Beckman, Bryce, and Cline 2011: 50–68
18	Südburg inscription/ hieroglyphic Hittite	Boğazköy	Šuppiluliuma II made three military campaigns along Mediterranean coast, including Luk(k)a-land	Hawkins 1995: 59
19	Thutmose III Annals, year 5 campaign/ Egyptian	Karnak	Seizing two Levantine ships	Breasted 1906.2: §§454–462

TABLE 8.1 Late Bronze and early Iron Age texts mentioning ships, sea battles, and other hostile maritime activities (cont.)

No.	Text nos./ language	Findspot	Subject	References
20	Papyrus Harris I	Near Medinet Habu	Ships "made for the sea," manned by archers	Grandet 1994: 230
21	*Tale of Wenamun*			Lichtheim 1976: 224–229

Wilkinson (2010: 56) suggests "the Egyptians were adept at recording things as they wished them to be seen, not as they actually were."

In an innovative study of the Medinet Habu reliefs, Ben-Dor Evian (2016) maintains that most historical reconstructions of the battles between the Egyptians and sea peoples have ignored the basic iconic and narrative principles of ancient Egyptian art. Consequently, the scenarios we have are full of misconceptions about the sequence and geographic settings of the land and naval battles, as well as the very nature of the sea peoples.

Two further Egyptian texts, however, may somehow be related to piracy (Sauvage 2011: 432–433). The first is from Thutmose III's fifth campaign in year 29 (late fifteenth century BCE), after which the pharaoh seized two ships laden with servants, metals, wood, etc. (Sethe 1906: 686–687). The second, from the reign of Ramesses III (early twelfth century BCE), is the Papyrus Harris I, which mentions the construction of ships made for the sea and manned by archers. Finally, the eleventh-century BCE Egyptian *Tale of Wenamun* includes certain events that may suggest pirate-like activity (Lichtheim 1976: 224–229; Gilboa 2015: 248–250). On his venture to Byblos, some of Wenamun's goods were stolen by one of his own crew at Dor on the Carmel Coast; eventually, Wenamun confronted a ship of the Tjeker at sea, seizing goods to replace those he had lost. Although eleven ships of the Tjeker confronted Wenamun as he prepared to leave Byblos, he was able to set sail for Egypt, but was blown off course to Alašiya. The confrontation between Wenamun and the Tjeker on the high seas is the only episode that might be related to piracy, but even then, we would expect the Tjeker—not Wenamun—to be the pillagers.

Wachsmann (2000b: 809) has referred to "the ever present danger of shore-based pirates/privateers/enemy ships" recorded in the Amarna letters; elsewhere he presented a series of possibly relevant cuneiform texts and Linear B documents (Wachsmann 1998: 123–130). It must be emphasized, however, that it remains a matter of opinion whether any of these documents are actually concerned with piracy or pirates. Nonetheless, there are three main groups of people whose activities could be regarded as piratic in nature: the Lukki (men of the Lukka-lands), the *miši*, and the men of Arwad (to which Linder 1981: 38–39 adds the Ahhiyawa). If the Šikila, who "live on ships," are equated with the Šekelesh (Tjeker), known from the Egyptian documents of Merneptah, Ramesses III, and Wenamun (Artzy 1997: 5; Singer 1999: 722), they, too, conducted seaborne raids on coastal towns.

What do the documentary records tell us of these peoples? In Amarna letter (EA) 38, the king of Alašiya protests to the pharaoh that the Lukki had repeatedly attacked various towns on Cyprus in addition to raiding Egyptian-controlled territory (Moran 1992: 111; Table 8.1: 9). Akkadian letters RS 20.238 and RS 94.2523 + RS 94.2530 (Table 8.1: 3, 6) both refer to Ugarit's navy or ships and the Lukka-lands (and Hatti). Bryce (2016: 73) sees in the latter a situation in which the Hittites engaged the services of the Hiyawa-men (Ahhiyawa?) to provide support (by land and sea) in the increasingly vulnerable frontier zones of their kingdom in the south and southwest. If the Lukka-lands formed part of the region extending from western Pamphylia through Lycia, on the southern coast of Anatolia (Bryce 2005: 56), this rocky, semi-mountainous area included numerous bays and coves that could well have served as a haven for pirates (see, also, Singer 2006: 251–252, 258).

The *miši* are mentioned in the Amarna letters concerning Byblos and the Land of Amurru. Lambdin (1953), followed by Moran (1992: 174, 178), equated this term with Egyptian *mš'* (army, troops). Linder (1981: 39 n. 38) sought to extend the meaning of *mš'* to "warship" (based on its Old Kingdom meaning) and thus defined the *miši* as "men of the warships," or "marines." Artzy (1997: 5 n. 18) regarded them as "hired mariners ... who acted in the sea around Byblos and Amurru as coastal guards for the Egyptian overlords." Rib-Addi of Byblos often refers to the *miši*; for example, in EA 101 he tells the pharaoh that "the ships of the army [*miši*] are not to enter the land of Amurru" (see Table 8.1: 12 for references). In EA 105 the men of Amurru under King Abdi-Aširta have seized the ships of the *miši* and their cargo (Moran 1992: 178). With reference to a British Museum painted papyrus showing warriors with boar's-tusk helmets fighting alongside Egyptians (Schofield and Parkinson 1994), Wachsmann (1998: 130) suggested that "the *miši* ships mentioned in the Amarna tablets may refer to Aegean (Mycenaean?) ship-based mercenaries in the employ of the Egyptian court at Amarna" (see, also, Artzy 1997: 4). Such an association, however, is certainly not implied by any of the documents in question.

Five Amarna letters mention the men and ships of Arwad (Table 8.1: 12) and demonstrate that they, too, engaged in naval warfare during the fourteenth century BCE. They were involved in attacking and establishing a naval blockade of Amurru (EA 104–105), intercepting ships from Byblos at sea (EA 105), sacking the port of Ullasa (northern Lebanon?) (EA 105), blockading ports to prevent the delivery of grain (EA 98), and attacking the port of Ušu in support of Sidon, against the activities of Tyre (EA 149). EA 101 is a difficult letter to interpret: its author (probably Rib-Adda) asks the pharaoh to seize the ships of the men of Arwad to prevent them from attacking Byblos. Vidal (2008: 10–12) interprets this letter to mean that Ṣumur (main town of Amurru), with Egyptian support, had replaced Arwad as a key trading port, leading the men and ships of Arwad to act as mercenaries using "marauding practices and piracy" to survive; he thus compares them with Artzy's (1997) "economic mercenaries." Whilst none of the Amarna letters demonstrates that the men of Arwad were pirates, Vidal (2008: 11) stresses that Arwad—a small (some 40 ha) island—could have provided some of the essential features (isolation, inaccessibility, and refuge) of a piratic base for piratic practices.

From all the documentary evidence concerning the activities of these sea peoples and their ships, one thing is clear: Late Bronze polities were unsuccessful in curbing raids on coastal ports or establishing any dominance on the high sea. Seaborne raiders took port towns by surprise, at times sacking and destroying them, at other times taking hostages. Most scholars who have written on piracy in the Late Bronze Age have necessarily based their arguments on the plundering of coastal towns, including ports like Ugarit, Byblos, and Ṣumur, as well as unknown coastal sites on Cyprus (Alašiya) and Lesbos (Lazpa). It must be reiterated, however, that piratic activities, as understood today, are at least partly predicated upon sea-based encounters.

There are few instances of such activity in the documentary evidence:
- KBo XII 38 (sea battle between ships of Alašiya and the Hittites) (Table 8.1:14);
- RS 20.238 (ships of Ugarit somehow engaged in or against the Lukka-lands) (Table 8.1: 3);
- EA 105 (ships of Arwad intercept three Byblian ships at sea) (Table 8.1: 10);
- EA 114 (Byblian ships seized at sea by a likely coalition involving Amurru and Beirut) (Table 8.1: 11);
- RS 20.18 and RSL 1 ("enemy" ships threaten Ugarit and its ships) (Table 8.1: 1, 7);
- the *Tale of Wenamun* (seizure of goods from a Tjeker ship at sea) (Table 8.1: 21).

Perhaps such acts of plunder and the seizing of captives point to the economic lure of piracy, as well as the positive correlation between piracy and trade. As Artzy (1997, 1998) argued long ago, certain fringe groups facilitated trade within and amongst various Late Bronze Age polities and exchange networks. Their expertise in navigation, trade, or simply possession of a boat made them an essential part of these trade networks, "intermediaries" whose activities impacted positively as well as negatively on coastal settlements throughout the Levant.

If we define piratic activity as an irregular, ongoing, and economic activity that involves maritime mobility, the use of ships, and plundering for personal benefit, then the activities outlined in contemporary Late Bronze Age documents may be construed that way. Moreover, it must be acknowledged that it is no mean feat to identify pirates in Late Bronze or early Iron Age material or textual evidence, not least because such people were, perhaps, first and foremost, not pirates per se but rather merchants, mariners (like Artzy's "hirelings," "economic mercenaries," or "intermediaries"), or even rulers (like Odysseus and Menelaus, kings who plundered at will, at least on occasion). The boundary between pirates, corsairs, privateers, buccaneers, or even organized naval endeavors is difficult enough to disentangle in medieval and later documents, when the indifference of any given state or its rulers, if not their participation in such activities, is far from clear.

This situation is compounded when it comes to the material record of the Late Bronze and early Iron Ages, where most arguments have been based on the presumed representations of warriors on ships, or the interpretation of defensible coastal sites, or other, even less tangible and "symbolic," associations. Such archaeological reasoning relies more on subjective assertion than convincing demonstration. Unlike the case in post-Roman times, we have no evidence to show that Bronze Age grain merchants, for example, turned an occasional hand to seaborne marauding during the growing season, or that spice merchants finalized a successful trading season by raiding shipments of wine or silks, or that naval commanders replenished their personal coffers by moonlighting as pirates (Backman 2014: 180). Unlike any case that we can make for the eastern Mediterranean in the Late Bronze or early Iron Ages, post-Roman Mediterranean piracy "showed all the fluidity, pragmatism, and at times contradiction of other forms of Mediterranean life. ... It thrived on many of the same elements of cross-cultural adaptation as did Mediterranean trade and intellectual exchange. ... It was widely regarded as a risk of doing business, a problem to be regulated and managed rather than solved" (Backman 2014: 182).

5   Conclusion

Virtually all the recent literature postulating the existence of piracy or the activity of pirates during the Late Bronze Age assumes and asserts their existence, and perhaps the authors will prove to have been right in doing so. Adding an analysis of the relevant, contemporary documentary evidence as I have attempted to do may seem to corroborate their arguments. Nonetheless, I would emphasize three points:

1) There is no word or term in the rich textual record at our disposal that can be equated with either "pirates" or "piracy."
2) There is no unequivocal association between the wide sweep of material culture that has been linked to Late Bronze Age piracy and what has been termed a "culture of piracy" (Hitchcock and Maeir 2016: 247, 259).
3) There is little correlation between sea-based encounters as known from any later period and the actions or representations called into evidence for the Late Bronze Age.

Thus, if we use the terms "pirates" and "piracy" for the Late Bronze Age, we should do so more cautiously, setting aside the type of intellectual inflation that art theorists label "post-critical" (e.g., Foster 2015). Being critical, however, may also require a certain detachment from the prevailing argument, and it seems prudent to remind those who are leading the discussion that we are not always all on the same side, in the same way.

References

Artzy, M. 1997. Nomads of the Sea. In: Swiny, S., Hohlfelder, R., and Swiny, H.W., eds.: *Res Maritimae: Cyprus and the Eastern Mediterranean from Prehistory through Late Antiquity* (Cyprus American Archaeological Research Institute, Monograph 1). Atlanta: 1–16.

Artzy, M. 1998. Routes, Trade, Boats and "Nomads of the Sea." In: Gitin, S., Mazar, A., and Stern, E., eds. *Mediterranean Peoples in Transition: Thirteenth to Tenth Centuries BCE*. Jerusalem: 439–448.

Aykurt, A. and Erkanal, H. 2017. A Late Bronze Age Ship from Liman Tepe with Reference to the Late Bronze Age Ship from Izmir/Bademgediği Tepesi and Kos/Seraglio. *Oxford Journal of Archaeology* 36: 61–70.

Backman, C.R. 2014. Piracy. In: Horden, P. and Kinoshita, S., eds. *A Companion to Mediterranean History*. Chichester, UK: 170–183.

Beckman, G., Bryce, T., and Cline, E.H. 2011. *The Ahhiyawa Texts* (Writings from the Ancient World 28). Atlanta.

Ben-Dor Evian, S. 2016. The Battles between Ramesses III and the "Sea-Peoples": When, Where and Who? An Iconic Analysis of the Egyptian Reliefs. *Zeitschrift für Ägyptischen Sprache* 143: 151–168.

Ben-Dor Evian, S. 2017. Ramesses III and the "Sea-Peoples": Towards a New Philistine Paradigm. *Oxford Journal of Archaeology* 36: 267–85.

Bordreuil, P., ed. 1991. *Une bibliothèque au sud de la ville : les textes de la 34e campagne* (Ras Shamra-Ougarit 7). Paris.

Braudel, F. 1972. *The Mediterranean and the Mediterranean World in the Age of Philip II*. 2 vols. New York.

Breasted, J.R. 1906. *Ancient Records of Egypt*. 5 vols. Chicago.

Broodbank, C. 2013. *The Making of the Middle Sea: A History of the Mediterranean from the Beginning to the Emergence of the Classical World*. London.

Bryce, T. 2005. *The Kingdom of the Hittites*. Oxford.

Bryce, T. 2016. The Land of Hiyawa (Que) Revisited. *Anatolian Studies* 66: 67–79.

Caraher, W., Moore, R.S., and Pettegrew, D.K. 2014. *Pyla-Koutsopetria 1: Archaeological Survey of an Ancient Coastal Town* (American Schools of Oriental Research, Archaeological Reports 21). Boston.

Cesarano, D.A. 2008. *Mycenaean Corsairs: A Reassessment of Late Helladic II Piracy*. MA thesis. University of Delaware. Delaware.

Cifola, B. 1994. The Role of the Sea Peoples and the End of the Late Bronze Age: A Reassessment of Textual and Archaeological Evidence. *Orientis Antiqui Miscellanea* 1: 1–23.

Dietrich, M., and Loretz, O. 1981. Untersuchungen zu Statue und Inschrift des Königs Idrimi von Alalaḫ: Die Inschrift des Königs Idrimi von Alalaḫ. *Ugarit-Forschungen* 13: 201–268.

Emanuel, J.P. 2016. Maritime Worlds Collide: Agents of Transference and the Metastasis of Seaborne Threats at the End of the Bronze Age. *Palestine Exploration Quarterly* 148: 265–280.

Foster, H. 2015. *Bad New Days: Art, Criticism, Emergency*. London.

Gabrielsen, V. 2013. Warfare, Statehood and Piracy in the Greek World. In: Jaspert, N. and Kolditz, S., eds. *Seeraub im Mittelmeerraum: Piraterie, Korsarentum und Maritime Gewalt von der Antike bis zur Neuzeit* (Mittelmeerstudien 3). Paderborn: 133–153.

Galvin, P.R. 1999. *Patterns of Pillage: A Geography of Caribbean-Based Piracy in Spanish America, 1536–1718* (American University Studies Series 25: Geography Vol. 5). New York.

Gilan, A. 2013. Pirates in the Mediterranean: A View from the Bronze Age. In: Jaspert, N. and Kolditz, S., eds. *Seeraub im Mittelmeerraum: Piraterie, Korsarentum und Maritime Gewalt von der Antike bis zur Neuzeit* (Mittelmeerstudien 3). Paderborn: 49–66.

Gilboa, A. 2015. Dor and Egypt in the Early Iron Age: An Archaeological Perspective of (Part of) the Wenamun Report. *Egypt and the Levant* 25: 247–274.

Grandet, P. 1994. *Le Papyrus Harris I (BM 9999)*. 2 vols. (Bibliothèque d'étude 109.1, 2). Cairo.

Günel, S., and Herbordt, S. 2014. Mykenische Kraterfragmente mit figürlichen Darstellungen und ein Siegelabdruck eines hethitischen Prinzen aus der spätbronzezeitlichen Siedlung von ÇineTepecik. *Archäologischer Anzeiger* 2014(1): 1–14.

Güterbock, H.G. 1967. The Hittite Conquest of Cyprus Reconsidered. *Journal of Near Eastern Studies* 26: 73–81.

Hawkins, J.D. 1995. *The Hieroglyphic Inscription of the Sacred Pool Complex at Hattusa (Südburg)* (Studien zu den Boğazköy-Texten, Beiheft 3). Wiesbaden.

Hitchcock, L.A., and Maeir, A.M. 2014. Yo-ho, Yo-ho, A Seren's Life for Me! *World Archaeology* 46: 624–640.

Hitchcock, L.A., and Maeir, A.M. 2016. A Pirate's Life for Me: The Maritime Culture of the Sea Peoples. *Palestine Exploration Quarterly* 148: 245–264.

Hitchcock, L.A., and Maeir, A.M. 2017. Fifteen Men on a Dead Seren's Chest: Yo Ho Ho and a Krater of Wine. In Batmaz, A., Bedianashvili, A., Michalewicz A., and Robinson, A., eds. *Context and Connection: Essays on the Archaeology of the Ancient Near East in Honour of Antonio Sagona* (Orientalia Lovaniensia Analecta 263). Leuven: 147–159.

Jung, R. 2009. Pirates of the Aegean: Italy—The East Aegean—Cyprus at the End of the Second Millennium BC. In: Karageorghis, V., and Kouka, O., eds. *Cyprus and the East Aegean: Intercultural Contacts from 3000 to 500 BC. An International Archaeological Symposium Held at Pythagoreion, Samos, October 17th–18th 2008.* Nicosia: 72–93.

Korfmann, M. 1986. Troy: topography and navigation. In: Mellink, M., ed. *Troy and the Trojan War: A Symposium Held at Bryn Mawr College, October 1984.* Bryn Mawr, PA: 1–16.

Lackenbacher, S., and Malbran-Labat, F. 2016. *Lettres en akkadien de la "Maison d'Urtenu": fouilles de 1994* (Ras Shamra-Ougarit 23). Louvain.

Lambdin, T.O. 1953. The Miši-People of the Byblian Amarna Letters. *Journal of Cuneiform Studies* 7: 75–77.

Leeson, P.T. 2009. *The Invisible Hook: The Hidden Economics of Pirates.* Princeton.

Lesko, L.H. 1980. The Wars of Ramesses III. *Serapis* 6: 83–86.

Lichtheim, M. 1976. *Ancient Egyptian Literature* 2: *The New Kingdom.* Berkeley.

Linder, E. 1981. Ugarit: A Canaanite Thalassocracy. In: Young, G.D., ed. *Ugarit in Retrospect.* Winona Lake, IN: 31–42.

Liverani, M. 1990. *Prestige and Interest: International Relations in the Near East ca. 1600–1100 BC.* Padua.

Luraghi, N. 2006. Traders, Pirates, Warriors: The Proto-history of Greek Mercenary Soldiers in the Eastern Mediterranean. *Phoenix* 60: 21–47.

Miroschedji, P. de. 2012. Egypt and Southern Canaan in the Third Millennium BCE: Uni's Asiatic Campaigns Revisited. In: Gruber, M., Ahituv, S., Lehmann, G., and Talshir, Z., eds. *All the Wisdom of the East: Studies in Near Eastern Archaeology and History in Honor of Eliezer D. Oren* (Orbis Biblicus et Orientalis 255). Fribourg–Göttingen: 265–292.

Molloy, B.P.C. 2016. Nought May Endure but Mutability: Eclectic Encounters and Material Change in the 13th to 11th Centuries BC Aegean. In: Molloy, B.P.C., ed. *Of Odysseys and Oddities: Scales and Modes of Interaction between Prehistoric Aegean*

Societies and Their Neighbours (Sheffield Studies in Aegean Archaeology 10). Oxford: 343–383.

Monroe, C. 2011. "From Luxuries to Anxieties": A Liminal View of the Late Bronze Age World-System. In: Wilkinson, T.C., Sherratt, S., and Bennett, J., eds. *Interweaving Worlds: Systemic Interactions in Eurasia, 7th to the 1st Millennia BC*. Oxford: 87–99.

Moran, W.L. 1992. *The Amarna Letters*. Baltimore.

Mountjoy, P. 2011. A Bronze Age Ship from Ashkelon with Particular Reference to the Bronze Age Ship from Bademgediği Tepe. *American Journal of Archaeology* 115: 483–488.

Nougayrol, J., Laroche, E., Virolleaud, C., and Schaeffer, C.F.A. 1968. *Ugaritica* 5 (Mission de Ras Shamra 16). Paris.

Otten, H. 1963. Neue Quellen zum Ausklang des hethitischen Reiches. *Mitteilungen der Deutschen Orient-Gesellschaft* 94: 1–23.

Roberts, R.G. 2014. Changes in Perceptions of the "Other" and Expressions of Egyptian Self-Identity in the Late Bronze Age. In: Knapp A.B. and van Dommelen, P., eds. *The Cambridge Prehistory of the Bronze and Iron Age Mediterranean*. New York: 352–366.

Samaras, V. 2015. Piracy in the Aegean during the Postpalatial Period and the Early Iron Age. In: Babbi, A., Bubenheimer-Erhart, F., Marín-Aguilera, B., and Mühl, S., ed. *The Mediterranean Mirror: Cultural Contacts in the Mediterranean Sea between 1200 and 750 B.C.* (Tagungen 20). Mainz: 189–204.

Sauvage, C. 2011. Evidence from Old Texts: Aspects of Late Bronze Age International Maritime Travel and Trade Regulations in the Eastern Mediterranean? In: Duistermaat, K., and Regulski, I., eds. *Intercultural Contacts in the Ancient Mediterranean* (Orientalia Lovaniensia Analecta 202). Louvain: 427–437.

Schofield, L., and Parkinson, R.B. 1994. Of Helmets and Heretics: A Possible Egyptian Representation of Mycenaean Warriors on a Papyrus from el-Amarna. *Annual of the British School at Athens* 89: 157–170.

Sethe, K. 1906. *Urkunden der 18. Dynastie* (Urkunden des Aegyptischen Altertum 4, Band 3). Leipzig.

Sherratt, S. 1998. "Sea Peoples" and the Economic Structure of the Late Second Millennium in the Eastern Mediterranean. In: Gitin, S., Mazar, A., and Stern, E., eds. *Mediterranean Peoples in Transition: Thirteenth to Early Tenth Centuries BCE*. Jerusalem: 292–313.

Sherratt, S. 2016. From "Institutional" to "Private": Traders, Routes and Commerce from the Late Bronze Age to the Iron Age. In: Moreno García, J.C., ed. *Dynamics of Production in the Ancient Near East*. Oxford: 289–302.

Singer, I. 1999. A Political History of Ugarit. In: Watson, W.G.E., and Wyatt, N., eds. *Handbook of Ugaritic Studies* (Handbuch der Orientalistik, Abteilung 1, Der Nahe und Mittlere Osten, Band 39). Leiden: 603–733.

Singer, I. 2006. Ships Bound for Lukka: A New Interpretation of the Companion Letters RS 94.2530 and RS 94.2523. *Altorientalische Forschungen* 33: 242–262.

Souza, P. de. 1999. *Piracy in the Graeco-Roman World*. Cambridge.

Stanley Price, N.P. 1979. *Early Prehistoric Settlement in Cyprus: A Review and Gazetteer of Sites, c.6500–3000 BC* (British Archaeological Reports, International Series 65). Oxford.

Vidal, J. 2008. The Men of Arwad, Mercenaries of the Sea. *Bibliotheca Orientalis* 65: 5–15.

Virolleaud, C. 1965. *Le palais royal d'Ugarit* 5 (Mission de Ras Shamra 11). Paris.

Wachsmann, S. 1981. The Ships of the Sea Peoples. *International Journal of Nautical Archaeology* 10: 187–220.

Wachsmann, S. 1998. *Seagoing Ships and Seamanship in the Bronze Age Levant*. College Station, TX.

Wachsmann, S. 2000a. To the Sea of the Philistines. In: Oren E.D., ed. *The Sea Peoples and Their World: A Reassessment* (University Museum Monograph 108; University Museum Symposium Series 11). Philadelphia: 103–143.

Wachsmann, S. 2000b. Some Notes on Mediterranean Seafaring during the Second Millennium BC. In: Sherratt, S., ed. *The Wall Paintings of Thera Vol. 2*. Athens: 803–824.

Wachsmann, S. 2013. *The Gurob Ship-Cart Model and Its Mediterranean Context*. College Station, TX.

Weeden, M. 2013. After the Hittites: The Kingdoms of Karkamish and Palistin in Northern Syria. *Bulletin of the Institute of Classical Studies* 56(2): 1–20.

Wilkinson, T., 2010. *The Rise and Fall of Ancient Egypt*. London.

CHAPTER 9

Oxhides, Buns, Bits, and Pieces: Analyzing the Ingot Cargo of the Cape Gelidonya Shipwreck

Joseph W. Lehner, Emre Kuruçayırlı, and Nicolle Hirschfeld

For Michal. Your passion for exploring through scientific analysis who traveled the Late Bronze Age seas, carrying what and how and why has rubbed off on us, into the second and even third generations now.

1 Introduction

The ship that sank at Cape Gelidonya (Turkey) ca. 1200 BCE is one of only three excavated wrecks dating to the Late Bronze Age, though this was an era of intensive overseas exchange in the Mediterranean. It was also one in which the metal craft economy facilitated multiple scales of interaction, from households to polities, and the cargo found on the seabed at Cape Gelidonya consists primarily of copper and tin in the form of ingots and ingot fragments, copper alloy implements, and scrap metal intended for recycling. The ship belonged to a tinker traveling a circuit along the coasts of Cyprus, Syria, and southern Anatolia (Bass et al. 1967).

The shipwreck was first excavated in 1960 and those discoveries were well published in 1967 (Bass et al. 1967). But meanwhile there have been substantial new discoveries on the seabed and rediscoveries in the museum storerooms (Bass 2012, 2013; Bass and Hirschfeld 2013). Because this cargo represents an assemblage deliberately collected in antiquity it is fitting now to collate the discoveries of the past half century back into their original whole and study and publish the corpus in its entirety. New techniques of scientific analysis are also now possible. Identification of ingot typologies and scientific analysis of the copper's composition and its microscopic structure will provide further information about where the smith obtained his copper, the various means of metal production, and how and why it was broken up for circulation.

2 The Team and Our Sponsors

Intensive (re)study of the ingot cargo from the Cape Gelidonya shipwreck began in 2013, when Lente Van Brempt devoted a summer to building an inventory of the ingot fragments. She published an excellent preliminary analysis of the material in her Ph.D. thesis and her catalog has served as an invaluable starting point for further study (Van Brempt 2016: especially Chapter 8 and Appendix VIII).[1] In summer 2016, we were able to commence a program of conservation at the INA Bodrum Research Center by the capable hands of Asu Selen Özcan and under the supervision of chief conservator Esra Altınanıt Biçer, funded first by the Institute of Nautical Archaeology and then the Council of American Overseas Research Centers.[2] That same summer, Kenneth and Adair Small contributed funds that made it possible for Emre Kuruçayırlı and Joseph Lehner to travel to Bodrum, look through the collection, and begin designing a research protocol. A grant from the Brennan Foundation has provided the funds for a pilot program to implement that protocol, a project carried out in 2017 and continuing into 2019. We also continue to expand our team of collaborators, including first Zofia Stos and now also Moritz Jansen and Sabine Klein. We would stop in our tracks if it were not for the generosity of the many people who have granted or facilitated access to their institutes and laboratories.[3] And, finally, there are the graduate students (see below) who have volunteered time and expertise and have sparked us with their enthusiasm and questions.

The following report is not intended to be comprehensive or final; rather, it is a summary discussion of work in progress. The complete data and detailed description of analytical methodology will appear in a future publication.

3 Project Goals

The defining characteristic of the Cape Gelidonya shipwreck cargo is the predominance of copper and copper alloy materials, including over 1,200 individual ingots and ingot fragments. While copper metal and object production extend back in time as far as 10,000 years ago, ingot production became more common only during the Bronze Age ca. 3000–1200 BCE, when societies across the eastern Mediterranean and Near East became increasingly interconnected. Copper ingots are typically the primary product of copper smelting, and their

---

1 Special thanks to Lina Kassianidou, for the great lengths she went to, to come with her graduate student to Bodrum, and to Cemal Pulak, whose observations were critical especially during that first summer of sorting.
2 CAORC's Responsive Preservation Initiative for Cultural Heritage Resources.
3 Tuba Ekmekçi, Bodrum Research Center, Institute of Nautical Archaeology; Gülsu Şimşek and Barış Yağcı at KUYTAM (Surface Science and Technology Center, Koç University).

production permitted a widespread trade of copper metal for later remelting and working. By the Late Bronze Age, ca. 1700–1200 BCE, when societies in these areas developed a spectrum of larger-scale states, the consumption of copper and copper alloys drove a burst of industrial production and extensive trade. The end of the Late Bronze Age is defined by political collapse and extensive reorganization of production and trade, eventually leading to the rise of regionalized Iron Age kingdoms, city-states, and large territorial empires in the Near East. The Cape Gelidonya cargo fits directly in this crucial time period of social upheaval, and we are primed to examine how metals and metallurgy helped to define the social context during the end of the Bronze Age. By examining the assemblage in multiple scales using multiple techniques, we aim to track processes of continuity and change across three domains documented in this ingot cargo, including production, trade, and consumption. In effect, we are examining the life histories of copper metal from the ores and primary production to trade, transport, and consumption of ingots, scrap, and finished objects and, finally, their accumulation as a cargo and chance deposition on the seabed at Cape Gelidonya. This cargo is an exceedingly rare and well-preserved assemblage, permitting scholars to examine the cross-cutting relations of technology and ancient economies within the framework of the social dynamics that define the end of the Bronze Age.

3.1 Copper Production

Metal production involves a network of technologies from mining, smelting, melting, to metalworking. Evidence demonstrates that producer communities involved in the production of copper in the eastern Mediterranean and Aegean exhibit significant variation in how technologies were adopted and organized, demonstrating that by the end of the Bronze Age, production strategies were specialized and interconnected. Previous research has shown that by the end of the Bronze Age copper from these regions was typically produced by smelting ores in crucibles or furnaces, using charcoal to produce simultaneously the temperatures and atmospheric conditions required to reduce ores into copper metal. Copper production is highly sensitive to two fundamental issues: raw material availability (e.g., ore mineral types, timber for charcoal, and ancillary ceramic materials) and the human sociocultural context, which includes technological traditions, scale, tempo, and social organization of production.

The analysis of the Cape Gelidonya metal cargo offers insight into this process. If our interpretation of the wreck as the remains of a tinker is correct, then we are able to link indirectly the potentially different producer communities of primary ingot copper and finished copper/copper-alloy tool and scrap to a mobile specialist metal producer on the ship. This interconnection is certainly not directly related, but rather one that is linked through the complex economic and social relations that typify the Late Bronze Age. Assessing where the primary resources originated, how the ingots and tools were produced, and how these two interrelate permits us to define and describe the constellation of producer networks that are materialized in the metal cargo of the wreck. The near and far relations represented here are fundamental in understanding not only quality and quantity of the cargo but also the social world in which the ship's agents were involved and lived.

Previous analyses of the metal cargo provide clear evidence for different producer communities. Already at the time of the first archaeological publications on the Cape Gelidonya wreck, Bass (1961: 275; 1967: 77) used several lines of evidence to link the ingot cargo to production in Cyprus. This was nominally challenged by subsequent analyses by Maddin and Muhly in 1974 of a single oxhide ingot recovered in 1959, a year before Bass's excavations at Cape Gelidonya. On the basis of spectrographic analysis that measured elevated concentrations of cobalt (ca. 0.2 wt%), Maddin and Muhly concluded that Cyprus may not have been the original source, pointing rather to the Ergani massive sulfide deposit in southeastern Anatolia (Muhly and Maddin 1974: 28). After elemental and metallographic analyses of several more ingots from Bass's excavations, Muhly concluded more conservatively that it would not be possible to distinguish a provenance for the source copper (Muhly, Stech Wheeler, and Maddin 1977: 361). The issue of ingot and scrap metal provenance was further tested with the application of lead isotope ratio analysis by the Isotrace Laboratory at Oxford. These analyses demonstrated that the sampled oxhide and bun- ingots were highly consistent with Cypriot copper sources (Stos-Gale et al. 1998), while scrap metal and finished objects had a much wider distribution reflecting sources across the eastern Mediterranean, Aegean, and Anatolia (Stos 2009).

Our ongoing work examines further how communities produced the ingot cargo and in particular the assemblage of ingot fragments, many of which display characteristics that distinguish them from the complete ingots. This work seeks to build on the previous analysis of the more complete and diagnostic ingots to determine typological, compositional, microstructural, and isotopic differences. A more comprehensive view of the total ingot assemblage permits us to examine not only the raw materials used in ingot production, but also the technological choices that were employed in their production. Tracking variations in the raw materials and technologies provides insight into the baseline range of ingot compositions represented by the cargo and how these data differ from earlier ingot assemblages recovered from the greater region.

3.2 Copper Trade

Our second focus is the logistics and organization of copper trade. The social processes involved in the economy of ingot production to their distribution and eventual collection as a cache and ultimately cargo on the ship was probably mediated through multiple interested parties. Temporally, this necessarily includes networked moments of exchange both before and during the creation of the ship's cargo. With this perspective, we broaden our view from the motivations of the ship's agents to looking at the cycle of copper production up to the point of its collection on the ship.

Evidence suggests, for example, that many of the larger oxhide ingots (ca. 25 kg each) must have been produced by pouring smaller volumes of molten copper into a mold multiple times, because there is currently no evidence for crucibles and furnaces in which this volume of copper could have been melted. Were these larger ingots produced by pooling raw copper from multiple sources within a greater region or were they produced in the single location using a single source (ex. Knapp 2000: 38–47)? All of this happened before the ingots entered the context of the ship cargo. If the isotopic, compositional, and microscopic characteristics are the same for different ingot types in the Cape Gelidonya assemblage and for different ingots of the same type, then the ingots were most likely produced in the same area using shared technological traditions; however, if the ingots display significant variations between and within ingot types, then it is more likely that different sources and technologies were employed for their production. This has direct implications for understanding how the copper was mobilized and collected as cargo, whether as a single event or several separate events of provisioning.

3.3 Consumption

Our third area of research is an examination of how the ingot cargo reflects a variety of copper consumption patterns, both on the scale of the ship and interregionally. Consumption in this sense refers to how the copper was broken down and cached into a single cargo. As an important step in between the production and exchange of ingots and their eventual remelting and potential alloying to produce finished objects, these patterns are fundamental to the interpretation of the metal cargo. The primary data set that reveals consumption is the typological and microscopic data. From these, we can observe how people handled copper, including the fragmentation and collection of increasingly smaller pieces. We know now, by a raw count of individual objects, that the great majority of the copper ingot assemblage is fragmentary—a characteristic that sets the Cape Gelidonya metal cargo apart from that of the earlier

Uluburun shipwreck, which was composed of mostly complete objects. Caches of fragmentary ingots are well known from terrestrial settlements across the central and eastern Mediterranean, and they likely represent storage of copper commodities or workshops. At a smaller scale, we can observe microscopic markers of hammering and flattening of particularly small ingot fragments and pieces that are most consistent with casting spillage. If we can rule out post-depositional fragmentation of the ingots, then we are required to understand how and where the ingots were fragmented, how they were provisioned, and how they were ultimately consumed.

Thus, we can begin to understand the ingot cargo on multiple levels of analysis: within types (e.g., oxhide, bun-shaped, and slab-shaped ingots), between types, and between assemblages (e.g., from Cape Gelidonya, Uluburun, and terrestrial sites). These data allow us to evaluate not only the specific characteristics of the Cape Gelidonya cargo but also longer-term processes of cultural continuity and innovation involved in production, trade, and consumption of copper across different social contexts.

4   Catalog

Kuruçayırlı and Lehner have now cataloged the entirety of the copper ingot cargo, including precise weights and other metrics related to ingot morphology. To date, the catalog numbers 1,212 ingots and ingot fragments: 270 oxhide, 174 bun, and 20 slab ingot types; 748 fragments could not be attributed to any known types due to the lack of diagnostic features. Since nearly all objects have been properly cleaned of concretion, it is now possible to report that the total copper ingot weight is about 1,135 kg, 80% of which are oxhide ingots or oxhide fragments, 12% bun ingots or bun fragments, 1.65% slab ingots, and 8% are non-diagnostic fragments. Along with typology and physical measurements of the ingots, the catalog includes detailed descriptions of surface features, such as inclusions, blisters, and porosity, so as to provide as much information as possible about how the ingots were produced, handled, traded, and consumed.

In addition, our team works closely with specialists in 3D modelling, including Dominique Langis-Barsetti (University of Toronto) and Samuel Martin (University of Arkansas), who have scanned over 160 ingots and ingot fragments to produce three-dimensional real-scale digital models (Fig. 9.1). In addition to creating a highly detailed documentary record, these digital records will enable remote study of the objects. Three-dimensional scans of the objects offer a novel way to observe ingot morphology. These models preserve the shape and texture of the artifacts and create new measuring techniques

FIGURE 9.1 Results of a 3D model of oxhide ingot IN 103; raw data showing point cloud (top); 3D model in false color (middle); texturized model using photographic data (bottom)

that enable acquisition of highly accurate morphometrics and visualization of micro-topographical features related to symbolic impressions/incisions, hammering, chiseling, corrosion crusts, and other forms of superficial changes to the original cast structure.

5   Bulk Composition, Microscopy, and Microanalysis

The most significant aspect of the pilot study has been the selective sampling of ingot fragments for laboratory analysis. All 1,212 cataloged pieces were first scanned using a portable XRF (PXRF) analyzer to determine their qualitative elemental compositions. This information was a weighty factor in the selection of 107 samples for quantitative analyses, which represent all known types from the site. Of these, 77 have been examined by means of compositional analysis, 46 have been designated for metallographic analysis, and 100 for lead and copper isotope analysis.

5.1   *ICP-MS Analysis*

In this first round of analysis, 77 of the samples were analyzed for elemental composition using an Agilent 7700x ICP Mass-Spectrometer (ICP-MS) at the KUYTAM laboratory at Koç University in Istanbul (Kuruçayırlı, Lehner, and Hirschfeld 2017). Particular attention was paid to selecting a representative assemblage, consisting of 30 oxhide, 22 bun, and 5 slab ingots, and 20 nondiagnostic ingot fragments. Some of these—20 oxhide, 12 bun, and all 5 slab ingots—were selected because they had previously been chosen for lead isotope analysis (Stos-Gale et al. 1998; Stos 2009). The authors have established a collaboration with Stos and we plan to publish jointly all the results of both methods of analyses.

The results demonstrate that the sampled ingots and ingot fragments were cast of unalloyed copper with generally low impurity contents. The only exception is iron that is found in concentrations of 1.0–3.12 wt% in six samples. Despite the immiscibility of copper and iron, significant concentrations of iron in copper metal have been widely observed and are likely explained by the opportunity for the copper to pick up the iron through the smelting process (Craddock and Meeks 1987). Furthermore, the known presence of slag inclusions, including mineral phases of magnetite (Fe_3O_4), fayalite (Fe_2SiO_4), and iscorite (Fe_7SiO_{10}), as observed in the Uluburun ingots (Hauptmann et al. 2002: 6-7) would also increase the bulk composition of iron in the ingot metal. The elevated concentrations of iron may be due to small inclusions of slag in the sample. Producers would remove slags through remelting, hammering, and deslagging by poling or scraping slag away as it floated on the surface of molten copper while in a crucible. Higher concentrations of iron, and therefore slag, indicate that the copper in these selected ingots is relatively impure.

The ICP-MS analysis detected high tin contents in a bun ingot quarter (BI 112) and in four of the five slab ingots studied—a result consistent with Stos (2009: 168). Tin bronze ingots are exceptionally rare in the Aegean and Near East (see Moorey et al. 1988: 47; Kenoyer and Miller 1999: 118; Begemann et al. 2001: 51), and it is not clear whether they represent recycled tin bronze scrap or were intentionally produced. On the other hand, the fact that slab ingots were cast of tin bronze rather than unalloyed copper supports Pulak's suggestion that these items may have been partially shaped blanks for agricultural tools, perhaps plowshares (C. Pulak, personal communication; see, also, Bass 1967: 82).

5.2   *Metallography Results*

Forty-six objects were selected for metallographic analysis at KUYTAM. This analysis requires that samples are taken from the object with their original orientation preserved so that observations under the microscope are more accurate. This is especially important for the Cape Gelidonya ingot cargo because most of these objects were cast in open molds; solidification and crystallization occurred relative to the mold surface. Therefore, sample location and orientation were noted for each object sampled.

Preliminary analysis demonstrates the excellent preservation of copper ingot microstructure. All samples prepared so far show prominent as-cast structures, including nonmetallic inclusions, dendrites, and interdendritic infills enriched in impurities of arsenic and sulfur. These data indicate that these ingots were not altered much after casting; there are exceptions where past intentional ingot breakage and fragmentation by cold hammering left diagnostic deformations in the microstructure. Here we report on three distinct samples to demonstrate how this work is highly informative and necessary to interpret the Cape Gelidonya ingot assemblage.

5.3   *Quarter Bun Ingot BI 112*

BI 112 (95/20) was previously analyzed by Stos who discovered not only that it had a unique lead isotopic composition incompatible with known Cypriot ores, but also that it was composed of an alloy of copper and tin (ca. 12 wt% tin) (Stos 2009: 170). Bulk elemental analysis using ICP-MS by Kuruçayırlı and Lehner confirmed the significant presence of tin (ca. 15.6 wt%). Bun ingots are very rarely composed of copper tin alloys, with only a couple other examples known across the Mediterranean and Near East. Scholars typically assume that ingots were produced of pure metals, whether tin or copper, and that they were only later alloyed together when producing finished objects. Our results now confirm that, sometimes, copper alloys were used to produce bronze ingots for exchange; however, it is not possible to determine certainly whether this bun ingot was the product of intentional alloying of raw copper and tin or whether its composition was the product of recycling tin bronze objects like tools and weapons.

That said, the high concentration of tin between 10 and 16 wt% is consistent with the intentional melting of raw copper and tin together to form a true tin bronze bun ingot. The higher concentration of tin in BI 112 therefore suggests that the ingot may not have lost significant amounts of tin in the melting and casting process. The high content of tin is further demonstrated by microscopy, where the polished and etched section near the outer rim of the object shows typical as-cast structures of tin bronze preserved in the microstructure (Fig. 9.2) including α + δ eutectoid structures typical of tin bronzes with elevated quantities of tin (> 10 wt%). Past lead isotope analyses by Stos at Oxford (see section below) further demonstrated that this ingot is inconsistent with Cypriot copper ores, unlike most other oxhide and bun ingots from Cape Gelidonya analyzed at the lab. Rather, the ingot is currently most consistent with copper ores from the Central Taurus Mountains. At present, these results raise an important question about the possibility of bronze ingot production and further raises the possibility that intentionally produced tin bronze ingots circulated in the region in the Bronze Age, contrary to the current prevailing scholarly opinion.

5.4 Ingot Fragment FR 78

Due to the lack of any preserved edges, it is difficult to determine whether ingot fragment FR 78 is from an oxhide or bun ingot (Fig. 9.3). What is particularly interesting about this fragment is that both its surfaces, top and bottom, exhibit high degrees of flattening, possibly due to intentional breaking of the ingot into smaller fragments. Figure 9.4 compares the 3D surface texture of FR 78 with IN 115, an oxhide ingot handle fragment with prominent blistering on the surface that exhibits no working. Here it is possible to see how working effectively reduced the blistery surface of FR 78.

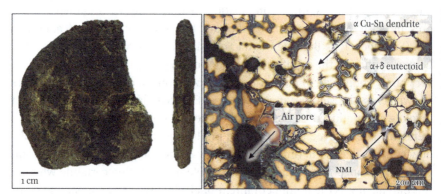

FIGURE 9.2 3D model of quarter bun ingot fragment BI 112, showing bottom surface and side profile (left); metallographic section etched with alcoholic FeCl3 showing classic α-bronze dendritic structure with coring, interdendritic α + δ eutectoid, sulfide nonmetallic inclusions (nmi), and air pores; bulk composition is tin bronze (ca. 10–15 wt% Sn) (right)

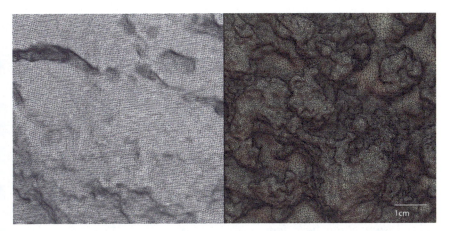

FIGURE 9.3 3D model of nondiagnostic ingot fragment FR 78 (99 wt% Cu), showing bottom surface and side profile; note that both surfaces are flattened due to working (left); metallographic section etched with alcoholic FeCl3 showing classic α-Cu dendritic structure with some coring, interdendritic regions rich in arsenic and sulfur, air pores, and a partially corroded and worked top surface (right)

FIGURE 9.4 3D scanned microtopography of top ingot surfaces; ingot fragment FR 78 with heavy working (left), and oxhide ingot IN 115 with preserved blistery surface and no working (right)

The metallograph depicted in Figure 9.4 (right) shows typical cast structures with a worked surface. The partially corroded surface reveals high microporosity and deformed dendrites of α-copper, best visible with their nearly parallel orientation. The presence of an interdendritic phase rich in arsenic and sulfur shows how slower cooling after casting led to the precipitation of these phases. Arsenic and sulfur content almost certainly comes from the original ores, and these are typical elements associated with chalcopyrite known from the massive sulfide deposits of Cyprus.

5.5 Ingot Fragment FR 359

Ingot fragment FR 359 is another nondiagnostic piece, whose lack of any preserved edge makes it difficult to determine what type of ingot it represents (Fig. 9.5). The fragment exhibits exceptional working on both the top and bottom surfaces, and its exceptional thinness (ca. 0.9 cm) is unique among the oxhide and bun ingots from Cape Gelidonya. Judging from its microstructure, there is only microporosity and little to no intragranular corrosion. Exceptionally long dendrites of α-Cu are evenly dispersed throughout the metallographic section and through the section of the entire fragment, indicating a regular and slow cooling. This is also evinced by the precipitation of interdendritic phases rich in arsenic and sulfur, which are comparable to FR 78.

5.6 Nonmetallic Inclusions

Nonmetallic inclusions are typically precipitations of the original metal composition. These form and disperse as the molten metal cools and provide important insights into the thermodynamics of the smelting, melting, and casting processes. Typically, nonmetallic inclusions can be divided into three separate material types: iron-rich slag inclusions remnant from the original smelting process, copper oxides in the form of cuprite (CuO_2), and sulfides like chalcocite (Cu_2S) and chalcopyrite ($CuFeS_2$). Slag inclusion content is usually dependent on the original smelting technology and/or the time and attention given to further purify the copper with slag removal techniques, during the molten stage or even through hot and cold working of the metal after casting. Slag inclusions will be preserved when excess slags are not removed from the original

FIGURE 9.5   3D model of nondiagnostic ingot fragment FR 359 (99 wt% Cu), showing bottom surface and side profile; note that both surfaces are flattened due to working (left); metallographic section etched with alcoholic FeCl3 showing classic α-Cu dendritic structure with some coring, interdendritic phases rich in arsenic and sulfur, air pores (right)

smelt and are not further removed during the remelting into larger ingots. Oxides like cuprite will develop in the presence of air and come in two types: One forms as corrosion products on the surfaces of the ingots and interdendritically after deposition. The other type develops when excess oxygen is present during the casting process, usually as films on the surface of the pores or, again, interdendritically, as precipitations upon cooling. Sulfide inclusions will also precipitate when excess sulfur is present in the copper melt, and these derive from the use of sulfidic ores, which is a known practice during the Late Bronze Age (Jansen et al. 2017).

Previous analyses of copper ingots from other sites, including especially the late fourteenth-century BCE Uluburun shipwreck site, demonstrate that most ingots are composed of pure copper with significant inclusions of slag and copper oxides (Hauptmann, Maddin, and Prange 2002; Hauptmann, Laschimke, and Burger 2016). The angular slag inclusions present even in large oxhide ingots indicate that they were almost certainly produced by small volumes of copper poured into a large mold multiple times. This suggests that the oxhide ingots were produced as an intermediate step meant primarily to aid in the transport of bulk copper. Oxide inclusions furthermore indicate that the copper of these ingots was remelted from smaller volumes in the presence of air before final casting.

Preliminary analysis of the nonmetallic inclusions in the Cape Gelidonya copper ingot assemblage shows that, contrary to the Uluburun ingots, there are very few slag inclusions. Ingot production techniques must have changed somehow during the century or so separating the two shipwrecks. Additionally, prominent inclusions of copper oxides like cuprite and an increased presence of copper sulfide inclusions suggest that there were changes in smelting technology or ore source. The lead isotope analyses carried out by Stos (mentioned above) suggest the latter. We will investigate this further in a newly formulated collaboration with Moritz Jansen of the University of Pennsylvania Museum of Anthropology, who will conduct copper isotope ratio research at the Deutsches Bergbau Museum in Bochum and Goethe University in Frankfurt, Germany together with Sabine Klein.

5.7   *Isotope Analyses*

Research on copper isotopes is in its beginning stages globally, but we currently know that minute differences in copper isotope composition are directly related to the original mineralogy of the copper, whether oxide or sulfide (Jansen et al. 2018). Since we are beginning to understand that most of the Cape Gelidonya copper ingots were produced from Cypriot copper, we can now start to differentiate the *kinds* of ores producer communities selected and to determine whether or not particular sources were expended or selected over others over time.

Previous analyses by Stos at Oxford University have shown a pattern best seen when comparing ingots and non-ingots (scrap metal, objects, etc.) from the Cape Gelidonya shipwreck (Stos-Gale et al. 1998; Stos 2009: 166–172). All ingots except for one (BI 112, described above) derive from Cypriot ores, most likely the Apliki source in the Solea region. BI 112, a bun ingot composed of a copper-tin alloy and not pure copper like most other ingots, is not compatible with Cypriot ores but rather more consistent with Tauride ores of southern Anatolia. This result, together with the fact that non-ingots show a wide distribution of lead isotope abundance ratios, indicates that whereas the raw copper ingots form a tight cluster around Cyprus, the rest of the metal cargo from the Cape Gelidonya shipwreck was highly varied in terms of metal acquisition networks. These data are compatible with the explanation that the shipwreck likely represents the practice of metal collection and trade across several regions, rather than a single shipment originating in a single place. George Bass's original interpretation, that the Cape Gelidonya cargo belonged to a metal tinker, still holds.

Notably, however, Bass did not examine the fragmented ingots, which represent, by far, the largest constituent of the cargo. The new isotope work in collaboration with Jansen and Klein will test these ideas further, in addition to helping detangle the issue of ore selection and use as it changes during the Bronze Age.

6 Conclusion

Three and a half millennia after their production and more than half a century after the initial discovery on the seabed, the cargo of ingots and ingot fragments from the Cape Gelidonya shipwreck continues to yield new information and provoke further questions. Conservation and detailed recording of each piece, finally to be completed in 2019, for the first time provide a comprehensive catalog of the many and varied constituents of the original shipment. Pending funding, 3D images will be made available online for all to see, helping to improve how archaeological objects are studied remotely. The completion of the catalog provides us the means to sample the assemblage in the most ideal way—across known categories and compositional groups. Building on typological studies undertaken in the 1960s and lead isotope analyses in the 1990s, we have now demonstrated that PXRF, ICP-MS, and metallographic analyses are viable and productive methods for further research of the Cape Gelidonya metal cargo. We will use the results of our pilot program as a basis for seeking further funding to carry out the larger analytical program that we have now developed fully. During our work, we have formed a collaboration that will allow us to add copper isotope analysis to our toolkit. In doing so we hope not only to add to our understanding of the production and distribution processes of this ingot cargo, but also to participate in the development and testing of this new analytical method. Moving forward, especially with our isotope program, we will be able not only to test further the production strategies and provenance of the copper, but also, hopefully, to add ultimately diagnostic nuance to the use life of the ship and how metals fit into the greater picture of the end of the Bronze Age in this dynamic region. The little ship that exemplified the technologies of the Bronze Age continues to contribute to the newest technologies of the twenty-first century.

References

Bass, G.F. 1961. The Cape Gelidonya Wreck: Preliminary Report. *American Journal of Archaeology*, 65(3): 267–276.

Bass, G.F.; Throckmorton, P.; Du Plat Taylor, J.; Shulman, A.R.; and Buchholz, H.-G. 1967. *Cape Gelidonya: A Bronze Age Shipwreck*. Transactions of the American Philosophical Society 57(8). Philadelphia: The American Philosophical Society.

Bass, G. F. 2012. Cape Gelidonya Shipwreck. In Cline, E.H., ed. *The Oxford Handbook of the Bronze Age Aegean*. Oxford: 797–803.

Bass, G.F. 2013. Cape Gelidonya Redux. In: Aruz, J. Graff, S.B., and Rakic, Y., eds. *Cultures in Contact: From Mesopotamia to the Mediterranean in the Second Millennium b.c.* New York: 62–71.

Bass, G.F. and Hirschfeld, N. 2013. Return to Cape Gelidonya. *PASIPHAE. Rivista di Filologia e antichità egee* 7: 99–104.

Begemann, F., Schmitt-Strecker, S., Pernicka, E., and Lo Schiavo, F. 2001. Chemical Composition and Lead Isotopy of Copper and Bronze from Nuragic Sardinia. *European Journal of Archaeology* 4(1): 43–85.

Craddock, P. T. and Meeks, N.D. 1987. Iron in Ancient Copper. *Archaeometry* 29(2): 187–204.

Hauptmann, A., Laschimke, R., and Burger, M. 2016. On the Making of Copper Oxhide Ingots: Evidence from Metallography and Casting Experiments. *Archaeological and Anthropological Sciences* 8(4): 751–761.

Hauptmann, A., Maddin, R., and Prange, M. 2002. On the Structure and Composition of Copper and Tin Ingots Excavated from the Shipwreck of Uluburun. *Bulletin of the American Schools of Oriental Research* 328: 1–30.

Jansen, M., Hauptmann, A., Klein, S., and Seitz, H.-M. 2017. The Potential of Stable Cu Isotopes for the Identification of Bronze Age Ore Mineral Sources from Cyprus and

Faynan: Results from Uluburun and Khirbat Hamra Ifdan. *Archaeological and Anthropological Science* 10(6): 1485–1502. https://doi.org/10.1007/s12520-017-0465-x (accessed February 27, 2019).

Jansen, M., et al. (2018). Copper and lead isotope characterization of Late Bronze Age copper ingots in the Eastern Mediterranean: results from Gelidonya, Gournia, Enkomi and Mathiati. *Bronze Age Metallurgy on Mediterranean Islands: volume in honor of Robert Maddin and Vassos Karageorgis*. A. Giumlia-Mair and F. Lo Schiavo. Autun, Editions Mergoil: 552–577.

Jansen, M., Hauptmann, A., Klein, A., and Seitz, H.-M. 2018. Copper and lead isotope characterization of Late Bronze Age copper ingots in the Eastern Mediterranean: results from Gelidonya, Gournia, Enkomi and Mathiati. In: Giumlia-Mair, A. and Lo Schiavo, F., eds. *Bronze Age Metallurgy on Mediterranean Islands: volume in honor of Robert Maddin and Vassos Karageorgis*. Autun: 552–577.

Kenoyer, J.M. and Miller, H.M.-L. 1999. Metal Technologies of the Indus Valley Tradition in Pakistan and Western India. In: Pigott, V.C., ed. *The Archaeometallurgy of the Asian Old World* (University Museum Monograph 89). Philadelphia: 107–152.

Knapp, A.B. 2000. Archaeology, Science-Based Archaeology and the Mediterranean Bronze Age Metals Trade. *European Journal of Archaeology* 3(1): 31–56.

Kuruçayırlı, E., Lehner, J.W., and Hirschfeld, N. 2017. Gelidonya Burnu Batığı'nın (M.Ö 1200) Metal Kargosu: Bakır Külçelerin Tipolojik ve Arkeometalürjik İncelemesi. *Arkeometri Sonuçları Toplantısı* 33: 229–248.

Moorey, P.R.S., Curtis, J.E., Hook, D.R., and Hughes, M.J. 1988. New Analyses of Old Babylonian Metalwork from Tell Sifr. *Iraq* 50: 39–48.

Maddin, R. and J.D. Muhly. 1974. Some Notes on the Copper Trade in the Ancient Mid-East. *Journal of Metals* 26(5): 24–30.

Muhly, J.D., Stech Wheeler, T., and Maddin, R. 1977. The Cape Gelidonya Shipwreck and the Bronze Age Metals Trade in the Eastern Mediterranean. *Journal of Field Archaeology* 4(3): 353–362.

Stos, Z.A. 2009. Across the Wine Dark Seas ... Sailor Tinkers and Royal Cargoes in the Late Bronze Age Eastern Mediterranean. In: Shortland, A.J., Freestone, I.C., and Rehren, T., eds. *From Mine to Microscope: Advances in the Study of Ancient Technology*. Oxford: 163–180.

Stos-Gale, Z.A., Gale, N.H., Bass, G., Pulak, C., Galli, E., and Sharvit, J. 1998. The Copper and Tin Ingots of the Late Bronze Age Mediterranean: New Scientific Evidence. In: Kimura, H., ed. *The Fourth International Conference on the Beginnings of the Use on* [sic] *Metals and Alloys: May 25–27, 1998, Kunibiki Messe, Matsue, Shimane, Japan* (BUMA-IV). Sendai, Japan: 115–126.

Van Brempt, L. 2016. *The Production and Trade of Cypriot Copper in the Late Bronze Age, from Ore to Ingot: Unraveling the Metallurgical Chain*. Ph.D. dissertation. University of Cyprus. Nicosia.

CHAPTER 10

The Presence of the Past: Ruin Mounds and Social Memory in Bronze and Early Iron Age Israel and Greece

Joseph Maran

1 Introduction

This paper focuses on a communal reference to the past directed toward ancient monuments that from generation to generation were integrated into narratives that elucidated their significance in more or less different ways. By way of example, I will turn to the curious phenomenon of ruins of third- and second-millennium BCE monumental buildings in Israel and Greece that exerted an impact on social memory despite lying seemingly dormant for many centuries and sometimes even—as we shall see—for as long as a millennium.

As sociologist of space Martina Löw (2001: 198–210; 2008) has emphasized, places come into being through the perception of changing arrangements of material objects and living beings, but can continue to exist even after these arrangements have vanished, often through the mere symbolic effects of these arrangements. The 9/11 Memorial in New York City and the Temple Mount in Jerusalem demonstrate how the memory of buildings can be preserved even if—or precisely because—the structures themselves no longer exist. It is the void left by these former buildings that lends significance to their sites and turns them into reference points toward which various forms of social practices are directed. Although the explanation of the meaning of a place may change over the course of time, it is the very act of recollecting and reascribing meaning through social memory and the practices derived from it that make certain places persist for such a long time (Juneja 2009; Cosmopoulos 2015: 162–163).

At Hazor, in northern Israel, the ruins of the Late Bronze Age monumental Building 7050 form the center of the Upper City of the site (Area A) (Ben-Tor et al. 2017: 86–104, 112–130). The building, which was destroyed in the course of the thirteenth century BCE by a fierce conflagration, is interpreted as either a ceremonial palace or a temple (Ben-Tor 2006a, 2013, 2017; Zuckerman 2006, 2010, 2017; Bonfil and Zarzecki-Peleg 2007; Ben-Tor and Zuckerman 2008). Its destruction, which included the mutilation of statues and ritual vessels (Ben-Tor 2006b), is assumed to have been carried out through "a systematic

© KONINKLIJKE BRILL NV, LEIDEN, 2020 | DOI:10.1163/9789004430112_012 annihilation campaign, against the very physical symbols of the royal ideology and its loci of ritual legitimation" (Zuckerman 2007). What is of particular interest here is the way in which the building's ruin was treated after the destruction. After a hiatus of about 150 years (Ben-Ami and Ben-Tor 2012: 24–26; Ben-Tor and Bechar 2017: 3), the plot on which the building had stood saw only minimal construction along its margins, while the center of the ruin was left with no architectural covering during Iron Age I and II (Ben-Ami 2012a: 65–71, 93, pls. 2.1, 2.13, 2.21; 2012b: pls. 3.1, 3.13, 3.22, 3.36; Ben-Ami and Ben-Tor 2012: pl. 1.1; Sandhaus 2012: pls. 4.1, 4.15), despite its central position in the Upper City of Hazor.

When analyzing the remains of Building 7050 one may notice a certain symmetry in the ruin. The height of the stumps of the walls seems to rise from north to south toward the central room, then to drop again from north to south. This symmetry is also observable, albeit less clearly, along the east–west axis, suggesting that, at some point, the burnt debris had been intentionally shaped into a mound. As far as I know, it is unclear how soon after the structure's final destruction this artificial shaping of the ruin took place, but as Doron Ben-Ami,

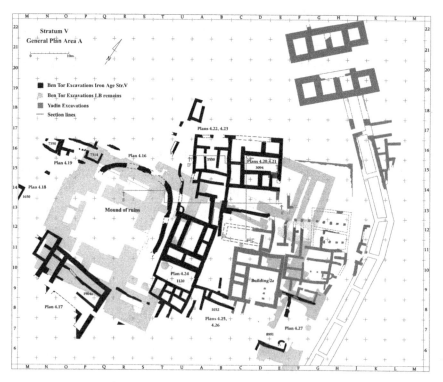

FIGURE 10.1   Hazor (Israel), Area A; plan of Stratum V with the Building 7050 ruin mound
AFTER SANDHAUS 2012: PL. 4.15

Amnon Ben-Tor, and Deborah Sandhaus have demonstrated, there can be no doubt that most of the "mound of ruins" was deliberately left uninhabited by the onset of the Iron Age (Ben-Ami and Ben-Tor 2012: 26; Sandhaus 2012: 286, 306; Ben-Ami 2013). All three have interpreted this as indication of a special attitude toward the place, one possibly paired with some sort of formal prohibition on building on top of it. This may, in fact, explain why the mound in Stratum V was finally encircled by a wall (Fig. 10.1). Sharon Zuckerman (2011: 393) has therefore argued that the remains of Late Bronze Age Hazor "became part of a value-laden ancestral landscape, rich in meaning for the societies living within it. People who frequented the site treated the ruins with awe, which materialized in ritual activities performed amidst the ruins. These activities might be understood as acts of appropriation of the remains, and their constant reinvention and reinterpretation was later to be incorporated into a vivid biblical narrative of the fate of a once magnificent political and religious Canaanite center."

2   The Hazor Building 7050 Ruin Mound and Early Helladic "Ritual Tumuli"

In the context of the southern Levantine Bronze Age, the shaping of a mound out of the remains of Hazor Building 7050 seems to be highly unusual, but the practice bears a striking resemblance to the ways in which the ruins of certain monumental buildings of Early Helladic and Mycenaean Mainland Greece were treated. The closest parallels lie in some of the so-called ritual tumuli (Forsén 1992: 36–37) of the Early Helladic period in the Peloponnese. Although the term "tumulus" unfortunately bears connotations of funerary structures (Weiberg 2007: 154), such ritual tumuli were not constructed for funerary purposes, but rather served as foci for forms of social communication the nature of which we are not yet in a position to specify. The best-known example of such is the House of the Tiles tumulus at Lerna. The House of the Tiles was the first identified example of the architectural type of the Early Helladic Corridor House, after which the second half of the Early Helladic (EH) II phase (ca. 2500–2200 BCE) was named "Period of the Corridor Houses" (Wiencke 1989). After the destruction of the House of the Tiles, a tumulus was modeled out of its ruin and bordered by a circle of stones at the end of EH II (Banks 2013: 23–31). The way in which the ruin was artificially shaped into a tumulus closely resembles the situation at Hazor, as the height of the stumps of the building's walls clearly rises toward the center before dropping symmetrically on either side, along both the north–south and west–east axes. While the perimeter of the mound was not significantly encroached on by building activities in the first subphase of the ensuing phase EH III settlement, it was covered by houses several decades later (Banks 2013: 31). Elizabeth Banks (2013: 31) thus concluded that, contrary to the assumptions of the excavator John L. Caskey (1956: 165; 1986: 14), the EH III inhabitants did not construct the tumulus out of reverence for the House of the Tiles. Even if correct, her claim does not exclude the possibility that the tumulus became the focus of social memory much later. This indeed seems to have been the case, as two shaft graves—by far the most elaborate funerary structures of Early Mycenaean Lerna—were dug within or very close to the perimeter of the House of the Tiles tumulus. This suggests that some sort of awareness of the existence of the 500-year-old tumulus must have survived (Whittaker 2014: 200; Maran 2016: 161). I would therefore agree with Erika Weiberg (2007: 170), who states that "the mound would have continued for some time to be a marker of the area and, as such, a likely focus for at least oral tradition as a visual preservation of the historicity of the site."

Until a few decades ago, the House of the Tiles tumulus appeared to be a singular case. Since then, however, similar Early Helladic "ritual tumuli" formed out of ruins have come to light at Thebes in Boeotia and Tiryns in the Argolid. Another example of such a tumulus, at Olympia, was not shaped out of a ruin but rather built of soil and stones.

A large apsidal building with three rooms was uncovered during the construction of the extension of the Archaeological Museum of Thebes, which is situated at the northern edge of the Kadmeia, the old town of Thebes (Fig. 10.2). The building, which dates to late EH II and is bordered on the north and east by a fortification wall, probably served both private and public functions (Aravantinos and Psaraki 2011a: 409–410; Psaraki 2014). Although there is no evidence of a previous conflagration, the structure seems to have been abandoned. After some of its mud-brick walls had already started collapsing, the bodies of at least twelve individuals were buried together in the southeast corner of its central room and the southwest corner of its east room (Aravantinos and Psaraki 2011a: 403; 2011b: 285). The dead do not seem to have been buried with particular care, but they did receive grave furnishings that point to a date toward late EH II. According to Aravantinos and Psaraki (2011a: 403–404), "directly after the abandonment of the house and the mass burial, solid layers of mud bricks were laid carefully, filling the space between the upper structure of the defensive wall and the surviving walls of both the apsidal building and the other outdoor constructions. ... The surviving shape of the mound gives the impression of a terrace of approximately 800 sq. m., which slopes to the northwest and to the north." There is no indication that the mud-brick mound, which I shall call the "Apsidal Building tumulus," was encircled by a wall or row of stones. The northern part of the Apsidal Building tumulus uncovered by

THE PRESENCE OF THE PAST 181

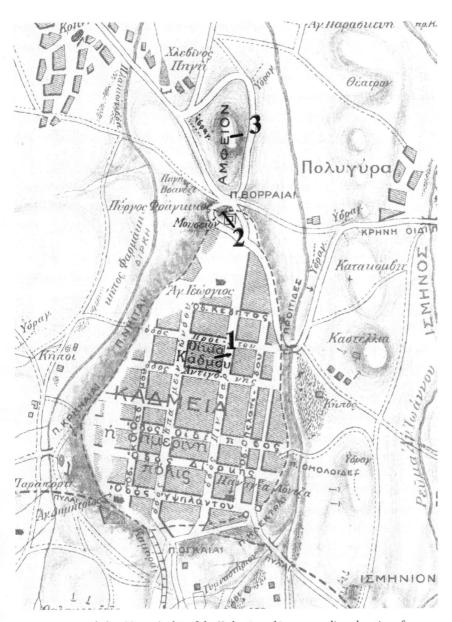

FIGURE 10.2   Thebes (Greece); plan of the Kadmeia and its surroundings; location of monuments mentioned in the text: (1) House of Kadmos ruin mound; (2) Apsidal Building mound; (3) Ampheion tumulus
AMENDED AFTER KERAMOPOULLOS 1917

the excavation, which was used as a burial plot in Middle Helladic times (Aravantinos and Psaraki 2011a: 404; 2011b: 285–287), was flattened in the Late Helladic period and built over by a fortification wall in Late Helladic (LH) IIIA–B

(Aravantinos and Psaraki 2011a: 404). In light of this evidence, it is likely that the uncovered part of the Apsidal Building tumulus was intentionally spared any overbuilding between EH III and the early Mycenaean Palatial period because of the respect it commanded as a monument (Aravantinos and Psaraki 2011b: 288; Psaraki 2014: 100–101).

The Apsidal Building tumulus was constructed at the end of EH II immediately opposite the already existing tumulus on the Ampheion Hill (Fig. 10.2: nos. 2 and 3, respectively), which was likewise built of mud bricks and lies about 150 m to the north of the Kadmeia, from which it is separated by a narrow valley (Spyropoulos 1981; Aravantinos and Psaraki 2011a: 405–407). The Ampheion tumulus is not attributed here to the group of ritual tumuli, as it was used from late EH I or early EH II on as a marker of regular burials, whereas the Apsidal Building tumulus served as a marker of both a building and an extraordinary mass burial (Aravantinos and Psaraki 2011a: 406–408). Both tumuli, however, are closely related not only through their manner of construction but also by their position (Aravantinos and Psaraki 2011a: 408; Konsola 2014: 94). The Apsidal Building tumulus lies on the hill of the so-called Frankish Tower, also known as the "first hill" of four separate hilltops within the Kadmeia of Thebes (Keramopoullos 1909: 107–111; Dakouri 1998: 10–14). The first hill rises on the northern end of the Kadmeia, above the valley that separates it from the Ampheion Hill. Evidence of Early Helladic and Mycenaean fortification walls built independently of each other at the same point suggests that the area of the first hill formed the northern border of the respective settlements of the Kadmeia by the third and second millennia BCE. Based on their topographical positions, between EH III and LH III both tumuli must have been visible from a distance to visitors who approached Thebes from the north, and must have appeared as twin monuments from various vantage points. Daniel W. Berman (2004: 17–19) has argued that the myth of the founding of Thebes by Amphion and Zethus may go back to Mycenaean times and be older than that of the foundation of Kadmos. This makes it possible that, at some point in the second millennium BCE, the two opposing tumuli were identified as the graves of the legendary twin founders. In this context it would be helpful to know how long the Apsidal Building Tumulus retained its symbolic meaning after the construction of the fortification wall on top of it during the Mycenaean Palatial period. In the fifth century BCE at the latest, literary sources speak of a grave of Amphion (Berman 2015: 82–84; see, also, Kühr 2006: 126–127), while Pausanias mentions a grave of Amphion and Zethus that scholars since Antonios D. Keramopoullos (1917: 383–385, 460) have identified as the Ampheion tumulus (Spyropoulos 1981: 28–34; Symeonoglou 1985: 192–193; Loucas and Loucas 1987; Aravantinos and Psaraki 2011b: 280; Berman 2015:

83, 99, 154). The fact that these sources do not mention a separate grave of Zethus (Berman 2015: 99 with n. 63) may indicate that the Apsidal Building Tumulus was already forgotten by the classical period, at the latest, and only the Ampheion tumulus was remembered as the grave of the mythical founders.

The extremely long duration of certain social memory patterns attached to Early Helladic ritual tumuli is best exemplified by the sanctuary of Olympia. A long discussion surrounds the question of whether the major Greek sanctuaries of the early first millennium BCE date back to Mycenaean times or were established only later. To answer this question, research has generally relied on evidence that suggests continuity in cult practices from Mycenaean times. In the last two decades, however, new discoveries at Olympia have underlined the need to consider far more subtle links to the past that do not necessarily manifest themselves in a continuity of cult practices and are based on concepts of time that differ greatly from archaeological chronologies. Although the beginnings of the sanctuary of Olympia do not seem to date back to the Mycenaean period (Eder 2006), as was once believed, there is good reason to assume that those who founded the sanctuary in the tenth century BCE perceived it as standing in a direct line of continuity with the distant past. As the excavations under the direction of Helmut Kyrieleis (2002, 2006) have shown, the sanctuary of Olympia was probably founded at a site of an EH II ritual tumulus that had not been formed from an architectural ruin, but rather of a mound of earth bordered by row of stones. When the sanctuary was established in the Protogeometric period, the Pelopion tumulus was already over 1,000 years old and only partly visible because it had been covered by EH III and Middle Helladic houses as well as alluvial deposits. All the same, the preserved parts of the tumulus that were not destroyed or covered by buildings or alluvial sediments were sufficiently prominent to be chosen as the focal point of the sanctuary of the so-called Altis many centuries later. The architectural reference of the Pelopion temenos to the Early Helladic tumulus proves beyond doubt the intentionality of the choice of the much older monument's location as the core of the sanctuary. Kyrieleis (2002: 216–218; 2006 25–27, 55–62) has persuasively argued that certain narrative traditions associated with the tumulus must have enabled its integration into new mythological contexts and led to its identification as a grave of a hero, around which the sanctuary was founded, which in Archaic times at latest came to be associated with the mythical hero Pelops (Kyrieleis 2006: 55–61; Ekroth 2012).

The recent reinterpretation of old excavation evidence from Tiryns suggests that the case of Olympia is unlikely to be an isolated phenomenon (Maran 2016). As is well known, the successive Mycenaean Great Megara of the fourteenth and thirteenth centuries BCE were built exactly on the same spot, one on which the Early Helladic Rundbau had stood over 800 years earlier. Thanks to recent research by Peter Marzolff (2004, 2009), it is possible to distinguish two phases of this building's history. During the first, the architects seem to have intended to build a strong tower whose façade was structured by means of carefully built buttresses. During the second, which followed a conflagration, the buttresses were concealed by a massive mud-brick wall, ca. 4.5 m wide, that surrounded an inner circular wall. According to Marzolff (2009: 186–187), the massive mud-brick wall need not have served as a load-bearing element, but rather as a sort of glacis. Until recently and based on a similar line of reasoning, I attributed the correspondence between the position of the Rundbau and the Great Megaron to decisions made independently of each other in Early Helladic and Mycenaean times. Situated on the highest topographical point of the hill, the monumental structures ensured the greatest possible visibility, which, too, contributed to their importance. This strategic factor can certainly still be deemed important, but what seems likelier now is a significantly more intricate and indirect link between these two monuments from vastly different eras. As at Lerna, so here it seems that after the destruction of the circular building around 2200 BCE, a hitherto unrecognized tumulus was formed out of the ruins and encircled by a stone wall (Maran 2016: 160–166). In this respect it is even possible that the Rundbau's second building phase was already part of the structure's transformation into a tumulus, as the concealment of the Rundbau's buttresses by a glacis-like mud-brick structure recalls the way in which the apsidal building in Thebes was turned into a tumulus through the filling of its open spaces with mud bricks.[1]

The Rundbau tumulus served as a major point of reference for social memory from EH III through the Middle Helladic and Early Mycenaean periods, making it a decisive link between the far-apart eras of the Early Helladic "Period of the Corridor Houses" and the Mycenaean Palatial period (Maran 2016: 166–169). The tumulus must have stood as a recognizable monument at least until the early Mycenaean period, when, at some point between the seventeenth and fifteenth centuries BCE, the construction of buildings slowly began to encroach on the tumulus and at least one Early Mycenaean cist grave was cut into its foundations. Subsequently, in the fourteenth century BCE the ruling Mycenaean elite decided to instrumentalize the remains of the tumulus for new political ends by drawing on the discourses associated with it. By placing the central structure of the palace directly above the tumulus, the architects

---

[1] This possibility occurred to me only after the publication of Maran 2016.

were able to integrate it visually into a long chain of tradition (Maran 2016: 167–169).

3   The Memorialization of Mycenaean Palatial Ruin Mounds

There is no indication that the Rundbau tumulus was still remembered after the first Great Megaron was built over it. The very ruins of Mycenaean palaces, however, sometimes became focal points of social memory.[2] After the total destruction of the last palace at Tiryns at the end of LH IIIB, only the area of the Great Megaron and its court were reclaimed in new architectural plans. Building T rose in the eastern portion of the ruins of the Great Megaron, while the palatial round altar in the Great Court was transformed into a square platform (Maran 2001). Prior to the construction of Building T, the still upright walls of the eastern and western palatial wings were demolished and the remaining ruins of the palace were leveled (Maran 2012). This left Building T surrounded on three sides by the shallow mound of the palace ruins (Fig. 10.3), which remained visible in the Iron Age and became the focus of those cult practices in the Great Court that led to the second reconstruction of the altar (Müller 1930: 137–139) and the deposition of cult paraphernalia in the so-called bothros (Gercke 1975: 159–161). There is no evidence that the Tiryns palace ruin mound was carefully shaped in the same way as the ruin mounds at Lerna or Hazor, nor does it seem to have been encircled by a row of stones or a wall. All the same, the ruin mound of the palace at Tiryns was also not built over in classical antiquity, and even Byzantine construction does not seem to have interfered with it. This also explains why in many areas Schliemann found the remains of the heavily burnt palace right below the surface (Schliemann 1886: 8–9). It seems as though the intention was to preserve the palace ruin mound in the condition that it had retained since the Late Mycenaean period. In contrast to Hazor, however, the entire acropolis at Tiryns seems to have been turned into a place of memory left largely uninhabited between the early Iron Age and Roman times.

Another example of a reference to past ruins lies in a palatial Mycenaean building complex, destroyed in a conflagration, that Keramopoullos uncovered at the center of the Kadmeia of Thebes and called the "House of Kadmos" (Figs. 10.2: no. 1; 10.4; Keramopoullos 1909, 1917: 338–340; Symeonoglou 1985:

---

2 The case of Megaron B at Eleusis, excellently studied by Cosmopoulos 2015: 132–151, 162–166, demonstrates that nonpalatial Mycenaean buildings, too, sometime became reference points for social memory many centuries later.

FIGURE 10.3   Tiryns (Greece); palace ruin mound with Building T; situation in 1908
AMENDED AFTER MÜLLER 1930: PL. 31

40–47; Dimakopoulou and Konsola 1995: 23; Dakouri 1998; Dakouri-Hild 2001). In this way he identified the ruin with the building that had been destroyed, according to Greek literary tradition, when Zeus revealed himself to Semele, who was then consumed by the flames ignited by Zeus's lightning, while the infant Dionysus, to whom Semele was about to give birth, was saved by the god (Symeonoglou 1985: 40–47; Moggi and Osanna 2010: 287–290; Berman 2015: 103–104). According to this tradition, the burnt palace of Kadmos was subsequently maintained as an open-air sanctuary dedicated to Dionysus (Symeonoglou 1985: 45–46; Kühr 2006: 221–222, 248–250; Berman 2015: 23–24, 103–104). Inside it lay the remains of a building with the bridal chambers of Semele and Harmonia, Kadmos's wife, which were regarded as ἄβατον (*abaton*), that is, closed to visitors due to their sanctity (Keramopoullos 1909: 114–115 with n. 1; Symeonoglou 1985: 45–47; Moggi and Osanna 2010: 288–289; Berman 2015: 153).

It is indeed quite likely that the ruin of the structure uncovered by Keramopoullos, which, in its present state, measures approximately 40 × 15 m (Dakouri-Hild 2001: 84), was intentionally preserved as such after the building's destruction, even if the explanations for its survival in Mycenaean times may have been quite different from those offered by the later literary tradition. To this day visitors are surprised at the height of the ruins of the House of Kadmos, which are situated at approximately the same elevation as a Frankish building a few meters to the south and rise so far above the modern horizon that it is nearly impossible to believe that they are the remains of a building that is over 3,000 years old (Fig. 10.4). Two reasons lie behind this situation: first, the House of Kadmos was built on the "second hill"—one of the four hilltops of the Kadmeia—which means that the building was situated on a topographically higher level than were the other contemporary, or even later, palatial buildings around it (Keramopoullos 1909: 107–111; Dakouri 1998: 1–14; Dakouri-Hild 2010: 698); second, the ruin of the House of Kadmos was not covered with buildings after its destruction, probably in LH IIIB1 (Dakouri-Hild 2001: 95–101 with further literature). Keramopoullos was surprised that throughout the excavation he did not encounter any architectural remains from the Mycenaean period or classical antiquity above this ruin (Keramopoullos 1909: 111–112). The ruin was not even torn down in the Byzantine era (Keramopoullos 1909: 119–120). According to Keramopoullos's convincing explanation of this highly unusual situation, the remains were intentionally preserved as a monument after the building's destruction. Today we can specify that the ruin was neither dismantled nor overbuilt in the Final Palatial period (LH IIIB2), and that people held on to this resolve in LH IIIC and all of post-Mycenaean antiquity despite the site's centrality within the topography of the Kadmeia. Only a deliberate

FIGURE 10.4   Thebes (Greece); view (from south) of the House of Kadmos ruin, medieval architecture, and surrounding modern buildings of the Kadmeia
PHOTO BY MELANIE STRUB, MARCH 2017

decision not to touch the ruin can explain the fact that traces of burnt construction material (mud bricks, lime, clay, and wood) are still preserved here and there at a significant height above the stone socles of the walls (Dakouri 1998: 40–41; Dakouri-Hild 2001: pls. 15: a, b; 18: a, c). Such remains would have been removed or damaged by any attempt to build on top of this plot (Keramopoullos 1909: 112). The condition of the building's walls likewise suggests that the remains of the House of Kadmos must have risen as a mound from the surrounding terrain, which, given its exposed position on the "second hill," must have been highly visible. The House of Kadmos ruin mound also does not seem to have been encircled by a stone row or a wall, and, in contrast to Hazor and Lerna, the preserved heights of the house's walls do not suggest that their ruins were molded into a mound with sloping sides. Rather, the ruin mound seems to have had a rather amorphous contour. The difference in its appearance from Early Helladic ritual tumuli or Hazor Building 7050 ruin mound may be linked to the wish to preserve not simply a mound, but a ruin of a building identifiable as such centuries after its destruction (Keramopoullos 1909: 114).

4   Ruin Mounds and Social Memory

Of the Bronze Age monuments presented here (Table 10.1), with the exception of the Pelopion tumulus at Olympia, all were shaped out of the ruins of large buildings. Major conflagrations were the cause behind the destruction of most of these buildings. Only in the case of the Thebes Apsidal Building are there no signs of destruction, though even here the mass burial in the building points to a disaster prior to the construction of the tumulus. This suggests that any association between buildings and dramatic local events increased the likelihood of remembrance by later generations. In the case of the Thebes Apsidal Building tumulus, additional mud bricks were used for constructing the tumulus and filling the interstices between walls. This construction method offers a link to the Thebes Ampheion tumulus, a monument that served funerary purposes. If the second building phase of the Rundbau already formed part of the tumulus construction, then we have evidence of the use of mud bricks at Tiryns as well. In the case of Hazor and some Early Helladic ritual tumuli, ruins were carefully shaped into mounds with sloping sides, generally delimited from their surroundings by a circular row of stones or a wall (Hazor Building 7050 ruin mound [since Stratum V], Lerna House of the Tiles tumulus, Tiryns Rundbau tumulus), though sometimes without such a boundary (Thebes Apsidal Building tumulus). Neither example of a preserved ruin of a Mycenaean palace discussed here (Tiryns palace ruin mound, Thebes House of

TABLE 10.1 Comparative chart of the monuments discussed in this article

Monument	Date	Destruction by fire	Date	Shape of mound	Burials	Building above	Visibility
Olympia Tumulus	EH II	–	EH II	Earth tumulus encircled by row of stones	–	EH III (partly)	?
Lerna House of the Tiles	Late EH II	x	EH II/III	Ruin shaped into mound, encircled by wall	LH I	EH III (partly)	x
Thebes Apsidal Building	Late EH II	–	EH II/III	Mud-brick mound over ruin	MH	LH	x
Tiryns Rundbau	Late EH II	x	EH III	Ruin shaped into mound, encircled by stone wall	LH I–II	LH	x
Hazor Building 7050	13th c. BCE	x	LBA/Iron	Ruin shaped into mound, encircled by wall	–	Iron II	x

TABLE 10.1 Comparative chart of the monuments discussed in this article (cont.)

Monument	Date	Destruction by fire	Date	Shape of mound	Burials	Building above	Visibility
Thebes House of Kadmos	LH IIIB1	x	–	Ruin unshaped	–	–	x
Tiryns Palace	LH IIIB2	x	–	Ruin shaped into flattened, irregular mound	–	LH IIIC	x

Kadmos ruin mound) reveals evidence of either careful shaping or a stone boundary. Both were given not a symmetrical but rather an amorphous contour. In the case of the House of Kadmos, this may have been done in order to preserve the impression of the building's ruin for future generations. Due to the discovery of the mass burial, the Thebes Apsidal Building tumulus is the only one of the cases examined here that stands at the threshold between a ritual and a funerary tumulus. The singularity of this burial and the size of the mud-brick mound support, in my opinion, the excavators' conclusion that the monument belongs within the group of Early Helladic ritual tumuli.

Once the particular mounds discussed here were shaped into their form, nothing was built over their core area for a long time (Hazor Building 7050 ruin mound, Thebes Apsidal Building tumulus and House of Kadmos ruin mound, and Tiryns Rundbau tumulus and palace ruin mound). Elsewhere, mounds were covered with buildings soon after their construction (Olympia Pelopion tumulus, Lerna House of the Tiles tumulus). Remarkably, in three cases (Thebes Apsidal Building tumulus, Lerna House of the Tiles tumulus, and Tiryns Rundbau tumulus) Middle Helladic and/or Early Mycenaean burials were cut into them long after the mounds were shaped. The Tiryns palace ruin mound offers the sole example of a building (Building T) that was built into a ruin and stood surrounded by a ruin mound. Due to their position on topographically exposed hilltops, nearly all the monuments presented here (Hazor Building 7050 ruin mound, Tiryns Rundbau tumulus and palace ruin mound, Thebes Apsidal Building mound, and House of Kadmos ruin mound) enjoyed wide visibility, thereby increasing the likelihood that they served as points of reference in later periods. Only the Olympia Pelopion tumulus was situated not on a hill but in an alluvial plain; yet, the fact that it rose from relatively flat surroundings also guaranteed it a certain degree of visibility.

The foundation of a sanctuary referring to the Olympia Pelopion tumulus, the construction of the central palatial buildings over the Tiryns Rundbau tumulus, and the cutting of Middle Helladic or Early Mycenaean graves into the Thebes Apsidal Building tumulus, the Tiryns Rundbau tumulus, and the Lerna House of the Tiles tumulus are all indications that such monuments were capable of exerting an impact on social memory in periods separated by extremely long intervals. This was the case at Lerna and Olympia even though the tumuli were extensively covered by architecture and/or alluvial deposits. Such long-term impact conflicts with notions of linear evolution and continuity prevalent in archaeology. Were we unaware of the Pelopion temenos, we would probably not have considered the possibility of a link between monuments separated by nearly a millennium based solely on the available archaeological evidence, as in the centuries immediately following the construction of the ritual tumuli, these monuments were not always respected and were thus gradually covered by buildings and natural sediments. Still, what was left of them, combined with at least a residual awareness of their significance, seems to have been enough to provoke discourses on their meaning many centuries later (Aravantinos and Psaraki 2011a: 409–410).

Obviously, the way in which society constructs and reconstructs the past does not follow a linear trajectory. As Maurice Halbwachs (1992: 46–53) already recognized, what remains of the past is only what a society at a given moment can recollect within its particular frame of reference. What and how it remembers and how it relates to it, is assessed differently from generation to generation. As in the case of social memory in general, an analysis of the relation between monuments and the formation of social memory has been impeded by the focus of research on undifferentiated collectives and the integrative effects of social memory. The notion of architecture serving as a "storage of memory" (Assmann 1999, 2006) or a "lieu de mémoire" (Nora 1984) has tended to essentialize the relation between memory, monuments, and collective identities, and to emphasize the integrative role of sites, architecture, and landscapes for society at large. At the same time, however, it disregards or downplays the contested, antagonistic, and often exclusionary ways in which such memory is constructed in intersocietal practices and discourses by groups with marked differences in resources, power, and interests (Juneja 2009: 12–36; Maran 2011). The ambiguity of social memory as an arena in which integrative and divisive intersocietal currents clash becomes especially apparent in the memorialization of past monuments, which encompasses a material engagement with ruins and abandoned places as sites of the active creation of social memory. From generation to generation and from group to group, such monuments are integrated into narratives that explain their significance in more or less different ways, thereby making the coexistence of disparate explanations for them a distinct possibility. Depending on intersocietal discourses in which the past is recollected, features once regarded as important may recede into the background or even sink into seeming oblivion. Through narrative traditions and the physical recognition of monuments, however, seemingly forgotten features may suddenly be reinvigorated and turn into important factors, because faced with new social and political circumstances, certain groups may assign them significance. As they are closely tied to specific social and political circumstances, the explanations arising from their memorialization are subject to constant change; certain views prevail while others are marginalized or excluded. It is therefore crucial to stress the dynamic, fluid, and contested character of processes that allow for the coexistence of different constructs of the past (Juneja 2009). At various times, mounds at Olympia, Lerna, Thebes, and Tiryns may have been regarded as graves of historical or mythical beings (cf. Pelops at Olympia, Amphion and Zethus at Thebes), or as the remains of a palace or temple destroyed during mythical events, as is documented, for example, by the identification of the House of Kadmos ruin mound and its designation as *abaton* due to its sanctity in classical literary tradition. The perceived sacred nature of the events commemorated may also have led to a ban on inhabiting the Hazor Building 7050 ruin mound (Ben-Ami and Ben-Tor 2012: 26), though such a decision may also have been motivated by the sacrilegious nature of the event that provoked the destruction, as, for example, the wrath of the gods. The spatial and visual interrelation between the Ampheion tumulus and the Apsidal Building tumulus in Thebes also serves as a reminder that when it came to the narratives linked to these two monuments it was not that important whether they had originally belonged to a leveled building or to a funerary or ritual tumulus. Moreover, the faithful transmission of a specific meaning was not all that crucial to the long-term preservation of the monument's memory. What counted was the fact that people recognized these monuments as something special and tried to bestow meaning upon them by integrating them into narratives. Irrespective of the specific explanations given to these monuments, their physical presence alone was a decisive factor in authenticating the explanations assigned to them.

Acknowledgements

Michal Artzy has championed an approach that assesses the archaeology of the Bronze and Iron Ages of Israel in its broader Mediterranean setting. In this way she was able to gain new insight into patterns of connectivity that linked distant societies. Thank you, Michal, for the many years of your friendship and inspiration! I am indebted to the late and much-missed Sharon Zuckerman for introducing me to beautiful Hazor and for many creative discussions. I thank Debby Sandhaus and Vasilis Aravantinos for valuable advice and information. Amnon Ben-Tor generously allowed the reproduction of the plan of Hazor Stratum v, for which I am grateful. In this article I follow the Iron Age chronology used in the Hazor series. I would like to thank Sveta Matskevich, who gave me the idea for Table 10.1 and designed it. Special thanks go to Irina Oryshkevich for improving the English of this article and to Maria Kostoula for preparing and remastering the illustrations included in the article.

References

Aravantinos, V., and Psaraki, K. 2011a. Mounds over Dwellings: The Transformation of Domestic Spaces into Community Monuments in EH II Thebes, Greece. In Borgna, E. and Müller-Celka, S., eds. *Ancestral Landscapes: Burial Mounds in the Copper and Bronze Ages (Central and Eastern Europe–Balkans–Adriatic–Aegean, 4th–2nd millennium B.C.). Proceedings of the International Conference Held in Udine, May 15th–18th 2008* (Travaux de la Maison de l'Orient 58). Lyon: 401–413.

Aravantinos, V., and Psaraki, K. 2011b. Οι Πρωτοελλαδικοί Τύμβοι της Θήβας (The Early Helladic Tumuli of Thebes). In: Katsanopoulou, D., ed. *Helike IV: Ancient Helike and Aigialeia. Protohelladika: The Southern and Central Greek Mainland*. Athens: 279–293.

Assmann, A. 1999. *Erinnerungsräume: Formen und Wandlungen des kulturellen Gedächtnisses*. Munich.

Assmann, A. 2006. *Der lange Schatten der Vergangenheit: Erinnerungskultur und Geschichtspolitik*. Munich.

Banks, E.C. 2013. *Lerna, a Preclassical Site in the Argolid*, Vol. 6: *The Settlement and Architecture of Lerna IV*. Princeton.

Ben-Ami, D. 2012a. The Early Iron Age II (Strata X–IX). In: Ben-Tor, A., Ben-Ami, D., and Sandhaus, D. eds. *Hazor 6: The 1990–2009 Excavations. The Iron Age*. Jerusalem: 52–153.

Ben-Ami, D. 2012b. The Iron Age II (Strata VIII–VII). In: Ben-Tor, A., Ben-Ami, D., and Sandhaus, D. eds. *Hazor 6: The 1990–2009 Excavations. The Iron Age*. Jerusalem: 154–285.

Ben-Ami, D. 2013. Hazor at the Beginning of the Iron Age. *Near Eastern Archaeology* 76(2): 101–104.

Ben-Ami, D. and Ben-Tor, A. 2012. The Iron Age I (Stratum "XII/XI"): Stratigraphy and Pottery. In: Ben-Tor, A., Ben-Ami, D., and Sandhaus, D. eds. *Hazor 6: The 1990–2009 Excavations. The Iron Age*. Jerusalem: 7–51.

Ben-Tor, A. 2006a. Ceremonial Palace, Not a Temple. *Biblical Archaeology Review* 32(5): 8, 78–79.

Ben-Tor, A. 2006b. The Sad Fate of Statues and the Mutilated Statues of Hazor. In: Gitin, S., Wright, J.E., and Dessel, J.P., eds. *Confronting the Past: Archaeological and Historical Essays on Ancient Israel in Honor of William G. Dever*. Winona Lake, IN: 3–16.

Ben-Tor, A. 2013. The Ceremonial Precinct in the Upper City of Hazor. *Near Eastern Archaeology* 76(2): 81–91.

Ben-Tor, A. 2017. A Ceremonial Palace, Not a Temple. In: Ben-Tor, A., Zuckerman, S., Bechar, S., and Sandhaus, D., eds. *Hazor 7: The 1990–2012 Excavations. The Bronze Age*. Jerusalem: 139–140.

Ben-Tor, A. Ben-Tor, A. and Bechar, S. 2017. Introduction. In: Ben-Tor, A., Zuckerman, S., Bechar, S., and Sandhaus, D., eds. *Hazor 7: The 1990–2012 Excavations. The Bronze Age*. Jerusalem: 1–3.

Ben-Tor, A., and Zuckerman, S. 2008. Hazor at the End of the Late Bronze Age: Back to Basics. *Bulletin of the American Schools of Oriental Research* 350: 1–6.

Ben-Tor, A., Zuckerman, S., Bechar, S., Bonfil, R., Weinblatt, D., and Sandhaus, D. 2017. The Late Bronze Age. In: Ben-Tor, A., Zuckerman, S., Bechar, S., and Sandhaus, D., eds. *Hazor 7: The 1990–2012 Excavations. The Bronze Age*. Jerusalem: 66–144.

Berman, D.W. 2004. The Double Foundation of Boiotian Thebes. *Transactions of the American Philological Association* 134: 1–22.

Berman, D.W. 2015. *Myth, Literature, and the Creation of the Topography of Thebes*. Cambridge.

Bonfil, R. and Zarzecki-Peleg, A. 2007. The Palace in the Upper City of Hazor as an Expression of a Syrian Architectural Paradigm. *Bulletin of the American Schools of Oriental Research* 348: 25–47.

Caskey, J.L. 1956. Excavations at Lerna, 1955. *Hesperia* 25: 147–173.

Caskey, J.L. 1986. Did the Early Bronze Age End? In: Cadogan, G., ed. *The End of the Early Bronze Age in the Aegean* (Cincinnati Classical Studies, N.S. 6). Leiden: 9–30.

Cosmopoulos, M.B. 2015. *Bronze Age Eleusis and the Origins of the Eleusinian Mysteries*. Cambridge.

Dakouri, A.C. 1998. *The House of Kadmos at Mycenaean Thebes: A Preliminary Re-Examination of the Architecture*. MA thesis. Durham University. Durham. http://etheses.dur.ac.uk/4747/ (accessed March 30, 2019).

Dakouri-Hild, A. 2001. The House of Kadmos in Mycenaean Thebes Reconsidered: Architecture, Chronology, and Context. *The Annual of the British School at Athens* 96: 81–122.

Dakouri-Hild, A. 2010. Thebes. In: Cline, E.H., ed. *The Oxford Handbook of the Bronze Age Aegean*. Oxford: 690–711.

Dimakopoulou, K. and Konsola, D. 1995. Αρχαιολογικό Μουσείο της Θήβας—Οδηγός (Archaeological Museum of Thebes: Guide). Athens.

Eder, B. 2006. Die spätbronze- und früheisenzeitliche Keramik. In: Kyrieleis, H., ed. *Olympia 1875–2000. 125 Jahre deutsche Ausgrabungen. Internationales Symposion, Berlin 9.–11. November 2000*. Mainz: 141–246.

Ekroth, G. 2012. Pelops Joins the Party: Transformations of a Hero Cult within the Festival at Olympia. In: Brandt, J.R. and Iddeng, J.W., eds. *Greek and Roman Festivals: Content, Meaning, and Practice*. Oxford: 95–137.

Forsén, J. 1992. *The Twilight of the Early Helladics: A Study of Disturbances in East-Central and Southern Greece towards the End of the Early Bronze Age* (Studies in Mediterranean Archaeology, Pocket Book 116). Jonsered.

Gercke, P. 1975. Die Geometrische Keramik. In: Jantzen, U., ed. *Führer durch Tiryns*. Athens: 155–161.

Halbwachs, M. 1992. *On Collective Memory*. Chicago–London.

Juneja, M. 2009. Architectural Memory between Representation and Practice: Rethinking Pierre Nora's *Les lieux de mémoire*. In: Sengupta, I., ed. *Memory, History, and Colonialism: Engaging with Pierre Nora in Colonial and Postcolonial Contexts* (German Historical Institute London Bulletin Supplement 1). London: 11–36.

Keramopoullos, A.D. 1909. Η οικία του Κάδμου (The House of Kadmos). *Archaiologike Ephemeris* 1909: 57–122.

Keramopoullos, A.D. 1917. Θηβαϊκά (Thebaika). *Archaiologikon Deltion* 3: 1–503.

Konsola, D. 2014. Η πρωτοελλαδική Θήβα. Επισκόπηση και αξιολόγηση των ερευνών (Early Helladic Thebes. Overview and Assessment of the Finds). In: Aravantinos V. and Kountouri, E., eds. *100 Χρόνια Αρχαιολογικού Έργου στη Θήβα. Οι πρωτεργάτες των ερευνών και οι συνεχιστές τους. Συνεδριακό κέντρο Θήβας, 15–17 Νοεμβρίου 2002* (100 Years of Archaeological Work in Thebes. The Pioneers of Research and Their Followers. Conference Center Thebes, 15–17 November 2002). Athens: 85–96.

Kühr, A. 2006. *Als Kadmos nach Boiotien kam: Polis und Ethnos im Spiegel thebanischer Gründungsmythen*. Stuttgart.

Kyrieleis, H. 2002. Zu den Anfängen des Heiligtums von Olympia. In: Kyrieleis, H., ed. *Olympia 1875–2000. 125 Jahre deutsche Ausgrabungen. Internationales Symposion, Berlin 9.–11. November 2000*. Mainz: 213–220.

Kyrieleis, H. 2006. Die Ausgrabungen am Pelopion 1987–1996. In: Kyrieleis, H., ed. *Anfänge und Frühzeit des Heiligtums von Olympia* (Olympische Forschungen 31). Berlin–New York: 1–139.

Löw, M. 2001. *Raumsoziologie* (Suhrkamp Taschenbuch Wissenschaft 1506). Frankfurt am Main.

Löw, M. 2008. The Constitution of Space: The Structuration of Spaces through the Simultaneity of Effect and Perception. *European Journal of Social Theory* 11(1): 25–49.

Loucas, I. and Loucas, E. 1987. La tombe des jumeaux divins Amphiôn et Zéthos et la fertilité de la terre béotienne. In: Laffineur, R., ed. *Thanatos: les coutumes funéraires en Egée à l'âge du Bronze, actes du colloque de Liège (21–23 avril 1986)* (Aegaeum 1). Liège: 95–106.

Maran, J. 2001. Political and Religious Aspects of Architectural Change on the Upper Citadel of Tiryns: The Case of Building T. In: Laffineur, R. and Hägg, R., eds. *POTNIA: Deities and Religion in the Aegean Bronze Age. Proceedings of the 8th International Aegean Conference, Göteborg, Göteborg University 12–15 April 2000* (Aegaeum 22). Liège–Austin: 113–122.

Maran, J. 2011. Contested Pasts: The Society of the 12th c. B.C.E. Argolid and the Memory of the Mycenaean Palatial Period. In: Gauß, W., Lindblom, M., Smith, R.A.K., and Wright, J.C., eds. *Our Cups Are Full: Pottery and Society in the Aegean Bronze Age:*

Papers Presented to Jeremy B. Rutter on the Occasion of His 65th Birthday. Oxford: 169–178.

Maran, J. 2012. Architektonischer Raum und soziale Kommunikation auf der Oberburg von Tiryns—Der Wandel von der mykenischen Palastzeit zur Nachpalastzeit. In: Arnold, F., Busch, A., Haensch, R., and Wulf-Rheidt, U., eds. *Orte der Herrschaft: Charakteristika von antiken Machtzentren*. Rahden: 149–162.

Maran, J. 2016. The Persistence of Place and Memory: The Case of the Early Helladic Rundbau and the Mycenaean Palatial Megara of Tiryns. In: Bartelheim, M., Horejs, B., and Krausz, R., eds. *Von Baden bis Troia: Ressourcennutzung, Metallurgie und Wissenstransfer* (Oriental and European Archaeology 3). Vienna: 153–173.

Marzolff, P. 2004. Das zweifache Rätsel Tiryns. In: Schwandner, E.-L. and Rheidt, K., eds. *Macht der Architektur, Architektur der Macht. Bauforschungskolloquium in Berlin vom 30. Oktober bis 2. November 2002 veranstaltet vom Architektur-Referat des DAI* (Diskussionen zur Archäologischen Bauforschung 8). Mainz: 79–91.

Marzolff, P. 2009. Der frühbronzezeitliche Rundbau von Tiryns. Architektonischer Einzelgänger oder Außenposten einer östlichen Koine? In: Kyriatsoulis, A., ed. *Bronze Age Architectural Traditions in the Eastern Mediterranean: Diffusion and Diversity. Proceedings of the Symposium, 7.–8.5. 2008 in Munich*. Weilheim: 185–207.

Moggi, M. and Osanna, M. 2010. *Pausania: Guida della Grecia*, Libro 9: *La Beozia*. Milan.

Müller, K. 1930. *Tiryns, Die Ergebnisse der Ausgrabungen des Instituts* 3: *Die Architektur der Burg und des Palastes*. Augsburg.

Nora, P. 1984. Entre mémoire et histoire: la problématique des lieux. In: Nora, P., ed. *Les lieux de mémoire* 1 : *La République*. Paris: XVII–XLIII.

Psaraki, K. 2014. Πρωτοελλαδική κεραμική από την πόλη της Θήβας. Ανασκαφή στο οικόπεδο επέκτασης του Αρχαιολογικού Μουσείου Θηβών (Early Helladic Pottery from the City of Thebes. Excavation on the Plot of the Extension of the Archaeological Museum of Thebes). In: Aravantinos, V. and Kountouri, E., eds. *100 Χρόνια Αρχαιολογικού Έργου στη Θήβα. Οι πρωτεργάτες των ερευνών και οι συνεχιστές τους. Συνεδριακό κέντρο Θήβας, 15–17 Νοεμβρίου 2002* (100 Years of Archaeological Work in Thebes. The Pioneers of Research and Their Followers. Conference Center Thebes, 15–17 November 2002). Athens: 97–115.

Sandhaus, D. 2012. The Iron Age II (Strata VI–V). In: Ben-Tor, A., Ben-Ami, D., and Sandhaus, D. eds. *Hazor 6: The 1990–2009 Excavations. The Iron Age*. Jerusalem: 286–401.

Schliemann, H. 1886. *Tiryns: der prähistorische Palast der Könige von Tiryns—Ergebnisse der neuesten Ausgrabungen*. Leipzig.

Spyropoulos, T.G. 1981. Αμφείον: Έρευνα καί μελέτη του Μνημείου του Αμφείου Θηβών (Ampheion: Research and Study of the Monument of the Ampheion at Thebes). Sparta.

Symeonoglou, S. 1985. *The Topography of Thebes from the Bronze Age to Modern Times*. Princeton.

Weiberg, E. 2007. *Thinking the Bronze Age: Life and Death in Early Helladic Greece* (Boreas 29). Uppsala.

Wiencke, M.H. 1989. Change in Early Helladic II. *American Journal of Archaeology* 93: 495–509.

Whittaker, H. 2014. *Religion and Society in Middle Bronze Age Greece*. Cambridge.

Zuckerman, S. 2006. Where Is the Hazor Archive Buried? *Biblical Archaeology Review* 32(2): 28–37.

Zuckerman, S. 2007. Anatomy of a Destruction: Crisis Architecture, Termination Rituals and the Fall of Canaanite Hazor. *Journal of Mediterranean Archaeology* 20(1): 3–32.

Zuckerman, S. 2010. "The City, Its Gods Will Return There...": Toward an Alternative Interpretation of Hazor's Acropolis in the Late Bronze Age. *Journal of Near Eastern Studies* 69: 163–178.

Zuckerman, S. 2011. Ruin Cults at Iron Age I Hazor. In: Finkelstein, I. and Na'aman, N., eds. *The Fire Signals of Lachish: Studies in the Archaeology and History of Israel in the Late Bronze Age, Iron Age, and Persian Period in Honor of David Ussishkin*. Winona Lake, IN: 387–394.

Zuckerman, S. 2017. Arguments for Identifying Building 7050 as a Temple. In: Ben-Tor, A., Zuckerman, S., Bechar, S., and Sandhaus, D., eds. *Hazor 7: The 1990–2012 Excavations. The Bronze Age*. Jerusalem: 138–139.

CHAPTER 11

In the Footsteps of the Phoenicians in Paphos

Jolanta Młynarczyk

I am delighted to offer this modest paper in honor of my distinguished friend Michal Artzy, whom I first met at the Zinman Institute excavations of Sha'ar ha-Amaqim in 1993 and with whom I have the pleasure to work at the Phoenician site of Tel 'Akko. The part of the research dealing with the Cypro-Classical to Hellenistic period in Paphos has been sponsored by the grant of the Polish National Research Centre (NCN) UMO. 2016/22/M/HS3/00351.

The important settlement of Paphos in the southwestern coastal area of Cyprus "appears to have originated in Middle Cypriot III/Late Cypriot I as the terminal station of the route that brought copper to the coast from the foothills of Troodos" (Iacovou 2013: 285). In terms of the Phoenician connections in Cyprus during the earlier part of the Iron Age, Paphos is still among less known regions; however, the early Phoenician presence in the southwest of Cyprus has been firmly attested by the material culture of the Cypro-Geometric period. In P. Bikai's opinion, it is even possible that "an early period of Phoenician trade … used western Cyprus as a stopping point" in the expansion toward the west (Bikai 1987: 70). Indeed, the earliest Phoenician pottery found on Cyprus ("Kouklia Horizon," ca. 1050 to 850[?] BCE) comes mostly from Kouklia, which is ancient Paphos, described as Palaepaphos from the Hellenistic period on. A quantity of Phoenician objects made their appearance in the tombs at Palaepaphos-Skales as early as the eleventh century BCE (Bikai 1994: 35); an enigmatic graffito on one of the vessels found there contained some Phoenician characters and was dated to the tenth century BCE (Lipiński 2004: 45, 69). These direct testimonies to the Phoenician connections, however, disappeared from the archaeological record at Paphos around the mid-eighth century BCE, and the Phoenician pottery of the "Kition Horizon" (750[?] to after 700 BCE) is altogether absent from the site (Bikai 1987: 69–70).

In the era of fully developed Cypriot kingdoms (Iacovou 1994), that is, in the Cypro-Archaic and Cypro-Classical periods (the latter corresponding to the Persian period in the continental Levant), there is no direct evidence of any Phoenician connections. All the names of the Paphian kings we know so far are Greek (e.g., Lipiński 2004: 68–69; Iacovou 2006a: 46, 48; 2006b: 319–321; Młynarczyk 2011: 645–646, n. 4–5). Moreover, it is known that the Paphians allied with Evagoras I, king of Salamis, against Milkyaton, the Phoenician king of Kition, in 391 BCE (Lipiński 2004: 94–95). Yet, despite the lack of direct testimonies to the Phoenician presence in Paphos during that period, several features in the sphere of the Paphian kingship and religion point in the direction of the Phoenician coast, especially Byblos. Most importantly, both areas shared the concept of hereditary kingship intimately linked to the priesthood of the protector deity ("kings and priests"; Maier 1989: 386) on the one hand, and the very nature of the goddess in question on the other ("a goddess of universal power"; Karageorghis 2005: 16). These similarities were doubtlessly rooted in the Late Bronze Age, probably in connection with the much-frequented trading network between Cyprus and the coastal Canaanites. The latter were coming to Cyprus from Ugarit, but also from other harbor towns, Byblos included, as proved by the account of Wenamun's trip from Byblos to Cyprus ca. 1075 BCE (Bikai 1994: 32–34).

Bikai has suggested (1994: 32) that there must have been some connection between the temples dedicated to Aphrodite at Byblos, Ashkelon, and Paphos. This view is most probably based partly on a well-known fifth-century BCE mention by Herodotus, who noted that the Phoenician sanctuary of Aphrodite Ourania at Ashkelon had been the model for the "sanctuary (of the goddess) in Cyprus" (Hdt. 1.105.2–3). It is plausible to assume that Herodotus meant the sanctuary in Paphos, which was an important religious center on Cyprus during his time, even if he did not give any specific place name. More importantly, the link between the religious life in Paphos and the Levantine coast is emphasized in the myths regarding Kinyras, the legendary pre-Greek king of Paphos (Karageorghis 2005: 14–17; Iacovou 2006a: 46, n. 94). As to Kinyras's place in the tradition of Paphos, seemingly contradictory accounts of Greek authors Theopompus (fourth century BCE) and Pausanias (second century CE) may reflect an actual historical sequence. According to Theopompus, upon the arrival of the Achaeans at Paphos, Kinyras's companions (likely with Kinyras himself) moved eastward to Amathus (Aupert 1997; Karageorghis 2005: 17). Then, a monumental temple to the goddess (Aphrodite, according to the *interpretatio Graeca*) was erected in Paphos by Agapenor the Arcadian (Paus. 8.5), which would have been during the Achaean "colonization." One has to note, however, that in the first–second centuries CE Tacitus (*Hist.* 2.3) mentioned a tradition that had attributed the temple foundation to Kinyras himself (Maier 1989: 377; Karageorghis 2005: 14). Indeed, a confirmation of the pre-Greek cultural background of Paphos was evinced, presumably, by "a few elements" of the Eteocypriot language found there (Aupert 1997: 21–22).

The Oriental, specifically Phoenician (Byblite), connections of Kinyras, even if reflected in just scraps of myths preserved in Greek and Latin literary sources, are widely recognized today (Karageorghis 2005: 15–16, 21–25; Ioannou 2015:

109), and, significantly, till the collapse of the Paphian kingdom in the last quarter of the fourth century BCE, the local rulers were considered as the descendants of Kinyras (e.g., Młynarczyk 2011: 646–647). As such, they were also priests of the patron goddess of Paphos, who was worshipped under the name of *Anassa/Wanassa*, meaning, literally, "a sovereign" (e.g., Maier 1989: 376; Karageorghis 2005: 40–42). *Anax* (m.) and *Anassa* (f.) were, in fact, royal titles used in Cyprus till the end of the Cypro-Classical period, as recorded by Aristotle (Iacovou 2006b: 328–329). Despite its Mycenaean spelling, the name *Anassa*, describing the great Paphian goddess (who was known as Aphrodite from the third century BCE on), is an exact counterpart of that identifying the great goddess of Byblos, Ba'alat Gubal, Lady of Byblos, as described in the dedication of the famous stele of Yehawmilk, king of Byblos, from the mid-fifth century BCE (Caubet, Fontan, and Gubel 2002: 65–66; Ioannou 2015: 110). Notably, a similar description of a Phoenician goddess, MLKTQDŠT (Holy Queen: apparently Astarte) occurs in a fourth-century BCE inscription from Kition (*CIS* I.86 A6; Masson and Sznycer 1972: 21–68). The inscription on the Yehawmilk Stele testifies to the bond of the royal and divine power, which is exactly the model of the Paphian kingship, unique in Cyprus, but attested on the Phoenician coast, specifically in Byblos and Sidon (Maier 1989: 376, 386, n. 34). This hereditary sacred kingship persisted in Paphos till the reign of its last ruler, Nikokles (Młynarczyk 1990: 68–70; Iacovou 2013: 287), who was described in a dedication of his (lost) statue as a descendant of the god-like Kinyras (Młynarczyk 1990: 71, n. 27). Even after the abolition of his kingdom, the Paphian priests of the goddess (who was worshipped under the name of Aphrodite by then) would retain the ceremonial title of Kinyrads for several centuries (Młynarczyk 1990: 113).

The last direct evidence of the Phoenicians in Paphos refers to an early part of the Hellenistic period. Among this is a dedication to "Astarte of Paphos," which confirms the supposed affinity between the cult of the goddess in Paphos and in Phoenicia (Karageorghis 2005: 36, 42; Ioannou 2015: 115). The fragmentary Phoenician inscription in question was found in the area of Palaepaphos; carefully incised into a stone slab, it has been dated on paleographic grounds to the third century BCE (Masson and Sznycer 1972: 81–86, pl. I: 3). The inscription commemorates an unspecified offering to Astarte of Paphos ('ŠTRT PP) in "this sanctuary." The findspot, a site known as Xylinos, is distant enough from the main sanctuary of the Paphian goddess to be taken as a proof of the existence of yet another cult place. An equation of Astarte of Paphos with the local Aphrodite has been confirmed by a Greek dedication to Aphrodite discovered nearby and doubtlessly pertaining to the same sanctuary (Masson and Sznycer 1972: 81, with references in n. 2).

Another bit of evidence of the Phoenician presence at Paphos relates to the beginning of the Hellenistic period and comes from the new harbor town, Nea Paphos, which was founded by the last king of the Kinyrad dynasty, Nikokles, after 320 BCE (Młynarczyk 1990: 67–73; 2011: 646). There, a simple pit grave, probably of a child, cut in the rock in the eastern necropolis of Nea Paphos, yielded a few pottery vessels, among them a proto-Rhodian amphora bearing a Phoenician graffito. The pottery items in question have been dated by D. Michaelides to the late fourth–third centuries BCE (Michaelides and Sznycer 1985: 251–252). The inscription, scratched onto the surface of the aforementioned amphora after firing, and whose paleography is suggestive of the fourth century BCE, gives the name and profession of its final owner as 'Abd-(?) GR, the smelter (*h-nsk*) (Michaelides and Sznycer 1985: 255). This document records an ethnic Phoenician artisan active in the newly founded town and specializing in the traditional Phoenician craft of metalworking.

Unfortunately, we lack any additional sound evidence regarding the Phoenician connections of Paphos in the Cypro-Classical and Hellenistic to Roman periods. Any possible testimony to these should be sought through further in-depth studies of the material culture and perhaps also religious customs of the Paphos region. As an example of such study, one may mention investigations into the repertoire of Paphian pottery in the late Cypro-Classical period. Among the table vessels doubtlessly manufactured at Palaepaphos and found there in a fill at the locality Evreti, dated to the second half of the fourth century BCE, the shapes of some plates, specifically Maier and von Wartburg's Types III and IX (1985: 109, fig. 5), have close parallels among ceramics of the Neo-Babylonian and Persian periods (dated ca. 580–380 BCE) discovered in Stratum 3 at Tell Keisan (Briend and Humbert 1980: pl. 20: 6–9, 13, 14). It is especially important to note that the Paphian plate belonging to Maier and von Wartburg's Type IX, most often debased Red Slip Ware (a ware that may be of Phoenician origin), is very rare elsewhere on Cyprus except for the earliest archaeological deposits found at Nea Paphos (Maier and von Wartburg 1985: 109, n. 44). All these suggest the survival of Phoenician influence on the Paphian pottery production at the turn of the Cypro-Classical period.

As another example of possible Phoenician connections in the new town of Paphos one may consider a unique cemetery containing the burials of dogs associated with those of humans. Discovered right outside the northwestern part of Nea Paphos and dated to the late Hellenistic and Roman periods, it is difficult to interpret properly, but at the same time strongly suggestive of some kind of persisting Phoenician presence or tradition (Raptou 2009).

References

Aupert, P. 1997. Amathus during the First Iron Age. *Bulletin of the American Schools of Oriental Research* 308: 19–25.

Bikai, P. 1994. The Phoenicians and Cyprus. In: Karageorghis, V., ed. *Proceedings of the International Symposium Cyprus in the 11th Century B.C.* Nicosia: 31–38.

Bikai, P.M. 1987. *The Phoenician Pottery of Cyprus.* Nicosia.

Briend, J. and Humbert, J.-B. 1980. *Tell Keisan (1971–1976): une cité phénicienne en Galilée* (Biblicus et Orientalis, Series Archaeologica 1). Fribourg–Göttingen–Paris.

Caubet, A., Fontan, É., and Gubel, E. 2002. *Art phénicien : la sculpture de tradition phénicienne.* Paris.

CIS Corpus Inscriptionum Semiticarum, Paris, 1867–1962.

Iacovou, M. 1994. The Topography of 11th Century B.C. Cyprus. In: Karageorghis, V., ed. *Proceedings of the International Symposium Cyprus in the 11th Century B.C.* Nicosia: 149–166.

Iacovou, M. 2006a. "Greeks," "Phoenicians" and "Eteocypriots": Ethnic Identities in the Cypriot Kingdoms. In: Chrysostomides, J. and Dendrinos, C., eds. *"Sweet Land": Lectures on the History and Culture of Cyprus.* Camberley: 27–59.

Iacovou, M. 2006b. From the Mycenaean Qa-si-re-u to the Cypriote Pa-si-le-wo-se: The Basileus in the Kingdoms of Cyprus. In: Deger-Jalkotzy, S. and Lemos, I.S., eds. *Ancient Greece from the Mycenaean Palaces to the Age of Homer.* Edinburgh: 315–335.

Iacovou, M. 2013. Paphos before Palaepaphos: New Approaches to the History of the Paphian Kingdom. In: Michaelides, D., ed. *Epigraphy, Numismatics, Prosopography and History of Ancient Cyprus: Papers in Honour of Ino Nicolaou.* Uppsala: 275–292.

Ioannou, C. 2015. D'Aphrodite à Astarté Paphia. *Cahier du Centre d'Etudes Chypriotes* 45 (*Hommage à Jacqueline Karageorghis*): 107–117.

Karageorghis, J. 2005. *Kypris: The Aphrodite of Cyprus. Ancient Sources and Archaeological Evidence.* Nicosia.

Lipiński, E. 2004. *Itineraria Phoenicia* (Studia Phoenicia 18, Orientalia Lovaniensia Analecta 127) Leuven–Paris–Dudley, MA.

Maier, F.G. 1989. Priest Kings in Cyprus. In: Peltenburg, E., ed. *Early Society in Cyprus.* Edinburgh: 376–391.

Maier, F.G. and Wartburg, M.-L. von 1985. Excavations at Kouklia (Palaepaphos): Thirteenth Preliminary Report: Seasons 1983 and 1984. *Report of the Department of Antiquities, Cyprus* 1985: 100–121.

Masson, O. and Sznycer, M. 1972. *Recherches sur les Phéniciens à Chypre.* Genève–Paris.

Michaelides, D. and Sznycer, M. 1985. A Phoenician Graffito from Tomb 103/84 at Nea Paphos. *Report of the Department of Antiquities, Cyprus* 1985: 249–256.

Młynarczyk, J. 1990. *Nea Paphos 3: Paphos in the Hellenistic Period.* Warsaw.

Młynarczyk, J. 2011: Descendants of the God-Like Kinyras: The Kings of Paphos in Archaeological Record. In: Demetriou, A., ed. *Praktika tou 4: Diethnous Kypriologikou Synedriou Lefkosia 29 Apriliou–3 Maiou 2008, Archaio tmema.* Lefkosia: 645–653.

Raptou, E. 2009. Nouvelles pratiques funéraires à Paphos hellénistique et romaine. *Cahiers du Centre d'Etudes Chypriotes* 39: 89–112.

CHAPTER 12

Informed or at Sea: On the Maritime and Mundane in Ugaritic Tablet RS 94.2406

Chris Monroe

1   Introduction: Secret Messages to the Notable Urtenu

The clay tablet cataloged RS 94.2406 was excavated at Tell Ras Shamra, Syria, in 1994 during French excavations directed by Marguerite Yon (Calvet 2000). Dennis Pardee published his translation of the cuneiform alphabetic inscription in *Context of Scripture* vol. 3 (2002) under the rubric "Archival Documents (West Semitic, text 3.45R)." It subsequently appeared in French with transliteration and brief philological commentary by coauthors Pardee and Pierre Bordreuil in *Manuel d'Ougaritique* 2004, and again in their 2009 English edition, *A Manual of Ugaritic* (henceforth *Manual*), where it is titled "Text 31: A Double Letter: The Queen to *Urtēnu* and *Ilîmilku* to the Same." Bordreuil and Pardee (2010: 4–6) offer further comments, as does Gzella (2010: 61–62), in the same volume, for its direct epistolary style. Sauvage and Pardee (2015) boldly identify the text as an "itinéraire maritime," following the 2002, 2004, 2009, and 2012 (*RSO* 18, no. 60) editions of the text, but notably ignore the critical reading of Dietrich and Loretz (2009), who label it *KTU* 2.88 with the terrestrial description, "Eine Villa für Ilimilku." Most recently, van Soldt (2016) devoted a chapter to the text in which he tentatively identifies the anonymous queen who figures in the letters.

Thus, it is with great caution I here try to ascertain what historicity should be given to the text(s) on this tablet, especially regarding its status as a royal maritime itinerary. In doing so, I adhere mainly to the transliteration, clear photographs, hand copies (see Fig. 12.1), and English translation in the 2009 *Manual*, while making reference to any differences from the French translation in *RSO* 18 or German translation of Dietrich and Loretz (2009). Beyond assessing the relative plausibility of its maritime context, the text may inform us regarding logistics of writing aboard ship. We are often at sea when trying to reconstruct histories of liminal nomadic maritime folk whose priorities did not necessarily include documentation; this nausea becomes particularly acute when dealing with the idiosyncrasies of Ugaritic.

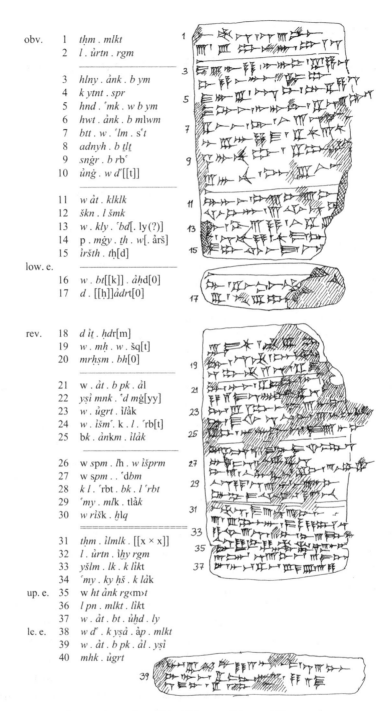

obv.	1	tḥm . mlkt
	2	l . ủrtn . rgm
	3	hlny . ȧnk . b ym
	4	k ytnt . spr
	5	hnd . ʿmk . w b ym
	6	hwt . ȧnk . b mlwm
	7	btt . w . ʿlm . sʿt
	8	adnyh . b ṭlṭ
	9	snġr . b rbʿ
	10	ủnġ . w dʿ[[t]]
	11	w ȧt . klklk
	12	škn . l šmk
	13	w . kly . ʿbd[. ly(?)]
	14	p . mġy . ṯh . w[. ȧrš]
	15	ỉršth . ṯh[d]
low. e.		
	16	w . bt[[k]] . ȧḥd[0]
	17	d . [[ḫ]]ȧdrt[0]
rev.	18	d ỉṯ . ḥdr[m]
	19	w . mḥ . w . šq[t]
	20	mrḥṣm . bh[0]
	21	w . ȧt . b pk . ȧl
	22	yṣỉ mnk . ʿd mġ[yy]
	23	w . ủgrt . ỉlȧk
	24	w . ỉšmʿ. k . l . ʿrb[t]
	25	bk . ȧnkm . ỉlȧk
	26	w spm . lh . w ỉšprm
	27	w spm . . . ʿdbm
	28	k l . ʿrbt . bk . l ʿrbt
	29	ʿmy . mlk . tlȧk
	30	w rỉšk . ḥlq
	31	tḥm . ỉlmlk . [[x × x]]
	32	l . ủrtn . ỉḥy rgm
	33	yšlm . lk . k lỉkt
	34	ʿmy . ky ḥš . k lȧk
up. e.	35	w ht ȧnk rg⟨m⟩t
	36	l pn . mlkt . lỉkt
	37	w . ȧt . bt . ủḥd . ly
le. e.	38	w dʿ . k yṣȧ . ȧp . mlkt
	39	w . ȧt . b pk . ȧl . yṣỉ
	40	mhk . ủgrt

FIGURE 12.1   Copy and transliteration of RS 94.2406 (*KTU* 2.88)
FROM DIETRICH AND LORETZ 2009: 148–149

Like most tablets from Ugarit, RS 94.2406 gives neither year-name nor other internal dating, and the writing is laconic—almost a form of shorthand, failing to provide, for example, the name of one of the senders (the queen's, of all people) and lacking patronymics for the other author and its recipient. Where the tablet was excavated is key to its interpretation. The find spot is the *Maison d'Ourtenu,* so-called because at least ten letters addressed to Urtenu were found there (Calvet 2000; Malbran-Labat 2010). The stately manor, in the south-central residential quarter, outside the palace, is the site of an archive containing over 600 tablets, second in number only to the combined finds from the palace archives (*Manual*: 7). Other tablets and the archaeological material from this house date Urtenu's career to Ugarit's last two kings, Niqmaddu III and Ammurapi, or about 1210 to 1185 BCE (Calvet 2000). The pottery from the house, including Mycenaean chariot kraters, some in the so-called Rude Style, dates to the late thirteenth and early twelfth centuries. Other texts from the house mention Ramesses II, Merenptah, and Seti, pharaohs from the same period. Given the various tablets addressed to an unnamed governor, or *sakinu,* found in this same house, Urtenu is all but positively identified as this governor. As such, he was the most important official after the king, overseeing most administrative and economic state business (Singer 1999; van Soldt 2002; Monroe 2009: esp. 238–289). Urtenu's residence was, as Yon puts it, a "large house of very fine quality"—one befitting a governor—that compares with those of other Ugarit elites such as Yabninu and Rap'anu, and emulates the manner of construction seen in the palace (Yon 2006: 87–88, fig. 51). At over 200 sq m and featuring extensive ashlar masonry, a second story, vaulted tomb, and impressive catalog of riches, including a cylinder seal and chariot parts (Calvet 2000), its excavation took eleven more years after the large epigraphic discoveries of 1994. Urtenu's archive is rich and international in its scope, and includes business dealings with Egypt, Cyprus, Hatti, Carchemish, and Emar and the Phoenician towns of Tyre, Sidon, Byblos, and Beirut. Several deals involve Queen Sharelli's Egyptian son-in-law and agent, Shipti-Baalu (Singer 1999: 658), their relationship signifying the merchant-royal symbiosis that prevailed at Ugarit, as well as commercially favorable conditions set by the Egyptian-Hittite peace treaty of 1259.

2 Reading the Letters

To this well-positioned figure named Urtenu arrived our double letter, containing two messages from two of Ugarit's most influential persons: first, the queen, anonymous here; second, a namesake of Ugarit's most famous scribe, Ilimilku, whose colophon appears on tablets of the Baal Cycle and the Aqhat and Kirta myths (Hawley, Pardee, and Roche-Hawley 2015). The meanings vary depending on which translation one chooses. Bordreuil and Pardee translate as follows (*Manual*: 245–246; the translation into English is mine):

> Message of the queen: To Urtenu say:
> "I was on the sea when I sent this document to you. Today I'm lodged at MLWM, tomorrow at Adaniya the third day at Sunnajara, and the fourth at Unuju. You are now informed."
> [Matters in lines 11 through 20 are unclear due to breaks, but supposedly involve disaster, Urtenu's belongings, and a house.]
> "As for you, not a word must escape your mouth until [broken personal name] arrives. Then I will send a message to Ugarit. Should I hear that (she) has not agreed to guarantee you, then I'll send another message. Now a vessel (or two), and (two pair of unknown objects) are ready. If she does not guarantee you, and does not come to me, she will send a message to the king, and you can kiss your head good-bye."
> [Second message, starting on line 31]
> Message of Ilimilku: To Urtenu, my brother, say: "May it be well with you. Concerning the fact that you sent me the message, 'Send me a message quickly,' now I have dictated this message in the presence of the queen. What you must do is to seize the house for me. Moreover, you must recognize that the queen also has left. But you must keep absolutely quiet about this at Ugarit."

By Dietrich and Loretz's treatment (2009: 148–152), the same messages read thus:

> Message of the queen: To Urtenu say: "Now I am on the day on which I have given this letter to you—on this very day I am lodged at *Mlwm*, and hurrying the next day to *Adyn*, the third day at *Sngr*, and on the fourth day at *Ung*. So take note!"
> [Lines 11–21 are unclear but concern some housecleaning matter that has ended up with the queen instead of Urtenu.]
> ("As for you, from your mouth nothing may be said until my arrival. Then I will write to Ugarit. And if I hear that [she] does not speak for you, I will write (again). You should also set up the bowls. Both the date cake and the bowls are prepared. Since she does not speak for you, (and) she does not come before me, (but) writes to the king—your authority is lost!")
> [Second message, from line 31]

Message from Ilimilku: To Urtenu, my brother, say: "I wish you well! Since you have written to me: 'Write in a hurry!' I have for my part written my message in the presence of the queen. You hold the house for me now! Know that the queen is out of town too. For your part—from your mouth you may say nothing in Ugarit!"

As one can see, the second message changes very little based on the translator, and differences in the first message are of major consequence only due to how one reads a single word, *ym*, read fairly as either "day" or "sea." According to the *Manual*, and Sauvage and Pardee (2015), events taking place at the end of Ugarit's history plausibly include the queen escaping to Hittite territory via the sea while inviting the governor to conspire (perhaps with the help of Ilimilku and an unknown woman) against the king's wishes. Such events fit comfortably into the dire circumstances assumed to characterize the early twelfth century. Dietrich and Loretz's translation is prosaic by comparison, lacking sea travel, necessarily, or a queen escaping from a doomed city. Two elites are concerned about domestic matters while away at places that we can only tentatively find on a map.

I see no way to declare unequivocally which translation is correct without sufficient comparanda that at present do not exist. It comes down to plausibility and subjectivity. Readers should refer to the primary editions for full philological commentary, but that would not solve the crux of the matter, which is how one reads *b ym* in lines 3–10. Dietrich and Loretz take the philologically conservative view that since this expression means "on the day" in other texts, then it should be read that way here and consistently, in other words, the same in line 3 as in line 5 and then, by ellipsis, in lines 8 and 9 where *ym* is omitted but assumed to go with words for "third (day)" and "fourth (day)." This logic serves well for lines 5–10 (the stops of an itinerary), but it also forces them to read lines 3–4 (*hlny. ank b ym / k ytnt. spr*) rather awkwardly as "now I am on the day on which…" ("Nunmehr bin ich an dem Tag, an dem…"), where the "on the day" is confusingly redundant and wordy compared to more direct phrasing such as "today I. …" Van Soldt (2016: 110) follows Dietrich and Loretz here, and his wording also shows the difficulty of avoiding "the sea" in the phrasing: "Behold, I, on the day that I gave this document (to be sent) to you, on this day I am staying in Mlwm." The reading of line 3 in the *Manual* (as in Sauvage and Pardee 2015) is lexically more unusual, unattested in other letters, and differs from the reading of the same phrase in line 5, but it allows a syntactically straightforward opening in "(now) I was on the sea when…," which seems like a phrase that should be ubiquitous at Ugarit instead of a single, putative instance.

3 Who Is the Queen?

Ugarit's violent end is well known and largely uncontroversial, despite continued debate over the timing and nature of the broader eastern Mediterranean crisis (Knapp and Manning 2016). Archaeology provides ample evidence for the destruction, and the urgency is apparent in many letters, including some in the Urtenu archive (RS 88.2009, on military reinforcements from Hatti; RS 94.2002 + 2003, on grain relief from Egypt; RS 34.152, on famine, plausibly at Emar). During the reign of Ugarit's last king, Ammurapi, the city tried to reestablish good relations with Egypt as the Hittite empire lost its grip on Syria. Itamar Singer (1999: 712–716) similarly hypothesized widespread famine in the eastern Mediterranean, including an Akkadian letter found at Tel Aphek that references Egyptian grain en route to Ugarit. Other evidence for an ecological downturn comes from Akkadian texts from Emar (Zaccagnini 1995) and palynological analyses from Tell Tweini (in coastal northern Syria) suggesting an arid phase starting around 1200 BCE (Kaniewski, Guiot, and Van Campo 2015). An oft-cited Akkadian tablet, RS 20.238 (*Ugaritica* 5: no. 24, once thought to be still in the kiln as the city was destroyed) is perhaps the most dramatic witness, from an anonymous king of Alashiya, writing: "Now the ships of the enemy have come. They have been setting fire to my cities and have done harm to the land." Niqmaddu III, the recipient, was supposed to do something about this, but his unfortunate reply to Alashiya is that his own ships are off in distant Lukka (later known as Lycia).

Since the Amarna Age things had been rather *plus ça change*. Ugarit had moved from the Egyptian sphere into Hittite vassalage under Suppiluliuma in the later fourteenth century, and there seems to have been a relationship of commercial convenience. In a thirteenth-century treaty with Tudhaliya IV of Hatti, King Ammistamru II purchased Ugarit's exemption from the Hittite war against Assyria for 50 talents of gold (*Manual*: 13; *PRU* 4: 150–151). Perhaps as part of this relatively laissez-faire policy toward a vassal, Hatti excused Ugarit from the usual practice of dynastic intermarriage, since no Hittite princess or queen appears in the Ugarit court until Ehli-Nikkalu's name surfaces in two Akkadian legal documents that divide her estate with Ammurapi (*PRU* 4: 208–210). Bordreuil and Pardee assume that this division of property followed a royal divorce, a likely context for events transpiring on our tablet. And, thus, in *RSO* 18 and in Sauvage and Pardee (2015), Ehli-Nikkalu is said to be the anonymous queen at sea during the last days of Ugarit. On the other hand, Itamar Singer (1999: 701) points out that neither divorce nor marriage is stated in those legal documents, and, thus, Ammurapi may have simply inherited his deceased father's estate while Ehli-Nikkalu, as a consequence of becoming widowed by

Niqmaddu III, received her movable wealth to take back to Hatti; moreover, Ehli-Nikkalu need not have been in Ugarit any later than the *start* of Ammurapi's reign (Singer 1999: 703–707), putting the events of our letter twenty years before Ugarit was put to the torch. This interpretation gains support from van Soldt's (2016) recent reconstruction wherein the most likely queen to have been involved in the matters of RS 94.2406 is Sharelli, whose impressive international dossier is already known from several tablets that also include references to Urtenu and Ilimilku (Singer 1999: 696–700). As with the translation of *b ym*, such a reconstruction of dramatic events and personae remains at the mercy of the queen's scribe, who failed to specify her name or the king's. Of course, there was no need to tell Urtenu these things. He was certainly informed; it is we who remain at sea.

4 Lost in Transmission: From Wooden Boards to Clay Tablets

Returning to lines 3–10 of the tablet and taking the maritime itinerary as plausible, I admit that what first grabbed my attention was the potential of a letter having been issued while on the sea. To my knowledge, no other text from the Bronze Age or in all of preclassical antiquity makes such a claim. What explains such a singularity, if anything? Low literacy among ancient mariners probably factors; sailing and boatbuilding leave time for little else, even now. Certainly, there were exceptional circumstances and people involved in our case. Did the royals never go to sea themselves, except in extraordinary cases? It is frankly amazing we do not know this. Given the maritime orientation of Ugarit's economy, that it took nearly seventy years of excavation to find this single, putative reference is mightily counterintuitive, and yet poor documentation of maritime life is practically a constant over time and space, at least until the Renaissance.

In the case of Ugarit, the relative absence of maritime documentation may be the result of systematic loss, due to the way information was transmitted from port to capital. If most shipboard and dockside recording was done on perishable media such as wood or papyrus, with only the most important records being copied onto clay for archival or legal concerns held in Ugarit, then indeed, one would expect there to be very few maritime matters found in Ugarit's tablets. Indeed, the odds would seem in favor of our text never having made it back to Ugarit, except that it concerned, perhaps, the most consequential person there, namely Urtenu. How it reached his house from the queen's location is not at all obvious. Bordeuil and Pardee (*Manual*: 246–247) state that "the messenger carrying the tablet [...] took a ship back to Ugarit from the port serving 'Adaniya." Sauvage and Pardee (2015) painstakingly demonstrate the nautical plausibility of this town being near the present Adana in Cilicia, and it makes sense that a Hittite port might have had the necessary facilities for scribes, messengers, and sailors. But, at the same time, one must admit we know little about any of these places, and the message may have departed from any of the other three towns in the itinerary. Whichever town it came from, can we even say what its original form was? On what medium was the queen's original dictation recorded, and was it copied before Urtenu received the clay tablet RS 94.2406? Dietrich and Loretz (2009: 150) suggest that the tablet's many corrections are consistent with its having been inscribed outside the city. One might take this even further and posit an unstable shipboard setting; but that would create the unlikely and unwise prospects of either storing wet tablets aboard a rocking ship or baking them aboard. There is still no archaeological evidence for hearths in ships' galleys until the seventh-century CE Yassi Ada shipwreck (van Doorninck 2005)

The only writing equipment from a Bronze Age ship is a pair of wooden writing boards or *diptychs* found on the shipwreck at Uluburun, Turkey (Pulak 2008: 367–368). The more complete of the Uluburun diptychs measures 9.5 × 13.5 × 0.9 cm, and used three cylindrical ivory hinges to open flat, exposing two recessed boxwood surfaces that were filled with beeswax impregnated with yellowish orpiment. No other writing boards from the Bronze Age have been recovered, though ivory or bronze hinge parts have been found at Megiddo, Byblos, Ugarit, and even Pylos, in the Peloponnese. Writing boards are mentioned at Ugarit (RS 19.053 = *PRU* 6 20), as "tablet of wax" *ṭuppa ša iškuri*. They also occur at Emar as Akkadian ^{giš} *lē'u* (less commonly, giš.ḫur = Akk. *uṣurtu* "drawing"), in Middle Assyrian rations, and as the source for material inscribed on Middle Babylonian *kudurru*s. They occur most frequently at Boğazköy, where they also had specific styli for inscribing the wax (Symington 1991: 120–122). Their appearance in *Iliad* 6.102 ("But he quickly sent him off to Lycia, gave him tokens, murderous signs, scratched in a folded tablet, and many of them too, enough to kill a man") could reflect either eighth-century or Late Bronze Age practices, and, in either case, show the role of the wooden tablet as a device for sending long-distance messages. Symington (1991: n. 36) cites the common phrase in Hittite notations on tablet copies: "according to the word(ing) of the wooden tablet." The medium was clearly widespread and long used, despite the near lack of preserved Bronze Age examples. Moreover, it was a common recording device in Hatti, including its frontier towns Carchemish and Emar. Thus, it seems more than plausible that a message from Cilicia (Kizzuwatna in the Hittite realm), would have been recorded first on wood, before copied onto clay at Ugarit. As Symington (1991: 121) observes, this is how Queen

Puduhepa wrote to her counterpart in Egypt or Alashiya about the marriage of her daughter to Ramesses II (Beckman 1999: no. 22E). That scribes at Ugarit used writing boards to write to one another is also shown by the final paragraph of RS 19.053 (*PRU* 6: 19–21), lines 20–26, following Symington (1991: 121–22): "Hear me about this other matter. The shoe which you gave me—if a tablet of wax is to your liking, I will indeed give you (one), but the tablet (of wax) which is with you, return to its owner." Despite the mundane mysteries of this text, it shows that some scribes at Ugarit (as in Assyria) owned writing boards. Another Akkadian letter, RS 34.136, sent from the king of Carchemish to the king of Ugarit, contains an explicit reference in lines 21–24 to the importance of the writing board in recording shipment contents; it was meant to be read aloud to the recipient upon arrival: "Now, the writing board which they delivered to me, let them read (it) out before you" (Symington 1991: 123). Symington's discussion of the Uluburun boards ends with a Neo-Assyrian reference to a writing board used to tally up a river shipment (1991: 123).

Cemal Pulak (2008) does not think the Uluburun boards were actually prepared aboard ship, though, like me at that time, he may not have been aware of our text, which plausibly, if uniquely, documents some sort of writing being done at sea. In light of RS 94.2406 I now think it entirely plausible that the queen had her double letter drafted aboard ship on a wooden tablet, which traveled some unknown route, possibly that reconstructed by Sauvage and Pardee (2015) before being copied onto clay at Ugarit.

5 Flying or Buying?

That the queen was somewhere in Cilicia is plausible enough, but to answer why she needed to take the risk of sharing this information with Urtenu requires some reconstruction. No other texts come from the queen while aboard ship, though another letter from the Urtenu archive, RS 94.247 (*Manual*: no. 32; see, also, Watson 2010: 168–169), features the *sakinu* supplying the queen at an unknown location with various dry and wet comestibles. Such supplies may have been vital, and perhaps this sort of condition underlies the imperative Ugaritic construction, *w d*, that ends her noted itinerary, and which might be read more literally "so know it" (as Dietrich and Loretz's "So nimm (dies) zur Kenntnis!"), instead of the less urgent "you are now informed." Whatever else was sent the queen's way, in terms of maritime trade she was dealing in the most valuable commodity of all: information. But are *we* informed, as Urtenu no doubt was, or just corrupted by our knowledge of how the story at Ugarit ends?

The sections in lines 11–15 that follow the queen's itinerary may or may not be crucial to how we understand the whole matter, but there is considerable disagreement over its meaning. Urtenu is exhorted to do something with his belongings in line 11, and then to do something else with his name in line 12. In line 13 verbal roots for "to finish," and "to serve," are likely present before one comes to the arrival of a "disaster" in line 14, at least according to readings in the *Manual* and Sauvage and Pardee (2015). Dietrich and Loretz (2009: 151) see this quite differently. The word translated as "disaster" is *th*, which was the subject of some consternation in the past due its occurrence toward the end of *KTU* 2.33 (lines 25, 29, and 37), an urgent letter to the queen regarding an enemy, a battle, and two thousand horses that did not show up where they were needed. In each of the three lines, Pardee (1984) translated *th* as simply "X," as in "X has been declared against me," "the children in X," and "let the X happen." After a fulsome philological commentary on the first 21 lines, Pardee offers this pessimistic appraisal of the letter's ending: "Lines 22–38 provide proof enough, were it needed, that even with a perfectly preserved text our knowledge of Ugaritic is not yet good enough to produce indisputable interpretations" (1984: 219). Dietrich and Loretz (2009: 151), on the other hand, have been confident for some time that this word was translated from the Akkadian cognate *šē'u* "neighbor" with an attached pronominal suffix *-h*. Thus understood, *th* is appropriately not listed in the 2003 *Dictionary of the Ugaritic Language* (*DULAT*); instead, it seems far more plausible that what "arrived" in line 14 was a neighbor (which also makes more sense for *KTU* 2.33, as in "the children of the neighbor" and "let the neighbor come"). "Disaster" would seem to fit an 1185 BCE crisis scenario, but given the domestic context (house, vessels, servant) noted in these sections of the letter, a neighbor creates less trouble for the philologist or historian.

The section in lines 16–20 involves a house but has defied attempts at coherent translation. That it is set apart with line dividers tells us that it is probably another task for Urtenu, one distinct enough from the previous to warrant its own section. The next two sections running from line 21 to 30 concern a woman's guarantee, or "entering into" (Ug. '*rbt*) that occurs three times in lines 24 and 28 and seems to be critical in determining Urtenu's fate. Lines 21–22 read: "As for you, nothing whatsoever escapes your mouth until [...] arrives," the break no doubt obscuring the identity of the woman who is Urtenu's potential guarantor. Lines 23–25 are fairly clear: "Then I will send a message to Ugarit [...] Should I hear that [she] has not agreed to guarantee you, then I'll send a(nother) message." The technical expression here, like its Akkadian cognate *erēbu*, is based on the verb "to enter" and occurs not infrequently in loan contracts (*DULAT*: 180–181).

The final section of the queen's letter, lines 26-30, continues spelling out the conditions of this guarantee and Urtenu's tasks. First, we have two lines whose reading is obscure and probably crucial to understanding the text clearly. Three items are mentioned: the first item could be restored as *kaspu* for silver, or stand as a type of bowl known as *sippu* or *sappu* (*DULAT*: 765-766), which perhaps contains the second item. The third item, here in the dual, is also unknown. It is not clear if the woman's guarantee depends on the receipt of these items, but that would be the logical implication, since lines 28-30 (in the *Manual*) state that "(if) she does not guarantee you, does not (agree to) come to me, she will send a message to the king and you can kiss your head goodbye." While it makes for dramatic reading, kissing and goodbye are not in the text (as the RSO 18 translation, "ta tête est partie" recognizes), and the idiom may be misleading when a far less severe conclusion may be equally plausible. The end of line 28 and beginning of 29 repeat the negated verb *la 'arabat,* but now with the preposition *'imma,* all of which would read more literally, "if she does not go in with you, and does not go in with me, and goes (instead) to the king, (then) your head is lost." Context is everything in Ugaritic, and if we do not let the assumption of crisis determine context, then *rashu* need not refer to the anatomical "head," but "capital or principal," as in initial or first, and as in investment, all readings known in the Akkadian cognate *rēšu,* found in Old Babylonian letters and even Old Akkadian texts (*CAD* R: 288-289). This more commercial reading would perhaps explain the purpose of the items referred to in lines 26-27, as well as explain the motivation for the mystery woman's guarantee or pledge.

So, to summarize what could be an equally plausible reading of events in the first letter on RS 94.2406, the queen—perhaps Sharelli, as posited by van Soldt (2016), and whose vast international correspondence enjoyed "special prestige," according to Singer (1999: 696-700)—was at sea making deals rather than making her escape from a collapsing Ugarit. Urtenu would be keeping silent so that the "mystery woman" might have a freer hand to invest in the queen's venture without interference from the king; she was probably a royal. Should the king have found out, heads may not have literally rolled, but Urtenu's stake would have been lost and the whole deal might have fallen through— a minor collapse compared to what was coming, but unfortunate. As I argue elsewhere (Monroe 2009), it was probably unseemly for royals to be participating openly in commercial ventures; that was an activity for agents and businesspeople. Thus, the matter here might not have been life and death, but profit and loss, just more business correspondence between the governor and queen, as was Text 32 in the *Manual.*

6   An Epic Companion?

Ilimilku's message to Urtenu, the second letter on the tablet, can be translated as it already has been in the *Manual* or by Dietrich and Loretz, and as such fits my reading of the first letter. The interpretive problem of context and its determining force is similar to the first letter. Urtenu states his expectation of a quick reply to a prior message. Whether this was taking place in a business context or during a disaster or invasion, the information exchanged in these letters must have been quite valuable. Finding a safe haven for the queen and her chosen few in Hittite Cilicia may have been complicated, even more so if one assumes the sea was teeming with pirates and marauding Sea Peoples. More interesting perhaps is the apparent ability of the queen to escape the kingdom unnoticed, either for survival or commerce, though this need not be taken to support the misconception that the queen had a special harbor residence in Ras Ibn Hani (van Soldt 2006: 16). That she had somebody named Ilimilku along is especially intriguing in the wake of epigraphical information coming out of Urtenu's house. Bordreuil and Pardee are careful not to claim that this must have been the same Ilimilku who wrote the famous myths; but the Baal Cycle fragment found in Urtenu's house bearing Ilimilku's colophon, which they do mention (Bordreuil and Pardee 2010: 19–20), makes the identification all the more plausible and nearly irresistible.

7   Answers Written on the Water

Conclusions in the traditional sense are a bit elusive. The vagaries of the Ugaritic writing system, coupled with our knowledge of the disastrous outcome awaiting Ugarit and its neighbors, I fear may leave us incapable of reading these texts with adequate objectivity. To balance ambiguous alternatives in hopes that better information will come along also seems like dubious historiography at best. Nevertheless, what is common to these alternative interpretations of RS 94.2406 is a role for writing that is decidedly powerful as an information technology. It is a role that complements the one uncovered by neo-Marxist and Weberian readings of Mesopotamian writing from earlier periods wherein literacy functioned as part of the state apparatus for economic administration, coercion, and maintaining the charismatic bases of royal legitimacy, Like the Old Assyrian letters from Kültepe, epistolary at Ugarit was a practical tool used to access vast information networks and the wealth generated therein.

Kevin McGeough (2007) applied network analysis to the Ugaritic texts, representing each prominently attested individual as a node, sized according to his or her number of contacts and linked by lines to other such nodes. Such an approach graphically reinforces the identification of numerous powerful households at Ugarit, including those of Urtenu, other commercial agents, and the queen, all of whom acted, however, as dependents of the palace, the most dominant of economic actors. McGeough's analysis and conclusions mostly concern the heterarchical organization of royal power and how prior studies have obscured this. Royal power at Ugarit was thus decentralized via a network of local exchange relationships involving multiple households and institutions.

My own view (Monroe 2009, based on a 2000 dissertation; Monroe 2015) sees an Ugarit wherein the power of exchange was exerted through a network of local and long-distance relationships involving multiple households and institutions that sometimes included the palace. In studying the modes of wealth accumulation practiced by entrepreneurs at Ugarit and in the Late Bronze Age inter-societal system as a whole, I found eight significant dimensions to the social relations and means of exchange. Literacy, here meaning the ability to correspond in writing, is a particularly crucial dimension, since it facilitated the creation of social networks and legal protections that reduced risk, anxiety, and transport costs for all concerned. Knowing how to correspond was a prerequisite for entry into more elite networks of information and influence that flowed in and out of Ugarit. Nodal figures like Urtenu, and other figures with access to royal capital, were successful at combining multiple strategies of accumulation that could either include or exclude the king. And as our current text implies, the king could not own or control the information networks that he only accessed through officials and exchange specialists, many of whom clearly had independent interests. Both models of political economy at Ugarit (the network-based of McGeough, and my *social relations of exchange*) acknowledge the limits of palatial power and knowledge. As articulated so well by Artzy (1997), royals were wary of entrepreneurial types, whose activities were often destabilizing. RS 94.2406 may show us how entrepreneurs empowered with writing were even more elusive and dangerous.

Finally, and returning to Bordreuil and Pardee's *Manual* reading, one can hardly overlook the self-determinative agency in the queen's ability to communicate with the governor and thus maintain a lifeline of information, under either dire or sensitive circumstances. To conduct such a venture without the king's knowledge (or even the governor's, until it was revealed to him by Ilimilku) reveals the extraordinary value of information and the crown's inability to monopolize it. Moreover, this singular text plausibly implies another level of sophistication in what many have already remarked was an elaborate international information network—namely that letters could be sent and received while at sea. Bronze Age harbors, from the northern and prominent Ugarit down to the southern, modest Tel Nami (Israel) functioned as thresholds where conditions of risk, ambiguity, and liberality contributed to innovation and even social transformation. Extending the technology of writing to the maritime world was a powerful act, in this case conducted by a well-connected woman living by the sea.

Acknowledgments

I want to thank David Owen and the rest of a 2011 audience at Cornell, where some of these ideas were first presented in a paper entitled "'You Are Now Informed': Ugaritic Text RS 94.2406 and the Limits of Power and Knowledge at the End of the Bronze Age." I am also indebted here especially to the scholarship of Pierre Bordreuil, Dennis Pardee, Itamar Singer, Wilfred van Soldt, and Dorit Symington. My critical engagement with their work is done with deepest respect. Finally, my appreciation goes to Michal Artzy, who with great patience and generosity gave me my start in Near Eastern archaeology at Tel Nami.

References

Artzy, M. 1997. Nomads of the Sea. In: Swiny, S., Hohlfelder, R.L., and Swiny, H.W., eds. *Res Maritimae: Cyprus and the Eastern Mediterranean from Prehistory to Late Antiquity* (Cyprus American Archaeological Research Institute Monograph Series 1). Atlanta: 1–16.

Beckman, G.M. 1999. *Hittite Diplomatic Texts* (2nd ed.) (Writings from the Ancient World 7). Atlanta.

Bordreuil, P. and Pardee, D. 2010. Textes alphabétiques inédits du Musée du Louvre. In: Soldt, H.W., van, ed. *Society and Administration in Ancient Ugarit*. Leiden: 1–15.

CAD. The Assyrian Dictionary of the Oriental Institute of Chicago. Chicago.

Calvet, Y. 2000. The House of Urtenu. *Near Eastern Archaeology* 63(4): 210–211.

Dietrich, M. and Loretz, O. 2009. Die keilalphabetischen Briefe aus Ugarit (i): KTU 2.72, 2.76, 2.86, 2.87, 2.88, 2.89 und 2.90 *Ugarit-Forschungen* 41: 109–165.

Doorninck, F. van. 2005. The Ship of Georgios, Priest and Sea Captain: Yassiada, Turkey. In: Bass, G.F., ed. *Beneath the Seven Seas*. New York: 92–99.

DULAT. Olmo Lete, G. del and Sanmartin, J. 2003. *A Dictionary of the Ugaritic Language in the Alphabetic Tradition*. 2 vols. (2nd rev. ed.). Leiden–Boston.

Gzella, H. 2010. Linguistic Variation in the Ugaritic Letters and Some Implications Thereof. In: Soldt, H.W., van, ed. *Society and Administration in Ancient Ugarit.* Leiden: 58–70.

Hawley, R., Pardee, D., and Roche-Hawley, C. 2015. The Scribal Culture of Ugarit. *Journal of Ancient Near Eastern History* 2(2): 229–267.

Kaniewski, D., Guiot, J., and Van Campo, E. 2015. Drought and Societal Collapse 3200 Years ago in the Eastern Mediterranean: A Review. *WIREs Climate Change* 6: 369–382. https://doi:10.1002/wcc.345 (accessed April 1, 2019).

Knapp, A.B. and Manning, S.W. 2016. Crisis in Context: The End of the Late Bronze Age in the Eastern Mediterranean. *American Journal of Archaeology* 120: 99–149.

KTU. Dietrich, M., Loretz, O., and Sanmartin, J. 2013. *The Cuneiform Alphabetic Texts from Ugarit, Ras Ibn Hani and Other Places* (3rd, enlarged ed.) (Alter Orient und Altes Testament 360/1). Münster.

Malbran-Labat, F. 2010. Pratiques marchandes dans le commerce ougaritain. In: Soldt, H.W., van, ed. *Society and Administration in Ancient Ugarit.* Leiden: 84–93.

Manual. Bordreuil, P. and Pardee, D. 2009. *A Manual of Ugaritic.* Winona Lake, IN.

McGeough, K.M. 2007. *Exchange Relationships at Ugarit* (Ancient Near Eastern Studies, Supplement 26). Leuven.

Monroe, C. 2009. *Scales of Fate: Trade, Tradition, and Transformation in the Eastern Mediterranean, ca. 1350–1175 BCE* (Alter Orient und Altes Testament 357). Münster.

Monroe, C. 2015. Tangled Up in Blue: Material and Immaterial Relations of Exchange in the Late Bronze Age World. In: Howe, T., ed. *Traders in the Ancient Mediterranean* (Publications of the Association of Ancient Historians 11). Chicago: 7–46.

Pardee, D. 1984. Further Studies in Epistolography. *Archiv für Orientforschung* 31: 213–230.

Pardee, D. 2002. Ugaritic Letters. In: Hallo, W.M. and Younger, K.L., Jr., eds. *The Context of Scripture,* Vol. 3: *Archival Works from the Biblical World.* Leiden: 87–115.

PRU 4. Nougayrol, J. 1956. *Le Palais Royal d'Ugarit 4: Textes accadiens des Archives Sud (archives internationales)* (Mission de Ras Shamra 9). Paris.

PRU 6. Nougayrol, J. 1970. *Le Palais Royal d'Ugarit 6 : Textes en cunéiformes babyloniens des archives du Grand Palais et du Palais Sud d'Ugarit* (Mission de Ras Shamra 12). Paris.

Pulak, C. 2008. The Uluburun Shipwreck and Late Bronze Age Trade. In: Aruz, J., Benzel, K., and Evans, J.M., eds. *Beyond Babylon: Art, Trade, and Diplomacy in the Second Millennium B.C.* New York: 289–305.

RSO 18. Bordreuil, P., Pardee, D., and Hawley, R. 2012. *Une bibliothèque au sud de la ville 3: Textes 1994–2002 en cunéiforme alphabétique de la Maison d'Ourtenou* (Ras Shamra-Ougarit 18). Lyon.

Sauvage, C. and Pardee, D. 2015. L'itinéraire maritime d'une reine d'Ougarit. Note sur le texte RS 94.2406—in memoriam Pierre Bordreuil. *Syria* 92: 239–254.

Singer, I. 1999. A Political History of Ugarit. In: Watson, W.G.E. and Wyatt, N., eds. *Handbook of Ugaritic Studies*. (Handbuch der Orientalistik 39). Boston.

Soldt, W.H. van. 2002. Studies on the *Sākinu*-Official (2): The Function of the Sākinu of Ugarit. *Ugarit-Forschungen* 34: 805–828.

Soldt, W.H. 2006. Studies on the *Sākinu*-Official (3): The *Sākinu* of Other Ugaritic Towns and of the Palace and the Queen's House, and the Findspots of the Tablets. *Ugarit-Forschungen* 38: 1–24.

Soldt, W.H. 2016. The Traveling Queen of Ugarit. In Matoïan, V. and Maqdissi, M.—al, eds. *Études ougaritiques* IV (Ras Shamra-Ougarit 24). Leuven: 95–108.

Symington, D. 1991. Late Bronze Age Writing Boards and Their Uses: Textual Evidence from Anatolia and Syria. *Anatolian Studies* 41: 111–123.

Ugaritica 5. Nougayrol, J., Laroche, E., Virolleaud, C. and Schaeffer, C.F.A. 1968 *Ugaritica* v: *nouveaux textes accadiens, hourrites et ugaritiques des archives et bibliothèques privées d'Ugarit* Paris.

Watson, W.G.E. 2010. From List to Letter: Notes on Letter-Writing Techniques in Ancient Ugarit. In: Soldt, H.W. van, ed. *Society and Administration in Ancient Ugarit*. Leiden: 164–178.

Yon, M. 2006. *The City of Ugarit at Tell Ras Shamra*. Winona Lake, IN.

Zaccagnini, C. 1995. On War and Famine at Emar. *Orientalia* 64: 92–109.

CHAPTER 13

A Fragmentary Small Copper Oxhide Ingot from Tell Beit Mirsim at the James L. Kelso Bible Lands Museum, Pittsburgh-Xenia Theological Seminary

Cemal Pulak

A leading scholar in the field of terrestrial, maritime, and coastal archaeology, as well as a preeminent teacher and researcher, Michal Artzy has worked in fields as diverse as neutron activation analysis of pottery, ancient metallurgy, and Bronze Age exchange. It is a great pleasure and honor to pay tribute to her multifarious and distinguished contributions embracing both traditional and new approaches to Near Eastern archaeology with this paper. While this study concerns only a single, partial copper ingot excavated from Tell Beit Mirsim about 90 years ago, the invitation to contribute to her *Festschrift* seemed a fitting opportunity to publish a first detailed account here, especially since the results illustrate how much more there is to be discovered and learned about sources and exchange of copper in the Bronze Age.

1 Introduction

Tell Beit Mirsim (henceforth TBM) is situated in the eastern region of the Judean Shephelah, or lowlands, and is spread over an area of 7.5 acres (Albright 1938: 1).[1] Under the directorship of William Foxwell Albright, four seasons of excavation between 1926 and 1932 by the Pittsburgh-Xenia Theological Seminary and the American School of Oriental Research in Jerusalem revealed at TBM likely evidence for metalworking activity in Stratum D, dated to Middle Bronze (MB) IIC (Albright 1938: 25). According to Albright, Stratum D, in the southeast (SE) quadrant of the tell, was "the best preserved section of a city from the first half of the sixteenth century B.C. yet excavated in Palestine."[2] The

---

1 Ben-Arieh (2004: 1) provides the map reference for the site as New Israel Grid 19100-200/ 59600-700.
2 Albright 1938: 41; date given specifically as ca. 1600–1560/1550 on p. 60. No major modification to the excavation strata and dates suggested by Albright appears to have been made; they are used as originally published by later studies; see, for example, Ben-Arieh 2004: 1.

metallurgical evidence comes from a house located in SE 23, D-9, and includes an open limestone mold with cavities for casting tools on three of its four largest surfaces (Albright 1938: 53, with pl. 43: b, d),[3] and two similarly sized limestone pot bellows found in close proximity, but incorrectly identified as crucibles in the report.[4] One of the pot bellows (no. 8) apparently crumbled to pieces during removal, but the other (no. 7) was recovered intact and drawn for publication (Albright 1938: pl. 31: 7). The stone mold and pot bellows were fashioned from a hardened chalk locally known as *nari*, which is noted in the report as a refractory material. Based on their material, as well as the low-level placement of their "'spouts," Albright identified these two vessels as crucibles for melting copper. Because no traces of copper were noted in either vessel, he concluded that they had not yet been used, finding support for his interpretation in the unfinished state of the nearby limestone mold.

Since the two vessels are actually pot bellows, rather than crucibles, they would not have been used directly for melting copper or any other metallurgical process and, thus, would be devoid of any copper residue.[5] In all likelihood, these pot bellows, usually used in pairs, would have supplied a forced draft to a furnace for melting copper or bronze for the purpose of casting metal objects.[6] The report does not indicate whether other metallurgical objects such as nozzles (tuyeres) for directing the forced air from the pot bellows into the furnace (or remnants thereof) were discovered during excavation. Albright does, however, suggest that these associated finds provide evidence for copper working in this stratum, but not whether they comprise the contents of a metallurgical workshop.

During a previous excavation season, a partial small oxhide-shaped copper ingot was also found some distance away from the stone mold and pot bellows. It was inside a house located in SE 32, D-2,[7] an 18–24 m distance from the house

---

3 That only three of the four sides were shaped to cast stone tools, and one side left blank, suggested to Albright that the mold was unfinished. One side of the mold was carved to cast an adze blade and three knives, another side, an adze and a brooch, and the third side, a knife blade 43 cm long.

4 See Albright 1938: 53–54, pl. 40: 7–8 for in situ photographs of the two stone pot bellows.

5 In fact, copper melts at 1085 °C, which is well above limestone's decomposition temperature of about 900 °C.

6 For Near Eastern pot bellows and manners of their use, see Davey 1979: 101–111; Tylecote 1981: 107–118. Pot bellows occur also in Cyprus (Kassianidou 2011), Anatolia (Müller Karpe 2000: 117), and Crete (Blitzer 1995: 508–509; Dimopoulou 1997: 435; Evely 2000: 363–365; Betancourt and Muhly 2006: 126).

7 For the index of objects in the plates, including their serial numbers (for copper ingot = SN 769), refer to Albright 1938: 96, and for the object listing by SN, see p. 82. Based on SN groupings within the object listing, it appears that the ingot was found during the 1928 field

in SE 23, as best as can be determined from the site plan (Albright 1938: 54, 137, pls. 41: 13; 51). The copper ingot reinforces the evidence for ongoing metallurgical activity in this part of the city and is the focus of this study.

2 The Small Oxhide-Shaped Copper Ingot from Tell Beit Mirsim

2.1 *Background*

Invited to give a lecture on October 12, 2012 at the Pittsburgh Theological Seminary, and when touring the Seminary's James L. Kelso Bible Lands Museum, I realized that one of the core collections of the museum consists of artifacts from the Late Bronze Age site of TBM, the partial copper ingot discussed here among them (Fig. 13.1). I am grateful to my gracious hosts, Ron E. Tappy, the G. Albert Shoemaker Professor of Bible and Archaeology and the museum director, and Museum Curator Karen Bowden Cooper, who kindly invited me to study and sample the TBM ingot.

Specifications and description of the TBM Ingot:
Location: James L. Kelso Bible Lands Museum
Registration no.: 1.0-435
Provenance: Tell Beit Mirsim, SE quadrant, Grid 32, Stratum D, Locus 2
Stratigraphic date: MB IIC
Condition: Approximately 2/3 complete
Dimensions: Max. l. 9.64 cm; max. w. 8.78 cm; min. w. 6.94 cm; thickness: 0.93–1.51 cm
Weight before cleaning and conservation: 246.64 g
Weight after cleaning and conservation: 233.31 g
Weight after sampling: 231.29 g
Weight of sample (total): 2.02 g (sampled: 17 October 2011 and 22 May 2013)
Volume of preserved ingot: 62.03 cm^3
Condition (based on reconstructed volume): ca. 61.5% complete
Maximum length of digitally reconstructed ingot: ca. 14 cm
Total volume of digitally reconstructed ingot: ca. 100.9 cm^3
Weight of digitally reconstructed ingot: ca. 358.2 g

A little over one third (ca. 38.5% on reconstructed volume basis) of the ingot was deliberately broken off in antiquity, presumably for use in a transaction or, more likely, for melting in the metalworking area near the ingot's findspot. Measuring only 9.64 cm in length (overall reconstructed length ca. 14 cm), it is

---

season, while the pot bellows and stone mold were excavated in 1932. It should be noted that all of these finds were located within Stratum D.

FIGURE 13.1   The Upper rough, "bubbly" surface and all four sides (upper left) and the flatter molded surface (upper right) of the copper oxhide ingot from TBM, as found and preserved in the collections of the James L. Kelso Bible Lands Museum. The red circle (upper right) indicates the portion examined under magnification; at bottom, magnified view (A) shows quartz grains (B), iron oxide particles (C), and mineralized grass or straw chaff (D, E).
PHOTOS BY RYAN LEE [UPPER] AND SUZANNE ECKERT [LOWER]; FIGURE LAYOUT BY RYAN THEIS

a small ingot, although still about one-third larger than the largest of the Cypriot copper oxhide ingots generally referred to as "miniature" or "votive" ingots. The TBM ingot has the typical "pillow" shape associated with the chronologically earlier oxhide ingots of Buchholz's Type I (Bass's Type Ib),[8] with gently incurving sides but with corner protrusions a little more pronounced and rounded than those of the typical pillow-shaped ingots.

More importantly, the TBM ingot is a much smaller version of the standard, full-sized pillow-shaped oxhide ingots, and smaller still than the five small

---

8   According to Buchholz's (1959: 6–7, fig. 2) typology, the Type I pillow-shaped ingots are the earliest of the oxhide-shaped ingots. Bass (1967: 53, fig. 55) expanded Buchholz's typology based on the oxhide ingots from the Cape Gelidonya shipwreck, but the chronology of the ingot types was not changed.

pillow-shaped ingots from the late fourteenth-century BCE Uluburun shipwreck.[9] Both surfaces of the TBM ingot are similar to those of full-sized copper oxhide ingots, and quite different from the smoother surfaces of miniature votive oxhide ingots from Cyprus and elsewhere. While some of the Cypriot miniature ingots are inscribed, the preserved portion of the TBM ingot bears no markings or inscriptions of any kind.

3 The Tell Beit Mirsim Copper Oxhide Ingot Conservation and Analyses

In the museum, the surfaces of the TBM ingot were concealed by excavation dirt and layers of copper corrosion (Fig. 13.1). Upon initial inspection, the occurrence of small patches of active chloride corrosion, commonly known as "bronze disease," necessitated the removal of all dirt and corrosion layers in order to stabilize the active corrosion areas, the application of a chemical barrier, and the environmental sealing of the ingot for safe, long-term storage.[10]

---

9 Five small or fractional pillow-shaped ingots of Type 1b were found on the late fourteenth-century BCE Uluburun shipwreck (Pulak 2000: 141–142; 2008: 307–308, fig. 185c; Ünsal, Pulak, and Slotta 2005: 59.8, 567.30–31), but as these are smaller versions of the standard pillow-shaped ingot type, they may not fully conform to the chronological typology proposed by Buchholz. For a small oxhide ingot of unique shape from the Uluburun shipwreck, see Ünsal, Pulak, and Slotta 2005: 568.32; Pulak 2008: 307–308, fig. 185e.

10 Based on a protocol signed between myself, on behalf of the Institute of Nautical Archaeology (INA), and the James L. Kelso Bible Lands Museum on November 13, 2010, the TBM ingot and several other copper alloy artifacts were sent to Texas A&M University (TAMU) on temporary loan for conservation purposes. The conservation of the artifacts was carried out under the overall supervision of Helen C. Dewolf of the Center for Maritime Archaeology and Conservation (CMAC) Laboratory and Nautical Archaeology Program (NAP) at TAMU; the collection was returned to the museum on April 5, 2013. The ingot was cleaned mechanically and areas of active corrosion were removed completely using dental tools, and the process was repeated during the final stages of conservation. Following mechanical cleaning, the ingot was soaked in successive baths of 5% sodium carbonate (Na_2CO_3) for several months, and the chloride levels were reduced from the initial 500+ ppm to well below 50 ppm. Layers of loosened corrosion products were mechanically cleaned with minimal brushing using tooth and fiberglass brushes. After final cleaning and rinsing in deionized water, the ingot was placed in a 2% benzotriazole (BTA) for 24 hours and immersed in molten microcrystalline wax as an environmental sealant. Upon the reoccurrence of several minute active corrosion spots after placing the ingot in an accelerated environmental chamber, the microcrystalline wax coating was removed and the ingot immersed in 2% formic acid under vacuum for four hours and rinsed, and the BTA and microcrystalline wax applications were repeated as before.

During the various stages of cleaning and conserving, a total of 13.33 g of dirt and corrosion products were removed from the ingot.

3.1 Pre-cleaning and Conservation Examination

Prior to the mechanical removal of surface deposits, the ingot was carefully examined with a high-power microscope for possible remnants of a clay or stone mold adhering to its surfaces.[11] The examination of the ingot's molded surface revealed that the surface "dirt" is high in clay minerals and likely consisted mostly of unfired clay. Its texture is not what one would expect to see in a fired-clay mold or even in an unfired-clay mold that has come into contact with molten copper. Clay exposed to high temperatures during firing hardens into ceramic, a process that is accompanied by some shrinkage resulting in gaps or separation between the clay matrix and surrounding minerals. Furthermore, this shrinkage imparts a somewhat "chunky" texture to the clay matrix. Neither of these features, both of which are readily observable under high magnification, could be seen in the clay on the ingot's molded surface (Fig. 13.1: a). As refractory clay would be expected to contain inclusions such as grog, sand, or straw chaff added to the clay before firing, the TBM ingot's clay was examined for evidence of such inclusions. The yellow-white particles in the ingot's clay are mostly quartz grains, as revealed by their color, five- to six-sided crystals in cross section, and uneven fracture (Fig. 13.1: b); the grog-like, reddish inclusions are highly oxidized, iron-rich mineral particles (Fig. 13.1: c); and the grass or straw chaff preserved in the clay matrix would have been mostly burned out, leaving a void if the clay had been fired or subjected to contact with molten copper instead of being preserved in a mineralized state (Fig. 13.1: d, e). All three inclusions, and the unfired clay itself, are consistent with excavation dirt and not indicative of fired refractory clay.

Moreover, unfired clay with identical inclusions was also observed on the rough or "bubbly" surface of the ingot, which would not have been in contact with the mold during the casting of the ingot. In conclusion, therefore, the dirt adhering to the ingot's surfaces must be natural TBM soil from the excavation and not remnants of a refractory-clay mold.

Top or "bubbly" surface of the ingot: The ingot's upper face, which was exposed during casting in an open mold is sometimes also referred to as the "bubbly" surface, due to the irregular texture formed by the effervescence of dissolved gasses such as oxygen, carbon monoxide, carbon dioxide, water vapor,

---

11   I am greatly indebted to Suzanne Eckert, formerly of the Department of Anthropology, TAMU, for undertaking this examination and expressing her opinion, which I refer to here.

A FRAGMENTARY SMALL COPPER OXHIDE INGOT

FIGURE 13.2   The TBM ingot after cleaning and conservation: the "bubbly" top surface and all four sides (left) and the flatter, molded surface (right)
PHOTOS BY LILIA CAMPANA; FIGURE LAYOUT BY RYAN THEIS

and sulfur dioxide in the molten copper during solidification in the mold. This face exhibits the same rough surface seen on full-sized copper oxhide ingots (Figs. 13.2, 13.3; Hauptmann, Maddin, and Prange 2002: 4). Viewed from this surface, the TBM ingot is slightly asymmetrical in shape, with one corner being wider and more rounded than the other. The bubbly surface is devoid of any obvious iron silicate slag particles or bits of charcoal observed on the bubbly surface of some Uluburun oxhide ingots (Hauptmann, Maddin, and Prange 2002: 6–7). A few small, dark patches slightly atop the ingot's crust are stable copper-corrosion products left on the ingot during its final cleaning and conservation in 2013. The bubbles are generally of uniform shape and size, except for three larger ones near and approximately midway between the two corner protrusions. Near what would have been the midpoint of the complete ingot, there is a gas pore that perforates the ingot. In the same approximate area, there is an irregular flattened patch (Fig. 13.3), corresponding to the slightly concave deformation (relative to the top surface) clearly visible in the ingot's longitudinal profile. The portions of the ingot on either side of this deformation are raised and form a shallow but visible V shape, even though about a third of the ingot is missing. Corresponding flattened patches occur on the ingot's bottom or molded surface, which are readily discernible from the ingot's naturally deformed surface features. These conspicuous flattened areas on both surfaces of the ingot indicate that it was struck with a hammer or some

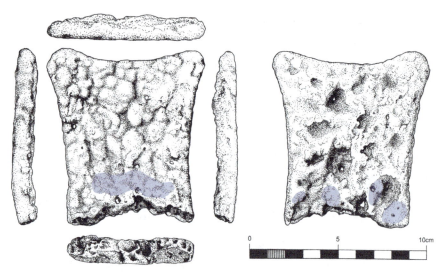

FIGURE 13.3 Drawing of the TBM ingot after cleaning and conservation: the "bubbly" top surface and all four sides (left) and the flatter, molded surface (right). Blue shading demarks flattened areas from striking the ingot for fracturing purposes
DRAWING BY HELEN C. DEWOLF

other heavy blunt tool. While the beating was likely repeated on both faces by alternately flipping the ingot (the reason for the presence of the flattened surface on the molded side), it was last struck on the top or bubbly surface when the ingot finally fractured into two pieces.[12] This indicates that the break was not accidental or a result of rough handling, but rather deliberate.

Molded or smooth surface of the ingot: The molded surface, the face of the ingot in contact with the mold when the ingot was cast, is relatively flat, but pocked with six deep (0.6–1.1 cm) conical or dome-shaped gas cavities, one of which pierces through the ingot, as well as four intermediate (0.2–0.4 cm deep) and four to five shallow (0.1–0.2 cm deep) cavities (Figs. 13.2, 13.3). The distribution and shape of these cavities suggest that, in addition to the dissolved gasses in the molten copper, they probably resulted from humidity left in the mold and carbon dioxide produced from the breakdown of limestone upon coming in contact with molten copper, as is often the case with calcination of limestone. Either way, it is an indication that the ingot was cast in a durable mold of clay or limestone, as opposed to a sand mold, which would have allowed

---

12 The plano-convex discoid or bun-shaped ingots from the Uluburun shipwreck were fragmented by the same method; Pulak 2000: 144–145; see, also, Hauptmann, Maddin, and Prange 2002: 19.

significant off-gassing when the ingot was cast, resulting in a non- or considerably less porous ingot composition. The mold must have been crudely made, as revealed by irregularities in the ingot's shape and its rounded, rather than sharp, edges.

Since an ingot is only a semi-finished rather than a final product in the circulation of metal, the resulting shape would not have been of great significance, and the choice of a clay versus stone mold for casting would simply have been based on practicality. The presence of gas pores, whether deliberate or inadvertent, provided some advantage in facilitating the fracturing of the ingot into smaller pieces for exchange or in expediting the melting in a crucible. Near the middle of the TBM ingot, close to the deliberately broken edge, there are four small flattened patches resulting from striking the ingot with a heavy, blunt tool to break it (Fig. 13.3). There is no visible scoring on either surface of the ingot near the break to suggest an attempt at a more even or uniform division.

Sides of the ingot: The ingot's preserved original sides exhibit a rounded profile with gentle curves, particularly so on the corner protrusions (Figs. 13.2, 13.3). These rounded sides and edges contrast with those of large oxhide ingots that have well-formed, mostly straight and sharp sides tapering outward slightly, which also form a purchase or grip for lifting the ingot. The rounded sides of the TBM ingot suggest that it was cast in a crudely made shallow mold about 1.5 cm deep. There is no indication that the molten copper flowed over or exceeded the mold edge. This may imply that only a limited quantity of molten copper was poured into the mold or that the copper had cooled a little, becoming more viscous before pouring, rather than that care was taken to avoid overflow and cast a perfect ingot. The slight upward curvature of the ingot at the break is a result of being struck with a heavy tool. Judging from its irregularity, the break was propagated mainly along gas cavities, some of which are now fully exposed. It appears that an attempt was made to break the ingot approximately in equal halves across its narrowest point, or waist, without scoring it to control the break, but that attempt failed partly due to the irregularity of the large gas cavities within the ingot.

3.2 *Porosity/Density Determinations*

After cleaning and conserving the ingot, it was laser scanned to generate a 3-D image, which then was used to determine the ingot's total volume.[13] The ingot's volume was recalculated after digitally filling in the gas cavities on the molded

---

13   The ingot was scanned by Chris Dostal, research associate at CMAC-NAP at TAMU, using a FARO Fusion coordinate measuring machine (CMM) with a Version 2 Laser Line Probe attachment, and volume calculated using Geomagic Studio 2014 software.

surface so that the surface appeared mostly flat, without cavities. This latter, flattened version is probably a better approximation of the ingot's original surface as cast, since the gas voids likely became exposed over time as the thin copper "skin" covering them corroded away. Since the volume of the ingot with exposed gas cavities is smaller than the volume with sealed gas cavities, the density of the former is higher than that of the latter.

Volume with exposed gas cavities on the molded surface: 62.03 cm^3
Volume with sealed gas cavities on the molded surface: 65.82 cm^3
Density with exposed gas cavities on the molded surface: 233.31 g ÷ 62.03 cm^3 = 3.76 g/cm^3
Density with sealed gas cavities on the molded surface: 233.31 g ÷ 65.82 cm^3 = 3.55 g/cm^3
Density of pure copper: 8.96 g/cm^3

As can be deduced from the low values for the density of the TBM ingot compared to that of pure copper, the ingot is highly porous. Some of the ingot's mass would have been lost due to copper corrosion. While there is no way to determine the exact amount of this loss, it would not have been high because of the ingot's small surface area relative to its large volume.

Nevertheless, both versions of the ingot's density are rather low, corresponding to only 42% and 39.6%, respectively, of the density of pure copper. Due to its high porosity, therefore, the TBM ingot weighs less than half of a comparable ingot cast of solid copper. Substantial porosity, in fact, is typical of ingots cast from freshly smelted, unrefined "blister copper" (Hauptmann, Maddin, and Prange 2002: 4). The metallographic analysis of the Uluburun oxhide and disc-shaped ingots revealed a porosity rate of about 20% or even higher. The same study further showed that the high levels of porosity in the Uluburun ingots combined with the high concentration of copper oxide inclusions helped explain the previously perplexing question of how ingots of a metal as ductile as copper could have been readily broken into fragments simply by repeated striking with a heavy blunt tool. The porosity provides a path for the propagation of cracks when external pressure, such as that which comes from hitting with a heavy tool, is applied. Any copper ingot is made all the more brittle by the presence of oxides, which render the copper matrix brittle (Hauptmann, Maddin, and Prange 2002: 19). These incidental factors facilitated the breaking of copper ingots for transaction purposes or for ease of use in metalworking.

The TBM ingot was digitally reconstructed to represent the complete object by mirroring and flipping the preserved part of the ingot over the place of the missing portion and adjusting it for the best fit (Fig. 13.4). From this we obtained

A FRAGMENTARY SMALL COPPER OXHIDE INGOT 231

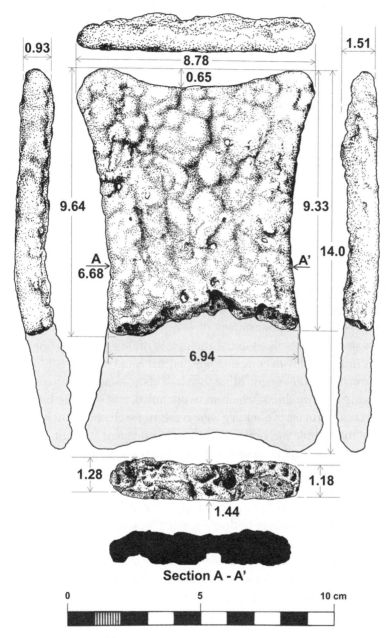

FIGURE 13.4 Drawing of the TBM ingot reconstructed by mirroring and flipping the preserved part of the ingot over the area of the missing portion; dimensions in cm
FIGURE LAYOUT BY RYAN THEIS

the volumes of the reconstructed complete ingot with exposed and sealed gas cavities on the molded surface and multiplied them by the density obtained for the 3-D versions of the preserved ingot with both exposed and sealed gas cavities, as the latter value is believed to be a better approximation to that of the original ingot.

Volume of restored ingot with exposed gas cavities on the molded surface: 100.89 cm^3

Volume of restored ingot with sealed gas cavities on the molded surface: 104.65 cm^3

Weight of restored ingot with exposed gas cavities: 100.89 cm^3 × 3.76 g/cm^3 = 379.35 g

Weight of restored ingot with sealed gas cavities: 104.65 cm^3 × 3.55 g/cm^3 = 371.51 g

3.3 Sampling and Chemical Analyses

The TBM ingot was sampled from its broken side to avoid altering or damaging the ingot's original profile and surfaces. A total of 2.02 g of copper was sampled from the ingot for quantitative and lead isotope analyses (LIA). Due to the ingot's high porosity and poor state of preservation, the sample was taken using stainless steel dental tools, as initial attempts at drilling produced fine metallic granules intermixed with corrosion powder that could not be easily separated from the metallic component. More than half of the sample taken consisted of copper corrosion products, which were discarded, and only the brightly colored metallic particles of about 1 g were retained for chemical analysis.

Part of this sample was sent to the Deutsches Bergbau-Museum in Bochum, Germany, for chemical analysis using inductively coupled plasma mass spectroscopy (ICP-MS), and another part was sent to the Institut für Geowissenschaften at Johann Wolfgang Goethe-University in Frankfurt am Main, Germany, for LIA using a multicollector inductively coupled plasma mass spectrometer (MC-ICPMS).[14] The results of both analyses are presented in Tables 13.1 and 13.2.

The quantitative-analysis results indicate that the TBM ingot was cast of unalloyed, unrefined copper. Tin was identified only in trace amounts. The rough, bubbly surface and high porosity of the ingot are characteristics of casting with newly smelted blister copper.

---

14   I am grateful to Ünsal Yalçın for the chemical analysis of the TBM ingot and for arranging the LIA to be conducted at Frankfurt am Main. The results of both analyses were sent to me on December 3, 2012.

TABLE 13.1   ICP-MS analysis results for the TBM ingot, given in ppm except for the copper (Cu), which is given as percentage (87.4%). The total percentage of all elements listed is 87.5%, with much of the total difference (12.5%) coming from undetected elements resulting from corrosion products in the sample. The high nickel (Ni) value is probably due in part to contamination from dental tools used in sampling (Bochum Sample no. 4502–12)

Ag	Sn	Sb	Te	Pb	Bi	U	Au	P
225	3	47	4	295	1	2	4	2
S	Fe	Co	Ni	Zn	Mn	As	Se	Cu (%)
180	23	6	325	15	1	510	460	87.4

magnified view (A) shows quartz grains (B), iron oxide particles (C)

TABLE 13.2   LI-ratio results from the TBM ingot (Bochum Sample no. 4502–12)

	^{206}Pb/^{204}Pb	^{207}Pb/^{204}Pb	^{208}Pb/^{204}Pb	^{207}Pb/^{206}Pb	^{208}Pb/^{206}Pb
Mean	2.42408	18.49462	15.66176	38.52427	0.84683	2.08301
SE (%)	0.00162	0.00308	0.00277	0.00321	0.00114	0.00154
SE (abs)| 0.00004	0.00057	0.00043	0.00124	0.00001	0.00003
SD (%)	0.00725	0.01345	0.01206	0.01399	0.00508	0.00687
SD (abs)| 0.00018	0.00249	0.00189	0.00539	0.00004	0.00014

The main impurities present in the ingot are arsenic, selenium, nickel, lead, silver, and sulfur, with trace amounts of antimony, iron, zinc, and cobalt. The remaining elements, including gold and tin, are all below 5 ppm. It is possible that some of the nickel may have been introduced as contamination from the stainless steel dental tools used during sampling.[15] The concentrations of the trace elements of the TBM ingot are generally higher than in Cypriot copper. The especially high silver level, along with the gold-silver ratio and the LI ratios, does not match that of Cypriot ores.[16] Metallurgical waste analyzed from

---

15   One of the dental tools was analyzed using a portable XRF (x-ray fluorescence) analyzer, which revealed 0.017% Ni. I thank Kevin Melia-Teevan, NAP-TAMU Research Assistant, for XRF analyses of the TMB ingot samples and the tools used in taking the samples.

16   I am grateful to Sophie Stos-Gale and Michael Bode for comparing the TBM chemical results with both published and unpublished data.

Faynan (Jordan) seems to be much higher in lead and iron content, and it therefore does not provide a good fit. The overall chemical composition of the TBM ingot seems similar to those of copper ores from Timnah (Israel), Oman, Bahrain, and the United Arab Emirates, but none of these provide an exact match. It should be noted, however, that chemical compositions can vary considerably even within the same ingot, and an interpretation based on the chemical composition of a single ingot cannot be taken as definitively characterizing the properties of its ore source, That is one reason why an assemblage of copper ingots like that from the Uluburun shipwreck is so invaluable and informative in determining copper sources and exchange routes.

The LI data for oxhide ingots from Crete, Sardinia, the Uluburun shipwreck, and TBM, as well as ores and metallurgical remains from Cyprus, Faynan, Timnah, and Oman, are plotted in Figure 13.5, shown in the usual two diagrams representing orthogonal plane sections through the three-dimensional space occupied by LIA data.[17] The LI-ratio results for the TBM ingot are not consistent with published copper ore results from Sardinia, the Aegean, Cyprus, or Turkey, nor with those from Yemen and the Arabian Peninsula. The TBM ingot's isotopic results are close, but lie outside the LI data for Cypriot copper ores. The results likely exclude Cyprus as its source, which also seems to be corroborated by its high silver content and silver-gold ratio. The LI data for some metallurgical waste from Timnah, like the Cypriot field, also seem to cluster near the TBM ingot LI values, but the ingot lies just outside the Timnah isotopic field. The widely scattered LI data from Oman seem to coincide with those of some oxhide ingots and, to some extent, with those of the TBM ingot; but whether Oman could have been a reasonable source for copper oxhide ingots cannot be determined at present. Although the available LI data from Wadi Faynan in southern Jordan (for example, Wadi Ratiye and Wadi Khalid) give a widely scattered LI-ratio distribution, and those from Oman are also spread fairly wide, they appear to incorporate the TBM ingot in their measured isotopic field. Yet, the chemical compositions of analyzed metallurgical waste from Faynan are much richer in lead and iron than the TBM ingot.[18] At this preliminary stage of research, therefore, it is not possible to make a definitive attribution for the copper source of the TBM ingot, as more LI data for copper ores are needed from the Near East before meaningful conclusions can be reached.

---

17   The LI-ratio diagrams were prepared by Michael Bode, Deputy Director of Materials Science at the Deutsches Bergbau-Museum, Bochum. I am grateful to Bode for preparing these diagrams for me on such short notice.

18   I thank Michael Bode for this observation. Any error in the interpretation of the diagrams is solely my own.

A FRAGMENTARY SMALL COPPER OXHIDE INGOT 235

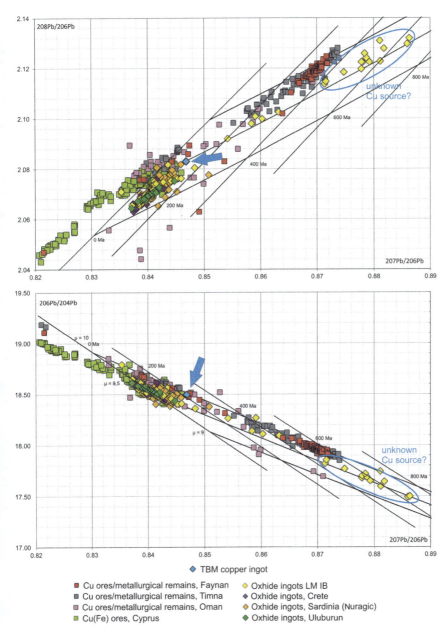

FIGURE 13.5   Lead isotope ratio plots of copper oxhide ingots from Crete, Sardinia, the Uluburun shipwreck, and TBM, along with ores and metallurgical remains from Cyprus, Faynan, Timnah, and Oman in two diagrams representing orthogonal plane sections (in two dimensions) through the three-dimensional space occupied by LIA data points
DIAGRAMS BY MICHAEL BODE

4 Miniature Copper Oxhide Ingots and the Small Tell Beit Mirsim Ingot in Context

Much of the copper exported from Cyprus during the Late Bronze Age was in the form of oxhide ingots. These have been found over a broad geographical range extending from southern France, Corsica, and Sardinia in the west to Urfa in southeastern Turkey and Mesopotamia in the east, and from southern Germany, the Danube, and the Black Sea in the north to Egyptian Thebes in the south.[19] The LIA results of the great majority of oxhide ingots dating to ca. 1400 BCE or later, including nearly all 354 from the Uluburun shipwreck (Pulak 2000: 147–150; Gale and Stos-Gale 2005: 121–127), are consistent isotopically with Cypriot copper ores, and some specifically with ores from the Apliki mining region in the northwestern part of Cyprus. The LI data of oxhide ingots dating after ca. 1250 BCE are also consistent isotopically with Cypriot copper ores, but almost exclusively with that of the Apliki mining region and not with any other Cypriot copper ore sources (Gale 2011: 214–215).[20] The chief exception to this are some oxhide ingots found in the pre-1400 BCE period, in Late Minoan (LM) IB or possibly also slightly earlier contexts of sites on Crete. These earliest oxhide ingots fall into two isotopically separate groups: one consists of ingots from Gournia, Mochlos, Kato Zakros, and Kato Syme having LI compositions consistent with those of Cypriot copper ores, and the second group consists of ingots from Hagia Triada, Tylissos, and Kato Zakros, which have LI ratios that are distinct from those of all Cypriot copper ores (Gale 2011: 218; Stos-Gale 2011: 222–226). The source of the copper ores for the second group remains unknown, but their LI values indicate they are geologically much older. While these values are somewhat scattered for some of the ingots, they likely exclude the immediate Mediterranean region as a possible source Fig. 13.5. Based on LIA results, therefore, the earliest oxhide ingots from Crete originate from at least two distinct geographical sources: one group with LI values consistent with those of Cypriot ores and another with LI results that are likely from as yet unidentified, non-Mediterranean source(s).[21]

---

19 For a map showing the geographical spread of oxhide ingot discoveries, see Sabatini 2016: 30, fig. 1. The map does not include the three oxhide ingots from Urfa (Pulak 2011).

20 While some of the Uluburun oxhide ingots overlap with the Apliki LI field, others are consistent with the LI data of the Skouriotissa and Mavrovouni mines located in the same region, and still others do not show clear LI overlaps with Cypriot ores, although all of the latter ingots are also of Cypriot origin. This result illustrates the need for a more extensive sampling of Cypriot ores to map more fully the islands LI characteristics.

21 Stos-Gale 2011: 222–226. The LI compositions for some of the early (LM IB) oxhide ingots from the Cretan sites of Hagia Triada, Kato Zakros, and Tylissos that are not consistent with those of Cypriot copper ores are listed in Stos-Gale 2011: table 22.2.

The earliest copper ingots known from Israel date to the Early Bronze IV (ca. 2400–2000 BCE) and are found in sites located in the Shephelah, where Tell Beit Mirsim is located, and the southern Hebron Hills in the Central Negev, and as far as Hazor in the north. These small (ca. 10–12 cm) bar-shaped ingots were made of unrefined iron-rich "black copper," and their LI ratios are consistent with copper ores from Wadi Faynan in Jordan (Yahalom-Mack 2014: 159, 161, 163 fig. 4, 173). More significant, however, are the plano-convex disc-shaped ingots from Hazor, dated stratigraphically to LB I. Two of them that have been radiocarbon dated to the seventeenth or sixteenth century BCE are noted as having LI ratios consistent with the copper ore deposit from Ambelikou on Cyprus, which was exploited during the Middle Cypriot period (Yahalom-Mack 2014: 160–161, 163 fig. 4, 170, 173). If correct, it would appear that these disc-shaped ingots represent the earliest forms in which copper was exported from Cyprus and predate the earliest known Cypriot oxhide ingots found in LM IB contexts in Crete. In all likelihood, therefore, copper was being exported from Cyprus in disc-shaped ingots before ingots in the oxhide shape were developed, and later became a Cypriot hallmark.

Although the TBM ingot is much smaller than the standard oxhide ingots, its MB IIC context, dated stratigraphically to the first half of the sixteenth century BCE, would appear to make it the earliest known ingot in the oxhide shape.[22] As noted by Bass (1973: 31), the general oxhide shape seems to appear first with the TBM ingot, which is at least as early as and likely earlier than any iconographic representation or actual examples of such ingots anywhere else. Even though the TBM oxhide ingot, as well as the slightly later examples from LM IB Crete, lacks the pronounced and elongated corner protrusions of later oxhide ingots, there is no doubt that its shape is associated with the general oxhide form, which Buchholz classified under his Type 1 ingots (Buchholz 1959: 6–7, fig. 2). Does the TBM ingot, then, represent the earliest known example of the oxhide shape?

As these early oxhide ingots are dated only by stratigraphic means, their absolute dates are not sufficiently precise to provide a reliable response to this query. Moreover, arguments have been advanced for antedating the end of LM IA and beginning of LM IB from the conventional date of ca. 1525–1500

---

22 The TBM ingot is included in the catalog of oxhide ingots made by Buchholz (1966: 66; 1988: 203) and Bass (1967: 57). In his list of all known miniature ingots, Knapp (1986: 26–27, table 1) includes the TBM ingot and marks its current location as "unknown." Further augmented lists are in Papasavvas (2009: 101–104) and Giumlia-Mair, Kassianidou, and Papasavvas (2011: 12–14).

BCE by approximately a century into the seventeenth century BCE.[23] Although this major date shift remains controversial, if accepted, it could mean that the TBM ingot and the early Cretan oxhide ingots are approximately contemporaneous. Even so, as with many of the LM IB Cretan ingots, the LI values of the TBM ingot do not appear to overlap with those of known copper ore sources on Cyprus or elsewhere in the Mediterranean. The very few Bronze Age sites where Cypriot copper is known to have been mined, smelted, and processed are too early to have been the source of these oxhide ingots, and the LI values of their ores are not consistent with those of the oxhide ingots (Gale 2011: 218; Stos-Gale 2011: 226). As already noted, the sources of the geologically older copper ores used in many early oxhide ingots must lie outside the immediate Mediterranean region. This, then, begs the question of where the oxhide ingot shape was first developed—a shape that eventually became the hallmark or "brand" of Cypriot export copper. Based on the results of LIA, since only 18% of the copper alloy objects analyzed to date from Late Minoan Crete are consistent with Cypriot ores, both Cypriot and non-Cypriot copper oxhide ingots reached Crete probably along with tin ingots to make bronze (Stos-Gale 2011: 228). As there is no source of tin on Crete, Cyprus, or anywhere else in the eastern Mediterranean that could have been exploited in meaningful quantities during the Middle and Late Bronze Ages, it must have been imported from non-Mediterranean sources (Weeks 1999; Pulak 2000: 153–155). It is of interest, therefore, that much of the approximately one ton of tin carried on the late fourteenth-century BCE Uluburun shipwreck consisted of complete and quarter-cut sections of ingots in the oxhide shape (Pulak 2000: 150–153).[24] Ingots, in general, are cast merely to facilitate the storage and transport of a given quantity of a specific metal, and they do not represent finished products. It makes little sense, then, to melt ingots only to cast them anew in different forms or shapes; there is no compelling archaeological, chemical, metallurgical, or even ethnographic evidence to suggest that this was ever done. Thus, both the Uluburun tin ingots, and the non-Cypriot LM IB copper ingots would appear to have been cast in their original oxhide shape in a region or regions outside the Mediterranean. The oxhide shape itself, therefore, likely developed somewhere in the Near East or Middle East earlier than its occurrence on Cyprus. However, until more analytical work is done to expand the LI database on copper ore sources in the Near East and farther afield, the

---

23 For archaeological and scientific arguments for and against this chronological shift, see Betancourt 1998; Bietak 2003; and Manning et al. 2006 for details and summary of scholarship on dating this period.
24 Tin ingots in non-oxide shapes, both complete and fragmentary, were also found.

specific origin of the oxhide shape will remain speculative (Stos-Gale 2011: 228). To this corpus of early, non-Mediterranean copper oxhide ingots we may now add the small example from TBM.

The identification of miniature copper ingots as small-scale versions or models of the full-sized oxhide ingot is indisputable. These miniature ingots realistically reproduce the standard oxhide ingot in nearly every morphological feature except for the latter's rough, irregularly textured surfaces, which are produced naturally during casting. Whether this omission was by preference or unintentional is not known. With minimal additional effort, however, the characteristic rough ingot surface could have been duplicated readily on the miniature ingots if it were deemed sufficiently important or necessary (Giumlia-Mair, Kassianidou, and Papasavvas 2011: 15). Based on the occurrence of Cypro-Minoan signs on some of the miniature ingots,[25] it has long been suggested that they functioned as dedicatory votives (Buchholz 1959: 19–20) or offerings to deities associated with metallurgy (Catling 1971: 29–30) such as those represented by the Ingot God and the Bomford Goddess (Papasavvas 2009: 93–101; 2011). It has also been suggested that miniature oxhide ingots were symbolic indicators of metallurgical sites or related to the elite engaged in copper production (Knapp 1986: 25–29; Hadjisavvas 2011: 24). More recently, they have been interpreted as marked commercial samples denoting the high quality and origin as "pure Cypriot copper" (Ferrara and Bell 2016). No full-sized oxhide ingot or fragments thereof have been found in cultic contexts; processing and redistribution of metal appears to have been undertaken in secular buildings such as those in Kalavasos, Maroni, and Alassa on Cyprus. This distribution pattern appears to be mirrored by the miniature ingots with only two exceptions—one example from Enkomi (Inv. no. Enk. 885) and a fragmentary ingot from Alassa (Hadjisavvas 2011: 23–24, fig. 3.3). For this reason, the notion of miniature ingots as votive or cultic objects has come into question (Webb 1999: 241, 297, 300). Some have assigned them a more practical role, such as weights for scales, because the miniature ingots were seen as conforming to weight systems used during the Bronze Age (Zwicker 1990: 10–11; Kassianidou 2005: 135). A recent metrological assessment of seven miniature ingots from Cyprus, however, has disproved this view, as the

---

25   Papasavvas (2009: 102) notes that there are only four inscribed miniature ingots out of sixteen examples, all of which are from Enkomi, with one additional example from Egypt. Papasavvas (2009: 102) also notes that even though it was a common practice to inscribe both full-sized and miniature oxhide ingots, the specific Cypro-Minoan signs on the miniature ingots do not appear on the full-sized ones. I would also add that this is the case for the discoid plano-convex or bun-shaped ingots from the Uluburun and Cape Gelidonya shipwrecks.

examined ingots vary significantly in size and weight. This led the authors of that study to reconsider their use as cultic artifacts, even if their contexts do not appear to support fully this proposition at this time (Giumlia-Mair, Kassianidou, and Papasavvas 2011: 15, 17). Until more conclusive evidence becomes available, the function of miniature ingots will continue to remain a matter of debate (ibid.: 13).

Based exclusively on their diminutive sizes, all known examples of miniature oxhide ingots have been lumped into a single group, irrespective of their likely different functions. Differences among some of the miniature oxhide ingots are striking. At least eighteen objects are listed as miniature ingots, although this number would increase if other, atypical, examples, as well as those found outside the Mediterranean region, were included in the group.[26] Among the corpus of eighteen miniature ingots, four model ingots that were found in Egypt stand out. These model ingots are said to be of "sheet copper," and at least one is inscribed with two cartouches of the Pharaoh Siptaḥ. All four were found in foundation deposits, undoubtedly representing a small quantity of copper that was meant to be taken out of circulation permanently.[27] Other miniature ingots are said to have been cast of refined copper in the lost-wax technique,[28] and still others, such as the TBM ingot, were cast with blister

---

26   Knapp (1986: 26–27, table 1) lists fifteen miniature ingots. Papasavvas (2009: 102–104) adds two more to the list from Alassa and Mathiatis hoards for a total of seventeen, and provides detailed information on where some of the Cypriot ingots were found. For details of the last two ingots, both of which are fragmentary, see, for the Mathiatis Hoard ingot, Kassianidou 2009: 52, 80, fig. 17; and Giumlia-Mair, Kassianidou, and Papasavvas 2011: 13–14, fig. 2.2: 1936/VII-17/9i; and for Alassa, Hadjisavvas 1986: 66, pl. XVIII: 6; 2011: 23–24 fig. 3.3. Hadjisavvas (2011: 23) and Zwicker (1992: 166, pl. XXXII: 4) mention an additional fragment of a miniature ingot from Alassa, which brings the total to eighteen. Of this total, eleven of the miniature ingots originate from Cyprus. This number would increase if additional miniature oxhide and oxhide-like ingots from areas outside the Mediterranean are also included; see Sabatini 2016a, 2016b: 42–45. A miniature ingot of unknown context from Bulgaria may be added to this list (Doncheva 2012: 689, 714 fig. 16).

27   These four model miniature ingots were found in each of two foundation deposits of Pharaoh Siptaḥ and in two of Pharaoh Twosret, dated to between the end of the thirteenth century and the first quarter of the twelfth century BCE. They are the only miniature ingots to have been found in Egyptian foundation deposits. These ingots are said to be of copper, but they have not been chemically analyzed. O'Connor 1967: 173–174 figs. 161–162; Papasavvas 2009: 104.

28   Catling (1964: 268) notes that miniature ingot 1936/VI-19/1 from Enkomi was perhaps cast by the lost-wax technique but does not provide an explanation for this. This reference may be the source for a similar view expressed by Papasavvas (2009: 101) and Giumlia-Mair, Kassianidou, and Papasavvas (2011: 15) in casting these miniature ingots. As I am unaware of a technical study on the casting techniques employed in the production of these miniature ingots, presumably some of them could also have been cast in simple, open molds.

copper coming directly from a smelting furnace, as was the case with full-sized oxhide ingots.

Only by direct examination of the miniature ingots themselves, or through their published high-quality photographs and detailed illustrations of both surfaces, can reliable assessments of their physical and metallurgical features be made; but this is seldom possible. Good quality photographs of Cypriot ingots showing only one surface of a fragmentary miniature ingot from Mathiatis and six intact ingots from Enkomi (Giumlia-Mair, Kassianidou, and Papasavvas 2011: 14, fig. 2.2) reveal that only one ingot (Enk. 885) has an irregular, porous, molded surface somewhat resembling that of the TBM ingot;[29] however, the ingot's surface porosity could have resulted from a poor choice of mold material rather than from casting with blister copper. If, for example, an open limestone mold was used, the carbon dioxide formed by calcination or breakdown of the mold upon contact with molten copper could have caused the surface porosity, even if pure, refined copper was used. The same would be true if a clay mold with high moisture content was used. By contrast, had this ingot been cast in a sand mold or by the lost-wax technique, it would have likely had smoother surfaces throughout.

Other than size, the most visible difference between the standard, utilitarian copper oxhide ingots and most miniature ones is in the relatively smooth surfaces of the latter. It is stated that the miniature ingots were cast by the lost-wax method, and that the craftsmen creating the wax model of the ingots made no effort to replicate the rough texture of the original ingots, even though this would have been fairly easy to do before investing a wax model for casting (Giumlia-Mair, Kassianidou, and Papasavvas 2011: 15). I am unaware of a metallurgical study analyzing the casting methods of miniature ingots, but, presumably, their smooth surfaces may be the main reason why they are thought to have been cast by the lost-wax technique, which may well have been the case for some of them. It is equally possible that some of the miniature ingots were cast, instead, in simple open molds, rather than by the lost-wax technique. Based on the chemical analysis of a single miniature ingot as bronze (De Jesus 1976: 231–232), it was assumed that all miniature ingots were cast of bronze (Knapp 1986: 28; Papasavvas 2009: 101). Thanks to the recent chemical analysis of seven miniature ingots from Cyprus, this now is known not to be the case, as the examined ingots did not reveal even a trace amount of tin (Giumlia-Mair, Kassianidou, and Papasavvas 2011: 15–16). As indicated above, this is true for the TBM ingot as well. At least in one instance, a miniature ingot from Enkomi was

---

29   For an illustration and catalog of this ingot, see Giumlia-Mair, Kassianidou, and Papasavvas 2011: 14, fig. 2.2, 18.

further modified after casting by repeated striking with a blunt, heavy tool to flatten it, as revealed by tool impressions on its surface.[30] Moreover, the purity of the miniature ingots' copper indicates that they were cast with remelted copper rather than with blister copper coming directly from the smelting furnace. Since remelted copper would have significantly fewer dissolved gasses compared to copper coming from the smelting furnace, the resulting casts would have smoother surfaces compared with the standard oxhide ingots or, in this instance, with the small TBM ingot.

What is certain, however, is that these miniature oxhides are not ingots per se, but merely finished products cast specifically to represent the oxhide ingot shape in which copper was exported from Cyprus. In other words, unlike copper oxhide ingots, which are only semi-finished products used for storing and transporting raw metal, miniature ingots are purpose-made models produced using the same methods and pure metals used to cast other prized metal objects, such as pins, weapons, and figurines. Size, then, is not the main difference between the miniature oxhide ingots and standard, utilitarian oxhide ingots, of which the TBM ingot is a small example. It would be more appropriate, therefore, to refer to small utilitarian ingots made of raw materials like the TBM ingot as presumably "fractional" or "diminutive" ingots, rather than as "miniature" ingots. Regardless of their function, it should be noted that several of the miniature ingots were found in fragmentary form, indicating that they doubled as utilitarian objects when needed, but as scrap metal and not as ingots. Their fragmentation was more likely the result of some ritualistic act or, because all metal had a high scrap value, they eventually found their way into the melting pot when the purpose for which they were made was fulfilled or when a dire need for copper arose in times of shortage, As such, miniature Cypriot oxhide ingots cast of pure copper served a symbolic purpose, the meaning of which is lost to us. The Egyptian miniature ingots made of "sheet copper" served a similar symbolic purpose but were used differently, as foundation deposits that were not meant to be recovered, unlike the cast miniature Cypriot oxhide ingots that were put back into circulation as metal, when the need arose. The TBM ingot was therefore utilitarian and not symbolic, functioning as a semi-finished ingot cast of blister copper, intended to be remelted and cast into a final product. Although it represents a smaller quantity of raw copper, the TBM ingot predates the phenomenon of the "miniature oxhide ingot", meaning it should be removed from the corpus of miniature ingots and seen for what it was meant to be: a functional, fractional ingot.

---

30   See ingot Inv. no. Enk. 774 in Giumlia-Mair, Kassianidou, and Papasavvas 2011: 14, fig. 2.2.

References

Albright, W.F. 1938. *The Excavations of Tell Beit Mirsim*, Vol. 2: *The Bronze Age: 1936–1937* (The Annual of the American Schools of Oriental Research 17). Cambridge, MA.

Bass, G.F. 1967. *Cape Gelidonya: A Bronze Age Shipwreck* (Transactions of the American Philosophical Society 57, Part 8). Philadelphia.

Bass, G.F. 1973. Cape Gelidonya and Bronze Age Maritime Trade. In: Hoffner, H.F., Jr., ed. *Orient and Occident: Essays Presented to Cyrus H. Gordon on the Occasion of His Sixty-Fifth Birthday*. Neukirchen-Vluyn: 29–38.

Ben-Arieh, S. 2004. *Bronze and Iron Age Tombs at Tell Beit Mirsim*. Jerusalem.

Betancourt, P.P. 1998. The Chronology of the Aegean Late Bronze Age: Unanswered Questions. In: Balmouth, M.S. and Tykot, R.H., eds. *Sardinian and Aegean Chronology: Towards the Resolution of Relative and Absolute Dating in the Mediterranean. Proceedings of the International Colloquium "Sardinian Stratigraphy and Mediterranean Chronology," Tufts University, Medford, Massachusetts, March 17–19, 1995* (Studies in Sardinian Archaeology 5). Oxford: 291–296.

Betancourt, P.P. and Muhly, J.D. 2006. The Pot Bellows. In: Betancourt, P.P. *The Chrysokamino Metallurgy Workshop and Its Territory* (Hesperia Supplements 36). Princeton: 125–132.

Bietak, M. 2003. Science versus Archaeology: Problems and Consequences of High Aegean Chronology. In: Bietak, M., ed. *The Synchronisation of Civilisations in the Eastern Mediterranean in the Second Millennium B.C.* (Denkschriften der Gesamtakademie 19; Contributions to the Chronology of the Eastern Mediterranean 1). Vienna: 23–33.

Blitzer, H. 1995. Minoan Implements and Industries. In: Shaw, J.W. and Shaw, M.C., eds. *Kommos: An Excavation on the South Coast of Crete*, Vol. 1, Part 1: *The Kommos Region and Houses of the Minoan Town: The Kommos Region, Ecology, and Minoan Industries*. Princeton: 403–536

Buchholz, H.G. 1959. Keftiubarren und Erzhandel im zweiten vorchristlichen Jahrtausend. *Prähistorische Zeitschrift* 37: 1–40.

Buchholz, H.G. 1966. Talanta:. Neues über Metallbarren der ostmediterranen Spätbronzezeit. *Schweizer Münzblatter* 16(62): 58–72.

Buchholz, H.G. 1988. Der Metallhandel des zweiten Jahrtausends in Mittelmeerraum. In: Heltzer, M. and Lipiński, E., eds. *Society and Economy in the Eastern Mediterranean (c. 1500–1000 B.C.)*. Leuven: 187–228.

Catling, H.W. 1964. *Cypriot Bronzework in the Mycenaean World*. Oxford.

Catling, H.W. 1971. A Cypriot Bronze Statuette in the Bomford Collection. In: Schaeffer, C.F.A., ed. *Alasia: Première Série* (Mission Archéologique d'Alasia, Tome IV). Paris: 15–32.

Davey, C.J. 1979. Some Ancient Near Eastern Pot Bellows. *Levant* 11: 101–111.

Dimopoulou, N. 1997. Workshops and Craftsmen in the Harbour-Town of Knossos at Poros-Katsambas. In: Laffineur, R. and Betancourt, P.P., eds. *TEXNH: Craftsmen, Craftswomen, and Craftsmanship in the Aegean Bronze Age: Proceedings of the 6th International Aegean Conference, Philadelphia, Temple University, 18–21 April 1996* (Aegaeum 16/2). Liège: 433–438, Pls. CLXVII–CLXXIV.

Doncheva, D. 2012. The Northern "Journey" of Late Bronze Age Copper Ingots. In: Paunov, E. and Filipova, S., eds. *Herakleous soteros thasion: Studia in honorem Iliae Prokopov sexagenario ab amicis et discipulis dedicata (Studies in Honour of Ilya Prokopov for His 60th Birthday, from His Friends and Pupils)*. Veliko Tarnovo, Bulgaria: 671–714.

Evely, R.D.G. 2000. *Minoan Crafts: Tools and Techniques. An Introduction* (Studies in Mediterranean Archaeology 92/2). Gothenburg.

Ferrara, S. and Bell, C. 2016. Tracing Copper in the Cypro-Minoan Script. *Antiquity* 90(352): 1009–1021.

Gale, N. 2011. Copper Oxhide Ingots and Lead Isotope Provenancing. In: Betancourt, P.P. and Ferrence, S.C., eds. *Metallurgy: Understanding How, Learning Why: Studies in Honor of James D. Muhly*. Philadelphia: 213–219.

Gale, N.H. and Stos-Gale, Z.A. 2005. Zur Herkunft der Kupferbarren aus dem Schiffswrack von Uluburun und der spätbronzezeitliche Metallhandel im Mittelmeerraum. In: Yalçın, Ü., Pulak, C., and Slota, R., eds. *Das Schiff von Uluburun: Welthandel vor 3000 Jahren*. Bochum: 117–131.

Giumlia-Mair, A., Kassianidou, V., and Papasavvas, G. 2011. Miniature Ingots from Cyprus. In: Betancourt, P.P. and Ferrence, S.C., eds. *Metallurgy: Understanding How, Learning Why. Studies in Honor of James D. Muhly*. Philadelphia: 11–19.

Hadjisavvas, S. 1986. Alassa: A New Late Cypriot Site. *Report of the Department of Antiquities* 1986: 62–67.

Hadjisavvas, S. 2011. Broken Symbols: Aspects of Metallurgy at Alassa. In: Betancourt, P.P. and Ferrence, S.C., eds. *Metallurgy: Understanding How, Learning Why. Studies in Honor of James D. Muhly*. Philadelphia: 21–27.

Hauptmann, A., Maddin, R., and Prange, M. 2002. On the Structure and Composition of Copper and Tin Ingots Excavated from the Shipwreck of Uluburun. *Bulletin of the American Schools of Oriental Research* 328: 1–30.

Jesus, P.S. de 1976. Report on the Analyses of the "Makarska" Tools and Some Implications. *Studi Micenei ed Egeo-anatolici* 17: 221–233.

Kassianidou, V. 2005. Was Copper Production under Divine Protection in Late Bronze Age Cyprus? Some Thoughts on an Old Question. In: Karageorghis, V., Matthäus, H., and Rogge, S., eds. *Cyprus: Religion and Society, from the Late Bronze Age to the End of the Archaic Period*. Möhnesee-Wamel: 127–142.

Kassianidou, V. 2009. Oxhide Ingots in Cyprus. In: Lo Schiavo, F., Muhly, J.D., Maddin, R., and Giumlia-Mair, A., eds. *Oxhide Ingots in the Central Mediterranean*. Rome: 42–81.

Kassianidou, V. 2011. Blowing the Wind of Change: The Introduction of Bellows in Late Bronze Age Cyprus. In: Betancourt, P.P. and Ferrence, S.C., eds. *Metallurgy: Understanding How, Learning Why. Studies in Honor of James D. Muhly*. Philadelphia: 41–47.

Knapp, A.B. 1986. *Copper Production and Divine Protection: Archeology, Ideology and Social Complexity on Bronze Age Cyprus* (Studies in Mediterranean Archaeology, Pocket-Book 42). Gothenburg.

Manning, S.W., Ramsey, C.B., Kutschera, W., Higham, T., Kromer, B., Steier, P., and Wild, E.M. 2006. Chronology for the Aegean Late Bronze Age 1700–1400 B.C. *Science* 312(5773): 565–569.

Müller Karpe, A. 2000. Zur Metallverarbeitung bei den Hethitern. *Der Anschnitt* 13 (*Anatolian Metal* 1): 113–124.

O'Connor, D. 1967. Model Ingots in Egyptian Foundation Deposits. In: Bass, G., *Cape Gelidonya: A Bronze Age Shipwreck* (Transactions of the American Philosophical Society 57, Part 8). Philadelphia: 172–174.

Papasavvas, G. 2009. The Iconography of the Oxhide Ingots. In: Lo Schiavo, F., Muhly, J.D., Maddin, R., and Giumlia-Mair, A., eds. *Oxhide Ingots in the Central Mediterranean*. Rome: 83–132.

Papasavvas, G. 2011. From Smiting to Smithing: The Transformation of a Cypriot God. In: Betancourt, P.P. and Ferrence, S.C., eds. *Metallurgy: Understanding How, Learning Why. Studies in Honor of James D. Muhly*. Philadelphia: 59–66.

Pulak, C. 2000. The Copper and Tin Ingots from the Late Bronze Age Shipwreck at Uluburun. *Der Anschnitt* 13 (*Anatolian Metal* 1): 137–157.

Pulak, C. 2008. The Uluburun Shipwreck and Late Bronze Age Trade. In: Aruz, J., Benzel, K., and Evans, J.M., eds. *Beyond Babylon: Art, Trade, and Diplomacy in the Second Millennium B.C.* New York: 288–310, 313–321, 324–333, 336–342, 345–348, 350–358, 366–378, 382–385.

Pulak, C. 2011. Three Copper Oxhide Ingots in the Şanlıurfa Archaeology Museum, Turkey. In: Betancourt, P.P. and Ferrence, S.C., eds. *Metallurgy: Understanding How, Learning Why. Studies in Honor of James D. Muhly*. Philadelphia: 293–303.

Sabatini, S. 2016a. Late Bronze Age Oxhide and Oxhide-like Ingots from Areas Other than the Mediterranean: Problems and Challenges. *Oxford Journal of Archaeology* 35(1): 29–45.

Sabatini, S. 2016b. Revisiting Late Bronze Age Oxhide Ingots: Meanings, Questions and Perspectives. In: Aslaksen, O.C., ed. *Local and Global Perspectives on Mobility in the Eastern Mediterranean*. Athens: 15–62.

Stos-Gale, Z.A. 2011. "Biscuits with Ears": A Search for the Origin of the Earliest Oxhide Ingots. In: Betancourt, P.P. and Ferrence, S.C., eds. *Metallurgy: Understanding How, Learning Why. Studies in Honor of James D. Muhly*. Philadelphia: 221–229.

Tylecote, R.F. 1981. From Pot Bellows to Tuyeres. *Levant* 13: 107–118.

Ünsal, Y., Pulak, C., and Slotta, R. 2005. *Das Schiff von Uluburun: Welthandel vor 3000 Jahren*. Bochum.

Webb, J.M. 1999. *Ritual Architecture, Iconography, and Practice in the Late Cypriot Bronze Age* (Studies in Mediterranean Archaeology, Pocket-Book 75). Jonsered.

Weeks, L. 1999. Lead Isotope Analyses from Tell Abraq, United Arab Emirates: New Data Regarding the "Tin Problem" in Western Asia. *Antiquity* 73: 49–64.

Yahalom-Mack, N., Galili, E., Segal, I., Eliyahu-Behar, A., Boaretto, E., Shilstein, S., and Finkelstein, I. 2014. New Insights into Levantine Copper Trade: Analysis of the Ingots from the Bronze and Iron Ages in Israel. *Journal of Archaeological Science* 45: 159–177.

Zwicker, U. 1990. Archaeometallurgical Investigation on the Copper and Copper-Alloy Production in the Area of the Mediterranean Sea (7000–1000 B.C.). *Bulletin of the Metals Museum* 15: 3–32.

Zwicker, U. 1992. Nondestructive and Other Investigations on Metal Objects of the Archaeological Museum Nicosia. In: Ioannides, G.C., ed. *Studies in Honour of Vassos Karageorghis*. Nicosia: 165–178.

CHAPTER 14

Lévi-Strauss and the Royal Ancestor Cult in the Bronze Age Levant

Marisa Ruiz-Gálvez

Michal Artzy is, for me, one of most admired Ladies of Mediterranean Archaeology. I am in wonderment of her brilliant ideas, her ability to join the pieces of the archeological record, to offer an appealing, well-formed interpretation, and her gift of captivating her audience and readers; but especially enviable are her energy and vibrant character. I hope that my contribution does justice to her merits.

1   Introduction

In one of the two essays comprising his book *The Way of the Masks*, C. Lévi-Strauss developed a model of a cognatic, bilateral kinship that he called *société á Maison*, "House society," following a formula adopted from medieval Europe. Lévi-Strauss considered the "House" a general kinship category, defining it as follows:

> "A moral person, holder of a property, made at the same time of material and immaterial goods, which is perpetuated by the transmission of its name, its fortune and titles through a lineage, either real or fictional, considered legitimate, on condition that such continuity could be" expressed either in the language of kinship or of the alliance, or in both.
>   LÉVI-STRAUSS 1981: 150

The House society model was first applied in the 1990s to the Maya social organization to explain the evolution from weak to strong states (Gillespie 2000; Joyce 2000). Since then, the model has been used to define seemingly very different societies as the Kwakiult and Yurok (Lévi-Strauss 1981), the Early Bronze Age Levantine societies (Chesson 2003), the Minoans (Driessen 2010, 2012), and the late Iron Age Gallaecians (González-Ruibal 2006). More recently, this model was also employed for defining societies of the Bronze and Iron Age

Levant, as well as Mycenaean, Villanovan, Etruscans, and Nuragic societies (González and Ruiz-Gálvez 2016).

The application of the House society model to seemingly diverse social groups is possible due to the flexibility of the "House," as it uses many different strategies to recruit its members, and because these strategies can be deployed as much by the common people as by the elite (Gillespie 2007: 38). Also, as the House is a highly competitive system, the model helps to explain dynamics of emergence and collapse of sociopolitical entities, as it is the House, and not its members, that has rights and duties (Lévi-Strauss 1981). Thus, we recently defined House societies as heterarchical systems, more complex than chiefdoms, but where power is still performed in a corporate way, where the ruler is only a *primus inter pares* as the assemblies of elders or high-ranking families constrain his power (González-Ruibal and Ruiz-Gálvez 2016).

As Lévi-Strauss (1981) pointed out when examining the Kwakiult and Yurok kinship systems, House societies are neither patrilineal nor matrilineal, but cognatic or bilateral, as both the father's and the mother's patrilineages are equally relevant, since rights to the House's name and property could be transferred through both lineages.

House societies emerge in complex agricultural systems (i.e., irrigation, plow agriculture, or specialized herding), where available soil is scarce and/or population densities, high, so that land control and land ownership become critical. In that sense, House societies comply with Goody's (1976) model of complex agrarian systems connected with the dowry institution and with monogamous and endogamous marriage. As Goody explains, complex agricultural systems allow the concentration of the best soils in few hands. Since irrigation, plow agriculture, and specialized herding all relied on male labor, estate and property are transmitted through the patrilineage, while women from wealthy families are dowered and used as pawns in a strategy of homogamous or hypergamous marriages geared toward the preservation and enlargement of the House's patrimony. This is due to the fact that, although women did not inherit property, they did transmit property rights to their offspring in the absence of a male heir in the family. In this way, Ávalos (1995: 619, 626) cites Numbers 27:1–11, where Yahweh orders Moses to allow females to inherit in absence of males and, though infrequent, there are references in the Bible to the *bet 'em*, "House of the mother" (Genesis 24:28). Institutions as the dowry, levirate, sororate, birthright, and forced bachelorhood of the junior sons as well as of those daughters who cannot be dowered, so that the inheritance is not split up, are all characteristics of these systems (Goody 1976). As these institutions are intended to enlarge and improve the patrimony and prestige of the House, rather to than to enrich the head of the household (or less so), the system described by Goody corresponds to Lévi-Strauss's house society.

Following Lévi-Strauss, many scholars outlined the physical features that define a kinship group as a House society (Macdonald 1987; Carsten and Hugh-Jones 1995; Joyce and Gillespie 2000; Beck 2007). The Houses are economic and social entities within which there is unequal access to property and prestige, and whose wealth and perdurability is conveyed through their elaborate architecture, as much as in the use of emblems, or through the song or recitation of their myths and exploits (Lévi-Strauss 1981: 152; González-Ruibal 2006: 163).

The agglomerated pattern of urbanism, shaping whole neighborhoods, has also been pointed out as the expression of corporate structures, where lesser members and affines group around the main House (Schloen 2001: 150–151, 302; Chesson 2003: 90–94; Driessen 2010: 50–57), as seen in the third-millennium Middle Euphrates towns and cities, where the Sumerian term KÁ referred to both the city gate and the people who lived in its vicinity (Ristvet 2011: 5; 2015: 57).

The ancestor cult was expressed in elaborate rituals performed by the head of the House, by the construction of an intramural pantheon, or by both, and also by the use of heirlooms and exotics as objects with biography (Kopytoff 1986; Whitley 2002), which help to preserve the memory of the family's heroic past.

González-Ruibal and I (2016) have recently demonstrated that the Levantine societies of the late third to the first millennium BCE all possess these characteristics. But how and when did all these features appear?

2 From Collective to Individual Rule

Based on the settlement pattern analysis of different Early Bronze Age Levantine sites, Chesson (2003: 86) suggested that the emergence of competitive Houses was governed by a corporate civic council. Notwithstanding, many scholars, including Chesson herself (2003: 94), Peltenburg (2007–2008), and Morandi Bonacossi (2014: 426ff.), perceived significant social changes that occurred during the Early–Middle Bronze Age transition. The mortuary record of Bab edh-Dhra' shows the emergence of a House identity from Early Bronze (EB) II–III onward (Chesson 2003: 95–97; de Miroschedji 2009: 105). Other authors (Porter 2002; Peltenburg 2007–2008: 224ff.; Schwartz 2012, 2013: 505–517) demonstrate how mortuary patterns in the Middle Euphrates Valley reflect ideological changes that occurred in the area, with burial plots devoted to restricted kinship.

It seems that the corporate structures of authority, typical of tribal institutions (Fig. 14.1), began to evolve into other structures, based on a more restricted kinship affiliation. Nevertheless, some collective structures survived when the state arose, and the early second-millennium Mesopotamian city-states enjoyed a heterarchical system of government. The existence of assemblies of elders as well as other institutions that shared governing responsibilities with the king, to some extent, is well known (Blanton and Fargher 2007; Ristvet 2011: 7). According to Sanders (2012: 198), the West Semitic lexicography of the second millennium reveals the strong weight of the tribe still underlying the state institutions. Thus, in Mari, as well as in Emar, the component *lim* (people/tribe) appears in names of kings or divinized individuals. On

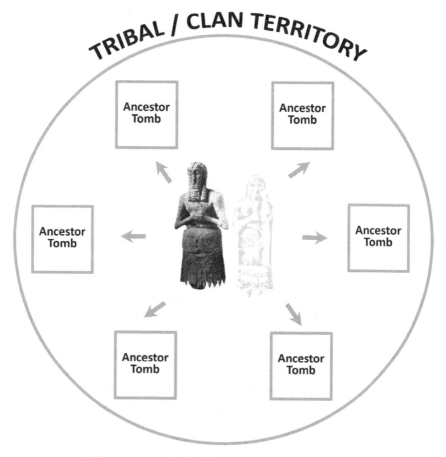

FIGURE 14.1   Collective source of rule; the king shares power with his clan representatives

the other hand, the coastal city-states as Ugarit, evolved into typical Syrian detribalized monarchies, albeit preserving a terminology associated with people as political actors and council institutions (Ávalos 1995: 622; Sanders 2012: 206). Assemblies of elders pervaded also the first-millennium kingdoms of Phoenicia and Israel (Ávalos 1995: 622).

Sites as extensively investigated as Ebla may provide textual and archaeological clues about the appearance of individual lineages emerging from the collective ethics.

The Ebla marriage and coronation texts offer us an insight into the roots of power and authority in Ebla (Biga 1998, 2007–2008: 256; Biga and Capomacchia 2012; Servadio 2009: 36ff.; Ristvet 2011: 8ff.; 2015: 40ff.; Archi 2013: 223; Matthiae 2015: 112ff.). The ARET 11 series includes two texts referring to the wedding and coronation ceremonies of the last two kings of Early Bronze Ebla (2400–2350 BCE). One of these texts includes the rite of incorporation of the bride, King Išar-Damu's cousin, whose father was a brother of the late King Irkab-Damu. On the night before the ritual begins, the bride-to-be camps outside the city; at dawn she crosses Kura's Gate, named for the protector god of the city, and ascends to Kura's Temple, where she takes off her clothes and dresses as a bride. She then brings offerings to Kura and the other gods of Ebla from her father's house, and proceeds to the palace where the wedding ceremonies are performed. The gestures of crossing Kura's Gate, undressing, and putting on new clothes are part of a rite of incorporation (van Gennep 1986).

Even more interesting is the pilgrimage from Ebla to Binaš that the royal couple embarks on after their wedding, visiting the royal pantheon accompanied by their retinue and the statues of the city gods, Kura and Barama. This four-day pilgrimage includes six sojourns in different cities in which the couple makes offerings and performs ceremonies in the tombs of other heroic ancestors. During these ceremonies, the royal couple is transformed into a divine couple.

ARET 7.150 describes another pilgrimage to a more distant city called Darib, with the offering of ten rams to the gods and to the last ten deified kings of Ebla (Biga 2007–2008: 267; Ristvet 2011: 12; 2015: 68–69; Matthiae 2015: 112ff.). As several scholars have suggested (Ristvet 2011: 9; Archi 2013: 232; Matthiae 2015: 116), the towns included in the pilgrimage are all close to Ebla and could have demarcated the ancestral territory of the dynasty. Thus, as the reading of another text, Tablet 74.120, suggests, some of the ancient rulers of third-millennium BCE Ebla were seminomads of the Syrian steppe (Bonechi 2001: 62).

Several aspects of these rituals are meaningful for my argument:
1) At least in one case, ARET 11.2, the bride, Tabur-Damu, and the groom, Išar-Damu, are cousins (Biga 1998: 84), and as part of her rite of incorporation, Tabur-Damu brings offerings to the city's god from her father's

House. Archi (2013: 228) emphasizes that the ceremony was perceived as the wedding of the queen. These aspects recall Goody's (1976) dowry marriage system and Schloen's (2001: 258) patrimonial kingdoms, where every household emulates the structure of the kingdom. Both, as explained above, are specific features of a House society.

2) The pilgrimage to the royal couple's ancestral territory was a mnemonic device to maintain the memory of the dynastic origins, but it also suggests that the power of the ruler was still deeply entangled in extensive kinship or clan ties.

Nevertheless, things seem to have changed at the time of Išar-Damu, the last king of Ebla recorded in the archives, if Matthiae (2015: 114ff.) is correct in identifying him as the king for whom the hypogeum excavated under Royal Palace G was built. The tomb was found empty and, although it may have been plundered, Matthiae thinks that it was meant to be the dynastic pantheon of Išar-Damu and his descendants, but was never used because the city of Ebla was abruptly destroyed. As the aforementioned author points out (ibid.: 116), this fact marks a profound change from extended to restricted affiliation, which Peltenburg (2007–2008: 237) describes as a "privatization of the ancestors."

Other important changes conducive to the deification of Ebla's queens seem to have been undertaken by Išar-Damu (Pinnock 2015: 140). Matthiae (2015: 116) interpreted the standard with two female figures that was discovered in a store of Palace G, as Queen Tabur-Damu mourning in front of a deified queen's statue, identified as Dusigu. Dusigu was Išar-Damu's mother and one of King Irkab-Damu's harem ladies, who, after the king's death, managed to set her son on the throne and become a regent when he was young (Biga 2003: 355–358; Matthiae 2015: 116). Pinnock (2015: 139–140) notes that the Ebla archives of the EB IV allude to kings who were deified in the past but not to queens, and that it was only during Išar-Damu's reign that queens were first deified too.

It was at the very beginning of the Middle Bronze Age that the tendency toward an intramural location of the royal pantheon seems to have become prevalent. This is the case for Palace G in Ebla (Matthiae 2015), for Qatna (Pälzner 2007, 2015), Tuttul, the small palace of Mari (Peltenburg 2007–2008: 232), and possibly for other palaces such as Alalakh—although the chamber tomb there was already plundered when Woolley found it (Woolley 1953: 75–76)—Jericho, and Byblos (Nigro 2009a, 2009b).

These changes into a restricted affiliation of the ruling dynasty could also explain the placing of almost life-size king and queen statues at the entrance of the administrative area of Palace G in Ebla. According to Pinnock (2015: 135), more than they were royal portraits, they may have represented archetypes of the monarchy. Thus, and following my point, it is from that point on that the palace complex emerged as a seat of the administrative and cultic functions of the dynasty represented by the hypogeum under Palace G. This is the kind of entity that we could more accurately call a house, or better yet, a royal House.

Burials within the urban area are not infrequent in many Syrian cities from the late third millennium BCE, the time of the Ebla archives (Biga 2007–2008: 254–255). Nevertheless, they became even more frequent during the Middle Bronze Age. It was then that subterranean tombs were built beneath the main palaces at Megiddo, Jericho, Tel Ta'anach, Kamid el-Loz, Alalakh, and Byblos (Nigro 2009a: 368–374, n. 12). It is also then that three interconnected royal hypogea were dug beneath the throne room of the Western Palace at Ebla. At least one of them could be identified as the tomb of Immeya, King of Ebla. Among its lavish grave goods, a bone talisman stands out, thanks to the scene carved on it and interpreted as the deification banquet of a deceased king (Matthiae 2015: 117). Interestingly, the character is portrayed holding a shepherd's crook,[1] a symbol connected to the House ideology in the ancient Near East from the end of the third millennium BCE on (González-Ruibal and Ruiz-Gálvez 2016: 401). But, especially significant is the fact that the hypogea were located in the Western Palace, for several reasons: This cardinal point is symbolically connected with the sunset and the underworld and was therefore the seat of the crown Prince, who was in charge of the royal funerals; it was also located next to the temple of Rashap, Lord of the Underworld, where the deified kings were worshipped (Matthiae 2015: 144ff.) A central room with a continuous bench running along three of its four walls and two rooms at the rear of the complex, for food processing, suggest its use for Kispû/Marzeâh meals. The location of royal tombs under the palace's floor connects the palace with the Mesopotamian concept of a cosmic center, the seat of the gods and of the deified monarchs and, therefore, a meeting point between the heavenly world, the world of the living, and the underworld. In a similar way, Schwartz (2013: 505) interprets the Middle Bronze elite burial area at Umm el-Marra—a circular enclosure on the top of the site—as a cosmic center (Fig. 14.2)

The Mari palace is an example of such a cosmic center, with the cultic areas devoted to Ištar and other gods and goddesses, and kispû rituals regularly performed in the throne room. In Pfälzner's words, "the palace of Mari was a place of the gods as well as that of the kings" (Pfälzner 2015: 421; see, also, Charpin 2012).

In Mari as much as in Ugarit, Qatna, and other second-millennium Syrian kingdoms, the Amorite kings made use of the divinization of deceased kings to support claims for rule, based on the divine source of kingship. And, as the

---

1 I thank Isabel Muntalt (Pompeu Fabra University, Barcelona) for calling my attention to this detail.

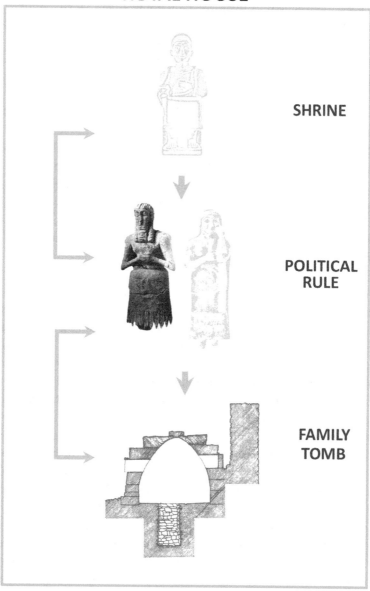

FIGURE 14.2   Individual source of rule based on the royal house as a cosmic center

divine royal ancestors also resided in the palace, the palace itself became a sacred building from which the king's ancestors continued to rule and provide prosperity for their people (del Olmo 2006, 2012; Pfälzner 2015).

The following features may be considered criteria to identify palaces and royal dynasties as House societies:
- Bilaterality: This explains the divinization not only of dead kings but, in some cases, also of dead queens, as in the case of Dusigu (González-Ruibal and Ruiz-Gálvez 2016: 387).
- Houses functioning as shrines or temples and the investment in the material wealth of the house.
- A concern with the past: The Middle Bronze palace of Qatna was built above a previous Early Bronze burial area, and some of the burials were integrated into its foundations (Pfälzner 2015: 433); the Old Babylonian palace of Mari rested on a cultic area (Charpin 2012), and the MB I royal tombs lay below the MB II Royal Palace (Nigro 2009b); Jericho, Ugarit, Qatna, Megiddo, and Kamid el-Loz, among other Middle Bronze palaces, accommodated royal hypogea beneath them (Nigro 2009a; Pfälzner 2015).

Moreover, the House society model is mimicked by the affluent families of the kingdom. A well-preserved MB II neighborhood in the southwestern sector of the Lower Town of Ebla provides us with a good insight of the kinship structure of the time (Ascalone, Peyronel, and Spreafico 2014). Houses are agglomerated; though they share dividing walls, they differ in size and plan and only some of them have a first floor apart from a ground floor. Houses were constantly refitted, enlarged, or partitioned, according to the family growth and other social or hierarchical changes within it. Many of the houses, such as the northeastern house in the central insula, stored a great amount of food, which suggests that the families that lived in them owned agricultural plots close to the city. This could be confirmed by finds recovered in three houses: a tablet, a cylinder seal, and three scale weights connected, perhaps, to the administration of the landed patrimony.

All these features also correspond with the definition of Houses as economic and social entities, with the agglomerated pattern of urbanism as a blueprint of a system of extended kinship, with lesser members and affines occupying small buildings around the main House, as described in Schloen's "House of the father" model (2001: 105–107, 336–337; see, also, Ur 2010: 412).

A further clue for the emergence of a House society system in northern Mesopotamia and the Levant is provided by the erection of family pantheons belonging to aristocratic families inside the urban precinct, below or next to their houses. This is the case of a chamber tomb discovered under Street L in Ebla, used for several generations and dated to MB II, the time of the Royal Pantheon of the Western Palace. Some evidence suggests that funerary banquets were held during the burials, emulating, perhaps, the royal rituals (Moglianzza and Polcaro 2010). Familial tombs with an entrance from the street are also known in

Middle Bronze Ugarit (Marchegay 2008: 107), and van der Toorn (1996: Chapter 3) describes an ancestor cult practiced by families and burials under the house floor beginning in the Old Babylonian period.

3 Epilogue: Why Did House Societies Emerge in the Early–Middle Bronze Age Transition?

There is probably not a single answer for this question as many factors must have contributed to this development. One of them may have been instability resulting from the 4.2 ka BP climatic event with its ensuing draught and soil degradation. These, in turn, probably brought about changes in resources management, resulting in a higher concern for the control of landed property and growing contacts between urban populations and seminomadic groups. The latter may have contributed to the formation of what Porter (2007) and Burke (2014, 2017) call the Amorite koine or the Amorite identity.

Among the cultural features described above, the patrimonial model and the concept of the ruler as a shepherd of his people (Schloen 2001: 120–121) could certainly have a relevant role. From the days of Sargon I onward, the Akkadian kings were given the epithet of shepherd, and the Ugaritic god Hilal was also called "Lord of the shepherd crook." This epithet seems to be connected to the idea that the gods were the real owners of the kingdom and the kings were the shepherds appointed to watch over the gods' patrimony (Schloen 2001: 120–121; González-Ruibal and Ruiz-Gálvez 2016: 400–401).

The harsh climatic conditions, including a drastic decline in rainfall regime caused by the 4.2 ka BP climatic event, impacted dry farming systems that were practiced together with pastoralism and trade by the Amorites, who, according to the texts, were settled in northern Mesopotamia and the Levant at the end of the third millennium BCE (Porter 2007: 108; Burke 2017: 267–270). Paleoclimatic records show increased human control of aquifers in both regions in the Early–Middle Bronze Age transition as a result of the interplay of climate- and man-induced environmental changes (Pustovoytov and Riehl 2016). Although in Burke's view (2014: 358) the formation process of the Amorite cultural and social koine had begun earlier, many of its features—strategies aimed to avoid splitting the landed patrimony; the ancestor cult; and the stress on endogamous, bilateral, patriarchal, and patrilocal kinship systems—might have been fueled or strengthened by the need to control critical resources, resulting in deep structural changes.[2]

---

2 My deep gratitude goes to my colleague Eduardo Galán for helping me with the illustrations.

4 Summary

In the present paper I contend that the Kingdom of Ebla, as many other kingdoms in the Levant and northern Mesopotamia, had evolved from a tribal to a more restricted system of affiliation, compatible with Schloen's (2001) model of patrimonial kingdom or Lévi-Strauss's (1981) House society system. Key facts can be summarized as follows:
- House societies are heterarchical systems, more complex than chiefdoms but less complex than states, which are hierarchical and class-based systems. This is due to the fact that House societies, as relics of their tribal roots, are corporate systems in which an elders or city assembly shares and counterbalances the king's power.
- House societies emerge where resources are scarce or critical for subsistence and controlling them becomes a power-wielding strategy, such as rights on salmon fishing in Yurok and Kwakiult societies, or rights on good arable land, in semiarid regions as those of the Mediterranean and the Near East.
- Although there is no unique reason that explains the emergence of a House society system during the Early–Middle Bronze Age transition in northern Mesopotamia and the Levant, it seems reasonable to assume that stress put on dry farming systems by severe droughts and reduced rainfall that were a consequence of the 4.2 ka. BP climatic event, may have triggered underlying processes of profound social and affiliation changes.
- Marriage in EB IV, as typical in societies with complex agricultural systems, was already based on a dowry system (Goody 1976) and endogamous alliances among close relatives, to reinforce allegiances of the kin group. This is demonstrated in the marriage and coronation texts from Ebla. Nevertheless, the pilgrimage to the royal couple's ancestral territory proves that kingship was still rooted in broad tribal ties.
- From the Early–Middle Bronze Age transition on, the northern Mesopotamian and Levantine kingdoms can be called Houses. The house of the king becomes an archetype of kingship, a kind of axis mundi, or meeting point between heaven, earth, and the underworld, in the sense that it was the seat of political rule (the throne room), cult (ancestor cult) and dynastic rights to govern (mausoleum of deified kings).

Affluent Houses emulate the "House of the king" model (Schloen 2001: 120–121, 331). In this way, agglomerated houses with a common dividing wall in MB II Ebla suggest that extended families lived together in a neighborhood. The fact that only one of the houses seems to have been larger and equipped with a second floor, suggests a model similar to Schloen's (2001: 336–337) for Ugarit or Late Bronze Canaan/Iron Age Israel, among many others (Brody 2009; Faust 2012;

Gilboa, Sharon, and Zorn 2014). The erection of family tombs inside the Ebla precinct, next to or below the houses, can be understood in the same way, because House societies are competitive and unstable systems, within which affluent Houses compete with each other and with the royal House to seize prestige and power.

References

Archi, A. 2013. Ritualization at Ebla. *Journal of Ancient Near Eastern Religions* 13: 212–237.

Ascalone, E., Peyronel, L., and Spreafico, G. 2014. Family Daily Life at Tell Mardikh-Ebla (Syria) during the Middle Bronze Age. In: Lionel, M., ed. *La Famille dans le Proche-Orient ancien: réalités, symbolismes et images,* Winona Lake IN: 243–266.

Ávalos, H. 1995. Legal and Social Institutions in Canaan and Ancient Israel. In: Sasson, J.M., ed. *Civilizations of the Ancient near East.* New York: 615–631.

Beck, R.A., Jr. 2007. *Durable House: House Society Models in Archaeology.* Carbondale.

Biga, M.-G. 1998. Review of *Testi rituali de la regalità (archivio L.2769)* by Pelio Fronzaroli. *Journal of the American Oriental Society* 118(1): 82–84.

Biga, M.-G. 2003. The Reconstruction of a Relative Chronology for the Ebla Texts. *Orientalia* 72(4): 345–367.

Biga, M.-G. 2007–2008. Buried among the Living at Ebla? Funerary Practices and Rites in a XXIV Cent. B.C. Syrian Kingdom. *Scienze dell'Antichità* 14(1) : 249–275.

Biga, M.-G. and Capomacchia, A.M.G. 2012. I testi di Ebla di Aret XI: Una Rilettura alla Luce dei Testi Paralleli. *Revue d'Assyriologie et d'Archéologie Orientale* 106(1) :19–32.

Blanton, R. and Fargher, L. 2007. *Collective Action in the Formation of Pre-modern States.* New York.

Bonechi, M. 2001. The Dynastic Past of the Rulers of Ebla. *Ugarit-Forschungen* 33: 53–64.

Brody, A.J. 2009. "Those Who Add House to House": Household Archaeology and the Use of Domestic Space in an Iron II Residential Compound at Tell en-Naṣbeh. In: Schloen, J.D., ed. *Exploring the Long Durée: Essays in Honor of Lawrence Stager.* Winona Lake, IN: 45–56.

Burke, A. 2014. Entanglement, the Amorite *Koiné,* and Amorite Cultures in the Levant. *ARAM* 26(1–2): 357–373.

Burke, A. 2017. Amorites, Climate Change and Negotiation of Identity at the End of the Third Millennium BC. In: Höffmayer, F., ed. *The Late Third Millennium in the Ancient Near East: Chronology, C14 and Climate Change* (Oriental Institute Seminars 11). Chicago: 261–309.

Carsten, J. and Hugh-Jones, S., eds. 1995. *About the House: Lévi-Strauss and beyond.* Cambridge.

Charpin, D. 2012. "Temple-palais" et chapelles palatiales en Syrie au troisième et deuxième millénaires avant J-C. *Revue de Assyriologie et d'Archéologie Orientale* 106(1): 73–82.

Chesson, M.S. 2003. Household, Houses, Neighborhoods and Corporate Villages: Modelling the Early Bronze Age as a House Society. *Journal of Mediterranean Archaeology* 16(1): 79–102.

Driessen, J. 2010. Spirit of Place: Minoan Houses as Major Actors. In: Dullen, P., ed. *Political Economies of the Aegean Bronze Age.* Oxford: 35–64.

Driessen, J. 2012. A Matrilocal House Society in Pre and Postpalatial Crete? In: Carinci, E., Curuzza, N., Militello, R., and Palio, O., eds. *Minoidos. Tradizione e identità minoica tra produzione artiganale, practice cerimoniali e memoria del passato. Studi offerti a Vicenzo La Rosa per il suo 70° cumpleanno.* Padova: 1–9.

Faust, A. 2012. *The Archaeology of Israelite Society in Iron Age II.* Winona Lake, IN.

Gennep, A. van 1986. *Los ritos de paso.* Madrid.

Gilboa, A., Sharon, I., and Zorn, J.R. 2014. An Iron Age I Canaanite/Phoenician Courtyard House at Tel Dor: A Comparative Architectural and Functional Analysis. *Bulletin of the American Schools of Oriental Research* 372: 39–80.

Gillespie, S. 2000. Beyond Kinship: An Introduction. In: Joyce, R.A. and Gillespie, S.D., eds. *Beyond Kinship: Social and Material Reproduction in House Societies.* Philadelphia.

Gillespie, S. 2007. When Is a House? In: Beck, R.A., Jr., ed. *The Durable House: House Society Models in Archaeology* Carbondale: 25–49.

González-Ruibal, A. 2006. House Societies vs. Kinship-Shaped Societies: An Archaeological Case for Iron Age Europe. *Journal of Anthropological Archaeology* 25(1): 144–173.

González-Ruibal, A. and Ruiz-Gálvez, M. 2016. House Societies in the Ancient Mediterranean (2000–500 BC). *Journal of World Prehistory* 29(2): 383–437.

Goody, J. 1976. *Production and Reproduction: A Comparative Study of the Domestic Domain.* Cambridge.

Joyce, R.A. 2000. *Gender and Power in Pre-Hispanic Mesoamerica.* Austin.

Joyce, R.A. and Gillespie, S.D., eds. 2000. *Beyond Kinship: Social and Material Reproduction in House Societies.* Philadelphia.

Kopytoff, I. 1986. The Cultural Biography of Things: Commoditization as Process. In: Appadurai, A., ed. *The Social Life of Things.* Cambridge: 64–91.

Lévi-Strauss, C. 1981. *La vía de las máscaras.* Méjico.

Macdonald, C., ed. 1987. *De la hutte au palais: sociétés "à maison" en Asie du Sud-Est insulaire.* Paris.

Marchegay, S. 2008. Les Pratiques funéraires à Ougarit au IIe millénaire: bilan et perspectives des récherches. In: Calvet, Y. and Yon, M., eds. *Ougarit au Bronze moyen et au Bronze récent* (Travaux de la Maison de l'Orient et de la Méditerranée 47). Lyon: 97–118.

Matthiae, P. 2015. The Royal Ancestor's Cult in Northern Levant between Early and Late Bronze Age: Continuity and Problems from Ebla to Ugarit. *Bulletin d'Archéologie et d'Architecture Libanaises Hors-Série* 10: 111–134.

Miroschedji, P. de 2009. Rise and Collapse in the Southern Levant in the Early Bronze Age. *Scienze dell'Antichità* 15: 101–129.

Moglianzza, S. and Polcaro, A. 2010. Death and Cult of Dead in Middle Bronze Age II Ebla: An Archaeological and Anthropological Study on Shaft Tomb P.8680 near Southern Palace (Area FF). In: Matthiae, P., Pinnock, F., Nigro, L., and Marchetti, N., eds. *Proceedings of the 6th International Congress on Archaeology of the Ancient Near East*, Vol. 3. Wiesbaden: 431–445.

Morandi Bonacossi, D. 2014. The Northern Levant (Syria) during the Middle Bronze Age. In: Killebrew, A.E. and Steiner, M., eds. *The Oxford Handbook of the Archaeology of the Levant (c. 8000–320 BCE)*. Oxford: 408–427.

Nigro, L. 2009a. The Built Tombs of the Spring Hill and the Palace of the Lords of Jericho ('ḎMR RḤ') in the Middle Bronze Age. In: Schloen, J.D., ed. *Exploring the Longue Durée: Essays in Honor of L.E. Stager*. Winona Lake, IN: 361–376.

Nigro, L. 2009b. The Eighteenth Century BC Princes of Byblos and Ebla and the Chronology of the Middle Bronze Age. *Bulletin d'Archéologie et d'Architecture Libanaises Hors-Série* 10: 159–175.

Olmo, G. del 2006. De la tienda al palacio// de la tribu a la dinastía. Evolución del poder político en el mundo semítico antiguo. In: Borbone, P.G., Mengozzi, A., and Tosco, M., eds. *Loquentes Linguis: Studi Linguistici ed Orientali in Onore di Fabrizio A. Pennacchetti*. Wiesbaden: 219–236.

Olmo, G. 2012. Littérature et pouvoir royal à Ougarit: sens politique de la littérature d'Ougarit. *Études Ougaritiques* 2: 242–250.

Pälzner, P. 2007. Archaeological Investigations in the Royal Palace of Qatna. In: Morandi Bonacossi, D., ed. *Urban and Natural Landscapes of an Ancient Syrian Capital* (Studi Archeologici su Qatna 1). Udine: 29–64.

Pfälzner, P. 2015. A House of Kings and Gods: Ritual places in Syrian palaces. *Bulletin d'Archéologie et d'Architecture Libanaises Hors-Série* 10: 413–442.

Peltenburg, E. 2007–2008. Enclosing the Ancestors and the Growth of Socio-political Complexity in Early Bronze Age Syria. In: Bartoloni, G. and Benedettini, M.G., eds. *Buried among the Living*. Rome: 215–247.

Pinnock, F. 2015. Ancestor's Cult and Female Roles in Early and Old Syrian Syria. *Bulletin d'Archéologie et d'Architecture Libanaises Hors-Série* 10: 135–156.

Porter, A. 2002. Communities in Conflict, Death and the Context for Social Order in the Euphrates Valley. *Near Eastern Archaeology* 65(3): 156–173.

Porter, A. 2007. You Say Potato, I Say ... Typology, Chronology and the Origins of the Amorites. In: Kuzucuoğlu, C. and Marro, C., eds. *Sociétés humaines et changement climatique à la fin du troisième millénaire: une crise a-t-elle eu lieu en Haut Mésopotamie?* (Varia Anatolica 19). Istanbul: 69–115.

Pustovoytov, K. and Riehl, S. 2016. The Early Bronze Age/Middle Bronze Age Transition at the Aquifer Geography in the Near East. *Journal of Archaeological Science* 69: 1–11.

Ristvet, L. 2011. Travel and the Making of North Mesopotamian polities. *Bulletin of the American Schools of Oriental Research* 361: 1–31.

Ristvet, L. 2015. *Ritual, Performance and Politics in the Ancient near East*. Cambridge.

Sanders, S. 2012. From People to Public in Iron Age Levant. In: Wilhelm, G., ed. *Organization, Representation and Symbols of Power in the Ancient Near East*, Winona Lake, IN: 191–211.

Schloen, J.D. 2001. *The House of the Father as Fact and Symbol: Patrimonialism in Ugarit and the Ancient Near East* (Harvard Semitic Museum Publications; Studies in the Archaeology and History of the Levant 2). Winona Lake, IN.

Schwartz, G.M. 2012. Era of the Living Dead: Funerary Praxis and Symbol in Third Millennium BC Syria. In: Pfälzner, P., ed. *(Re-)constructing Funerary Rituals in the Ancient Near East*. Wiesbaden: 59–78.

Schwartz, G.M. 2013. Memory and Its Demolition: Ancestors, Animals and Sacrifice at Umm el-Marra, Syria. *Cambridge Archaeological Journal* 23(3): 495–522.

Servadio, G., ed. 2009. *Ancient Syrian Writing: Preclassical and Classical Texts*. Damascus.

Toorn, K. van der 1996. *Family Religion in Babylonia, Syria and Israel*. Leiden–New York–Cologne.

Ur, J.A. 2010. Cycles of Civilization in Northern Mesopotamia, 4400–2000 BC. *Journal of Archaeological Research* 18: 387–431.

Whitley, J. 2002. Objects with Attitude: Biographical Facts and Fallacies in the Study of Late Bronze Age and Early Iron Age Warriors Graves. *Cambridge Archaeological Journal* 12(2): 217–232.

Woolley, A. 1953. *A Forgotten Kingdom*. Baltimore.

CHAPTER 15

Phoenicians and Corinth

Susan Sherratt

This paper is written for Michal Artzy, whom I first met almost 30 years ago, and who has been the kindest of friends and a constant source of inspiration ever since. As I (and others) are well aware, and as many of her publications make clear, Michal knows far more about ancient maritime matters and ships and their representations than I am ever likely to (see, e.g., Artzy 2003), but I hope she will like the Phoenician trading ship that I venture to identify at Corinth in this tribute.

1   Introduction

I have been thinking recently about the relationship between Phoenician mariners and Corinth because, although it seems clear that Phoenician ships were using the long open sea route via southern Crete (particularly Kommos) to the far west of the Mediterranean from the end of the tenth century BCE onward, it seems inconceivable to me that they did not also make use of the route via the Isthmus of Corinth, probably already from the ninth century, but certainly in the eighth and subsequent centuries. Here I find myself fighting against a long-standing prejudice on the part of much classical scholarship, which, for much of the twentieth century, denied the possibility of Phoenician activity in the Aegean until at least the end of the eighth century, and, until relatively recently, of Phoenician precedence over Greek activity in the central and western Mediterranean. Things, however, have gradually been changing, and, as Martin Frederiksen noted as many as 40 years ago, "the Phoenicians are on the way back" (Frederiksen 1976–1977: 43; cf. Ridgway 1994: 38–40). While this observation was made specifically in relation to the evidence for physical Phoenician presence on Pithecusae (Ischia) and in Etruria, it also referred more generally to a resurgent interest in Phoenicians, particularly in the central and western Mediterranean. Since then, Phoenicians have continued to make their way back to southwestern Spain from the beginning of the ninth century onward (González de Canales, Serrano, and Llompart 2006; Nijboer and van der Plicht 2006; and various papers in Celestino, Rafel, and Armada 2008), to Sardinia (Oggiano 2000; Ridgway 2006: 244–249), to Euboea in the later eleventh to ninth centuries (Papadopoulos 1997, 2011; Theurillat 2007), to Crete from at least the tenth century (Shaw 1989; Stampolidis and Kotsonas 2006) and even, if perhaps not much before the eighth century, to the northern Aegean (Kasseri 2012; though, see, also, Papadopoulos 2005: 588–592). Moreover, the idea that Greeks, particularly "enterprising Euboeans," were solely responsible for bringing oriental objects into the Aegean and for distributing their own pottery around the Mediterranean in the early Iron Age (e.g., Popham 1994; Boardman 1996) now begins to seem increasingly implausible (González de Canales, Serrano, and Llompart 2006: 25–26 ; Ridgway 2006: 247; Kourou 2012).

2 Phoenicians, Corinth, and Pottery

My interest in the Phoenicians and Corinth has been sparked by a number of stimuli over the years. In the first place, there is the well-known association between Phoenician and Corinthian ceramic and other material in the central Mediterranean, not least at eighth-century Pithecusae (Ridgway 1992: 111–118), so far seemingly the earliest Greek settlement in the central Mediterranean (Buchner 1966) and, according to Strabo (5.4.9), founded by Chalcidians and Eretrians from Euboea; and it occurred to me to wonder about the routes by which these different types of pottery got there. A breakdown of imported pottery from the Valle di San Montano cemetery (Ridgway 1992: 72–82, figs. 18–20, tables 3–5)—although the absolute numbers are small—suggests that, while its majority (63.8% of a total of 285 pots) came from Corinth,[1] the remainder (some 36%) came from beyond the isthmus—from Rhodes, the Levant, and Euboea, in that order.[2] Given that pottery is a commodity that is typically

---

1 The "Argive monochrome" lekythoi found in the cemetery have been counted as coming from Corinth, since it seems possible that at least some of these may have been made in or around Corinth (Stillwell and Benson 1984: 14; Kourou 1987). For these pots and their possible contents, see Kourou 1988.
2 If these numbers are broken down into two consecutive periods (Late Geometric I [ca. 750–725 BCE] and Late Geometric II [ca .725–700 BCE]; see Ridgway 1992: 69), it can be seen that in the earlier period, although the overall number of imported pots (27) is much smaller and the dominance of Corinthian pottery (17) continues, a somewhat larger number proportionally (7) starts its journey in the Levant and outnumbers Euboean imports (3). In the later period (a total of 258 imported pots) aryballoi from Rhodes are second in frequency to Corinthian pots, followed by Euboean and Levantine products (see Ridgway 1992: figs. 12, 18, 30, tables 4, 5, pl. 5). It is perhaps worth noting that the imported pots from the Valle di San Montano cemetery that had traveled furthest were often ones that traveled for the sake of their contents, rather than simply as pots: for example, the Rhodian "Kreis-und-Wellenband" aryballoi and Levantine flasks, both of which can be assumed to have contained perfumed

subject to seaborne tramping trade, picked up where it is available and disposed of as soon as a ready market is reached, it seems likely that at least a number of the ships that brought pottery to Pithecusae started in the southeastern Aegean, or even further east, and arrived in Pithecusae via the Isthmus of Corinth. In pre-Diolkos days this could well have involved ships of up to 16 m or so in length being hauled over the isthmus with the help of rollers,[3] but, in any case, it seems quite clear that the isthmus route was quite extensively used in even earlier periods, including the later thirteenth–eleventh centuries, when increases in settlement activity around the Corinthian and Saronic Gulfs and in the Ionian Islands, together with the distribution of amber and "Urnfield" and Cypriot bronze types suggest this (Harding and Hughes-Brock 1974: fig. 3; Mederos and Harrison 1996: fig. 5; Sherratt 2001: 235–236; 2000, fig. 5.1). The growth of Corinth, which can be traced from at least the late tenth century (Salmon 1996: 390) and of the Isthmian sanctuary from the eleventh century (Morgan 1999: 373) seem, at any rate, unthinkable without the isthmus.

Once we get rid of the idea, quite common until recently in classical circles, that only traders from a particular center could transport that center's pottery (see on this, e.g., Papadopoulos 1997: 193–194; Morris and Papadopoulos 1998: 254–258), it seems reasonable to suppose that eastern ships traveling via the Isthmus of Corinth may have conveyed at least some of the Corinthian pottery that pervades the central and western Mediterranean in the eighth and seventh centuries.[4] Corinthian pottery is by far the most frequent Greek pottery

---

oils (cf. Coldstream 1977: 228). In the settlement areas, however, imported pots that cannot have traveled with anything in them predominate among the fine pottery. In order of frequency these consist chiefly of Corinthian, Euboean, and Phoenician Red Slip, in addition to those of local manufacture (Ridgway 1992: 89).

3 The Diolkos—the trackway constructed so that ships could be hauled on wheeled trolleys over the isthmus—was probably built during the reign of the tyrant Periander ca. 600 BCE (Lewis 2001: 11–15), which in itself is a good indication that a sufficient number of ships had been using the isthmus for enough time for the need for it to be felt. A length of up to 16 m for a clinker-built ship being hauled on rollers has been suggested as feasible for the much later Varangian portage routes, which often included much longer haulage distances (Stalsberg 2001: 370). A couple of wrecks of eighth-century Phoenician merchant ships loaded with hundreds of wine amphorae and located in deep water off the southern end of the Levantine coast were ca. 14 m long (Ballard et al. 2002: 157) and, therefore, probably capable of being hauled across the isthmus without the Diolkos. See, also, Herodotus 7.24, where he remarks that Xerxes' men could have drawn their warships across the isthmus of the Athos peninsula without trouble, but that he chose instead to construct a canal as a means of displaying his power.

4 Cf. also van der Brugge 2016: 328. This must almost certainly be so in the case of the eighth-century Corinthian Geometric kotylai found together with Phoenician Red Slip juglets and an alabastron in Tomb 19 of the Laurita necropolis at Almuñécar on the Málaga coast of

found in the West and on the North African coast in this period, and also finds its way eastward into most parts of the Aegean (Salmon 1984: 101–109). That, indeed, easterners may have had a hand in positively developing the Corinthian pottery industry for export has been argued by Sarah Morris and John Papadopoulos (1998), who point out that the development of proto-Corinthian pottery, toward the end of the eighth century, owes much to oriental influence.[5] This can be seen in the prominence of shapes such as the globular aryballos[6] and the alabastron, which, along with contemporary lekythoi and Rhodian aryballoi, share the flat mushroom lip (and very probably the contents)[7] of earlier and contemporary Phoenician flasks and other small container shapes (cf., e.g., Ridgway 1992: figs. 8: 16–19; 12; 14: 8–13; 30; pls. 5, 7, 8). But it is evident also in the decorative style (first found on aryballoi), which includes oriental animals and the use of incision for outlines and details, and seems particularly evocative of engraved metalwork as represented, for example, by the Phoenician bronze and silver bowls that become increasingly widespread in the Mediterranean from the ninth century onward (Markoe 1985, 1996: 50–54; 2000: 148–150; Morris and Papadopoulos 1998: 252–254). Morris and Papadopoulos go on to discuss other possible indications of a Phoenician involvement with Corinth, which include the cult of Aphrodite Ourania (who might well be thought of as a goddess of navigation) as official protectress of the city.[8] It has been suggested by Charles Williams (1986) that this cult came directly from Phoenicia, and, indeed, Herodotus (1.105) tells us that the temple of Aphrodite Ourania at Ashkelon was the oldest of all temples of this goddess. Williams (1981) has also drawn attention to the existence of a number of stelae

---

southeastern Spain (Aubet 2001: 292). For other types of Greek pottery carried west by Phoenicians even earlier than this, see further below; and see Pseudo-Scylax's *Periplous* 112c [Lipiński 2004: 462–464] for Phoenician merchants selling Attic pottery at Kerne on the northwestern coast of Africa.

5 As a corollary to this, it is perhaps no coincidence that the possibly locally made Late Geometric pottery from the precinct of Tanit at Carthage seems to have affinities with the pottery of Corinth (Coldstream 1968: 386–387; cf. now Docter 2014).

6 The globular aryballos with a wide flat disc lip already appears in Corinthian pottery in the late ninth or early eighth century (see, e.g., Weinberg 1943: 18 no. 63, pl. x; cf. Coldstream 1968: 94–95, pl. 17: c), but it is only toward the end of the eighth century that it first acquires "Orientalizing" decoration.

7 For Corinth's fame in the distant past as a producer of iris-scented unguent, see the first-century writer Pliny (*NH* 13.2).

8 Perhaps the equivalent of the Phoenician Tanit, or one of those other versatile Levantine goddesses associated with marine navigation and the protection of seafarers, who have a tendency to run effortlessly into one another. On the question of temple prostitution in the temple of Aphrodite Ourania at Corinth, see Fauth 1988: 38.

shrines of sixth–fifth-centuries date, including one in the Potters' Quarter, some of them not dissimilar in general to stelae or cippi found on early Iron Age Crete and in the Punic West (Morris and Papadopoulos 1998: 258, pl. 21; cf. Stampolidis 1990; Moscati 2001), or to elements of the Phoenician shrine at Kommos (Shaw 1989: fig. 10). Morris and Papadopoulos (1998: 259–261) also consider various elements in the foundation and other mythology of Corinth, which could be construed as suggesting some close Phoenician connections (cf. West 1997: 58). Other hints at Phoenician involvement in the life and religious practices of Corinth are listed by Eckert (2016: 127, 129–133).

3   Phoenicians, Corinth, and Euboean and Attic Pottery

Before I go on to discuss another small piece of archaeological evidence that may indicate a close Phoenician relationship with Corinth, it is perhaps worth considering some of the Euboean and Attic pottery that was arguably carried westward on Phoenician ships. As González de Canales, Serrano, and Llompart (2006: 25) have pointed out, it seems unthinkable that the Euboean pendent semicircle skyphoi and the 15 pendent semicircle plates of the ninth or very early eighth century (which are rare in the Aegean, but relatively common at Tyre) that turn up at Huelva (González de Canales, Serrano, and Llompart 2006: 19, figs. 21–24) were carried all that way by Euboean Greeks. The same has been argued for a similar skyphos from Sant'Imbenia on Sardinia, which, like the Huelva material, was found in a thoroughly Phoenician context (Ridgway 2006: 244–247; Naso 2014: 171).[9] How, then, did these get there? Did they first go to Tyre (as a considerable number of such skyphoi and an impressive number of such plates did [Coldstream and Bikai 1988]), and were then transported westward via Kommos on southern Crete, along the southern open sea route, to the far west? This is certainly possible, but one problem is that, although there are a few Euboean pendent semicircle skyphoi on Crete, particularly at Knossos (Popham 1983: 281; Coldstream 1996: 403), there is no sign of any of the plates on that island, and even the skyphoi are absent from Kommos (Callaghan and Johnston 2000). One could probably argue that the inhabitants of Crete had little use for such plates, since the shape is a regular feature of eastern Mediterranean ceramic and metal repertoires rather than Aegean ones. But one could perhaps ask alternatively whether the plates that reached Huelva might have

---

9   For other examples of pendent semicircle skyphoi from the central Mediterranean, some almost as early as the Sant'Imbenia one and none of them later than the mid-eighth century, see Naso 2014.

traveled west over the Isthmus of Corinth. Although, against this, there are no Euboean pendent semicircle plates or skyphoi known from Corinth or the Isthmian sanctuary, in support of it we might cite the two plates from the Kerameikos cemetery in Athens (Kraiker and Kübler 1939: 130, pl. 52; Kübler 1943: 46, pl. 34), tucked in well to the west of the eastern entrance to the Saronic Gulf. These are accompanied by a few pendent semicircle skyphoi in Athens, and to the west of the Isthmus at Delphi (Lemos 2002: 46), which suggests that this may have provided a route westward. Together with these may have traveled the examples of late ninth/early eighth century Attic pottery, which also reached Huelva and other sites with close associations with Phoenicians in the western and central Mediterranean (González de Canales, Serrano, and Llompart 2006: 19, figs. 17–20; Kourou in press 2020). Later, from the mid-eighth century, early versions of Attic and Euboean "SOS" amphorae can also be seen to extend in their distribution from Huelva in the far west to the Levant (including Tyre) in the far east (Pratt 2015: figs. 11–14); and Pratt (2015: 231–232) is surely justified in finding further support for the suggestion, first put forward by Shefton (1982), that Phoenicians were heavily involved in distributing these around the Mediterranean. The association of later versions with Early Corinthian aryballoi, especially in the western Mediterranean, suggests that at least some of them traveled westward over the Isthmus of Corinth.

4 A Phoenician Ship at Corinth?

Finally, returning more narrowly to the question of Phoenicians and Corinth, I would like to draw attention to part of a ceramic plaque excavated at Penteskouphia, close to ancient Corinth, in 1879, among over 1,000 other plaques probably from a sanctuary of Poseidon, many of which show scenes of potters at work with potters' wheels and kilns. This particular plaque, now in Berlin (Furtwängler 1885: 90 no. 831; Fraenkel 1886: 3 pl. 8 no. 3a; Rayet and Collignon 1888: xv fig. 6; Basch 1987: 235, 237 no. 494; Casson 1995: fig. 98), has been dated by reason of its style to the seventh or sixth century. One side of the plaque shows a male figure identified by Furtwängler as Poseidon, with a human-headed bird flying behind him, and beneath this a man in a cave or hole digging something (perhaps clay) with a pickax (Fraenkel 1886: pl. 8: 3b) (Fig. 15.1). The other side shows the stern end of a ship with furled sail and brail rig, which Casson (1995: 69) has compared to the rigging of both Phoenician and Greek ships. Above the rigging, on either side of the mast, hangs a row of seven or more jugs of some material, while on top of the curved stern is a curious symbol consisting of a circular shape on top of a vertical pole, and above that a horizontal line. Behind

FIGURE 15.1
Terracotta plaque from the sanctuary of Poseidon at Penteskouphia, Corinth; Berlin Altes Museum, Antikensammlung no. 831 [P. 303] (other side of Fig. 15.2)
FRAENKEL 1886: PL. 8: 3B

this symbol is a row of three emblems that look like two-barred crosses, but could, given the difficulty of painting at this relatively small and crude scale, possibly be caducei (Fig. 15.2).

The main symbol on the stern of the ship has also been interpreted as a caduceus, or kerykeion, the short staff entwined by two serpents, and frequently shown in classical iconography as carried by heralds and often associated with the god Hermes or with Iris, the messenger of the gods—which, in some ways, might seem appropriate for a ship carrying goods or messages swiftly across the waves; however, by the seventh–sixth centuries, we would expect to be able to recognize a Greek caduceus without too much difficulty, and this symbol is clearly not one. Rather, it bears a much closer resemblance to the symbol found on the sterns of war galleys portrayed on Phoenician coins dating from the fifth century and later (Basch 1987: 320–325 nos. 675–682, 687; cf. Brody 2005: 179) than anything found in Greek iconography. This symbol consists of a crescent moon surmounting a sun disc, a motif that is often associated with the "sign of Tanit" on funerary and other stelae in the Punic West (Moscati 2001), and which can be related to an ancient Canaanite symbol (Tubb 1998: 146).[10]

---

10 For the association of the disc and crescent moon with Tanit, see Brody 2005: 179; 2008: 3. This symbol can also be found on funerary stelae from the eleventh–sixth centuries

FIGURE 15.2
Terracotta plaque from the sanctuary of Poseidon at Penteskouphia, Corinth; Berlin Altes Museum, Antikensammlung no. 831 [P. 303]; showing stern end of a ship (other side of Fig. 15.1)
FRAENKEL 1886: PL. 8: 3A

I would suggest that the main symbol on the stern is intended to indicate that this is a Phoenician ship. The symbol, which is recognizable from the portrayal of ships on Phoenician coins (see above) and from Phoenician and Punic funerary stelae, does not seem to appear on other contemporary Greek

al-Bass cemetery at Tyre (Sader 2005: 36–40, 52–53, figs. 17, 20, 34). The crescent on these and on the ships on Sidonian coins, as well as on stelae in the west, can point either upward or downward.

Some later Punic stelae combine the disc and crescent moon and the "sign of Tanit" with what we would recognize from Graeco-Roman iconography as caducei (e.g., British Museum ANE125117: a second–first centuries BCE stele with a dedication to Baal from the Tophet of Carthage, which also has a disc and crescent moon combination at the top of the stele [Tubb 1998: 140, fig. 98]; British Museum 1857,1218.30: fourth–second centuries, also from Carthage, and also with a disc and crescent moon at the top [Davis 1863: pl. 1: 2]; Quinn 2017: figs. 5.5, 5.6, from the Carthage Tophet). Much ink has been spilled for over more than a century on the question of whether the caduceus was originally a Greek or eastern symbol. For differing views on this, see, e.g., Frothingham 1916; Boetzkes 1967; Cross 1997, 31 n. 108. I would merely point out that it may well be in some way relatable to the image of a snake-legged goddess on a Canaanite gold pendant found by Michal Artzy at Tel Nami on the Carmel Coast and datable to the thirteenth century BCE (Artzy 1994: 125, fig. 4). This image, in turn, can be compared with those on a Mitannian seal impression on a letter in the Amarna archive and on some earlier Mitannian cylinder seals (Porada 1974–1977: 141–142, figs. 1b, 6–7), which Buchanan (1971) has associated with the underworld. That images like these (or at least their derivative, the caduceus) eventually become associated with Tanit seems likely (Brody 2005: 179).

representations of ships, including other plaques from Penteskouphia. Since almost half of the ship is missing, it is impossible to say what the other end looked like, but the shape of the stern, at least, seems similar to those of both Greek and Phoenician cargo and fighting ships in representations of the midfirst millennium (Basch 1987: 236–238 nos. 490, 493, 498; 321 nos. 675–678).[11] Was the plaque dedicated at a sanctuary of the god of the sea and protector of sailors by a Corinthian potter desirous of ensuring a safe journey for the Phoenician ship that carried his wares overseas, or was it dedicated by a Phoenician shipowner or captain, either based in Corinth or en route across the isthmus? The jugs suspended above the ship have been assumed to be Corinthian ceramic products (Rayet and Collignon 1888: xv), and they could perhaps be seen as somewhat crude and elongated representations of some examples of Corinthian trefoil-mouthed oenochoae (e.g., Amyx and Lawrence 1975: pls. 46–51), even though the jugs on the plaque appear to have taller conical feet. Their close similarity to jugs shown lying in a kiln on another plaque (Fraenkel 1886: 4, pl. 8 no. 19b; Rayet and Collignon 1888: xiv fig. 5) would suggest that they are local products, as does the possibility that clay is shown being dug up on the other side of our plaque, as well as the frequent associations between potters and plaques from the Penteskouphia sanctuary in general. On the other hand, jugs that could equally be seen to match these representations were being produced over a wide area of the Mediterranean world, including Greece, the Levant, and Etruria, in a variety of materials, including glass and metal as well as ceramics.

5 Concluding Remarks

There is not a great deal more that it is possible to say about this image, given the incomplete state of the plaque and the relative crudeness of the painting. Nevertheless, speculative though it may be, it perhaps adds yet another small fragment of evidence to those outlined earlier for Phoenicians operating at, or passing through, Corinth in the Archaic and preceding periods. If so, it probably should not surprise us. We have arguably become accustomed, until relatively recently, to thinking within our own specialized, and often protectionist, disciplines and geographical areas. Classical Greek archaeologists dealt only with Greeks in Greece and in lands (and at times) recorded as having been inhabited by Greeks; and Phoenicians (the province of Levantine archaeologists) threatened an alien intrusion into an otherwise ideologically self-contained world. As long as

---

11   For the belief that it is a merchant ship, see Chatzidimitriou 2010: 10–11.

separate archaeological disciplines did not regularly interact and intermingle, it was forgotten that people from different parts of the ancient world (ideally distinguishable archaeologically by their quite different material cultures) did, and just how mobile and cosmopolitan that world could be, even in the early centuries of the Iron Age. As Michal Artzy has shown for the Late Bronze Age, it takes excavation of a single harborside, as at Tell Abu Hawam, to show just how varied the origins of ships that called in there could be (Artzy 2006: 55).

Despite our archaeological obsessions with pottery, we need not worry (as some do) that Phoenician pottery is missing from Corinth in the early Iron Age and Archaic periods. Phoenicians were perfectly happy to use and/or reproduce other people's pottery, as the Cypro-Geometric and Euboean Subprotogeometric pots from sites such as Dor and Tyre, and the locally made "Greek" pottery from Carthage show (Coldstream and Bikai 1988; Gilboa 1999; Docter 2014); and, as long as these were available, they were content to use tableware and even small packaging vessels made elsewhere, in some cases—as the pendent semicircle plates reveal—made specially for them and designed to fit into their own repertoires (Coldstream and Bikai 1988: 39). The main goods for maritime trade that they produced in their home cities were other types of manufactures: fine textiles, glass and faience, elaborate carved ivories, and fancy metalwork. Trade in the pottery of others (including pottery as containers for other people's wine or unguents) was, to some extent, opportunistic—picked up because they were passing anyway and knew they could find a market (cf. Artzy 1985)—or, to a greater extent, because they were traders and designed their routes accordingly.

This brings us to the question of sea routes, which have only relatively recently been systematically considered, most recently of all (and occasionally rather mechanically) in the context of "network" approaches (Knappett, Evans, and Rivers 2008). Routes that link places purely by sea are one thing, but isthmuses and portages have always been just as important in long-distance seafaring and trading (Sherratt 2006), and, like mountain passes, act as funnels to attract sea travelers and thus provide stimuli to the local production of manufactured goods for maritime export by whoever is passing that way in either direction. The 5 km wide Isthmus of Corinth is undoubtedly the most famous and one of the shortest examples in the ancient world, and the ancients themselves were in no doubt that Corinth owed its prosperity as a commercial emporium to its situation on it (Thuc. 1.13), even if twentieth-century scholars of earlier generations might perversely have taken another view and, in Weberian fashion, argued that the city's wealth was built on its rich agricultural land rather than its location or even its commerce (Will 1955; Salmon 1984). It is my belief that Thucydides was right, and that Corinth would never have become so wealthy in the first half of the first millennium BCE had it not been for its isthmus. This linked the Aegean and eastern Mediterranean with the central and western Mediterranean, and I have tried to suggest that ships of many different origins, including Phoenician ones, traveled across it.

References

Amyx, D.A. and Lawrence, P. 1975. *Corinth*, Vol. 7, Part.2: *Archaic Corinthian Pottery and the Anaploga Well*. Princeton.

Artzy, M. 1985. Merchandise and Merchantmen: On Ships and Shipping in the Late Bronze Age Levant. In: Papadopoulos T. and Hadjistyllis, S., eds. *Πρακτικά του Δεύτερου Διεθνικούς Κυπρολογικού Συνεδρίου* (*Acts of the Second International Congress of Cypriot Studies*). Nicosia: 135–140.

Artzy, M. 1994. Incense, Camels and Collared Rim Jars: Desert Trade Routes and Maritime Outlets in the Second Millennium. *Oxford Journal of Archaeology* 13: 2, 121–147.

Artzy, M. 2003. Mariners and Their Boats at the End of the Late Bronze and the Beginning of the Iron Age in the Eastern Mediterranean. *Tel Aviv* 30: 232–246.

Artzy, M. 2006. The Carmel Coast during the Second Part of the Late Bronze Age: A Center for Eastern Mediterranean Transshipping. *Bulletin of the American Schools of Oriental Research* 343: 45–64.

Aubet, M.E. 2001. Spain. In: Moscati, S., ed., *The Phoenicians*. London: 279–304.

Ballard, R.D., Stager, L.E., Master, D., Yoerger, D., Mindell, D., Whitcomb, L.L., Singh, H., and Piechota, D. 2002. Iron Age Shipwrecks in Deep Water off Ashkelon, Israel. *American Journal of Archaeology* 106(2): 151–168.

Basch, L. 1987. *Le Musée imaginaire de la marine antique*. Athens.

Boardman, J. 1996. Euboeans Overseas: A Question of Identity. In: Evely, D., Lemos, I.S., and Sherratt, S., eds. *Minotaur and Centaur: Studies in the Archaeology of Crete and Euboea Presented to Mervyn Popham*. Oxford: 155–160.

Boetzkes, R. 1967. Kerykeion. In: *Paulys Realencyclopädie der classischen Altertumswissenschaft* XI.1: 330–342.

Brody, A.J. 2005. Further Evidence of the Specialized Religion of Phoenician Seafarers. In: Pollini, J., ed. *Terra Marique: Studies in Art History and Marine Archaeology in Honor of Anna Marguerite McCann*. Oxford: 177–182.

Brody, A.J. 2008. The Specialized Religions of Ancient Mediterranean Seafarers. *Religion Compass* 2: 444–454.

Brugge, C. van der 2016. The Silver Krater of King Phaedimus: A Small Piece of Tyrian History in the *Odyssey*. In Kleber, K. and Pirngruber, R., eds. *Silver, Money and Credit: A Tribute to Robartus J. van der Spek on the Occasion of His 65th Birthday*. Leiden: 319–332.

Buchanan, B. 1971. A Snake Goddess and Her Companions: A Problem in the Iconography of the Early Second Millennium B.C. *Iraq* 33(1): 1–18.

Buchner, G. 1966. Pithekoussai: Oldest Greek Colony in the West. *Expedition* 8: 4–12.

Callaghan, P.J. and Johnston, A.W. 2000. The Pottery from the Greek Temples at Kommos. In: Shaw, J.W. and Shaw, M.C., eds. *Kommos* Vol. 4: *The Greek Sanctuary*, Part 1. Princeton: 210–301.

Casson, L. 1995. *Ships and Seamanship in the Ancient World*. Baltimore.

Celestino, S., Rafel N., and Armada, X.-L., eds. 2008. *Contacto cultural entre el Mediterráneo y el Atlántico (siglos XII–VIII ane): La precolonización a debate*. Madrid.

Chatzidimitriou, A. 2010. Transport of Goods in the Mediterranean from the Geometric to the Classical Period: Images and Meaning. *Bollettino di Archeologia Online. Edizione speciale—Congresso di Archeologia A.I.A.C. 2008* http://bollettinodiarcheologiaonline.beniculturali.it/wp-content/uploads/2019/01/1_CHATZIDIMITRIOU.pdf.

Coldstream, J.N. 1968. *Greek Geometric Pottery*. London.

Coldstream, J.N. 1977. *Geometric Greece*. London.

Coldstream, J.N. 1996. Knossos and Lefkandi: The Attic Connections. In: Evely, D., Lemos, I.S., and Sherratt, S., eds. *Minotaur and Centaur: Studies in the Archaeology of Crete and Euboea Presented to Mervyn Popham*. Oxford: 133–145.

Coldstream, J.N. and Bikai, P. 1988. Early Greek Pottery in Tyre and Cyprus: Some Preliminary Comparisons. *Report of the Department of Antiquities, Cyprus* 1988(2): 35–43.

Cross, F.M. 1997. *Canaanite Myth and Hebrew Epic: Essays in the History of the Religion of Israel*. Cambridge, MA.

Davis, N. 1863. *Inscriptions in the Phoenician Character*. London.

Docter, R. 2014. The Phoenician Practice of Adapting Greek Drinking Vessels (Skyphoi and Kotylai). In: Graelis, R., Fabrikat, I., Krueger, M., Sardà S., and Sciotino, G., eds. *El problema de las 'imitaciones' durante la protohistoria en el Mediterráneo centrooccidental: Entre el concepto y el ejemplo*. Tübingen: 65–71.

Eckert, M. 2016. *Die Aphrodite der Seefahrer und ihre Heiligtümer am Mittelmeer*. Berlin.

Fauth, W. 1988. Sakrale Prostitution im vorderen Orient und im Mittelmeerraum. *Jahrbuch für Antike und Christentum* 31: 24–39.

Fraenkel, M. 1886. Thontäfelchen aus Korinth im Berliner Museum. *Antike Denkmaeler* 1: 3–4.

Frederiksen, M.W. 1976–1977. Archaeology in South Italy and Sicily, 1973–76. *Archaeological Reports* 23: 43–76.

Frothingham, A.L. 1916. Babylonian Origin of Hermes the Snake-God, and of the Caduceus. *American Journal of Archaeology* 20(2): 175–211.

Furtwängler, A. 1885. *Beschreibung der Vasensammlung im Antiquarium*, Vol. 1. Berlin.

Gilboa, A. 1999. The View from the East: Tel Dor and the Earliest Cypro-Geometric Exports to the Levant. In: Iacovou, M. and Michaelides, D., eds. *Cyprus: The Historicity of the Geometric Horizon*. Nicosia: 119–139.

González de Canales, F., Serrano, L., and Llompart, J. 2006. The Pre-colonial Phoenician Emporium of Huelva ca 900–770 BC. *Bulletin Antieke Beschaving* 81: 13–29.

Harding, A. and Hughes-Brock, H. 1974. Amber in the Mycenaean world. *Annual of the British School at Athens* 69: 145–172.

Kasseri, A. 2012. Φοινικικοί εμπορικοί αμφορείς από τη Μεθώνη Πιερίας (Phoenician Amphorae from Methone in Pieria). In: Kephalidou, E. and Tsiafaki, D., eds. *Κεραμέως Παίδες (Children of the Potter: Studies Offered to Professor Michalis Tiverios by His Students)* Thessaloniki: 299–308.

Knappett, C., Evans, T., and Rivers, R. 2008. Modelling Maritime Interaction in the Aegean Bronze Age. *Antiquity* 82: 1009–1024.

Kourou, N. 1987. A propos de quelques ateliers de céramique fine, non-tournée du type "argien monochrome." *Bulletin de Correspondance Hellénique* 111(1): 31–53.

Kourou, N. 1988. Handmade Pottery and Trade: The Case of the "Argive Monochrome" Ware. In: Christiansen, J. and Melander, T., eds. *Proceedings of the 3rd Symposium on Ancient Greek and Related Pottery, Copenhagen, August 31–September 4 1987*. Copenhagen: 314–324.

Kourou, N. 2012. Phoenicia, Cyprus and the Aegean in the Early Iron Age: J.N. Coldstream's Contribution and the Current State of Research. In: Iacovou, M., ed. *Cyprus and the Aegean in the Early Iron Age: The Legacy of Nicolas Coldstream*. Nicosia: 33–51.

Kourou, N. 2020 In press. Phoenicians and Attic Middle Geometric Pottery in the Mediterranean. Echoes of an Early Athenian Cultural Value. In: Bonadies, L., Chirpanlieva, I., and Guillon, E., eds. *Les Phéniciens, les Puniques et les autres : Echanges et identités entre le monde phénico-punique et les différents peuples de l'Orient ancien et du pourtour méditerranéen*. Paris: 159–178.

Kraiker, W. and Kübler, K. 1939. *Kerameikos: Ergebnisse der Ausgrabungen*, Band 1: *Die Nekropolen des 12. und 10. Jahrhunderts*. Berlin.

Kübler, K. 1943. *Kerameikos: Ergebnisse der Ausgrabungen*, Band 4: *Neufunde aus der Nekropole des 11. und 10. Jahrhunderts*. Berlin.

Lemos, I.S. 2002. *The Protogeometric Aegean*. Oxford.

Lewis, M.J.T. 2001. Railways in the Greek and Roman World. In: Guy, A. and Rees, J., eds. *Early Railways: A Selection of Papers from the First International Early Railways Conference*. London: 8–19.

Lipiński, E. 2004. *Itineraria Phoenicia* (Orientalia Lovaniensia Analecta 127). Leuven.

Markoe, G. 1985. *Phoenician Bronze and Silver Bowls from Cyprus and the Mediterranean*. Berkeley.

Markoe, G. 1996. The Emergence of Orientalizing in Greek Art: Some Observations on the Interchange between Greeks and Phoenicians in the Eighth and Seventh Centuries B.C. *Bulletin of the American Schools of Oriental Research* 301: 47–67.

Markoe, G. 2000. *Phoenicians.* Berkeley.

Mederos, A. and Harrison, R. 1996. "Placer de Dioses." Incensarios en soportes con ruedas del Bronce Final de la Península Ibérica. *Complutum Extra* 6: 237–253.

Morgan, C. 1999. *Isthmia 8: The Late Bronze Age Settlement and Early Iron Age Sanctuary.* Princeton.

Morris, S.P. and Papadopoulos, J.K. 1998. Phoenicians and the Corinthian Pottery Industry. In: Rolle, R., Schmidt, K., and Docter, R. eds. *Archäologische Studien in Kontaktzonen der antiken Welt.* Göttingen: 251–263.

Moscati, S. 2001. Stelae. In: Moscati, S., ed. *The Phoenicians.* London: 364–379.

Naso, A. 2014. Pendent Semicircle Skyphoi from Central Italy in the Light of the Archaeometric Results. In: Kerschner, M. and Lemos, I.S., eds. *Archaeometric Analyses of Euboean and Euboean Related Pottery: New Results and Their Interpretations.* Vienna: 169–179.

Nijboer, A.J. and Plicht, J. van der. 2006. An Interpretation of the Radiocarbon Determinations of the Oldest Indigenous-Phoenician Stratum thus Far, Excavated at Huelva, Tartessos (South-West Spain). *Bulletin Antieke Beschaving* 81: 31–36.

Oggiano, I. 2000. La ceramica fenicia di Sant'Imbenia (Alghero, SS). In: Bartoloni, P. and Campanella, L., eds. *La ceramica fenicia di Sardegna: Dati, problematiche, confronti.* Roma: 235–258.

Papadopoulos, J.K. 1997. Phantom Euboians. *Journal of Mediterranean Archaeology* 10(2): 191–219.

Papadopoulos, J.K. 2005. *The Early Iron Age Cemetery at Torone.* Los Angeles.

Papadopoulos, J.K. 2011. "Phantom Euboians": A Decade On. In: Rupp, D.W. and Tomlinson, J.E., eds. *Euboea and Athens: Proceedings of a Colloquium in Memory of Malcolm B. Wallace, Athens 26–27 June 2009.* Athens: 113–133.

Popham, M.R. 1983. Euboean Exports to al Mina, Cyprus, and Crete: A Reassessment. *Annual of the British School at Athens* 78: 281–290.

Popham, M.R. 1994. Precolonization: Early Greek Contact with the East. In: Tsetskhladze, G.R. and De Angelis, F., eds. *The Archaeology of Greek Colonisation.* Oxford: 11–34.

Porada, E. 1974–1977. Die Siegelzylinder-Abrollung auf der Amarna-Tafel BM 29841 im Britischen Museum. *Archiv für Orientforschung* 25: 132–142.

Pratt, C.E. 2015. The "SOS" Amphora: An Update. *Annual of the British School at Athens* 110: 213–245.

Quinn, J. 2017. *In Search of the Phoenicians.* Princeton.

Rayet, O. and Collignon, M. 1888. *Histoire de la céramique grecque.* Paris.

Ridgway, D. 1992. *The First Western Greeks.* Cambridge.

Ridgway, D. 1994. Phoenicians and Greeks in the West: A View from Pithekoussai. In: Tsetskhladze, G.R. and De Angelis, F., eds. *The Archaeology of Greek Colonisation: Essays Dedicated to Sir John Boardman*. Oxford: 35–46.

Ridgway, D. 2006. Early Greek Imports in Sardinia. In: Tsetskhladze, G.R., ed. *Greek Colonisation: An Account of Greek Colonies and Other Settlements Overseas*, Vol. 1. Leiden: 239–252.

Sader, H. 2005. *Iron Age Funerary Stelae from Lebanon*. Barcelona.

Salmon, J.B. 1996. Corinth. In: Hornblower, S. and Spawforth A., eds. *The Oxford Classical Dictionary* (3rd ed.). Oxford: 390–391.

Salmon, J.B. 1984 *Wealthy Corinth: A History of the City to 338 BC*. Oxford.

Shaw, J.W. 1989. Phoenicians in Southern Crete. *American Journal of Archaeology* 93(2): 165–183.

Shefton, B.B. 1982. Greeks and Greek Imports in the South of the Iberian Peninsula: The Archaeological Evidence. In: Niemeyer, H.G., ed. *Phönizier im Westen* (Madrider Beiträge 8). Mainz: 337–370.

Sherratt, A. 2000. Circulation of Metals and the End of the Bronze Age in the Eastern Mediterranean. In: Pare, C.F.E., ed. *Metals Make the World Go Round: The Supply and Circulation of Metals in Bronze Age Europe*. Oxford 82–98.

Sherratt, A. 2001. Potemkin Palaces and Route-based Economies. In: Voutsaki S. and Killen, J., eds. *Economy and Politics in the Mycenaean Palace States: Proceedings of a Conference Held on 1–3 July 1999 in the Faculty of Classics, Cambridge*. Cambridge: 214–238.

Sherratt, A. 2006. Portages: A Simple but Powerful Idea in Understanding Human History. In: Westerdahl, C., ed. *The Significance of Portages: Proceedings of the First International Conference on the Significance of Portages, 29th Sept–2nd Oct 2004, in Lyngdal, Vest-Agder, Norway, Arranged by the County Municipality of Vest-Agder, Kristiansand*. Oxford: 1–13.

Stalsberg, A. 2001. Scandinavian Viking-Age Boat Graves in Old Rus.' *Russian History* 28(1/4): 359–401.

Stampolidis, N.C. 1990. A Funerary Cippus at Eleutherna: Evidence of Phoenician Presence? *Bulletin of the Institute of Classical Studies* 37: 99–106.

Stampolidis, N.C. and Kotsonas, A. 2006. Phoenicians in Crete. In: Deger-Jalkotzy, S. and Lemos, I.S., eds. *Ancient Greece: From the Mycenaean Palaces to the Age of Homer*. Edinburgh: 337–360.

Stillwell, A.N. and Benson, J.L. 1984. *Corinth*, Vol. 15, Part 3: *The Potters' Quarter: The Pottery*. Princeton.

Theurillat, T. 2007. Early Iron Age Graffiti from the Sanctuary of Apollo at Eretria. In: Mazarakis-Ainian, A., ed. *Oropos and Euboea in the Early Iron Age: Acts of an International Round Table, University of Thessaly, June 18–20, 2004*. Volos: 331–344.

Tubb, J.N. 1998. *Canaanites*. London.

Weinberg, S.S. 1943. *Corinth: Results of Excavations Conducted by the American School of Classical Studies at Athens*, Vol. 7. Part 1: *The Geometric and Orientalizing Pottery*. Cambridge, MA.

West, M.L. 1997. *The East Face of Helicon: West Asiatic Elements in Early Poetry and Myth*. Oxford.

Will, E. 1955. *Korinthiaka: Recherches sur l'histoire et la civilisation de Corinthe des origines aux guerres médiques*. Paris.

Williams, C.K. 1981. The City of Corinth and Its Domestic Religion. *Hesperia* 50: 408–421.

Williams, C.K. 1986. Corinth and the Cult of Aphrodite. In: Del Chiaro, M.A. and Biers, W.R., eds. *Corinthiaca: Studies in Honor of Darrell A. Amyx*. Columbia: 12–24.

CHAPTER 16

The Aegean-Type Pottery from Tel Nami

Philipp W. Stockhammer

That I am able to write here about the Aegean-type pottery from Tel Nami owes everything to the generosity of Michal Artzy. Since I told her about my idea to study the appropriation of Aegean-type pottery in the southern Levant in 2008, she has not only continuously supported me with all possible kind of advice, but she also offered me to include in my research the Aegean-type pottery from Tel Nami, which became a key site in my overall argument. Moreover, she was the one who taught me how to differentiate Aegean-type pottery of Cypriot origin from that from Aegean and Levantine workshops—knowledge that was crucial for all my subsequent analyses of Aegean-type pottery. It is, therefore, my greatest pleasure and honor to write about the Aegean-type pottery from the settlement and the cemetery of Nami in a volume dedicated to Michal.

This contribution is part of a larger, comprehensive study that focuses on the appropriation of Aegean-type pottery in the southern Levant during the Late Bronze Age (Stockhammer forthcoming). In the following, I present and discuss altogether 31 Aegean-type vessels (represented mostly by single sherds) from Area G of the settlement on the tell itself and 31 (almost/mostly) complete Aegean-type vessels from the cemetery in Area O at Nami East (Table 16.1). In both areas rich evidence from the late thirteenth and early twelfth centuries was discovered. The respective excavations took place under the direction of Michal Artzy from the Recanati Institute for Maritime Studies and the Zinman Institute of Archaeology at the University of Haifa from 1986 to 1989 (Artzy 1990b). So far, there has been no final publication of the archaeological evidence from the site. I base my contextual information on the large number of articles on the evidence (Artzy 1990a, 1990b, 1991a, 1991b, 1992, 1993, 1994, 1995, 1997, 1998, 2006; Artzy and Zagorski 2012), as well as personal information that Michal Artzy communicated to me during my study.

1   Area G

At the highest point of the tell in Area G, the excavators were able to differentiate two Late Bronze Age horizons, which they called Phase G/3 and Phase G/2. The

TABLE 16.1 Catalogue of the Aegean-type pottery from Nami

NAM#	Area, locus, context, stratum	Collection no.	No. of sherds	Vessel type	Vessel part	Decoration	Date	Origin	Other
1	G0, 331, surface	36–89 235/4	1	Unclear	Body sherd	Unclear	Unclear	Unclear	Examination not possible
2	G1, 257, robber's trench	31–91 55/1	1	Bowl	Body sherd	Unclear	Unclear	Unclear	Examination not possible
3	G2, 144, glacis coating, IIIB	37–86 128/10	1	Minoan transport jar (FS 164)	Body sherd	Linear	LH IIIA–C	Crete	
4	G2, 266, Room F, debris, IIIB	65–92 405/3	1	Flask (FS 189)	Neck	Unclear	Unclear	Unclear	Examination not possible
5	G2, 266, Room F, debris, IIIB	65–92 408/2	5	Flask (FS 189)	Neck	Linear	LH IIIB2/C	Cyprus or Levant	
6	G2, 240, Room K, debris, IIIB	31–91 18/2	1	Stirrup jar	Body sherd	Unclear	Unclear	Unclear	Examination not possible
7	G2, 267, Room F, floor, IIIB	65–92 415/3	1	Stirrup jar	Body sherd, spout attachment	Linear, Simple Style	LH IIIB2/C	Probably Cyprus	

TABLE 16.1 Catalogue of the Aegean-type pottery from Nami (*cont.*)

NAM #	Area, locus, context, stratum	Collection no.	No. of sherds	Vessel type	Vessel part	Decoration	Date	Origin	Other
8	G2, 131, Room D, wall debris, IIIB	65–92 526/4	1	Medium-sized closed vessel	Body sherd	Linear	LH IIIB2/C	Probably Cyprus	
9	G2, 131, Room D, wall debris, IIIB	13–88 564/1	1	Closed vessel	Body sherd	Linear	LH IIIB2/C	Probably Cyprus	
10	G2, 131, Room D, wall debris, IIIB	13–88 564/2	1	Closed vessel	Body sherd	Unclear	Unclear	Unclear	Examination not possible
11	G2, 224, Room C, habitation level, IIIB	36–89 325/5	1	Stirrup jar	Handle	Unclear	LH IIIB2/C	Probably Cyprus	
12	G2, 275, Room H, floor, IIIB	65–92 474/1	1	Medium-sized closed vessel	Body sherd	Linear	LH IIIB2/C	Probably Cyprus	
13	G2, 26, Room G, floor, IIIB	100–97 688/4	1	Open or closed vessel	Body sherd	Linear	LH IIIB2/C	Probably Cyprus	
14	G2c, 191a, Room B, floor, IIIB	36–89 913/6	3	Stirrup jar	False neck	Unclear	LH IIIB2/C	Probably Cyprus	

TABLE 16.1 Catalogue of the Aegean-type pottery from Nami (cont.)

NAM #	Area, locus, context, stratum	Collection no.	No. of sherds	Vessel type	Vessel part	Decoration	Date	Origin	Other
15	G2d, 144, burnt mud-wall debris, IIIB	13–88 452/1	1	Flask (FS 189)	Body sherd	Concentric circles	LH IIIB2/C	Probably Cyprus	
16	G3, 65a, fill, IIIA	13–88 336/6	1	Probably one-handled conical bowl (FS 242)	Rim	Inside: monochrome; outside: linear or monochrome with reserved zone	LH IIIC Early	Probably Cyprus	
17	G3, 65a, fill, IIIA	13–88 336/5	1	Stirrup jar	Handle	Linear	LH IIIB2/C	Probably Cyprus	
18	G3, 16, destruction/fill, IIIA	37–86 157/5	1	Probably amphoroid krater	Handle	Unclear	LH IIIB2/C	Cyprus or Levant	
19	G3, 112, destruction/fill, IIIA	13–88 420/1	1	Krater, amphoroid or FS 281	Body sherd, base	Linear above base	LH IIIB/C	Cyprus or Levant	

TABLE 16.1 Catalogue of the Aegean-type pottery from Nami (*cont.*)

NAM#	Area, locus, context, stratum	Collection no.	No. of sherds	Vessel type	Vessel part	Decoration	Date	Origin	Other
20	G3, 108, habitation level, IIIA	13–88 405/2	1	Stirrup jar or flask	Handle	Monochrome	LH IIIB2/C	Cyprus or Levant	
21	G3, 65a, fill, IIIA	13–88 336/17	1	Closed vessel	Body sherd	Linear	LH IIIB2/C	Cyprus or Levant	
22	G3, 64, debris, IIIA	13–87 119/5	1	Open or closed vessel	Body sherd	Linear	LH IIIB2/C	Cyprus or Levant	
23	G3, 44, destruction/fill, IIIA	13–87 168/3	1	Open or closed vessel	Body sherd	Linear	LH IIIB2/C	Probably Cyprus	
24	G3, 117, foundation layer, IIIA	13–88 414/11	1	Open or closed vessel	Body sherd	Unclear	LH IIIB2/C	Cyprus or Levant	
25	G3, 112, destruction/fill, IIIA	13–88 484/4	1	Open or closed vessel	Body sherd	Linear	Unclear	Unclear	
26	G3, 187, fill, IIIA	36–89 302/1	1	Open or closed vessel	Body sherd	Unclear	Unclear	Unclear	Examination not possible

TABLE 16.1 Catalogue of the Aegean-type pottery from Nami (*cont.*)

NAM #	Area, locus, context, stratum	Collection no.	No. of sherds	Vessel type	Vessel part	Decoration	Date	Origin	Other
27	G3, 356, fill, IIIA	100–97 689/3	1	Straight-sided alabastron (FS 94)	Body sherd	Vertical stripes	LH IIIB2/C	Probably Levant	
28	G3, 377, floor, IIIA	100–97 723/3	1	Open or closed vessel	Body sherd	Unclear	Unclear	Unclear	Examination not possible
29	G3	13–87 713/14	1	Shallow bowl (FS 296)	Body sherd	Inside linear and Argonaut (FM 22), outside linear	LH IIIB2	Argolid or Cyprus	
30	G3, 65	13–87 163/1	1	Rounded alabastron (FS 84/85)	Almost complete (no handles)	Thin line and vertical bars below handle	LH IIIB2/C	Probably Levant	
31	G, 268	65–92 447/1	2	Amphoroid krater	Rim	Joining semicircles, hanging (FM 42)	LH IIIB2/C	Probably Cyprus	

TABLE 16.1 Catalogue of the Aegean-type pottery from Nami (cont.)

NAM #	Area, locus, context, stratum	Collection no.	No. of sherds	Vessel type	Vessel part	Decoration	Date	Origin	Other
32	O, 1, surface	0/2	1	Globular stirrup jar (FS 171 etc.)	Complete	Unpainted or decoration not preserved	LH IIIB2/C	Probably Cyprus	
33	O, 19	547/1	1	Straight-sided alabastron (FS 94)	Complete	Two zones with net (FM 57)	LH IIIB2/C	Probably Levant	
34	O, 57	48/2	1	Straight-sided alabastron (FS 94)	Complete	Unpainted or decoration not preserved	LH IIIB2/C	Probably Levant	
35	O, 58	52/2	1	Globular stirrup jar (FS 171 etc.)	Almost complete body (no spout, neck, handles)	Linear, Simple Style	LH IIIB2/C	Probably Cyprus	
36	O, 58	52/3	1	Globular stirrup jar (FS 171 etc.)	Complete	Linear, Simple Style	LH IIIB2/C	Probably Cyprus	

TABLE 16.1 Catalogue of the Aegean-type pottery from Nami (*cont.*)

NAM #	Area, locus, context, stratum	Collection no.	No. of sherds	Vessel type	Vessel part	Decoration	Date	Origin	Other
37	O, 58	43/3	1	Straight-sided alabastron (FS 94)	Complete	Unpainted or decoration not preserved	LH IIIB2/C	Probably Levant	
38	O, 61?	123/?	1	Straight-sided alabastron (FS 94)	Complete	Unpainted or decoration not preserved	LH IIIB2/C	Probably Levant	
39	O, 60 + 65	73/5	2	Straight-sided alabastron (FS 94)	Almost complete (parts of body sherd)	Unpainted or decoration not preserved	LH IIIB2/C	Probably Levant	
40	O, 65	138/?	>13	Globular stirrup jar (FS 171 etc.)	Base, body sherd (lower part of the vessel)	Linear, Simple Style	LH IIIB2/C	Probably Cyprus	
41	O, 66	112/4	1	Straight-sided alabastron (FS 94)	Complete	Unpainted or decoration not preserved	LH IIIB2/C	Probably Levant	

TABLE 16.1 Catalogue of the Aegean-type pottery from Nami (cont.)

NAM #	Area, locus, context, stratum	Collection no.	No. of sherds	Vessel type	Vessel part	Decoration	Date	Origin	Other
42	O, 66	104/1	1	Straight-sided alabastron (FS 94)	Complete	Unpainted or decoration not preserved	LH IIIB2/C	Probably Levant	
43	O, 75	119/13	1	Globular stirrup jar (FS 171 etc.)	Complete	Linear, Simple Style	LH IIIB2/C	Probably Cyprus	Artzy 2006: 53 fig. 6: 15
44	O, 75	119/1	1	Straight-sided alabastron (FS 94)	Complete	Unpainted or decoration not preserved	LH IIIB2/C	Probably Levant	
45	O, 75	113/5	1	Straight-sided alabastron (FS 94)	Complete	Unpainted or decoration not preserved	LH IIIB2/C	Probably Levant	
46	O, 75	113/6	1	Straight-sided alabastron (FS 94)	Almost complete (one handle and part of the rim missing)	Unpainted or decoration not preserved	LH IIIB2/C	Probably Levant	

TABLE 16.1 Catalogue of the Aegean-type pottery from Nami (cont.)

NAM #	Area, locus, context, stratum	Collection no.	No. of sherds	Vessel type	Vessel part	Decoration	Date	Origin	Other
47	O, 78	125/8	1	Globular stirrup jar (FS 171 etc.)	Complete	Linear, Simple Style	LH IIIB2/C	Probably Cyprus	
48	O, 65 + 73 + 79 + 120 + 144 + 147	1/2	?	Stemmed krater with horizontal handles	?	Net	LH IIIB2/C	Probably Levant	
49	O, 79	13–88 149/2	1	Globular stirrup jar (FS 171 etc.)	Complete (parts of the rim missing)	Unpainted or decoration not preserved	LH IIIB2/C	Probably Cyprus	
50	O, 79	13–88 149/1	1	Straight-sided alabastron (FS 94)	Complete	Unpainted or decoration not preserved	LH IIIB2/C	Probably Levant	
51	O, 80	101/2	1	Globular stirrup jar (FS 171 etc.)	Almost complete (part of spout missing)	Multiple stem (FM 19)	LH IIIB2/C	Cyprus	Artzy 2006: 53 fig. 6: 16; Artzy and Zagorski 2012: 8 fig. 3

TABLE 16.1 Catalogue of the Aegean-type pottery from Nami (cont.)

NAM#	Area, locus, context, stratum	Collection no.	No. of sherds	Vessel type	Vessel part	Decoration	Date	Origin	Other
52	O, 101	36–89 645/2	1	Globular stirrup jar (FS 171 etc.)	Complete	Linear, Simple Style	LH IIIB2/C	Probably Cyprus	
53	O, 113	89–36 634/1	1	Globular stirrup jar (FS 171 etc.)	Complete	Unclear complex	LH IIIB2/C	Probably Cyprus	
54	O, 121	89–36 705/1	1	Globular stirrup jar (FS 171 etc.)	Shoulder, neck, spout, one handle	Linear, Simple Style	LH IIIB2/ CF	Probably Cyprus	
55	O, 154	58–90 11/1	>3	Globular stirrup jar (FS 171 etc.)	Base, shoulder, neck, two handles, spout	Linear, Simple Style	LH IIIB2/C	Probably Cyprus	
56	O, 164, 176, 178, 183	65–92 164 209/1, 176/178 230/1, 178 247/1, 183 251/1	>15	Krater with horizontal handles (FS 281)	Base, body sherd, rim	Spiral	LH IIIB2/C	Cyprus	Artzy 2006: 53 fig. 6: 13; Artzy and Zagorski 2012: 8 fig. 3

TABLE 16.1 Catalogue of the Aegean-type pottery from Nami (*cont.*)

NAM #	Area, locus, context, stratum	Collection no.	No. of sherds	Vessel type	Vessel part	Decoration	Date	Origin	Other
57	O, 199	65–92 160/1	1	Globular stirrup jar (FS 171 etc.)	Complete	Linear, Simple Style	LH IIIB2/C	Cyprus	Artzy 2006: 53 fig. 6:14
58	O, 199	65–92 109/2	1	Globular stirrup jar (FS 171 etc.)	Complete	Linear, Simple Style	LH IIIB2/C	Probably Cyprus	
59	O, 199	65–92 109/1	1	Globular stirrup jar (FS 171 etc.)	Complete	Linear, Simple Style	LH IIIB2/C	Cyprus	Artzy 2006: 53 fig. 6:17
60	O, 199	65–92 161/2	1	Globular stirrup jar (FS 171 etc.)	Almost complete (one handle and part of neck missing)	Linear, Simple Style	LH IIIB2/C	Probably Cyprus	
61	O, 199	65–92 161/1	1	Straight-sided alabastron (FS 94)	Complete	Linear	LH IIIB2/C	Probably Levant	
62	O, ?	13–88 142/15	10	Globular stirrup jar (FS 171 etc.)	Base, body sherd	Linear, Simple Style	LH IIIB2/C	Probably Cyprus	

former is a Late Bronze (LB) IIB residential quarter, which Artzy dates to the late thirteenth century BCE, based on Cypriot imports (classic White Slip II, Base Ring II, White Shaved, Plain White Wheel-made). Of particular interest for my research is the Late Bronze Age sanctuary, which was built in Phase G/2 in this area. Most of the excavated part of the building comprises a rectangular, courtyard-like structure of 10 × 6.5 m, which was probably surrounded on all sides by walls. The sanctuary was accessible from the south; benches were placed along the west and east walls—the latter heavily damaged by modern disturbances. Abutting the north wall of the courtyard was a small square room that protruded into the courtyard. Artzy (1991a: 197; 1992: 44; 1995: 22, 35 n. 39) deduces the entire complex had a cultic function, based on various installations: south of the square room was an area paved with pebbles and the sherds of a large ceramic incense burner; next to it, the excavators discovered the deposition of a bronze lamp under a cairn and a placement of four stones in the form of a square, comparable to the Late Bronze Age temple of Tel Mevorakh (cf. Stern 1984: 5–6, 161–162 figs. 24, 25). In the center of the square room lay a large stone—probably a former pillar base in secondary use—on which stood a large basalt basin. Between the pillar base and the basin, smashed pottery was found, including a kernos.

According to Artzy, the sanctuary was violently destroyed, which led to the preservation of rich in situ finds, among them many vessels found on and next to the stone benches along the yard walls. Particularly notable among the numerous finds are stemmed bowls, which were used as incense burners, bronze arrowheads and probably also small spearheads, the scales of a bronze armor, earrings and pendants of silver and gold, and glass and carnelian beads. Many of the finds show the "international character" (Artzy 1995: 22) of the "polymorphic society" (Artzy 1997: 7) of Nami, such as Aegean-type arrowheads and a Cypriot kernos. The clay of one of the stemmed bowls was exceptionally tempered with ash and bones, which corresponds to the special function of this type of vessel. Bases of amphorae reworked into miniature bowls, as well as a seven-spouted lamp, underline the special character of the ceramic assemblage. A Canaanite-type golden pendant bears the representation of a goddess, which is reminiscent of Mitanni sealings. Among the foreign objects is also a Minoan-type conical cup. Artzy associates the vessel with the ritual sacrifice of pumice, which was found in the open court at Nami and was also deposited in various Cretan sanctuaries within such conical cups. She raises the question of whether this probably Minoan-influenced cultic ritual was practiced by Minoan seafarers or Minoan priests at Nami or if Syrian seafarers adapted such rituals in the Aegean and then continued practicing them in the Levant (Artzy 1991a: 197; 1991b, 1992: 44–45; 1994: 125–126; 1995: 22–23; Yoselevich 2006).

In addition to the objects associated with ritual practices, the shrine also contained rich evidence of metalworking, such as scrap metal, including fragments of a statuette, armor scales, and Cypriot rod tripods; tools for metalworking; fragments of crucibles; and kilns with traces of metal inside. In Artzy's view (1991a: 197; 1994: 126–127; 1995: 25; 1998: 440–441; 2000: 27–28), the scrap metal was not used to create new bronze objects, but rather ingots that were then traded by the sailors. Artzy (1994: 126; 1995: 23; 2000) compares the entanglement of religious practices and metalworking at Nami with Cypriot sanctuaries, since cult areas and metalworking sites were placed in the immediate vicinity also at Kition and Athienou on Cyprus: "We wonder if the mariners who have made use of the summit at Nami knew that metals were a welcome gift to the gods—hence to the priests who could have been metal workers—as was the pumice which was useful in smoothing and burning metal" (Artzy 1995: 23, 25).

Based on the current state of publication, it is not yet possible to shed more light on the multitude of ritual practices performed in the sanctuary of Nami and to trace their geographical origin. So far, however, the appropriation of Cretan cult practices can be assumed, as well as of Cypriot ideas about the connection between religious rituals and metalworking. The practices in Nami show a complex relational entanglement of very different worldviews and social practices, which, when performed in the sanctuary, were probably no longer perceived as foreign, but above all as necessary.

I have been able to examine and document in detail the Aegean-type vessels from the sanctuary (Phase G/2), together with the material from Phase G/3, at the University of Haifa in January 2009 (see Table 16.1: NAM#1–31). My subsequent analysis of the ceramic vessels is based on my own records and on drawings of the vessels by Ragna Stidsing, which were kindly provided to me by Michal Artzy.

I was able to study in person twenty-four out of the thirty-one Aegean-type vessels from Area G. The remaining seven fragments could only be analyzed on the basis of descriptions of form and ware. Thirteen specimens (NAM#3–15) can be assigned to Phase G/2 contexts and thirteen others (NAM#16–28), to Phase G/3. From most of the vessels only a single, small fragment is preserved; however, since complete, in situ vessels were preserved in the sanctuary, the fragmentary state of the Aegean-type vessels indicates that none of them was likely used in the last phase of the sanctuary.

All of these vessels might already have been used during Phase G/3 and might have then been relocated during the construction activities in Phase G/2. An exception here is only a round alabastron FS (= Furumark Shape; cf. Furumark 1941) 84/85 (NAM#30) from Phase G/3, which is completely preserved except for the handles. While essentially, by comparison to the Late Helladic (LH) IIIB models from the Aegean, the unusual, metope-like decoration on this vessel, consisting of two horizontal bands with irregular vertical bar groups in between them, points to a local, Levantine place of production. It is the only clear evidence of this vessel shape at Nami. According to my own terminology (Stockhammer 2012a), it presents a case of material entanglement. The kind of practices the vessel was used for in the sanctuary remains speculative. Alabastra probably contained viscous substances, e.g., perfumed ointments, for which a variety of uses in the cult are conceivable.

The Aegean-type ceramic finds are dominated by linear-painted sherds of small and medium-sized closed vessels. They make up to 69% of all indicative specimens. Except for the aforementioned alabastron (NAM#30) and a straight-sided alabastron (NAM#27), most of these sherds should be attributed to globular stirrup jars (FS 171 etc.) and vertical flasks (FS 189). Thirty-one percent of all identifiable sherds belong to open vessels: three kraters and three bowls, probably two amphoroid kraters (NAM#18; 31), a possible one-handled conical bowl (FS 242; NAM#15), and a shallow bowl (FS 296) with interior decoration (NAM#29). The Aegean-type ceramics from Area G thus find an excellent parallel in Dor Phases G/12 and G/11, where the Aegean-type assemblage is also dominated by linear-painted body sherds of small and medium-sized transport vessels, but there are also a few kraters and linear bowls (Stockhammer 2018).

The similarity of the Aegean-type pottery from Nami G/3 and G/2 and Dor G/12 and G/11 suggests a similar dating for both assemblages. None of the potsherds from Area G is necessarily later than LH IIIB, according to the chronology of Mycenaean pottery. The fragment of the shallow bowl of the FS 296 type with the interior decoration (NAM#29) should still be dated to LH IIIB2 (cf. Stockhammer 2017) and an Argolid workshop for its production seems possible. The bowl has an excellent parallel on Cyprus, at Kalavasos-Ayios Dhimitrios, where a shallow bowl with an almost identical motif on the inside was found in a Late Cypriot IIC context (South 1988: pl. 35: 4). Also comparable are LH IIIB and LH IIIC Early vessels with a stylized representation of argonauts from Tiryns and Megiddo (Stockhammer 2011). Most of the vessels from Area G were certainly not manufactured before the late thirteenth and early twelfth centuries BCE. Among the most recent pieces is the linear-painted rim fragment NAM#16. It might be identified as a one-handled conical bowl (FS 242), but one cannot exclude with certainty another linear-painted bowl of Aegean type (cf. Karageorghis 1965: 157–184 for the broad spectrum of such bowls found on Cyprus in late thirteenth- and early twelfth-centuries BCE contexts). Similar evidence is found in Dor G/11, where sherds of such bowls also belong to the latest Aegean-type vessels (Stockhammer 2018); however, due to their small rim diameter they are more likely to be linear shallow bowls (FS 242).

Based on my analysis, none of the Aegean-type vessels found in Area G can safely be attributed to an Argolid workshop. Almost all of them should be assigned to Cypriot and Levantine workshops according to their ware or painting. This corresponds fully to the picture obtained for the pottery from the Nami graves, which is based also on petrographic and neutron activation analyses. Since vessels of Aegean type from Cypriot and Levantine workshops are difficult to differentiate from those from Aegean workshops without scientific methods and a trained eye, I suggest a Cypriot place of production for all Simple Style stirrup jars from Nami. As far as the alabastra are concerned, I assume a workshop in the Levant, where local production of this shape started already in the course of the thirteenth century BCE. However, only scientific analysis will eventually be able to identify the places of production. The dominance of Cypriot- and Levantine-produced Aegean-type pottery in the assemblage corresponds fully to the overall situation of finds in the southern Levant around 1200 BCE (Stockhammer 2017, 2018).

The clearly identifiable body sherd of a Minoan transport stirrup jar (NAM#3) presents a noteworthy exception. David Ben-Shlomo, Eleni Nodarou, and Jeremy B. Rutter summarized the known fragments of such stirrup jars from the southern Levant. Most of the previously known Minoan transport stirrup jar from this region were found at Tell Abu Hawam and originate from central or south-central Crete (Ben-Shlomo, Nodarou, and Rutter 2011). The stirrup jar fragment from Nami is another piece of evidence and can also be attributed to a central Cretan workshop. It would go too far to interpret this sherd as another reference to Cretan practices (as evidenced by the conical cup of Cretan type and the possible pumice sacrifice). Transport stirrup jars may have been (re)used several times and did not necessarily reach Nami directly from Crete (cf. ibid.: 347–348).

2   Area O

In addition to the sanctuary at the top of the tell with its unusual spectrum of finds, the burial ground in Area O, Nami East, is of great interest with regard to issues of transcultural interaction.[1] The LB IIB necropolis is characterized by a

---

1   From the current state of the publication, neither the grave numbers, nor complete grave inventories are available for evaluation. I assigned individual vessels to specific graves on the basis of the locus numbers written on the vessels. Even in the case of the few graves for which

variety of grave types and burial practices. Some of the deceased were buried within so-called collared-rim jars. Despite ancient grave robbery, many of the burials still contained unusually rich offerings, including a plethora of bronze vessels and objects of gold, silver, ivory, and faience. Among the bronzes are a wine-drinking set, of which the pot was exceptionally shaped on the model of Cypriot White Shaved ceramic vessels; three stemmed bowls used as incense burners; the single scale of an armor; and four bronze lamps. A fifth bronze lamp was found in the sanctuary on the tell, which, like the incense burners, creates a link between the sanctuary and the necropolis. A signet ring with a Hittite inscription also indicates a special social position of those buried here. For three bronze knives Artzy assumes an Aegean origin, on the basis of their shape. Two of these were discovered in a grave together with several Aegean stirrup jars, a gold and silver diadem, rings, a toggle pin, beads, a possible kylix, and one of the aforementioned bronze lamps. Sherds of an Aegean-type krater were scattered around the grave, containing traces of bronze on their interior (Artzy 1990a, 1992: 45–46; 1994: 127–130; 1995: 25–29; Fox 1991).

Of particular interest is also the inventory of Tomb 69, which contained the richest assemblage of bronze grave goods in the cemetery, but no pottery of Aegean type (Artzy 1990a; Fox 1991: 123, 125): in the northeast corner of the tomb there was a bronze incense burner with bowl, a bronze lamp, and a small bowl. Other bronze vessels were placed to the west of the skeleton, namely three bowls, a strainer cup, a bronze Base Ring bowl, a jug, and a lamp. Georgia Lynne Fox (1991: 125) interprets the juxtaposition of cup and saucer as a beer-drinking service, although this is actually a classic bronze wine-drinking set in Egyptian tradition (Pritchard 1968: 103; Gershuny 1985: 46–47). An incense stand with pomegranate or poppy-capsule pendants was placed along the femoral bone of the skeleton, as well as two bronze scepters of approximately 30 cm in length, one of them with pomegranate decoration and the other with poppy-capsule decoration. The deceased was adorned with two gold earrings in the form of pomegranates. Artzy (1990a) interprets these offerings as an indication of the burial of a priest or a priestess.

So far, the rich ceramic inventory of the Aegean- and Cypriot-type vessels from the tombs of Nami remains largely unpublished. Some of these vessels were presented by Artzy (2006: 53 fig. 6: 13–17, 54 fig. 7: 8–10, 58 fig. 10: 11–12, 59 fig. 11: 6–9); however, without more detailed information on the context of the objects. Among the Cypriot vessels are White Shaved juglets as well as Base

---

Artzy lists burial goods, she emphasizes the provisional nature of the evaluation. A few grave finds are listed by Fox 1991 with regard to locus number and bronze grave goods.

Ring II and White Slip vessels. I was kindly allowed to study the Aegean-type vessels together with the associated material from the sanctuary in Haifa in January 2009. Moreover, Artzy generously provided me with unpublished information about the graves, as well as a variety of drawings made by Stidsing. In the catalogue of my contribution (Table 16.1: NAM#32–62), I have listed all known Aegean-type vessels from the burials.

Artzy (1994: 130, 140–141 n. 9) already recognized that the Aegean-type stirrup jars were made of very different wares and follow various workshop traditions. With the help of petrographic and neutron activation analyses, she was able to prove the sampled vessels were produced either in Levantine or Cypriot workshops, but not in Aegean ones. One krater (NAM#56), decorated stirrup jars, and Simple Style stirrup jars were identified as Cypriot products (Artzy 2005: 358; 2006: 52). Most vessels of Cypriot origin seem to have been produced on eastern Cyprus, perhaps in the Enkomi region (Artzy and Zagorski 2012).

The 31 Aegean-type vessels from the graves represent only three kinds of shapes, i.e., there are 17 stirrup jars, 12 straight-sided alabastra, and 2 kraters with horizontal handles (Table 16.1). Except for two more complex decorated pieces (NAM#51, 53), all other stirrup jars show linear decoration in Simple Style. The alabastra are all unpainted, except for one linear and one complex-painted vessel (NAM#33, 61). Both shapes are standardized in size and design. Notably, despite the large number of alabastra, no round alabastra were deposited in the graves, although such a vessel was found in the nearby sanctuary. The same is true for the Aegean-type flasks, which were found in Area G but not in Area O. Obviously, small, almost identically looking stirrup jars and straight-sided alabastra were selected for the burials. Both shapes occur as single pieces or in irregular combinations in the graves. Four stirrup jars and an alabastron were found in Grave/Locus 199, two stirrup jars and an alabastron in Grave/Locus 58, two alabastra in Grave/Locus 66, and a stirrup jar and an alabastron in Graves/Loci 75 and 79.

In contrast to the small, closed vessels, the sherds of both kraters were dispersed over several loci (NAM#48, 56). Artzy (1995: 28–29) notes that the sherds of krater NAM#56 were scattered around one of the rich graves. The place of deposition of the kraters suggests that they were not used as funerary objects, but for social practices in the context of the burial rituals. After their breakage, their fragments were dispersed over several burial pits. One of the two kraters (NAM#56) is very close to Aegean kraters in shape, the overall decoration, and the spiral motif. According to scientific analysis, the vessel was produced on Cyprus (Artzy 2006: 52, 53 fig. 6: 13). In the lower part of the vessel's interior, Artzy (1995: 28–29) detected ring-shaped traces of bronze, which may indicate the placement of a bronze bowl inside the krater. The second krater is quite unusual in its design (NAM#48); its lower part and handles show clear reference to Aegean kraters with horizontal handles (FS 281), but the bowl is set on an unusual trumpet-shaped foot, known from Levantine-type stemmed bowls. The painting, like the foot, also follows local tradition and the rim shape corresponds more to Levantine than to Aegean models. Another detail also underlines that the potter was certainly not trained in Aegean pottery tradition: in order to make the handle attachment thinner, the leather-hard clay was shaved away in a technique very similar to that well known from Cypriot Shaved Ware jugs. The common method applied by Aegean potters of perforating the handle attachment or finger imprinting the thickest point of the attachment were not employed. Therefore, I assume that this krater was produced as a material entanglement of Aegean and Canaanite features by a potter trained in Cypriot or Canaanite tradition.

Stemmed kraters are rare in the southern Levant. Vessels of comparable shape are known from Phase II of the Fosse Temple at Lachish and Stratum VII at Megiddo. Especially the bowl of a krater from Megiddo (Loud 1948: pls. 72: 3, 141: 9) seems to be a good comparison with the krater from Nami, even if its horizontal handles are placed significantly lower than on kraters of Aegean origin. The krater from Megiddo also depicts a typical Canaanite motif. The Lachish krater seems more distant in shape, as its bowl and handle are all in Canaanite tradition (Tufnell, Inge, and Harding 1940: pl. 48: 246).

Since no fragments of Aegean-type drinking vessels were found in Area O, the kraters were most likely not used for Aegean-related drinking practices. The bronze traces in the aforementioned krater NAM#56 are another indication that these vessels were primarily not used for mixing water and wine following Aegean traditions (cf. Stockhammer 2011, 2012b). Already Artzy (1994: 125) assumed that the two kraters, as well as the stemmed shallow bowls, were used as incense burners. The bronze incrustations in krater NAM#56 might have been caused by intense heating of the bronze bowl inside the krater during the burning of the incense or subsequent oxidation processes. Accordingly, the two kraters would not have been used as mixing vessels, but as incense burners during funerary rituals.

Artzy explains the exceptional material wealth of the Nami graves with the site's role as an international harbor and a node in the maritime trade routes along the Levantine coast and inland in the direction of Megiddo and Tel Beth-Shean, from which the best comparisons for the bronzes from the Nami graves also derive. Through Nami, bronze in the form of finished products and ingots was traded inland. Moreover, terebinth resin was brought from the highlands and camel caravans probably brought frankincense from southern Arabia to Nami. The importance of the trade of different kinds of incense is also indicated by the incense burners in the Nami graves (Artzy 1994: 131–135; 1995: 30–32; 1997: 9–10; 1998: 440–441).

Even though the Aegean-type pottery from Area G hardly permits any further interpretation due to its very fragmented state and though the tombs of Area O still need to be published in detail, the Aegean-type ceramic assemblage from Nami nevertheless reflects impressively the strong Cypriot influences in the southern Levant in the late thirteenth and early twelfth centuries BCE (cf. Stockhammer 2017). I have termed this horizon of interaction with Aegean-type pottery in the southern Levant the "Horizon Nami" (Stockhammer 2018, forthcoming), acknowledging Nami's potential to be a key site for understanding these crucial decades that transformed the eastern Mediterranean.

Bibliography

Artzy, M. 1990a. Pomegranate Scepters and Incense Stand with Pomegranates Found in Priest's Grave. *Biblical Archaeology Review* 16: 48–51.

Artzy, M. 1990b. Nami Land and Sea Project 1985–1988. *Israel Exploration Journal* 40: 73–76.

Artzy, M. 1991a. Nami Land and Sea Project 1989. *Israel Exploration Journal* 41: 194–197.

Artzy, M. 1991b. Conical Cups and Pumice: Aegean Cult at Tel Nami, Israel. In: Laffineur, R. and Basch, L., eds. *Thalassa: L'Égée préhistorique et la mer. Actes de la troisième rencontre égéenne internationale de l'Université de Liège, Station de Recherces sous-marines et Océanographiques (StaReSO), Calvi, Corse, 23–25 avril 1990* (Aegaeum 7). Liège : 203–206.

Artzy, M. 1992. Tel Nami, un grand port à l'âge du Bronze. *Le Monde de la Bible* 76: 42–46.

Artzy, M. 1993. Tel Nami. In: Stern, E., ed. *The New Encyclopedia of Archaeological Excavations in the Holy Land*, Vol. 3. Jerusalem: 1095–1098.

Artzy, M. 1994. Incense, Camels and Collared Rim Jars: Desert Trade Routes and Maritime Outlets in the Second Millennium. *Oxford Journal of Archaeology* 13: 121–141.

Artzy, M. 1995. Nami: A Second Millennium International Maritime Trading Center in the Mediterranean. In: Gitin, S., ed. *Recent Excavations in Israel: A View to the West. Reports on Kabri, Nami, Miqne-Ekron, Dor, and Ashkelon* (Archaeological Institute of America: Colloquia and Conference Papers 1). Dubuque: 17–40.

Artzy, M. 1997. Nomads of the Sea. In: Swiny, S., Hohlfelder, R.L., and Wylde Swiny, H., eds. *Res Maritimae: Cyprus and the Eastern Mediterranean from Prehistory to Late Antiquity. Proceedings of the Second International Symposium "Cities on the Sea," Nikosia, 18–22 October 1994* (Cyprus American Archaeological Research Institute

Monograph Series 1; American Schools of Oriental Research Archaeological Reports 4). Atlanta: 1–16.

Artzy, M. 1998. Routes, Trade, Boats and "Nomads of the Sea." In: Gitin, S., Mazar, A., and Stern, E., eds. *Mediterranean Peoples in Transition: Thirteenth to Early Tenth Centuries B.C.E. In Honor of Professor Trude Dothan*. Jerusalem: 439–448.

Artzy, M. 2000. Cult and Recycling. In: Åström, P. and Sürenhagen, D., eds. *Periplus: Festschrift für Hans-Günter Buchholz zu seinem achtzigsten Geburtstag am 24. Dezember 1999* (Studies in Mediterranean Archaeology 127). Jonsered: 27–32.

Artzy, M. 2005. Emporia on the Carmel Coast? Tel Akko, Tell Abu Hawam and Tel Nami of the Late Bronze Age. In: Laffineur, R. and Greco, E., eds. *Emporia*, Vol. 1: *Aegeans in the Central and Eastern Mediterranean. Proceedings of the 10th International Aegean Conference/10e recontre égéenne internationale, Italian School of Archaeology, Athens, 14–18 April 2004* (Aegaeum 25). Liège: 355–361.

Artzy, M. 2006. The Carmel Coast during the Second Part of the Late Bronze Age: A Center for Eastern Mediterranean Transshipping. *Bulletin of the American Schools of Oriental Research* 343: 45–64.

Artzy, M. and Zagorski, S. 2012. Cypriote "Mycenaean" IIIB Imported to the Levant. In: Gruber, M., Ahituv, S., Lehmann, G., and Talhir, Z., eds. *All the Wisdom of the East: Studies in Near Eastern Archaeology and History in Honor of Eliezer D. Oren, Festschrift Eliezer Oren* (Orbis Biblicus et Orientalis 255). Freiburg: 1–12.

Ben-Shlomo, D., Nodarou, E., and Rutter, J.B. 2011. Transport Stirrup Jars from the Southern Levant: New Light on Commodity Exchange in the Eastern Mediterranean. *American Journal of Archaeology* 115: 329–353.

Fox, G.L. 1991. *The Bronze Age Objects from Tel Nami, Israel: Their Conservation and Implications for Ancient Metallurgy in the Eastern Mediterranean*. MA thesis, Texas A&M University. College Station, TX.

Furumark, A. 1941. *The Mycenaean Pottery: Analysis and Classification*. Stockholm.

Gershuny, L. 1985. *Bronze Vessels from Israel and Jordan* (Prähistorische Bronzefunde II, 6). Munich.

Karageorghis, V. 1965. *Nouveaux documents pour l'étude du Bronze récent à Chypre: recueil critique et commenté* (Études Chypriotes 3). Paris.

Loud, G. 1948. *Megiddo II: Seasons of 1935–39* (Oriental Institute Publications 62). Chicago.

Pritchard, J.B. 1968. New Evidence on the Role of the Sea Peoples in Canaan at the Beginning of the Iron Age. In: Ward, W.A., ed. *The Role of the Phoenicians in the Interaction of Mediterranean Civilizations: Papers Presented to the Archaeological Symposium at the American University of Beirut, March 1967*. Beirut: 99–112.

South, A.K. 1988. Kalavasos-Ayios Dhimitrios 1987: An Important Ceramic Group from Building X. *Report of the Department of Antiquities* 1988: 223–228.

Stern, E. 1984. *Excavations at Tel Mevorakh (1973–1976)*, Vol. 2: *The Bronze Age* (Qedem 18). Jerusalem.
Stockhammer, P.W. 2011. An Aegean Glance at Megiddo. In: Gauss, W., Lindblom, M., Smith, R.A.K., and Wright, J.C., eds. *Our Cups Are Full: Pottery and Society in the Aegean Bronze Age. Papers Presented to Jeremy B. Rutter on the Occasion of His 65th Birthday*. Oxford: 282–296.
Stockhammer, P.W. 2012a. Conceptualizing Cultural Hybridization in Archaeology. In: Stockhammer, P.W., ed. *Conceptualizing Cultural Hybridization: A Transdisciplinary Approach. Papers of the Conference, Heidelberg, 21–22 September 2009* (Transcultural Research. Heidelberg Studies on Asia and Europe in a Global Context). Berlin–Heidelberg: 43–58.
Stockhammer, P.W. 2012b. Performing the Practice Turn in Archaeology. *Transcultural Studies* 1: 7–42. http://archiv.ub.uni-heidelberg.de/ojs/index.php/transcultural/article/view/9263/3238(accessedApril10,2018).
Stockhammer, P.W. 2017. How Aegean Is Philistine Pottery? The Use of Aegean-Type Pottery in the Early 12th Century BCE Southern Levant. In: Fischer, P.M. and Bürge, T., eds. *"Sea Peoples" Up-to-Date: New Research on Transformation in the Eastern Mediterranean in the 13th–11th Centuries BCE* (Denkschriften der Gesamtakademie 8). Vienna: 379–387.
Stockhammer, P.W. 2018. The Aegean-Type Pottery. In: Stern, E., Gilboa, A., Sharon, I., Zorn, R., and Matskevich, S., eds. *Excavations at Dor, Final Report*, Vol. IIB: *Area G, the Late Bronze and Iron Ages: Pottery, Artifacts, Ecofacts and Other Studies* (Qedem Reports 11). Jerusalem: 71–87.
Stockhammer, P.W. Forthcoming. *Materielle Verflechtungen—Zur lokalen Einbindung fremder Keramik in der ostmediterranen Spätbronzezeit* (Vorgeschichtliche Forschungen 26). Rahden, Westfalen.
Tufnell, O., Inge, C.H., and Harding, L. 1940. *Lachish 2 (Tell ed Duweir): The Fosse Temple* (The Wellcome-Marston Archaeological Research Expedition to the Near East 2). London.
Yoselevich, N. 2006. The Utilization of Chalices as Incense Burners on Boats and in Coastal Sites. *R.I.M.S. News* 32: 27–28.

CHAPTER 17

The Rag-and-Bone Trade at Enkomi: Late Cypriot Scrap Metal and the Bronze Industry

Stuart Swiny

When asked if I would like to contribute to a festschrift honoring Michal Artzy, I immediately thought it might be useful, and certainly appropriate, to update my unpublished contribution to the research workshop "Recycling, Hoarding and Trade in the Bronze 13th–11th Centuries BCE" that she organized at the University of Haifa in 1998. It was a fine, interesting, and stimulating conference, and for me it was yet another chance to spend some time in the company of old friends, Michal in particular.

This photograph (Fig. 17.1), in many ways iconic, sums up the conference, with a smiling Vassos Karageorghis shouldering a copper oxhide ingot in the manner of many of his distant ancestors, standing next to an equally happy

FIGURE 17.1   Vassos Karageorghis, former Director of the Department of Antiquities, Cyprus, and Michal Artzy at the Recycling Research Workshop in Haifa, 1998

Michal Artzy: two scholars who have contributed so much to our comprehension of the eastern Mediterranean in ancient times.

Michal and I first met in Cyprus some twenty-three years earlier when she joined us for a few days on the Bronze Age excavations at Episkopi-Phaneromeni, west of the town of Limassol. My wife, Laina, and I have been close friends with her ever since, and have enjoyed watching our respective offspring grow to adulthood.

The term "rag-and-bone trade" is a colloquialism not commonly used outside the United Kingdom, and even there today is mostly restricted to individuals of a certain age, since this profession ceased to exist after the Second World War. In fact, a yet more appropriate title for my contribution might be "Steptoe and Son in the Late Bronze Age" as a parody of the hugely popular 1960s BBC radio and television program *Steptoe and Son,* chronicling the adventures of a cockney junk merchant and his unfortunate offspring. Rag-and-bone men did not only deal in rags and bones and tended to specialize in all sorts of scrap, specifically metal, so the Steptoe's predecessors could indeed have plied their trade toward the end of the Late Bronze Age in the Mediterranean. Prior to this period, in Cyprus at least, there would hardly have been enough metal in circulation to have enabled the accumulation of "scrap," which, according to Webster's Unabridged Dictionary, is typically "metal fragments and pieces of stuff valuable only as a raw material."

The description of broken, unserviceable metal artifacts as a major class of goods worthy of a place in the Late Bronze Mediterranean trading system was first noted by George Bass (1967) in his publication of the Cape Gelidonya shipwreck. The finds from the excavation are well known but his discoveries bear repeating here.

Lying throughout the wreck in clusters, which suggested they had originally been stored in bags or baskets—a fact often overlooked—were numerous bronze tools, weapons, and household utensils. Two of the clusters were found beneath the copper oxhide ingots, for which the wreck soon became famous. Although there were some weapons and tools, the most common artifact type consisted of agricultural implements, especially socketed picks, hoes, or plowshares, supplemented by a single socketed spade. Some of the tools were intact, but most were broken and associated with ingot fragments, which implied they were being transported not as functional objects but metallurgical scrap. As a result of these discoveries, Bass suggested an association between scrap metal and the bronze industry, seemingly the first to do so (Bass 1967: 117, 163).

Of the approximately 409 metal items excavated on this late thirteenth-century BCE wreck, 58 were strictly considered as "scrap metal, or unworked bronze castings" (Bass 1967: 113–117), as illustrated in Figures 17.2a and 17.2b, or

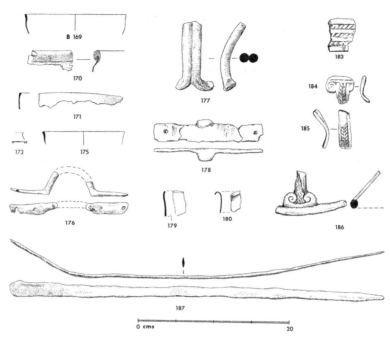

FIGURE 17.2A Fragmentary copper-based objects from the Gelidonya wreck, nos. 183–186 belonging to an offering stand
AFTER BASS 1967: FIG. 116

as fragments of offering stands of a type specifically associated with Cyprus, of which there were 4 fragments out of a total of 18 (Fig. 17.2a). Whereas it could be argued that the thin metal bowls or receptacles have corroded in places and become unserviceable as a result of their three millennia plus submersion in the sea, the more substantial handle, rim, and leg fragments were clearly broken before the ship sank.

Bass's interpretation of the Gelidonya wreck's fragmentary copper-alloy artifacts as metal scrap to be melted down and recast has been widely accepted (Karageorghis and Kassianidou 1999: 172, with references), and, indeed, the bronze- and copper-hungry Aegean world would have welcomed this category of cargo, arguably as much as the 91 ingots on board. Bass also suggested that, for stylistic and practical reasons, much of the metal must have come from Cyprus, as previously suggested by Catling (1964: 292–294).

It is interesting to point out that the Uluburun wreck, roughly a century earlier in date, carried no recognizable copper-based scrap (Pulak, personal communication, 2018), although it did contain a quantity of gold and silver scrap interpreted as bullion ("hackgold" and hacksilver) along with intact and damaged jewelry fashioned from the same materials (Pulak 2008: 357–358,

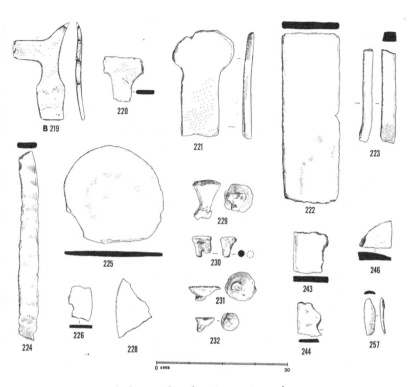

FIGURE 17.2B Unworked copper-based castings, waste, and scrap
AFTER BASS 1967: FIG. 126

fig. 114). With ten tons of copper ingots on board, copper-based scrap was perhaps not considered a valuable or desirable commercial item at this time.

Whether any copper-based scrap metal will be recovered from the recently discovered ingot carrying wreck west of Antalya that sank in the same general area as the abovementioned ships remains to be seen. So far, 73 "pillow type," fifteenth- to sixth-century BCE ingots and 4 bun ingots, presumably of copper, have been recorded (Öniz 2019).

The presence and function of scrap metal in the eastern Mediterranean was the subject of a recent study by Singer (2015). Scrap bronze is specifically mentioned in the Annals of Thutmose III in the lists of "giving gifts" from Isy (Singer 2015: 88). Despite the fact that most exports from the king of Alashiya to Egypt seem to be raw copper in the form of ingots, the most famous and substantial transaction being 1000 talents—estimated at 30 tons—scrap metal too is mentioned in the correspondence between Alashiya and Egypt. Singer (2015: 98) believes that scrap metal was used in the fourteenth century BCE as a medium of payment by a merchant or a ship's captain.

What then is the scrap metal situation in Cyprus in the Late Bronze Age? Examples of the island's metal assemblage have been recovered from the excavation of tombs and settlements alike. Burials do not seem to have contained scrap metal, at least in a recognizable form, which further emphasizes the utilitarian nature of this class of artifacts: they were destined to be melted down and recast anew and thus had no place as a funerary offering. Settlements, on the other hand, have yielded a range of objects that might, and indeed in the light of recent research, should be attributed to this category.

A study focusing on metal scrap and recycling at Kition was published by Karageorghis and Kassianidou (1999: 171–188). Although some evidence of metal scrap was noted (ibid.: 174), and it is suggested that the Kition workshops "would have been actively involved in the recycling of metal" (ibid.: 173), very little Late Cypriot (LC) IIC scrap metal was recorded from the temple area. This is perhaps because surprisingly few hoards were discovered at Kition.

The other great Late Bronze city, which lies below the fields surrounding Hala Sultan Tekke near Larnaca, has only since 2010 become the subject of consistent and large-scale renewed excavations (Fischer 2011), which have resulted in a wealth of material from both funerary and settlement contexts (Fischer and Bürge, 2014, 2017 with references). To date, however, little evidence for recycling has been noted despite the excavation of archaeometallurgical installations both in the past (Åström, 1982, 2000) and more recently (Fischer and Bürge forthcoming). Only two pieces of incontrovertible scrap in the form of two bent strips of copper-based metal came from the newly excavated general metalworking area, despite substantial quantities of different types of slag.[1]

Nothing recognizable as scrap is published from the settlement of Episkopi-Bamboula (Benson 1972: 125ff., pls. 34–37), although some metalworking, as demonstrated by crucible fragments and other clay objects (Benson 1972: 135, 137), was practiced at this LC III settlement.

The matter of "coppersmith's scrap" is discussed regarding Kalavasos-Ayios Dhimitrios (South 2012: 38, 41, fig. 5.7). This scrap consisted of folded pieces of copper-based vessels, some slag, and ingot fragments from within a building that may have been a coppersmith's workshop.

The situation is quite similar at the LC III settlements of Alassa-Pano Mantilares, and Paliotaverna, where a "coppersmith's workshop" was excavated as well as "scrap metal along with a handle fragment of an actual ingot" (Hadjisavvas 2011: 22). Hadjisavvas notes (ibid.: 24, 25) that the site was an important

---

1 I am most grateful to Peter Fischer for sharing information on, and images of, metal scrap from his excavations.

metallurgical center such as Kition or Enkomi, omitting, however, to include Hala Sultan Tekke, the other major coastal city site. The definitive study of Alassa's metallurgical remains by Van-Brempt and Kassianidou (2017: 479–485) mentions the existence of approximately 100 metal items from both excavated areas. They state that, in addition to intact and near intact artifacts, numerous fragments of sheets and rods, scrap, and other unidentifiable items made of copper alloys were recovered from the site (Van-Brempt and Kassianidou 2017: 480). Unfortunately, none of the scrap is illustrated or described in detail. The report concludes with the observation that no significant copper production, namely primary or secondary smelting, seems to have been undertaken at Alassa (ibid.: 485).

According to Zwicker (1988: 428), primary and secondary smelting, as well as melting, were undertaken at LC III Maa-Palaeokastro, where ingot fragments and incomplete objects are sometimes clustered together (Karageorghis and Demas 1988: 59, 218) and described as "scrap metal."

The largest exposure of Late Cypriot remains is at Enkomi-Ayios Iakovos, usually simply referred to as "Enkomi," where around 38,000 sq m of the site have been excavated. To provide an idea of the size of the excavated area, if the various trenches are amalgamated, the total fully excavated expanse would measure 215 by 175 m, a large exposure by any standard. The excavated remains at Enkomi span the entire Late Cypriot period, though we shall be concentrating on the later phases.

A study of the excavation reports from Enkomi shows that those published by the French mission under Claude Schaeffer provide little systematic and comprehensive information on the recovered metal assemblage. Notable finds, including hoards, are signaled out for special treatment, but no standard excavation report covering all finds was published. After Schaeffer ceased directing the project, Jacque-Claude Courtois began publishing material from the site (Courtois 1982, 1984). Unfortunately, the precise context of many of the finds is unrecorded and thus they are only given a broad date within the main periods.

The results of the Enkomi excavations directed by Porphyrios Dikaios, published between 1969 and 1971, on the other hand, are detailed in the extreme. His work was systematic in terms of excavation, recording and publication and, for that reason, the finds can easily be quantified. Unfortunately, the surface area of settlement that he excavated is only about one third the size of that investigated by the French mission.

All the metal finds published by Dikaios come from Levels IA to IIIC, which in terms of absolute dates correspond to sixteenth-century LC IA, up to LC IIIB, ca. 1150 BCE. Level IA yielded a single plowshare, perhaps intact, but certainly well worn (Dikaios 1969: pl. 153; 1971: 446). The remaining copper-based finds from Level I all belong to the end of the period and are thus of late sixteenth- to mid-fifteenth-centuries BCE date. They consist of a cache of six dagger or knife billets with trunnions, two drills, and a pointed implement, perhaps a damaged chisel. None of these items may be described as scrap (Dikaios 1969: pl. 153).

Level IIA, which the most recent scholarship (Crewe 2007: 73, table 1.1; Knapp 2013: 27, table 2) suggests should be dated to LC IIA2–IIB, or ca. 1450–1400 BCE, yielded evidence for copper smelting/melting and a mold, as well as four copper ingot fragments, but no other metal (Dikaios 1971: 450).

Level IIB (LC IIC, ca. 1400–1350 BCE according to Crewe 2007 and Knapp 2013) produced 30 copper-based objects (Dikaios 1971: 455, 456), consisting of an ax-head, two sickles, tweezers, a dagger handle, an arrow head, a sling bullet, a harness attachment, and a number of miscellaneous objects (Dikaios 1969: pl. 157: 12, 21, 35). Some were damaged, which is nothing unusual for excavated settlement material, but only the dagger handle (no. 28) could perhaps be described as scrap, though it was sufficiently intact to have been repaired and reused. It was found on its own beneath the floor of Room 12 of the ashlar building in Area I, and seems to have been discarded or overlooked as useless at a time when the site was undergoing a major building program.

This level yielded, in the words of Dikaios (1971: 511), "an unprecedented wealth and variety" of non-ceramic objects. Copper smelting and working were attested by workshops and molds for copper-based tools and weapons, but there is no mention or published images of scrap metal such as damaged, unserviceable objects. It is also significant that the small LC II hoard of four objects from the Quartier 3W (Point Topo. 438) excavated by the French mission and consisting of a large socketed shovel, two sickles, and a bangle or armband (Courtois 1982: 158; 1984: 38, figs. 7: 8; 8: 14, 17; 9: 4) lacks any identifiable scrap metal. There seems to be some confusion concerning the exact number of finds from the hoard, with Courtois once mentioning three (Courtois 1982: 158) and then four (Courtois 1984: 38), whereas Knapp Muhly, and Muhly (1988: table 2) list five. As borne out by the list above, the correct number is surely four.

The following Level IIIA (LC IIC–IIIA ca. 1300–1125/1100, according to Crewe 2007 and Knapp 2013) yielded a great quantity of copper-based metal, consisting of eighty-three items belonging to sixteen different types, namely eleven pins, one pair of tweezers, two sickles, thirteen weapons of various kinds, two ferrules, fragments of a tripod and a bowl, seven personal ornaments, four drills, four nails, and thirty-eight fragments of diverse, but mostly recognizable, objects, as shown in Figure 17.3. To this list should be added, according to

THE RAG-AND-BONE TRADE AT ENKOMI

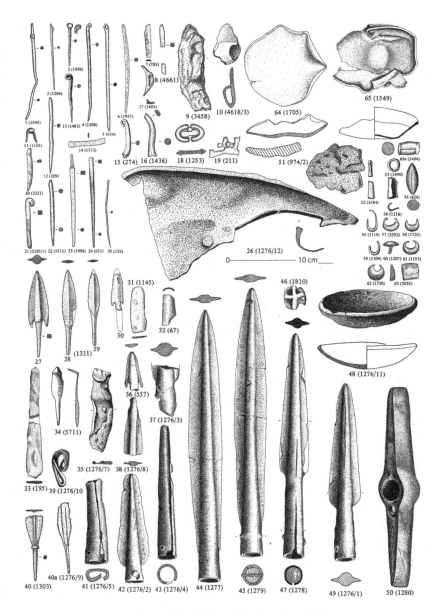

FIGURE 17.3   Selection of copper-based objects from Level IIIA (LC IIC–IIIA, c. 1300–1125/1100 BCE) at Enkomi
AFTER DIKAIOS 1969: PL. 163

Courtois (1982: 159), the statue of the Horned God, attributed on stratigraphic grounds to Level IIIB by Dikaios.

Dikaios (1971: 518) summarized the metal finds from this level with the comment that not only is bronze work represented by molds for tools and weapons, but also by much greater quantities of personal objects and weapons; however, as with the preceding levels, there is no mention of the existence of metal scrap. This is corroborated by a study of the published photographs and drawings of the objects (Dikaios 1969), which shows that most are intact or relatively well preserved (Figs. 17.3 and 17.4). With the exception of a sickle (Fig. 17.3: 35), two spear heads (Fig. 17.3: 37, 39), the fragment of a stand (Fig. 17.3: 26), a ferrule, and some miscellaneous objects, most of the metal objects were serviceable. A discrete concentration of finds in the destruction debris of Level IIIA, provides the only evidence for the gathering of unserviceable metal items outside of a hoard context at Enkomi.

Level IIIB, dated to LC IIIA or around 1100 BCE, boasted a more varied range of metal object types with 22 recorded, but less individual items since only 59 were published (Fig. 17.4). In addition to the types mentioned in connection with the assemblage from Level IIIA, there was a fibula, a fish hook, two miniature ingots, a bar about one meter in length, folded five times (Fig. 17.5), and an animal figurine, as well as one or two human figurines, depending on how the Horned God is dated, as noted above.

With the exception of the bent bar (Fig. 17.5; Dikaios 1969a: pl. 172: 1), two tools, and a bowl rim, these finds are mostly intact and would have been serviceable at the time of discard or loss. The number of metal finds is quite low in view of the surface excavated, and nothing suggests that they were being stored within individual households in anticipation of being recycled. Again, there is no mention of quantities of worn-out metal artifacts (Dikaios 1971: 533), suggesting that the overall composition of metal finds from Level IIIB lacked a category that could be described as scrap.

In his discussion of the metal industry, Courtois (1982: 155–175) focuses on the French excavations in Levels IIA to IIIC located in Quartier 6E, which provided evidence for metallurgical activity in several places, including in the Bâtiment à la Colonne and the structures surrounding it. He specifically states that the courtyards and corridors had numerous smelting installations with crucibles and tuyeres, and also mentions the discovery of molds for casting weapons, tools, and ornaments, as well as many individual finds, excluding those from the hoards (Courtois 1982: 163). Courtois notes that slag, as well as broken objects intended for remelting, was common. No further details were provided, however, and no drawings or photographs of any metal artifacts from Quartier 6E were published. To his credit, he did publish a sample of 351 copper-based objects in *Alasia III* (Courtois 1984: figs. 1–14), but there were many more (Courtois, personal communication, 1982).

This then is the situation concerning copper-based objects from Enkomi that were not concealed in hoards. If one presumes that the areas excavated by

THE RAG-AND-BONE TRADE AT ENKOMI

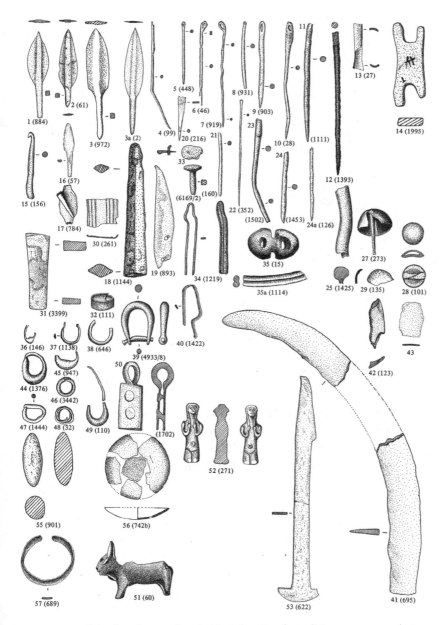

FIGURE 17.4 Selection of copper-based objects from Level IIIB (LC IIIA, c. 1100 BCE) at Enkomi, excluding no. 14
AFTER DIKAIOS 1969: PL. 171

Dikaios were generally representative in terms of quantity or general density of metal finds for the site as a whole, and that, had the French excavations been systematically published, they would have provided similar categories of

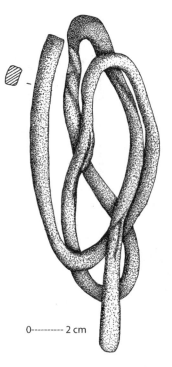

FIGURE 17.5
A 1 m long copper-based bar bent over five times from Level IIIB
AFTER DIKAIOS 1969A: PL. 172

0---------- 2 cm

artifacts, then it is clear that a major source of information on copper-based artifacts from Enkomi is provided by the contents of the numerous metal hoards.

The plan published in the seminal article by Knapp, Muhly, and Muhly (1988: fig. 6) on Late Bronze eastern Mediterranean hoards indicates the location of the hoards, ingots, and workshops, omitting those located in Quartier 6E just north of the House of Bronzes at Enkomi, clearly showing a correlation between hoards and metallurgical workshops.

Figure 17.6, reproduced from table 2 in Knapp, Muhly, and Muhly 1988, speaks for itself. With one exception, all the stratified Enkomi items listed here are of LC III date and those that are not securely stratified, such as the Foundry, Stylianou, and Gunnis hoards, belong, as suggested by Catling (1964: 278–291), to the same general date. As shown in Figure 17.6, the Enkomi hoards contain at least 315 items.

Since the original publication of this table in 1988, only one additional hoard has come to light in the form of a single deposit, at Alassa-Pano Mantilares, of LC IIIA date (Hadjisavvas 1996: 28; 2011: 23). It consists of several bronze weapons without any metal scrap and has been added to Figure 17.6.

For the first time in the eastern Mediterranean, Knapp, Muhly, and Muhly (1988: 233) asked some specific questions about the Late Bronze hoard

Site & Name of Hoard	Date (proposed)	Total No. of items	Tools: Smith	Tools: Agric	Tools: Woodwk	Weapons	Vessels & Stands	Ornamnt. Statuette	Ingots	Castings	Weights & Scales	Scrap Slag & Misc.
Enkomi "Foundry"		85	8	16	10	8	8		5	18	2	10
Enkomi "Gunnis"		18	2	10	6							
Enkomi "Maison des Bronzes"	LCIIIA	5			1	4						
Enkomi "Trésor de Bronzes"	LCIIIA	37		1	10	1		18			2	5
Enkomi "Stylianou"		28		13	3		3	6		1		2
Enkomi "Miniature"	LCIIIB	59				1	13	2		27	1	15
Enkomi "Weapon"	LCIIIA	33		1		25	2					5
Enkomi "Qrt.3W P.438"	LCII	5		4				1				
Enkomi "Qrt.3W P.783"	LCIIIA	7+				1	1+		2	+		3
Enkomi "Qrt.6W P.1458"	LCIIIA	41			3		12	1	1	1		23
Enkomi "Brunnen 212"	LCIIIA	23+		1	3	5	2	3	1		3	5+
Enkomi "Ingot"		3+	+				1		2+			+
Kition Floor III, Temple 4	LCIIIA	3		2								1
Mathiati		65	2	12	11	2			28	2		8
Pyla Kokkinokremos Gold Hoard	LCIIC	27					22			5		
Pyla Kokkinokremos Silver Hoard	LCIIC	3				1		2				
Pyla Kokkinokremos Bronze Hoard	LCIIC	43+	1		2	2	32	3	2		1	+
Sinda		11	2	2			3	3				1
Ayios Dhimitrios Bldg.III, A.219	LCIIC	15					1			14		
Myrtou Pigadhes	LCIIC/LCIIIA	6+	1			5						+
Hala Sultan Tekke Vyzakia	LCIIC	24*					14					2
Nitovikla (??)		3+		2		1+						
Enkomi Horned God Sanct.	LCIII	4		1			1					2
Cape Gelidonya (shipwreck)	LCIIC/LCIIIA	409	3	100	57	5	18	12	91	20	62	41
Alassa						3						

FIGURE 17.6 Content of Cypriot hoards with the cultural phases to which they are attributed; the Hala Sultan Tekke hoard included eight non-metal objects
AFTER KNAPP, MUHLY, AND MUHLY 1988: TABLE 2, WITH THE ALASSA HOARD ADDED

phenomenon and tried to explain why "things are the way they seem to be," noting that most hoards appear to be confined to a brief span about one hundred years long between ca. 1250 and 1150 BCE, bracketing the collapse of the major polities and urban centers of the Bronze Age world. They also emphasized that scrap metal is absent from earlier Aegean hoards, which mirrors the situation during the Prehistoric Cypriot Bronze Age (PreBA, Knapp 2013: 27, tab. 2, in broad terms corresponding to the twenty-fourth through the seventeenth centuries BCE). To date, few settlements of this period have been excavated and none have yielded concentrations of what might be described as scrap metal. Indeed, metal artifacts appear to be rare outside of funerary contexts. Many of the settlements, namely Marki-Alonia, Alambra-Mouttes, Politiko-Troullia, and Pyrgos-Mavrorachi, have, however, produced molds for casting tools, weapons, and what appear to be ingots (Frankel and Webb 2006: 216–217, fig. 67, pl. 57; Kassianidou 2017: fig. 2; Coleman et al. 1996: 135–136, fig. 31; Fall et al. 2008: 195, fig. 5; Belgiorno 2009; Swiny 2013: 236, fig. 8 with references). From two other settlements, Paramali S13-97 and Episkopi-Phaneromeni, which lack molds, come fragments of crucibles with copper prills attached (Swiny 1986: 68; Swiny and Mavromatis 2000: 435, fig. 2). All the sites with molds are in the general proximity of ore bodies and were presumably casting objects with copper mined from the nearby deposits. Paramali S13-97 and Episkopi-Phaneromeni, however, are far from ore bodies, yet they were evidently equipped to melt down raw material (i.e., ingots) or broken or worn-out copper artifacts, in order to recast them locally. It is important to note here that, finally, we have first-hand evidence for pre-Late Bronze ingots as represented by two ca. 165 g, elongated plano-convex castings from the PreBA settlement of Alambra-Mouttes. (Sneddon 2019: fig. 14). These ingots, almost certainly cast from the same mold, are comparable to the slightly earlier (ca. 2400–2000 BCE) bar-shaped ingots discovered in the central Negev, the oldest recorded in Israel (Yahalom-Mack et al. 2014: 159, fig. 17).

The absence of molds from the last-mentioned settlements does not mean that none existed, and indeed not all PreBA sites with evidence for metal working have produced molds. Under these circumstances, it is logical that no clusters of scrap metal have been recorded at PreBA settlements because this custom is clearly a ProBA phenomenon, at least in Cyprus.

Knapp, Muhly, and Muhly (1988: 235–237) thoughtfully break down the hoards into "utilitarian" caches hidden by merchants or metal workers with intent of recovery after a dangerous situation had passed, and "non-utilitarian" caches such as votive or building deposits, never intended to be retrieved.

THE RAG-AND-BONE TRADE AT ENKOMI

At Enkomi all the hoards belong to the "utilitarian" cache category and may be classified as "founder's" hoards, since they always display at least one of the

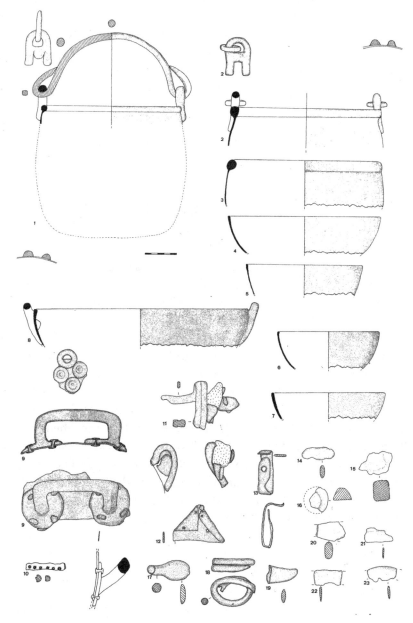

FIGURE 17.7   A good example of copper-based scrap from the Enkomi 1458 hoard, which included a total of 41 items
AFTER COURTOIS 1984: FIG. 13

criteria required to define a hoard of this type: namely, miscellaneous scrap metal and slag, castings, and ingots, either intact or fragmentary.

Figure 17.6 shows the breakdown of eleven hoards from Enkomi; the twelfth, listed as the "weapon hoard" with 33 items, is not a hoard at all but a concentration of metal from the destruction debris of Level IIIA. The categories of most significance to the present discussion are listed in the right-hand column described as "scrap, slag and misc.," and those close by to the left, labeled as "castings" and "ingots" since they are recorded in the majority of hoards. Indeed, nine out of the eleven hoards have scrap castings and ingot fragments, which, significantly, make up to 60% of the total number of items in a hoard, the average being 38%. This percentage is far higher than that of the non-hoard material and provides a good example of how the hoards represent specialist activity at Enkomi.

The items illustrated in Figure 17.7 are typical of the scrap, castings, and ingot fragments found at Enkomi and, with the exception of bowls nos. 3 to 7, all belong to the Quartier 6W Point Topo 1458 hoard.

Since most hoards are associated with metal workshops, there is obviously a connection between hoarding and metalworking on a practical level. But when it comes to collections of scrap metal gathered up in preparation for export on a vessel such as the one that sank off Cape Gelidonya, not surprisingly, there is a total lack of any large assemblages from any Late Cypriot site. The scrap found on the wreck must have come from somewhere, and urban centers seem the best source for many of the items, since large quantities of worn-out or broken objects would have been available there, and the installations required to remelt and cast were also present, as demonstrated by the archaeological remains at most of the above-discussed Cypriot sites. In the case of agricultural tools, these must have been collected in the countryside and then brought to the townships for recycling by the metalworkers or for export as in the case of the Cape Gelidonya ship's cargo. Somebody had to be responsible for scouring the villages for scrap metal, and who better than the likes of Steptoe and Son who may well have become the first nouveau riches thanks to the Late Cypriot rag-and-bone trade.

References

Åström, P. 1982 The Bronzes of Hala Sultan Tekke. In: Muhly, D.J., Maddin R., and Karageorghis, V., eds. *Early Metallurgy in Cyprus, 4000–500 BC*. Nicosia: 177–183.

Åström, P. 2000. A Coppersmith's Workshop at Hala Sultan Tekke. In: Åström, P. and Sürenhagen, D., eds. *Periplus: Festschrift für Hans-Günter Buchholz zu seinem achtzigsten Geburtstag am 24. Dezember 1999*. Jonsered: 33–35.

Bass, G.F. 1967. *Cape Gelidonya: A Bronze Age Shipwreck* (Transactions of the American Philosophical Society 57/8). Phadelphia.

Belgiorno M.R. 2009. Progetto Pyrame: Pyrgos ricerche archeologiche e archeometallurgiche, lo stato dell'arte a dicembre 2008. In: Belgiorno, M.R., ed. *Cipro all' inizio dell' Età del Bronzo*. Rome: 14–104.

Benson, J.L. 1972. *Bamboula at Kourion: The Necropolis and the Finds*. Philadelphia.

Catling H.W. 1964. *Cypriot Bronzework in the Mycenaean World*. Oxford.

Coleman, J.E., Barlow, J.A., Mogelonsky, M., and Scharr, K.W. 1996. *Alambra: A Middle Bronze Age Site in Cyprus. Investigations by Cornell University, 1975–1978* (Studies in Mediterranean Archaeology 118). Jonsered.

Courtois J.C. 1982. L'actiévité métallurgique et les bronzes d'Enkomi au Bronze récent (1650–1100 avant J.C.). In: Muhly, J.D., Maddin, R., and Karageorghis, V., eds. *Early Metallurgy in Cyprus, 4000–500 BC*. Nicosia: 155–175.

Courtois J.C. 1984. *Alasia III: les objets des niveaux stratifiés d'Enkomi (fouilles C.F.-A. Schaeffer 1947–1970)* (Éditions Recherches sur les Civilisations, mémoire 32). Paris.

Crewe, L. 2007. *Early Enkomi. Regionalism, trade and society at the beginning of the Late Bronze Age on Cyprus*. British Archaeological Reports. International Series 1706. Oxford: Archaeopress.

Dikaios, P. 1969a. *Enkomi Excavations, 1948–1958*, Vol. IIIA. Mainz am Rhein: Philipp von Zabern.

Dikaios, P. 1971. *Enkomi Excavations, 1948–1958*, Vol. 2. Mainz am Rhein.

Fall, P.L., Falconer, S.E., Horowitz, M., Hunt, J., Metzger, M.C., and Ryter, D. 2008. Bronze Age Settlement and Landscape of Politiko-*Troullia*, 2005–2007. *Report of the Department of Antiquities, Cyprus* 2008: 183–208.

Fischer, P.M. 2011. The New Swedish Cyprus Expedition 2010: Excavations at Dromolaxia Vizatzia/Hala Sultan Tekke. Preliminary Results. *Opuscula* 4: 69–98.

Fischer, P.M., and T. Bürge. 2014 The New Swedish Cyprus Expedition 2013: Excavations at Hala Sultan Tekke. Preliminary Results. *Opuscula* 7: 61–106.

Fischer, P.M., and T. Bürge. 2017. The New Swedish Cyprus Expedition 2016: Excavations at Hala Sultan Tekke (The Söderberg Expedition). *Opuscula* 10: 50–93.

Fischer, P.M., and T. Bürge. Forthcoming. The New Swedish Cyprus Expedition 2017: Excavations at Hala Sultan Tekke (The Söderberg Expedition). *Opuscula* 11.

Frankel, D. and Webb, J.M. 2006. *Marki Alonia: An Early and Middle Bronze Age Settlement in Cyprus. Excavations 1995–2000* (Studies in Mediterranean Archaeology 123/2). Sävedalen.

Hadjisavvas, S. 1996. Alassa: A Regional Center of Alashiya? In: Åström, P. and Herscher, E., eds. *Late Bronze Age Settlements in Cyprus: Function and Relationship* (Studies in Mediterranean Archaeology and Literature, Pocket Book 126). Jonsered: 23–38.

Hadjisavvas, S. 2011. Broken Symbols: Aspects of Metallurgy at Alassa. In: Betancourt, P.P. and Ferrence, S.C., eds. *Metallurgy: Understanding How, Learning Why: Studies in Honor of James D. Muhly*. Philadelphia: 21–27.

Karageorghis, V. and Demas M. 1988. *Excavations at Maa-Palaeokastro 1979–1986*. Nicosia.

Karageorghis, V. and Kassianidou, V. 1999. Metalworking and Recycling in Late Bronze Age Cyprus: The Evidence from Kition. *Oxford Journal of Archaeology* 18: 171–188.

Kassianidou, V. 2017. The Production and Trade of Cypriot Copper during the Bronze Age: New Data (in Greek). In: Papadimitriou, N. and Toli, M., eds. *Ancient Cyprus: Recent Developments in the Archaeology of the Eastern Mediterranean*. Athens: 111–134.

Knapp, A.B., Muhly, J.D. and Muhly, P.M. 1988. To Hoard Is Human: Late Bronze Age Metal Deposits in Cyprus and the Aegean. *Report of the Department of Antiquities, Cyprus* 1988: 233–262.

Knapp, A.B., 2013. *The Archaeology of Cyprus: From Earliest Prehistory through the Bronze Age* (Cambridge World Archaeology Series). Cambridge.

Öniz, H. 2019. A New Bronze Age Shipwreck with Ingots West of Antalya: Preliminary Results. *Palestinian Exploration Quarterly* 151: 3–14.

Pulak, C. 2008. The Uluburun Shipwreck and Late Bronze Age Trade. In: Aruz, J., Benzel, K., and Evans, J.M., eds. *Beyond Babylon: Art, Trade, and Diplomacy in the Second Millennium BC*. New York: 289–310, 357–358.

Singer, G.G. 2015. Scrap Metal in the Eastern Mediterranean during the Late Bronze Age. In: Mynářová, J., Onderka, P., and Pavúk, P., eds. *There and Back Again: The Crossroads II. Proceeding of an International Conference Held in Prague, September 15–18, 2014*. Prague: 85–127.

Sneddon, A. 2019. An Analog from the Prehistoric Bronze Age Site of Alambra Mouttes (Cyprus) for Adornments on the Enigmatic "Vounous Bowl". *Bulletin of the American Schools of Oriental Research* 382: 1–15.

South, A. 2012. Tinker, Tailor, Farmer, Miner: Metals in the Late Bronze Age Economy at Kalavasos. In: Kassianidou, V. and Papasavvas, G., eds. *Eastern Mediterranean Metallurgy and Metalwork in the Second Millennium BC: A Conference in Honor of James D. Muhly, Nicosia, 10th–11th October 2009*. Oxford: 35–47.

Swiny, S. 1986. *The Kent State University Expedition to Episkopi Phaneromeni 2* (Studies in Mediterranean Archaeology 139). Uppsala.

Swiny, S. 2013 The Legacy of Eve and James Stewart at CAARI and the Taxonomy of Cypriot Bronze Age Metal. In: Knapp, A.B., Webb, J.M., and McCarthy, A., eds. *J.R.B. Stewart: An Archaeological Legacy* (Studies in Mediterranean Archaeology 139). Uppsala: 229–239.

Swiny, S. and Mavromatis, C. 2000. Land behind Kourion. *Report of the Department of Antiquities, Cyprus* 2000: 433–452.

Van-Brempt, L. and Kassianidou, V. 2017. The Study of Metallurgical Remains from Alassa Panomantilares and Paliotaverna. In: Hadjisavvas, S. *Alassa: Excavations at the Late Bronze Age Sites of Pano Mantilaris and Paliotaverna 1984–2000*. Nicosia: 479–495.

Yahalom-Mack, N., Galili, E., Segal, I., Eliyahu-Behar, A., Boaretto, E., Shilstein, S., and Finkelstein, I. 2014. New Insights into Levantine Copper Trade: Analysis of Ingots from the Bronze and Iron Ages in Israel. *Journal of Archaeological Science* 45: 159–177.

Zwicker, U. 1988. Investigations of Material from Maa-*Palaeokastro* and Copper Ores from the Surrounding Area. In: Karageorghis, V. and Demas, M., eds. *Excavations at Maa-Palaeokastro 1979–1986*. Nicosia: 427–448.

CHAPTER 18

Sea Peoples from the Aegean: Identity, Sociopolitical Context, and Antecedents

Aleydis Van de Moortel

1   Introduction

In the course of her long and productive academic career, Michal Artzy through her discoveries and studies has made important contributions to our understanding of the Sea Peoples—those bands of seaborne raiders who attacked Egypt and the Levant in the course of the fourteenth–twelfth centuries BCE (esp. Artzy 1997, 2013). It is apt, then, to offer her a paper on this topic. Archaeological inquiry into the Sea Peoples began already in the mid-nineteenth century (Yasur-Landau 2010: 180). In recent decades new archaeological discoveries in the Levant, Aegean, and Italy (Jung 2017; Wiener 2017), as well as the adoption of fresh scholarly perspectives—and in particular postprocessual migration theory (Anthony 1990; cf. Yasur-Landau 2010)—have much advanced our understanding of the Sea Peoples phenomenon. Nowadays, a significant part of the debate has shifted toward issues of identity formation among the Sea Peoples settling in the Levant, but questions still remain about their origins as well as the historical and societal context of their raids and migrations. In the present study, I will address those last two questions. In particular, I want to discuss some new and old, but overlooked, evidence from the Aegean that throws light on the origins of some of these groups and shows that some of their warrior insignia go back as early as the Middle Bronze Age, and perhaps even the Early Bronze Age and Final Neolithic in the Aegean.

Raiders from the sea were first mentioned in the eastern Mediterranean in the early fourteenth century BCE, when Amenhotep III reinforced the Egyptian coastline against unnamed attackers (Bietak 2015: 31–32; Wiener 2017: 55). Later in that century, letters from Levantine rulers in the Amarna archive described seaborne assaults on Cyprus by a people called Lukka and on Byblos by a group of Shardana (Sandars 1985: 106–107; Wiener 2017: 55). Ca. 1290 BCE Shardana reportedly attacked Egypt with battle ships and were defeated by Ramesses II. In the late thirteenth and early twelfth centuries multiple groups were mentioned together, forming various confederations of Sea Peoples. In

SEA PEOPLES FROM THE AEGEAN

FIGURE 18.1   Double bird-headed ships of Sea Peoples with feathered headdresses and horned helmets depicted on the temple of Ramesses III at Medinet Habu
AFTER NELSON 1930: PL. 39

the time of pharaoh Merneptah (ca. 1220 BCE), Shardana, Lukka, and—for the first time—Ekwesh, Teresh, and Shekelesh joined Libyans and neighboring Meshwesh in an attack on Egypt, and were soundly defeated. Finally, ca. 1190 BCE, in year 8 of the reign of Ramesses III, four new peoples, called Peleset, Tjeker, Denyen, and Weshesh, joined the Shekelesh in an assault by land and sea (Sandars 1985: 120–132, 164). Ramesses III defeated this confederation in pitched battles, and famously memorialized those victories in monumental reliefs on his funerary temple at Medinet Habu, near Thebes, in Upper Egypt (Fig. 18.1). Other accounts mention the same pharaoh warding off seaborne attacks by Peleset and Teresh (Sandars 1985: 164–165). In addition to raiding, Sea Peoples served as mercenaries in Egypt and the Levant. Shardana became mercenaries of the king of Byblos after their attack on that city in the late fourteenth century. They also entered the service of pharaohs Ramesses II and III, even fighting on the Egyptian side in Ramesses III's great land battle of year 8 (Sandars 1985: 30–31, 120, 161, fig. 112). Unidentified foreign mercenaries aided Ramesses III in his first Libyan war of year 5 (ibid.: 117–118, 188, figs. 74, 122). Finally, the Papyrus Harris I, written shortly after Ramesses III's death, mentions that he employed Denyen, Peleset, Weshesh, and Shekelesh as mercenaries and stationed them in his garrisons (ibid.: 116–117, 165, fig. 72).

2   Origins of Sea Peoples

Already in the late nineteenth century scholars had used etymological arguments to link the Sherden/Shardana with Sardinia, Lukka with Lycia, Ekwesh/Aqajawasha with Achaea, Teresh/Tursha with Tyrsenoi (Etruscans), Shekelesh/Sikala with Sicily, and Peleset with the biblical Philistines and Aegean Pelasgoi

(Yasur-Landau 2010: 180). Some of these identifications have gained greater credibility as more written sources and archaeological evidence have become available. So, it is now widely accepted that the Lukka were the Bronze Age Lycians, whereas the Peleset settled in Philistia, and at least some of the Shardana appear to have moved to Sardinia. Scholarly opinion remains divided about the geographical association of the Denyen, whom most scholars associate with the land of Danuna in Cilicia, but one hypothesis links to Homer's Danaoi and the land of Tanaja used in Egyptian sources from Thutmose III onward to refer to Mycenaean Greece (Jung 2017: 24; cf. Cline and Stannish 2011: 7). It also has become increasingly clear that population movements were complex. Written sources tell us that Shekelesh occupied the area of Dor together with Tjeker, but other Shekelesh may have moved to Sicily where they were known as the Sikels. And recently discovered inscriptions from Aleppo and Tell Ta'yinat revealed that some of the Peleset founded a kingdom called Palastin or Walastin in the Hatay region of northern Syria (Meijer 2017).

Whereas it is becoming increasingly clear where various groups of Sea Peoples ended up, it still is difficult to determine where most of them originated. To judge by current archaeological and written evidence for foreign influxes into the eastern Mediterranean in the twelfth century BCE, most of the raiders came from somewhere in the Aegean and moved via Cyprus and Anatolia into Syro-Palestine and Egypt (Yasur-Landau 2010: 192–281). In addition, there is a persistent strain of Italian metal technology and consumption practices with respect to Italian-type pottery, tools, and fibulae that appeared first in the Aegean and then in the eastern Mediterranean in the fourteenth–twelfth centuries BCE, making it seem likely that also central Mediterranean peoples were among the attackers (Jung 2009, 2017). Both the Shardana and Shekelesh have been suggested as having come from Italy, but convincing archaeological proof is still lacking (Sandars 1985: 112; Jung 2017). The groups of Sea Peoples for which there is some etymological claim for an Aegean origin are the Ekwesh, Teresh, Peleset, Tjeker, Denyen, and Weshesh. If the Ekwesh, or Aqajawasha, can be equated with the Ahhiyawa from the Hittite texts and the Homeric Achaioi, they would have come from an area that encompassed part of Mycenaean Greece as well as a number of Aegean islands and the area of Miletus (Sandars 1985: 110–111, 200; Niemeier 2009: 17–18; Jung 2017: 24). If one accepts the hypothesis that the Denyen are to be associated with Tanaja and Homer's Danaoi, this group of people, who are called island dwellers by Ramesses III, would have originated in another area of the Greek mainland and adjacent islands (Sandars 1985: 133). Oreshko (2018: 49–50) recently has argued that Tanaja and the Danaoi should be associated with the southern Aegean and the Ahhiyawa/Achaioi with the central Aegean. Tjeker, Teresh, and Weshesh may have come from the area of the Troad, as their names are possibly connected with the Homeric Teucri and the Hittite terms Taruisha and Wilusha (Troy/Ilion), respectively (Sandars 1985: 111–112, 163, 170). The Peleset, whose Aegean origin is most widely accepted because of the strong evidence for Mycenaean material culture, domestic practices, and ritual in Philistia, have been linked etymologically with the Pelasgoi/Pelastoi, a pre-Greek people in the Aegean (Yasur-Landau 2010: 194–281; Singer 2013: 328–330; Jung 2017: 24–27).

In the present paper I want to further explore the origin of the Sea Peoples through their iconography, and argue that their antecedents in the Aegean go back to at least the Middle Bronze Age, if not the Final Neolithic. In particular, I will focus on their ships and headgear as shown in Egyptian depictions from the reigns of Ramesses II and III. When interpreting those images one must keep in mind that, even though there is evidence at times to associate specific attributes with particular groups of Sea Peoples, it is not always possible to exclude other groups from having had similar attributes, and this for two reasons: First, Egyptian artists are known to have confused characteristics of different ethnic groups (Stevenson Smith 1981: 245); and, second, it seems that considerable cultural mixing occurred among groups of Sea Peoples that lived together for some time (Jung 2009: 81–82; 2017: 30–31; Yasur-Landau 2010: 172–179).

3 Sea Peoples' Ships

Among the many Egyptian images of Sea Peoples, only Ramesses III's great sea battle relief at Medinet Habu shows their ships (Fig. 18.1). Only five ships are depicted, and all are similar, even though five ethnic groups are said to have participated in the attack (Peleset, Tjeker, Denyen, Weshesh, and Shekelesh) and the later Papyrus Harris I specifies that the Sea Peoples came with three different types of ships: *br*, *mnš*, and *aha* (Artzy 1997: 3). It thus is clear, as Artzy has pointed out, that the depiction of ships at Medinet Habu has been simplified. The engraved ships are warships and may have been *aha*, since this term was used a century earlier by Ramesses II to describe the vessels of Shardana attackers (Artzy 1997: 3). The characteristics of the *br* are unknown, and *mnš* must have been cargo ships (Basch 1987: 65–66; Wachsmann 1998: 47). The five depicted warships have a curved hull with angular extremities and a vertical stem and sternpost, both topped by a bird-headed figurehead facing outboard (Wachsmann 1998: 166–171, figs. 8.1–8.15). Like the Egyptian ships they have a raised foredeck and afterdeck, quarter steering oars, and a mast with mast top, downcurved yard, and brail lines.

There has been much debate about the geographical origin of these Sea Peoples ships with double bird-headed figureheads. Whereas at times they have been linked with the "bird boats" of central Europe (Wachsmann 1998), the lack of strong evidence for other direct connections with that area makes this hypothesis less likely (Jung 2017). The most viable current associations are with Italy and the Aegean. Even though many more double bird-headed ship representations have been adduced from Italy than the Aegean, it seems to me that many of those are dubious and the connection with Italy is not as strong as with the Aegean. Various Villanovan boat models from Italy have single and double bird-headed figureheads, but all postdate the era of the Sea Peoples and cannot be used to argue their origin (cf. Wachsmann 1998: 181, fig. 8.31). Jung has recently proposed that boat images with double figureheads already occur frequently in the Recent and Final Bronze Ages in Italy (contemporary with the Late Helladic (LH) IIIB and C phases in the Aegean, respectively), going back to the Middle Bronze (MB) III (contemporary with LH IIIA) and perhaps even the Early Bronze (EB) II (Jung 2017: 31–33, figs. 4: 2–4: 5). The incised images on the Final Bronze Age razors that he lists are schematic, however, and unconvincing as ship images. It also remains to be seen whether the plastic decorations on the Italian Recent Bronze Age cup handles of Damiani's Group XVIII, interpreted as "solar boats," represent actual ships or are merely variants of bird protome ornaments found in many forms on the rims and handles of Italian cups in this period and perhaps as early as the MB III phase (Damiani 2010: 273–324, pls. 93–115). More convincing are the images incised on the fragmentary EB II cup from Filo Braccio, on the Aeolian island of Filicudi, ^{14}C dated to the nineteenth century BCE, which indeed appear to represent eleven or twelve highly simplified angular boats, including three with double projecting figureheads (Martinelli et al. 2010: 308–312, figs. 15–16). The images are too schematic, however, to say for certain whether these are birds' heads or protomes of other animals. Even though unequivocal evidence for bird-headed ships remains to be found in Bronze Age Italy, one cannot deny that bird's heads played an important role in its iconography.

In contrast, images of ships with bird-headed figureheads are much at home in the Aegean towards the end of the Bronze Age, and can be traced back to the Middle Helladic (MH) II–III phase and possibly earlier. Moreover, they are associated with warriors with feathered headdresses and horned helmets comparable to the ones worn by the Sea Peoples depicted at Medinet Habu. Nearly all images are of ships with single figureheads, however, unlike the Medinet Habu reliefs, which show double figureheads. A few Aegean images of bird-headed ships date to the LH IIIB and Late Minoan (LM) IIIC phases: a terracotta ship model from Tanagra, Boeotia (Wachsmann 1998: 148–49, fig. 7.41), one from Tiryns (ibid.: 150, fig. 7.45), and a ship painted on a larnax from Gazi, Crete (ibid.: 136–139, fig. 7.19).[1] More numerous and widespread are finds dating to the various phases of the LH IIIC period (ibid.: 130–141, 182, figs. 7.8, 7.15–17, 7.19, 7.21, 7.25, 8.36; Mountjoy 2005), including ships painted on kraters from LH IIIB2/LH IIIC Early Bademgediği, near Izmir; LH IIIC Early/Middle Kos (Mountjoy 2005) and LH IIIC Middle Kynos, East Lokris (Fig. 18.2a; Dakoronia 2010: 16–18, figs. 21–23); as well as a fragment of a LH IIIC clay ship model from Kynos, East Lokris (Wedde 2000: 312, no. 334); a ship painted on a LH IIIC Middle kalathos fragment from Phylakopi (Wedde 2000: 326, no. 656); a LH IIIC Late pyxis from tholos Tomb 1 at Tragana, near Pylos; and a LH IIIC stirrup jar from Skyros (Wedde 2000: 326 no. 655). Similar bird-headed ships were painted on krater fragments found at Enkomi in Cyprus (Mountjoy 2005: 424, pl. 97d) and on a locally produced krater fragment from Ashkelon, in Philistia (Fig. 18.2b; Wachsmann 1998: 201–202, fig. 8A.1). These magnificent painted kraters no doubt were center pieces of male elite drinking parties where tales of heroic raids were told (cf. Deger-Jalkotzy 2006: 168, 174). Their geographic distribution forms a trail from both sides of the Aegean to Cyprus and Philistia that must mimic a Sea Peoples migration route.

Bird-headed ships appear to have a long pedigree in the Aegean. No images are known from the earlier Late Bronze Age, but one depiction arguably occurs

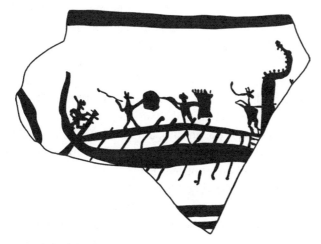

FIGURE 18.2A Single bird-headed ship with warriors wearing feathered headdresses depicted on a LH IIIC Middle krater from Kynos
AFTER DAKORONIA 2010: 17, FIG. 21

---

1 I agree with Wachsmann that the figurehead on the Gazi ship with the short vertical lines rising from its head resembles a simplified version of a birdheaded figureheads on the LH IIIC kraters from Bademgedigi, Kynos, and Enkomi; its elongated form bears resemblance to the LH IIIB2 ship model from Tiryns as well.

FIGURE 18.2B   Fragment of a locally produced LH IIIC1B krater from Ashkelon showing a warrior with round shield standing on a bird-headed figurehead
AFTER WACHSMANN 1998: 201–202, FIG. 8A.1

on a fragment of a large Matt-Painted barrel jar from Kolonna Stratum IX dated to the MH II–III phase (late eighteenth/seventeenth century BCE). It shows a warrior with a horned helmet standing on a large animal head that bears a close resemblance to the bird-headed figureheads of the LH IIIC kraters mentioned above (Fig. 18.3; Siedentopf 1991: 18–19, 55, 110, pl. 14 no. 75; Wachsmann 1998: 77–80, 82, 184, fig. 5.25). This scene also closely mimics that of a warrior with a round shield standing on top of a bird-headed figurehead on the krater fragment from Ashkelon (Fig. 18.2b). Siedentopf identifies the head on the Kolonna fragment as belonging to a snake-like sea monster, and Wedde assigns it to a fish (Wedde 2000: 238, 316, no. 510), but in view of its similarities with LH IIIC figureheads and especially the fragment from Ashkelon, I agree with Wachsmann that the Kolonna image is likely to be that of a warrior standing on a ship's figurehead.[2] Of roughly the same date as the Kolonna fragments are four partially preserved bird protomes from Mitrou, East Lokris, that decorated the rims of four Fine Gray Burnished (or Gray Minyan) carinated bowls or goblets (Fig. 18.4; Hale 2016: 260, 284, 286–287, fig. 15: 33). Most protomes have

---

2   Wedde rejects this identification because he believes that this scene was part of a metope arrangement that would not allow space for a ship; however, given the extreme rarity of pictorial decoration on Aeginetan Matt-Painted barrel jars, I believe that we cannot be certain about this metope arrangement. For one thing, pendent crosshatched triangles such as are depicted above the animal head are also found in open-field arrangements on jugs of Kolonna IX (Siedentopf 1991: pl. 63 no. 301).

FIGURE 18.3   Fragment of a MH II–III Matt-Painted barrel jar from Kolonna, Aigina, with a warrior with horned helmet standing on a bird-headed figurehead
AFTER SIEDENTOPF 1991: PL. 14: 75

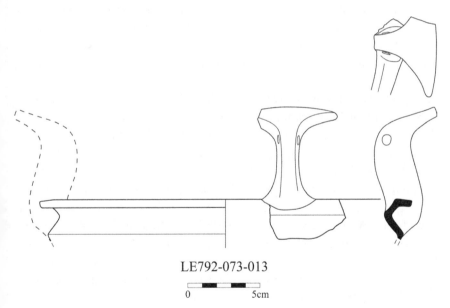

FIGURE 18.4   Fragmentary bird protome on a Fine Gray Burnished (or Gray Minyan) carinated bowl LE792-073-013 from Mitrou, East Lokris
DRAWINGS BY TINA ROSS, MITROU ARCHAEOLOGICAL PROJECT

plastic "eyes" set on either side of the head. They were found in various late Middle Helladic or very early LH I contexts and belonged to four different vases (Hale, personal communication). Even though they are not associated with ships, they suggest, like the Italian depictions, that the bird-headed emblem held some special importance for the groups that produced or consumed those vases. It is worth noting that Mitrou is located only 10 km east of the site of Kynos, which five centuries later produced the LH IIIC Middle "Sea Peoples" kraters with warriors with feathered headdresses standing on ships with bird-headed figureheads (see above). With their prominent flat beaks, the bird protomes from Mitrou appear to represent ducks or other waterfowl. It is conceivable that these aquatic birds with their ability to swim and fly held a special fascination for people who so relied on seafaring (cf. Yon 1992: 397—401). The feathered headdresses of several groups of Sea Peoples (see below) may represent the same fascination with the abilities of birds, and so may be the frequent depiction of water birds on Philistine Bichrome ware (e.g., Yasur-Landau 2010: 324, 327, figs. 8.16–8.24) as well as on LH IIIC and Geometric Greek pottery (cf. Wachsmann 1998: 184, fig. 8.42: C–D).

It is possible that ships with bird-headed figureheads had an even longer history in the Aegean. Whereas most images of Early Cycladic (EC) IIA longships carry fish emblems at the top of their bows, one or more of the recently discovered rock-cut ship engravings from the EC II settlement of Vathy, on the island of Astypalaia, have elongated projections that do not resemble fish as much as the stylized bird-headed figureheads of the LH IIIB clay model from Tiryns and the LM IIIB painted sarcophagus from Gazi (see above; Vlachopoulos and Matthaiou 2010–2013: fig. 6).[3] Further back in time, several boat engravings found at the Final Neolithic settlement of Strofilas, on Andros, have linear down-sloping figureheads that likewise cannot be fish emblems but resemble animal heads (Televantou 2014). Since the same settlement contained the engraved image of a duck (or duck-headed boat) in its sanctuary area, as well as a fragmentary shell pendant shaped like the head of a waterfowl (Televantou 2008: 49, 52, figs. 6.10, 6.21), it is plausible that also their ships had bird-headed figureheads. Furthermore, the fact that fish-headed and animal-headed figureheads coexisted in the EC II Cyclades makes it conceivable that these insignia referred to different cultural groups. The fish emblem may specifically have referred to Syros, because nearly all depictions of fish-headed longships on clay "frying pans" seem to have come from that island (Marthari 2017: 147–149).

---

3   The discovery of the Vathy engravings settles the long-standing debate about the directionality of Cycladic longships, because one of these ships for the first time is depicted with a steering oar, which shows that the lower extremity was the stern and the higher extremity with the emblem, the bow (Van de Moortel 2017).

In spite of the long history of bird-headed ships in the Aegean, a significant impediment to identifying them with the double bird-headed ships of the Sea Peoples of Medinet Habu has been the fact that nearly all Aegean images are of single figureheads, with the arguable exception of a painting with double bird-headed figureheads on a LH IIIC krater fragment from the lower town at Tiryns (Slenczka 1974: 29–30, no. 45, pl. 39.1e; Wachsmann 1998: 178–183, fig. 8.32).[4] An important breakthrough in this respect, however, has been Artzy's recent discovery of rock-cut graffiti of Aegean-type ships with angular bows and single bird-headed figureheads at Naḥal Meʻarot and Naḥal Oren, in the vicinity of the harbor of Tel Nami (Artzy 2013: 329–330, 336, 338, figs. 4.5–4.7). This area is located north of Tel Dor, which reportedly was occupied by Tjeker and Shekelesh. Given the non-Levantine, Aegean character of these ships and the Sea Peoples' connections of this area, it is very likely that these ships belonged to Sea Peoples. Their single figureheads provide support to those scholars who have suggested that the double figureheads of the Sea Peoples' ships depicted at Medinet Habu may be the result of Egyptian misunderstanding or artistic license (Jung 2017: 31). Another point worth considering in this respect is that some of the Final Neolithic, Early Bronze Age, and Late Bronze Age ship images from the Aegean do not have figureheads whereas others do. The same is true for the EB II ship engravings from Filicudi discussed above. This variation in imagery suggests that those figureheads were removable. Such devices would be reminiscent of the dragonheads of later Viking ships, which were removable and mounted only to indicate hostile intentions. It is conceivable that a similar practice existed in the Bronze Age Mediterranean. If that was the case, then the difference between single and double bird-headed ships may not have been that significant.

4 Feathered Headdresses

In addition to bird-headed ships, Sea Peoples depicted in Egypt are characterized by their armor. Round shields and sword types are shared by a variety of groups (Mehofer and Jung 2017). The main attribute that distinguishes groups of Sea Peoples is their headgear: some are depicted with horned helmets and others have a bushy type of headdress believed by most modern scholars to represent feathers. At Medinet Habu, Tjeker, Peleset, and Denyen are specifically identified by writing and shown with feathered headdresses (Sandars

---

4 Jung suggests that it may not be a ship but an elaborate whorl shell with bird protomes (Jung 2017: 31–32, n. 5). It seems to me, however, that this image is perfectly acceptable as a ship.

1985: 110–111, 131–132, figs. 68–69, 86–87). The other two groups said to have participated in the same invasion—Shekelesh and Weshesh—are not individually identified and thus we cannot be certain whether they wore feathered headdresses or horned helmets (see below).[5]

Even though a possible predecessor of the feathered headdress existed in Italy already in the fourteenth century BCE (Jung 2009, 2017: 31), it will be argued here that this headgear was more at home in the Aegean and went back to the late Middle Bronze Age (late eighteenth/seventeenth century BCE) in that region. Various depictions of men with stylized forms of this headgear have been found in the Aegean on thirteenth- and twelfth-century BCE vases. These include warriors associated with ships with single bird-headed figureheads on the LH IIIB2/LH IIIC Early to LH IIIC Middle krater fragments from Bademgediği, Kos, and Kynos discussed above. Men with similar headdresses are seen on fragments of a LH IIIB krater (Sandars 1985: 188–189, fig. 123; Mountjoy 2005: 426) and a larnax from Mycenae (Yasur-Landau 2010: 184, 186, fig. 5.73), as well as on a LH IIIC Middle krater fragment from Thebes (Andrikou et al. 2006: 44–49, 89, 175, no. 359, fig. 146), a LM IIIC fragment from Phaistos (Wachsmann 1998: 141, fig. 7.27), and the back side of the LH IIIC Warrior Vase from Mycenae (Sandars 1985: 189, fig. 125). Also, fishermen depicted on a LH IIIC krater from Kynos arguably have spiky headdresses (Yasur-Landau 2010: 91, 184, fig. 3.38). As a number of these vases had been locally produced, feathered headdresses may have had a widespread distribution on both sides of the Aegean.

A late Middle Bronze Age version of the same headdress can arguably be seen on the famous Phaistos Disc. Among the many stamped impressions on this disc are 19 human heads with "mohawks" that appear to be stylized representations of the feathered headdresses shown at Medinet Habu (Fig. 18.5; Pernier 1908: 281–283 no. 6). The authenticity of this clay disc has often been contested, but seems to be beyond a doubt, because several of its signs, including the heads with "mohawks," find comparanda on a golden ax from Arkalochori, which was excavated in 1934–1935, more than 25 years after the disc's discovery (Duhoux 1977: 15–16, 79–81, figs. 23–28). In addition, the disc was found encrusted with a limey deposit, which points to a lengthy stay underground (Duhoux 1977: 17, 81, fig. 29; see Cucuzza 2015; Anastasiadou 2016 for other arguments in favor of authenticity). In addition to the crested heads, two other signs on the disc are closely related to Sea People imagery, but were not

---

5 For a very tentative interpretation of the Shekelesh as wearing swept-back turbans, see Sandars 1985: 110–111, figs. 68, 69.

 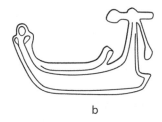 

a   b   c

FIGURE 18.5 Stamped images of a crested head, a ship, and a possible shield on the Phaistos Disc, probably of MM III date
AFTER PERNIER 1908: 281–283, 288, 291–292, NOS. 6, 25, 37

recognized as such by Pernier. As many as 14 out of 19 crested heads are accompanied by a circular sign with seven small circles inside (Fig. 18.5; Pernier 1908: 291–292, no. 37). Identified as a shield by Duhoux (1977: 45–46, 58 no. 12), it very much resembles the round shields with "bosses" brandished by early thirteenth-century Shardana mercenaries of Ramesses II (cf. Sandars 1985: 30, fig. 12). Moreover, the Phaistos Disc carries six stamped images of ships with an asymmetrical profile, slightly curved bottom, curved stern, short lower bow projection, and vertical stem topped by a horizontal linear emblem (Fig. 18.5; Pernier 1908: 288, no. 25), which are closely comparable to LH/LM IIIB–C Aegean warships, including those that carry warriors with feathered headdresses (see above; Van de Moortel 2017: Type D). Because of the small size of the images on the Phaistos Disc, it is impossible to tell whether or not the linear bow emblem was meant to be a bird-headed figurehead.

The disc's date is somewhat uncertain because of the imprecise excavation methods of the time. It was found together with a fragmentary Linear A tablet in a black, burned destruction level in basement Room 8 of Building 101 northeast of the Phaistian palace. This level is thought to represent debris fallen from above; it included two large restorable vases that now are dated to Middle Minoan (MM) IIIA and LM IA (Carinci and La Rosa 2013: 117, fig. 9.15). The dark discolorations on the disc indicate that it belongs to the burned debris. In the same part of the room, a cup fragment with dark-painted horizontal bands on a lustrous pale background was found that must be Late Minoan in date (Pernier 1908: 263–264, fig. 9; Duhoux 1977: 10, 79, fig. 21). This fragment may belong to the burned level or it may have been introduced by activities related to LM IIIB/C buildings identified by Militello about 10 m away (Militello, personal communication). Thus, the stratigraphic position of the disc does not entirely rule out a LM IIIB/C date for the disc, but its intact state and discolorations make it more likely that it was associated with the restorable MM IIIA–LM IA vases and the burned destruction. Moreover, a detailed study by Anastasiadou (2016) has revealed numerous correspondences of its images with MM IIB/III signs, strongly supporting its early MM III date. The disc, which had been deliberately fired, does not appear to be local, as its medium yellowish brown to brown color is unlike that of the locally produced pottery. Because of its Minoan-type signs, it seems likely that the disc came from elsewhere on Crete or the Minoanized Aegean. Thus, the similarities of its crested heads, shields, and ships with attributes of the Sea Peoples can be taken to argue that these were known in the wider Minoan world already in the late Middle Minoan period. Since the dominant Minoan iconography of the time is characterized by different ship hulls (Wedde 2000: Types II–IV; Van de Moortel 2017: Types B–C) and a conspicuous absence of warlike elements, the images on the Phaistos Disc may refer to a non-Cretan people with strong Minoan connections or perhaps to an as yet unknown group on Crete itself.

5 Horned Helmets

The other headdress worn by Sea Peoples in Egyptian imagery—the horned helmet—is most consistently associated with Shardana. Such helmets are sported by Shardana mercenaries of Ramesses II and III (Sandars 1985: 106), and also by a captive Shardana chieftain depicted in a Syrian war relief at Medinet Habu (Sandars 1985: 110–111, figs. 68, 69). In each instance, a disc-shaped emblem is shown between the horns. In contrast, other attackers and captives on the Medinet Habu reliefs have horned helmets without disc insignia (Sandars 1985: 158; Wachsmann 1998: 165–169, figs. 8.1, 8.4, 8.6, 8.8, 8.9, 8.11). Since the Shardana are not listed among those other attackers, it is conceivable that warriors with horned helmets without discs were not Shardana but Shekelesh or Weshesh (see above).

Because of their associations with Shardana, the origin of horned helmets has been sought in the central Mediterranean; however, they do not appear there until the eleventh century BCE (Jung 2017: 35). In contrast, the depiction of a warrior with a horned helmet on the barrel jar fragment from Kolonna discussed above (Fig. 18.3) demonstrates that such helmets were known in this part of the Aegean already in the MH II–III phase. Kolonna was a prosperous merchant town with widespread maritime trade connections at that time, and this image may represent one of its own warriors. This interpretation is supported by the fact that a horned boar's tusk helmet has been discovered in a MH II elite warrior's grave at Kolonna (Kilian-Dirlmeier 1995). A few LH IIIC kraters from the Greek mainland likewise depict horned helmets. These are the famous Warrior Vase from Mycenae, which shows warriors with such helmets (Sandars 1985: 189, fig. 124), and a krater from Pisaskion, in Messenia, depicting a hunter with such headdress (Yasur-Landau 2010: 90, 182, fig. 3.37). Pisaskion is located only a few kilometers from Tragana, where a LH IIIC Late pyxis painted with a bird-headed warship was found in a tholos tomb (Mountjoy 2005: 424, pl. 98a). The Warrior Vase from Mycenae is a particularly interesting document because it shows both types of Sea Peoples' headgear: on one side, warriors with horned helmets marching off to war and, on the other, a row of warriors with stylized feathered headdresses brandishing round shields and drawing spears for combat. These different poses may signify that two different, and perhaps opposing, groups are represented.

6 Concluding Remarks

It has been argued here that typical attributes of the Sea Peoples, such as ships with bird-headed figureheads, feathered headdresses, horned helmets, and possibly round shields, were symbols of group identity in various parts of the Aegean as early as the late Middle Bronze Age. Bird-headed ships may even go back to the Early Bronze Age and Final Neolithic in this region. The evidence is too scarce for us to be able to discuss the spatial distribution of these early groups. The fact, however, that these particular symbols of group identity did not become part of official Minoan or Mycenaean elite iconography of the LH/LM I–IIIA period indicates that these groups were suppressed by the palatial rulers. Yet, the striking similarities and apparent continuity in iconography across five centuries between late Middle Bronze Age and LB IIIB/C images in the Aegean suggest that somewhere in that region unbroken, yet to be discovered, traditions persisted of seaborne warrior groups with bird-headed ships and feathered headdresses or horned helmets. Continued warfare between emerging rulers and between palatial states in the Aegean, as evidenced by multiple waves of destruction in the fourteenth and thirteenth centuries BCE (Wiener 2017: 48–53), may at times have released single warrior groups such as the Shardana into the eastern Mediterranean—if indeed they came from the Aegean. It was only with the progressive breakdown of palatial powers, in the late thirteenth century BCE and at the transition to the twelfth century, that many more groups were able to reassert their independence and take to the seas once again. This time the potential push factors of past palatial oppression, violent anarchy after the collapse, and, climate change (Wiener 2017), in combination with the lures of the East, drew these groups to the eastern Mediterranean—first as raiders and mercenaries and then as settlers.

References

Anastasiadou, M. 2016. The Phaistos Disc as a Genuine Minoan Artefact and Its Place in the Stylistic Milieu of Crete in the Protopalatial Period. *Creta Antica* 17: 13–57.

Andrikou, E., Aravantinos, V.L., Godart, L., Sacconi, A., and Vroom, J. 2006. *Thèbes. Fouilles de la Cadmée* II.2. *Les tablettes en linéaire B de la Odos Pelopidou: le contexte archéologique. La céramique de la Odos Pelopidou et la chronologie du linéaire B* (Biblioteca di "Pasiphae." Collana di filologia e antichità egee 2.2). Pisa and Rome.

Anthony, D.W. 1990. Migration in Archeology: The Baby and the Bathwater. *American Anthropologist* 92: 895–914.

Artzy, M. 1997. Nomads of the Sea. In: Swiny, S., Hohlfelder, R.L., and Swiny, H.W., eds. *Res Maritimae: Cyprus and the Eastern Mediterranean from Prehistory to Late Antiquity* (Cyprus American Archaeological Research Institute Monograph Series 1). Atlanta: 1–16.

Artzy, M. 2013. On the Other "Sea Peoples." In: Killebrew, A.E. and Lehmann, F., eds. *The Philistines and Other "Sea Peoples" in Text and Archaeology* (Archaeology and Biblical Studies 15). Atlanta: 329–344.

Basch, L. 1987. *Le Musée imaginaire de la marine antique*. Athens.

Bietak, M. 2015. War Bates Island bei Marsa Matruh ein Piratennest? Ein Beitrag zur frühen Geschichte der Seevölker. In: Nawracala, S. and Nawracala, R., eds. *ΠΟΛΥΜΑΘΕΙΑ: Festschrift für Hartmut Matthäus anläßlich seines 65. Geburtstages*. Aachen: 29–41.

Carinci, F. and La Rosa, V. 2013. A New Middle Minoan IIIA Ceremonial Building and the So-Called "New Era" at Phaistos. In: Macdonald, C.F. and Knappett, C., eds. *Intermezzo: Intermediacy and Regeneration in Middle Minoan III Palatial Crete*. London: 107–121.

Cline, E. and Stannish, S.M. 2011. Sailing the Great Green Sea? Amenhotep III's "Aegean List" from Kom el-Hetan, Once More. *Journal of Ancient Egyptian Interconnections* 3(2): 6–16.

Cucuzza, N. 2015. Intorno alla autenticità dell' "Disco di Festòs." *Quaderni di Storia* 81(1): 93–124.

Dakoronia, F. 2010. *Kynos*. Athens.

Damiani, I. 2010. *L'età del Bronzo recente nell'Italia centro-meridionale* (Grandi contesti e problemi della Protostoria italiana 12). Florence.

Deger-Jalkotzy, S. 2006. Late Mycenaean Warrior Tombs. In: Deger-Jalkotzy, S. and Lemos, I., eds. *Ancient Greece: From the Mycenaean Palaces to the Age of Homer*. Edinburgh: 151–179.

Duhoux, Y. 1977. *Le Disque de Phaestos: archéologie, épigraphie, édition critique, index*. Leuven.

Hale, C.M. 2016. The Middle Helladic Fine Gray Burnished (Gray Minyan) Sequence at Mitrou, East Lokris. *Hesperia* 85: 243–295.

Jung, R. 2009. Pirates of the Aegean: Italy—the East Aegean—Cyprus at the End of the Second Millennium BC. In: Karageorghis, V. and Kouka, O., eds. *Cyprus and the East Aegean: Intercultural Contacts from 3000 to 500 BC. An International Archaeological Symposium Held at Pythagoeion, Samos, October 17th–18th, 2008*. Nicosia: 72–93.

Jung, R. 2017. The Sea Peoples after Three Millennia: Possibilities and Limitations of Historical Reconstruction. In: Fischer, P.M. and Bürge, T., eds. *"Sea Peoples" Up-to-Date: New Research on Transformations in the Eastern Mediterranean in the 13th–11th Centuries BCE. Proceedings of the ESF-Workshop Held at the Austrian Academy of Sciences Vienna 3–4 November 2014* (Contributions to the Chronology of the Eastern Mediterranean 35). Vienna: 23–42.

Kilian-Dirlmeier, I. 1997. *Das mittelbronzezeitliche Schachtgrab von Ägina* (Alt-Ägina 4.3). Mainz.

Marthari, M. 2017. Aspects of Pictorialism and Symbolism in the Early Bronze Age Cyclades: A "Frying Pan" with Longboat Depiction from the New Excavations at Chalandriani in Syros. In: Vlachou, V. and Gadolou, A., eds. *ΤΕΡΨΙΣ: Studies in Mediterranean Archaeology in Honour of Nota Kourou* (Études d'archéologie 10). Brussels: 147–160.

Martinelli, M.C., Fiorentino, G., Prosdocimi, B., d'Oronzo, C., Levi, S.T., Mangano, G., Stellati, A., and Wolff, N. 2010. Nuove ricerche nell'insediamento sull'istmo di Filo Braccio a Filicudi. Nota preliminare sugli scavi 2009. *Origini* 22 (N.S. 4): 285–314.

Mehofer, M. and Jung, R. 2017. Weapons and Metals: Interregional Contacts between Italy and the Eastern Mediterranean during the Late Bronze Age. In: Fischer, P.M. and Bürge, T., eds. *"Sea Peoples" Up-to-Date: New Research on Transformations in the Eastern Mediterranean in the 13th–11th Centuries BCE. Proceedings of the ESF-Workshop Held at the Austrian Academy of Sciences Vienna 3–4 November 2014* (Contributions to the Chronology of the Eastern Mediterranean 35). Vienna: 389–400.

Meijer, D.J.W. 2017. The Archaeological Ramifications of "Philistine" in Aleppo. In: Fischer, P.M. and Bürge, T., eds. *"Sea Peoples" Up-to-Date: New Research on Transformations in the Eastern Mediterranean in the 13th–11th Centuries BCE. Proceedings of the ESF-Workshop Held at the Austrian Academy of Sciences Vienna 3–4 November 2014* (Contributions to the Chronology of the Eastern Mediterranean 35). Vienna: 257–262.

Mountjoy, P.A. 2005. Mycenaean Connections with the Near East in LH IIIC: Ships and Sea Peoples. In: Laffineur, R. and Greco, E., eds. *Emporia: Aegeans in the Central and Eastern Mediterranean* (Aegaeum 25). Liège–Austin: 423–427.

Nelson, H.H. 1930. *Medinet Habu 1924–28, Part I: The Epigraphic Survey of the Great Temple of Medinet Habu (Seasons 1924–25 to 1927–28)*. Chicago.

Niemeier, W.-D. 2009. "Minoanisation" *versus* "Minoan Thalassocracy": An Introduction. In: Macdonald, C.F., Hallager, E., and Niemeier, W.-D., eds. *The Minoans in the Central, Eastern and Northern Aegean: New Evidence* (Monographs of the Danish Institute at Athens 8). Athens: 11–29.

Oreshko, R. 2018. *Ahhiyawa—Danu(na)*. Aegean Ethnic Groups in the Eastern Mediterranean in the Light of Old and New Hieroglyphic-Luwian Evidence. In: Niesiołowski-Spanò, Ł. and Węcowski, M., eds., *Change, Continuity, and Connectivity: North-Eastern Mediterranean at the Turn of the Bronze Age and in the Early Iron Age*. Wiesbaden: 23–56.

Pernier, L. 1908. Il disco di Phaestos con caratteri pittografici. *Ausonia* 3: 255–302.

Sandars, N.K. 1985. *The Sea Peoples: Warriors of the Ancient Mediterranean, 1250–1150 BC* (2nd ed). London.

Siedentopf, H.B. 1991. *Mattbemalte Keramik der Mittleren Bronzezeit* (Alt-Ägina IV.2). Mainz.

Singer, I. 2013. "Old Country" Ethnonyms in "New Countries" of the "Sea Peoples" Diaspora. In: Koehl, R.B., ed. *Amilla: The Quest for Excellence. Studies Presented to Guenter Kopcke in Celebration of His 75th Birthday* (Prehistory Monographs 43). Philadelphia: 321–333.

Slenczka, E. 1974. *Figürlich bemalte mykenische Keramik aus Tiryns* (Tiryns 7). Mainz.

Stevenson Smith, W. 1981. *The Art and Architecture of Ancient Egypt*. New York.

Televantou, C.A. 2008. Strofilas: A Neolithic Settlement on Andros. In: Brodie, N., Doole, J., Gavalas, G., and Renfrew, C., eds. *Horizon, Ὁρίζων: A Colloquium on the Prehistory of the Cyclades, Cambridge 2004*. Cambridge: 43–53.

Televantou, C.A. 2014. Strofilas Androu: I archaioteri poli tis Europis (Strofilas on Andros: The Oldest Town in Europe). *Istoria* (August 13, 2014). http://www.enandro.gr/2015-09-22-09-31-30.html (accessed May 28, 2019).

Van de Moortel, A. 2017. A New Typology of Bronze Age Aegean Ships: Developments in Aegean Shipbuilding in Their Historical Context. In: Litwin, J., ed. *The Baltic and Beyond: Proceedings of the 14th International Symposium on Boat and Ship Archaeology, Gdańsk, September 21–25, 2015*. Gdańsk: 263–268.

Vlachopoulos, A.G. and Matthaiou, A.P. 2010–2013. Neotera archaiologika Astypalaias. *Horos* 22–25: 375–386.

Wachsmann, S. 1998. *Seagoing Ships and Seamanship in the Bronze Age Levant*. College Station, TX.

Wedde, M. 2000. *Towards a Hermeutics of Aegean Bronze Age Ship Imagery*. Mannheim–Möhnesee.

Wiener, M.H. 2017. Causes of Complex Systems Collapse at the End of the Bronze Age. In: Fischer, P.M. and Bürge, T., eds. *"Sea Peoples" Up-to-Date: New Research on Transformations in the Eastern Mediterranean in the 13th–11th Centuries BCE. Proceedings of* the ESF-Workshop Held at the Austrian Academy of Sciences Vienna 3–4 November 2014 (Contributions to the Chronology of the Eastern Mediterranean 35). Vienna: 43–74.

Yasur-Landau, A. 2010. *The Philistines and Aegean Migration at the End of the Late Bronze Age*. Cambridge.

Yon, M. 1992. Ducks' Travels. In: Åström, P., ed. *Acta Cypria 2. Acts of an International Congress on Cypriote Archaeology Held in Göteborg on 22–24 August 1991*. Jonsered: 394–407.

Archaeological Periods

Bronze Age
  Abu-Hawam 120
  'Akko as a Phoenician center 128
  amulets 63
  ancestor cult in the Levant 247–57
  changes of island landscapes 111, 112
  collapse 312
  Cypriot pottery 99
  harbors 218
  on Lebanese coast 22
  Levantine society 247–48
  Lycians 320
  Mediterranean 327
  merchants 143, 155
  metallurgy 162, 163, 170, 174, 175, 238
  monumental structures 188
  piracy 144, 145, 147, 149
  ruin mounds affecting social memory 177–93
  ships 212, 322
  trade/exchange 221
  weight systems 239
  writing boards 212
Byzantine period 187
  Tel Keisan 81
  Miletos 112
  Tiryns 185
  Tyre 15

Chalcolithic period 22 n. 3

Early Bronze Age
  Aegean warrior insignia 318
  burial area at Qatna 255
  decline on Levantine coast 21
  Ebla 251
  Tell Fadous-Kfarabida 21
  foundation of Tyre 14–28
  Hama 21
  Levantine sites 249
  Levantine societies 247
  ship imagery 327, 331
  Sidon 21
Early Bronze Age I
  Tell Abu al-Kharaz 44
  burial 31, 43, 44
  Norşuntepe 39
  pottery 31, 37, 39, 44, 45
  socioeconomic changes 45
  subdivision of 45
  trade 43
Early Bronze Age IA
  Hassek Höyük 39
  Middle Euphrates (region) 39
  pottery 34, 36
  Tell Shiukh Fawqani 39
Early Bronze Age I–II
  contribution of pottery to chronology of period 31–46
Early Bronze Age II
  Tell Abu al-Kharaz 44
  'Ein Asawir 44
  Tell el-Far'ah (N) 44
  pottery 34, 39, 44, 45, 322
  Tel Qashish 45
  ship imagery 327
Early Bronze Age II–III
  Bab edh-Dhra' 249
Early Bronze Age III
  Tell Arqa 20
  pottery 21
  Tyre 19, 24
Early Bronze Age IV 237
  Tell Arqa 20
  Ebla archives 252
  marriage in 257
  pottery 21
  at Tyre 18, 19, 21
Early–Middle Bronze Age transition
  emergence of house societies 249, 256–57
Epipaleolithic period 105

Hellenistic period
  'Akko 81, 129
  Ḥorbat Ṭurit 135–36
  Paphos 199, 201–202
  Ras Ibn Hani 115
  texts 25
  Tyre 15

Iron Age   81, 185, 263
  'Akko as a Phoenician center   128
  Corinth   271
  Crete   266
  Cyprus   199
  Gallaecians   247
  Tel Hazor   179, 185
  Israel   257
  Tell Keisan   81, 95
  Levantine society   247–48
  masks   76 n. 10
  necropolis at al-Bass, Tyre   14,
    269 n. 10
  polities   163
  pottery   81, 83 n. 2, 99
  ruin mounds affecting social
    memory   177–93
  ships/ship imagery   145, 155
  stratigraphy at Tyre, 17, 17 Fig. 1.3
  trade from Phoenicia to Judah in the late
    Iron Age   69–78
  Tyre   15, 17, 22, 24
Iron Age I
  Tel Hazor   178
  Tell Keisan   83, 92, 99 n. 7
  Tiryns   185
Iron Age II   78
  Tel Hazor   178
  masks   72 n. 3
  Tell en-Naṣbeh   69
  Phoenician trade   76–77
Iron Age IIC
  pottery   73–74

Late Bronze Age   145, 164
  Aegean   143
  Tell Beit Mirsim   223
  Canaan   95, 257
  collapse   163
  copper export from Cyprus   236
  eastern Mediterranean   143
  economic decline   142
  Hala Sultan Tekke   304
  Tel Hazor   177, 179
  hoards   310–12
  Tell Keisan   83, 95, 99 n. 7
  kingship   200
  metallurgy   163, 173, 238, 304
  Tel Mevorakh   290

Tel Nami   278, 290
  piracy in Late Bronze Age eastern
    Mediterranean   142–56
  polities   154
  pottery   83 n. 2, 278
  ships/ship imagery   155, 271, 327
  shipwrecks   161
  texts/documents   144, 149, 155
  trade   99, 142, 154, 163, 301
  Tyre   18, 19, 21, 22, 24
  Ugarit   217
Late Bronze Age I   237
  'Akko   58
  Cypriot pottery   99
  Tel Mevorakh   87
  plano-convex disc-shaped
    ingots   237
Late Bronze Age I–II
  canine burials   60
  pottery   94
  Ugarit   93
Late Bronze Age IIB
  Tel Nami   290, 293
Late Bronze Age IIIB/C
  Aegean imagery   331

medieval period/Middle Ages
  Europe   247
  texts   155
  Tyre   15
  Venice   106, 119
Middle Bronze Age   99
  Aegean headgear   328
  Aegean iconography   331
  Aegean insignia   318, 331
  animal burials   58
  intramural burials   252–56
  metallurgy   238
  origin of the Sea Peoples   321
  palaces   225
  Tyre   18, 19, 21, 22, 24
  Ugarit   256
Middle Bronze Age I
  royal tombs at Mari   255
Middle Bronze Age II
  'Akko   56
  Cypriot pottery   99
  Ebla   255, 257
  palace at Mari   255

Middle Bronze Age IIA
  animal burials in rampart at Tel
    'Akko   54–65
  infant burial   63
  pig burial   60
Middle Bronze Age IIB   98
  donkey burials   59
  Megiddo   98
  Tel Mevorakh   98
Middle Bronze Age IIC
  'Akko   59
  Tel Beit Mirsim   221, 237
Middle Bronze Age IIC–Late Bronze I
  appearance of Monochrome vessels in the
    Levant   94
Middle Bronze Age III
  Cypriot pottery   99
  pottery   322
  ship imagery   322

Neolithic period   22, 22 n. 3, 105, 114
  Final Neolithic period   318, 321, 326, 327,
    331

Ottoman period
  'Akko   56
  Tyre   14, 15

Persian period   199
  'Akko   75 n. 5
  Ashkelon   77
  coins   76
  mask from Tell en-Naṣbeh   69–77
  pottery   73 n. 4, 74, 202
  province of Yehud   78
  religion at Tell en-Naṣbeh   74
  trade from Phoenicia to
    Judah   69–78
  at Tyre   15

Roman period
  Altinum   106, 119
  coins   27
  commerce   144
  changes of island landscapes   112,
    118
  Kom ed-Dahab   117
  Paphos   202
  texts   130
  Tiryns   185
  Tyre   15, 27 n. 6, 28

Index

¹⁴C (see radiocarbon dating)
4.2 ka BP climatic event   256, 257
Ababra, Tell   60
Abdi-Aširta   153
Abu Gurob   145
Abu Hawam, Tell   87, 89, 93, 94, 95, 98, 120, 130, 271, 293
Abu al-Kharaz, Tell   37, 44, 45
Acarköy   39
Achaea   319
Achaeans   200
Achaemenid period   74
Achaioi   320
Acheloos River   110, 112
Achilles Tatius   27 n. 5, 28
Achziv/Akhziv, Tel   75, n. 5, 130
Adamun   134
Adriatic Sea   143
Aegean
   copper production   163–64, 234
   drinking practices   296
   hoards   312
   iconography   145, 268, 269 n. 10, 322–31
   mercenaries   153
   Phoenician activity in   262–66
   possible origin of the Sea Peoples   318–31
   pottery and other artifacts   146, 292, 293, 295–96, 322–31
   region   143, 146, 147, 168, 272, 290, 302
   ships   145, 322–31
Aegean Sea   111
Aegean-type pottery   278–97
Aegina (Greece)   110, 111
Afis, Tell   35
African coast   265, 265 n. 4
Agapenor the Arcadian   200
Agathe/Agde   119
Ahhiyawa/Achaioi   153, 320
'Ain el Baqar   56
'Ajjul, Tell el-   59, 60, 87, 95
Akaki   95
Akkadian period   58, 62
Akkadian texts   61, 149, 152–54, 210, 212, 213, 215, 216, 251, 318

'Akko/Akko, Tel   54–65, 81, 89, 97, 98, 99, 128–39
   harbor of   56, 99, 130
   Total Archaeology Project   128, 129 n. 4, 138
'Akko Plain   76, 128–39
   reconstruction of its ancient environment   128–39
Al Rashidiyeh, Tell   21–22
Alalakh   253
Alambra   96, 97
Alambra-Mouttes   312
Alashiya/Alašiya. *See also* Cyprus   149, 152–54, 210, 213, 303
Alassa, Cyprus   239, 240 n.26
Alassa-Pano Mantilares   304, 310
Aleppo   320
Alexander the Great   22, 106, 115
Alexandria   108, 111, 115
Altinum   106
Amarna
   Letters   152–54, 269 n. 10, 318
   period   22, 210
Amathus   200
Ambelikou, Cyprus   237
Ambrosian Rocks   26, 27, 28
Amenhotep III (pharaoh)   318
Ammistamru II (king of Ugarit)   210
Ammon   77
Ammurapi (king of Ugarit)   207, 210–11
Amorite koine   256
Ampheion Hill tumulus, Thebes   182–83, 188, 193
Amphion, mythical founder of Thebes   182, 193
Amrit   106
amulets   62–64
Amuq Phase G   35, 43
Amuq Valley   31, 34, 43
Amurru   153–54
Anatolia
   animal cult in   60–61
   chronology   44
   coast   153, 161
   merchants   120

INDEX

metallurgy 164, 174, 222 n. 6
possible origin of the Sea Peoples 146, 320
ancestor cult in the Bronze Age Levant 247–57
anchorage at 'Akko 56
Annals of Thutmose III 303
Annals of Tyre 25
Aphek, Tel 92, 210
Aphrodite/Aphrodite Ourania 200–11, 265, 265 n.8
Apliki, Cyprus 236
Apsidal Building tumulus, Thebes 180–83, 188, 191, 193
Arabian Peninsula 234
Arad 44, 45
Archaic period 111, 183, 270, 271
Argolid 180, 292–93
Aristotle 201
Arkalochori 328
Arpera 91, 97
Arpera-Mosphilos 96
'Arqa/Arqa, Tell 20, 21, 95, 96, 97
Arslantepe 39, 43
Arwad 106, 110, 153–54
Arzawa 149
Ashkelon, Tel 37, 73 n. 4, 77 n. 14, 95, 96, 97, 200, 265, 323, 324
Astarte of Paphos 201
Atamrum (king of Andarig) 61
Athens 267
Athienou, Cyprus 98, 291
Athos peninsula 264 n. 3
'Atlit 96
Avaris. *See also* Dab'a, Tell el- 119
Awali delta 110
Aya Irini 85
Ayia Paraskevi 96
Ayios Iakovos 98
Azekah. *See* Zakariya, Tell

Baal 269 n. 10
Baal Cycle 208, 216
Ba'alat Gubal 201
Bab edh-Dhra' 249
Babylonian period 74, 78
Bademgediği Tepe 146, 323, 323 n. 1, 328
Bahrain 234
Balawat 24

Barama 251
Bass, al-, Tyre 14, 269 n. 10
Bâtiment à la Colonne, Enkomi 308
Beirut
  Cypriot pottery from 95
  mentioned in ancient texts 154, 207
Beit Mirsim, Tell
  copper oxhide ingot from 221–42
  Cypriot pottery from 91, 97
Berezan (Ukrain) 111
Bes 71
bet 'em, "House of the mother" 248
Beth-Shean, Tel 296
Bey Keuy 96
Binaš 251
Birgi River 117
Bīt-Gulu 60
Black Sea 111, 236
boats. *See* ships.
Boğazköy 212
Bomford Goddess 239
Brak, Tell 34, 58, 60
British Mandate period 136
Bronze Age. *See* Archaeological Periods at the end of the index
Bucchero Ware 94, 99
burial. *See also* tombs
  of animals 54–65, 202
  burial caves 31, 32, 37, 39, 43, 44
  of infants 54 n. 3, 58, 63, 202
  at the Kadmeia, Thebes 180
Burnat, Tel 63
Buto 44
Büyük-Menderes Delta 110, 112
Byblos 18, 21, 200, 201
  goddess of 201, 212
  hypogeum in 252, 253
  king of 201, 319
  mentioned in ancient texts 152–54, 200, 207, 318
  temple in 200
Byzantine period. *See* Archaeological Periods at the end of the index

caduceus/kerykeion 268, 269 n. 10
Chalcolithic period. *See* Archaeological Periods at the end of the index
Cape Gelidonya shipwreck 301, 314
  analysis of the ingot cargo of 161–75

Cape Gelidonya shipwreck (cont.)
    typology of ingots from   224 n.8, 239 n. 25
Carchemish   149, 207, 212, 213
Carmel Coast   152, 269 n. 10
Carmel Mountain   130
Carthage
    precinct of Tanit   265 n. 5
    Tophet   269 n. 10
Cassius Dio   144
cemeteries. *See also* necropoli
    at al-Bass, Tyre   14, 269 n. 10
    at Kerameikos, Athens   267
    at Tel Nami   278, 294
    at Paphos   202
    at Valle di San Montano   263, 263 nn. 1, 2
Central Negev   237, 312
Central Taurus Mountains   170
ceremonies and rituals   46, 59, 61–62, 179, 242, 249, 251, 253, 290–91, 321
    Cretan cult   290–91, 293
    cult of Lamaštu   61, 62–64
    funerary   59, 60, 249, 251, 255, 295, 296
Chalcidians   263
Chalcis, Euboea   111
chemical analysis   96, 164, 168–75, 221, 232–36, 241, 293, 295
chronology synchronization   37, 43, 44, 99
Cicero   144
Cilicia   212, 213, 216
Çine-Tepecik   146
coins   27, 28, 75, 76, 268, 269, 269 n. 10
colonies/colonization   105, 111, 114, 117, 200
Corinth
    Gulf of   264
    pottery   263–65, 263–64 n. 2, 264 n. 4, 265 n. 6, 267, 270
    in relation to Phoenicians   262–72
Corridor House (type)   179, 184
Corsica   236
Crete   76, 105, 222 n. 6, 234, 236–38, 262–63, 266, 293, 330
Crusader Cathedral at Tyre   15, 24
cult. *See* ceremonies and rituals
Cumae   111
Cyclades   326
cylinder seals   21, 207, 255
    Mitannian   269 n. 10, 290
Cypro-Archaic period   199

Cypro-Classical period   199, 201, 202
Cypro-Geometric period   199, 271
Cypro-Minoan signs   239
Cyprus. *See also* Alašiya   75 n. 5, 105, 106, 120, 147, 149, 153–54, 161, 199–202, 207, 222 n. 6, 225, 239, 291, 297, 320, 323
    copper from   164, 169–71, 173–74, 224–25, 233–34, 236–42, 300–14
    Cypriot pottery   81–99, 264, 278, 290, 292–96, 323
    Cypriot-type pottery   294
    mentioned in ancient texts   149, 207, 318

Dab'a, Tell el-. *See also* Avaris
    animal burials at   58–60
    Cypriot pottery from   96
Dalmatia   143
Danaoi   320
Danube   236
Danuna (land), Cilicia   320
Darib   251
Deir el-Balah   94
Delphi   267
Denyen   319, 320, 321, 327
Dhahrat el-Humraiya   96, 97
Dhiorios   96
digital reconstruction   119, 129, 130, 132–34, 136–37, 139, 166, 223, 230
Diolkos   264 n. 3
Dionysus/Bacchus   26, 186
Dius   25
Dor, Tel   75, 152, 271, 292, 320, 327
drinking practices   46, 76, 145, 294, 323
Dusigu (queen mother)   255

Eanna archive, Uruk   60
Early Assyrian period   62
Early Babylonian period   60 n. 7, 62
Early Bronze Age. *See* Archaeological Periods at the end of the index
Early Cycladic period   326
Early Cypriot III   95
Early Helladic period   179–84, 188, 191
Early Middle Euphrates 0 (culture)   33, 33n.1
Early Middle Euphrates 1–2 (culture)   34, 35
Early Mycenaean period   184, 191
Early Upper Euphrates   35
Eastern Roman Empire   28

INDEX 343

Ebla 21, 251, 257–58
   archives 251–53
   kingdom of 257
   royal ancestor cult at 251–53, 255
Egypt/ian 22, 43–46, 213, 236, 239 n. 25, 242, 294, 303, 318–20
   0 Dynasty 37, 38, 45
   animal burials in 59
   Cypriot pottery from 96
   First Dynasty 37, 44, 45
   iconography 152, 321, 327, 330
   mentioned in ancient texts 22, 152, 207, 210, 303
   peace treaty with Hittites 207
   pottery and other artifacts 19, 21, 31, 37–39, 44–45, 94–95, 240, 240 n. 27, 242
   texts 22, 145, 149, 152–54, 320
   and the Sea Peoples 318–21, 327, 330
   ships and ship models 145, 321
Ehli-Nikkalu 210–11
'Ein Asawir 31–46
Ekwesh/Aqajawasha 319–20
Emar 207, 210, 212, 250
'En Besor 44
Enkomi(-Ayios Iakovos), Cyprus 85, 90, 92–93, 94, 95, 96–97, 98, 146, 239, 239 n. 25, 240 n. 28, 241, 295, 323, 323 n.1
   bronze industry and trade at 300–14
Enlil 62, 64
Epipaleolithic period. *See* Archaeological Periods at the end of the index
Episkopi-Bamboula 304
Episkopi-Phaneromeni 312
Eretrians 263
Ergani massive 164
Eteocypriot language 200
Etruria 262, 270
Etruscan society 248
Euboea 111, 262, 263, 262–63 n. 2, 266–67, 271
Euphrates Valley/Basin 249
   pottery imported from 31–46
Evagoras I (king of Salamis) 199
Execration Texts 22
'Ezbet Helmi 60

Fadous-Kfarabida, Tell 21
Far'ah, Tell el- (N) 44, 45
Far'ah, Tell el- (S) 92, 95, 98

Farkha, Tell el- 39
Faynan, Wadi 234, 237
feathered headdress 322, 326, 327–29, 331
figureheads 321–29, 331
Filo Braccio, island of Filicudi 322, 327
Final Bronze Age 322
Fiora River 121
fishing weight 54, 54 n. 3
flint 19, 31
fortifications
   Tel 'Akko northern fortress 59
   animal burials in the Middle Bronze rampart at Tel 'Akko 54–65
   in Medinet Habu reliefs 146
   at Thebes (Greece) 180–82
   Troy as a "pirate fortress," 147
foundation deposits 240, 240 n. 27, 242
Frankish Tower, Kadmeia, Thebes 182

Galilee foothills 134
Galinoporni 96, 97
Gallaecian society 247
Gazi, Crete 323, 326
Geometric period 146, 264 n. 4, 326
Gezer 93, 95, 96, 97, 98
Ghamqe, Tell 106
Ghassil, Tell el- 95
Giens-Olbia 110, 113–15
GIS (Geographic Information System) 129, 132–33, 138–39
Giv'at Tantur 134–35, 137
Gordian III 28
Gournia 236
Great Megaron 183–84, 185
Greece 76, 120, 145, 177–93, 270, 320
Gu-la 60

Hagia Triada 236
Haifa-Akko Bay 128, 130
Hala Sultan Tekke 86, 90, 98, 304, 305
Halif, Tel 37
Hama 21
Hammu-Rabi (king of Kurda) 61
Harmonia 186
harbors 144
   at Tell Abu Hawam 120, 130, 271
   at Tel Achziv 130
   at Aegina 111
   at 'Akko 56, 99, 130

harbors (cont.)
   at Alexandria   115
   ancient harbor structures/
      installations   111, 114, 117, 119
   at Byblos   200
   contextualization and typology of ancient
      island harbors in the
      Mediterranean   105–21
   at Kom ed-Dahab   117
   at La Valletta   111
   on the Levantine coast   76, 77 n. 14
   at Miletos   112, 121
   at Tel Nami   218, 296, 327
   at Nea Paphos   202
   at Oiniadai   121
   at Paros   111
   at Pyla-Kokkinokremnos   147
   at Ras Ibn Hani   216
   at Ugarit   200, 218
Haror, Tel   58
Hassek Höyük   37, 39
Hatti   149, 153, 207, 210, 211, 212
Hazor, Tel   59, 87, 94, 97, 98, 177–79, 185, 188, 237
   Building 7050   177–79, 188, 191, 193
Hebron Hills   237
Hellenistic period. *See* Archaeological Periods
   at the end of the index
Herakles. *See also* Melqart   24, 26, 28
Hermes   268
Herodotus   24, 200, 264 n. 3, 265
Hesi, Tell el-   98
Hessek Höyük. *See* Hassek Höyük
Hilal (Ugaritic god)   256
Hiram I (king of Tyre)   24, 25
Hittite
   empire/territory   209, 210, 212, 216
   peace treaty with Egypt   207
   people   153, 154
   port   211–12
   rituals   61
   royalty   210–11, 212–13
   texts   149, 154, 212, 294, 320, 321
   war against Assyria   210
Hiyawa-men   153
Homer   144, 320, 321
Ḥorbat Ṭurit   135–36
Horned God statue, Enkomi   307–308
horned helmets   322, 324, 327–28, 330–31

House of Bronzes, Enkomi   310
"House of the father" model   255
House of Kadmos, Kadmeia, Thebes   185–91, 193
"House society" model   247–49, 252, 255, 257
House of the Tiles tumulus, Lerna   179–80, 188, 191
House of Urtenu   207
Huelva   266, 267

ICP-MS analysis. *See* chemical analysis
Idamaraṣ   61
Ilimilku   207–209, 211, 216, 217
Immeya (king of Ebla)   253
incense burners   290, 294, 296–97
Ingot God (statue)   239
ingots   291, 296, 303–306, 308, 310, 312, 314
   ingot from Tell Beit Mirsim   221–42
   ingot cargo from the Cape Gelidonya
      shipwreck   161–75, 301–302
   miniature ingots   225, 236–42
Ionia   76
Ionian Islands   264
Ionians (*Iaunaya/Iamnaya*)   144
Iris, messenger of the gods   268
Irkab-Damu (king of Ebla)   251–52
Iron Age. *See* Archaeological Periods at the
   end of the index
Išar-Damu (king of Ebla)   251
Ischia   110, 111, 262
islands
   Aegean Islands   320
   artificial   115, 120
   contextualization and typology of ancient
      island harbors in the
      Mediterranean   105–21
   intra-lagoonal   110, 111, 117–19
   Ionian Islands   264
   linked to the mainland by tombolos   110, 112–15
   maritime   110, 111, 121
   paleoislands   110, 111–12
Isola Grande   117
isotope analysis. *See* chemical analysis
Israel, kingdom of   251
Isthmus of Corinth   262, 264, 267, 271

Jemdet Nasr culture   43, 44
Jemmeh, Tell   59, 92, 94

INDEX

Jericho   37, 59, 252, 253, 255
Jerusalem   77
Jezirah area   39, 43
Jezirah culture   35, 43
Jezreel Valley   76, 130
Judah, Babylonian province   69–78
Judaidah, Tell   35, 39
Judean Highlands/Hills/hill country   69–70, 72 n. 3, 75–76

Kabri, Tel   96
Kadmeia, Thebes   180–82, 185, 187
Kalavasos, Cyprus   239
Kalavasos-Ayios Dhimitrios   292, 304
Kalopsidha   95, 96, 97, 98
Kamid el-Loz   253, 255
Karpass Peninsula   95, 96
Kato Syme   236
Kato Zakros   236
Kazaphani   93
Keisan, Tell   202
   Cypriot pottery from   81–99
Kerameikos, Athens   267
Khafajah   34
Khalid, Wadi   234
Khirbe, -el, Lod Valley. *See also* Nesher-Ramla Quarry   31
kingship   200–201, 253, 257
Kinyras (king of Paphos)   200–201
Kishon River. *See also* Naḥal Kishon   120
Kition, Cyprus   94, 147, 199–200, 201, 291, 304–305
Kizzuwatna   212
Knossos   266
Kolonna   324, 330
Kom ed-Dahab   111, 117
Kommos   266
Kos   323, 328
Kouklia. *See also* Palaepaphos   199
Kouklia-Mantissa   93
Koukounaries   147
Kourion-Bamboula   85, 94
*kudurru*s   212
Kültepe   216
Kura   251
Kura's Gate, Ebla   251
Kwakiult   247–48, 257
Kynos, East Lokris   146, 323, 323 n. 1, 326, 328

Kythera   96

La Valletta   111
Lachish   93, 95, 98, 296
Lady of Byblos   201
Lake Manzala   117
Lamaštu cult   61, 62–64
Land of Amurru   153
Lapithos-Ayia Anastasia   94
Last Glacial Maximum   120
Late Bronze Age. *See* Archaeological Periods at the end of the index
Late Cypriot (LC) period
   Enkomi   92
   Paphos   199
   pottery   87, 91–94, 95–98, 99 n. 7, 292
   scrap metal and bronze industry at Enkomi in   300–14
Late Geometric period   263 n. 2, 265 n. 5
Late Helladic (LH) period
   Kadmeia   181–82, 187
   pottery   146, 292, 323, 323 n., 324–25, 331
   ship imagery and models   145–46, 292, 322–23, 323 n. 1, 324–25, 329, 331
   Tiryns   185
Late Minoan period   236–38, 322, 326, 328, 329, 331
Late Mycenaean period   185
Late Pleistocene   105
Latmian Gulf   112
Lebanese coast   21, 22, 43, 75, 75 n. 7, 120
Lebanon Valley   43
Lerna   179–80, 184, 185, 188, 191, 193
Lesbos/Lazpa   154
Levant Period 3 (ARCANE periods)   44
Levantine coast   72, 75–76, 81, 106, 128, 130, 200, 264 n. 3. 296
Lévi-Strauss, C., House society model   247–57
Libyans   319
LiDAR (Light Detection and Ranging)   129, 132, 134–36, 139
Liman Tepe   146
limekilns   137
Linear A   329
Linear B   145, 149, 152
Lion harbor, Miletos   112
Lod, Tel   45–46
lost-wax technique   240–41

Lower Galilee 130
Lukka/Lukka-lands. *See also* Lycia 153–54, 210, 319
Lukka/Lukki (people) 149, 153, 318–20
Lycia. *See also* Lukka 153, 210, 212, 319, 320

Maa-Palaeokastro 147, 305
Magna Graecia 111
Maison d'Ourtenu. *See* House of Urtenu
Malatia-Elaziğ region 39
Malta 105, 111
Manzala Lagoon 117
Marduk 64
Mari 61, 250, 252–53, 255
Mari letters 61
Marki-Alonia 312
Maroni, Cyprus 239
Marsala 117
marzēaḥ 76, 253
masks 69–77
Mathiatis 240 n. 26, 241
Maya 247
medieval period/Middle Ages. *See* Archaeological Periods at the end of the index
Medinet Habu reliefs 145, 146, 149, 152, 319, 321, 322, 327, 328, 330
Mediterranean Sea 55, 105–21, 130, 143
Megadim, Tel 96, 97
Megiddo, Tel 44, 45, 93, 94, 95, 96, 97, 98, 99, 212, 253, 255, 292, 296
Melqart. *See also* Herakles 22, 24, 26, 28
Menander of Ephesus 25
Menelaus 155
mercenaries 153–55, 319, 329, 330, 331
Merenptah/Merneptah (pharaoh) 149, 153, 207, 319
Meshwesh 319
Mesopotamia 65, 236, 253, 256, 263
 animal cult 60–62
 chronology 39, 43–44
 cult of Lamaštu 62–64
 pottery 34–37, 39–43
 societal development 249–57
Mesopotamian period 35
metal
 artifacts. *See also* ingots 31, 69, 161–75, 212, 221–42, 265, 269 n. 10, 290, 294, 296, 300–14, 328

blister copper 230, 232, 240–42
bronze industry on Cyprus 300–14
copper production 163–66, 223, 239, 305
hoards 240 n. 26, 304–306, 308, 310–14
metalworking 163, 202, 222–23, 230, 291, 304, 306, 308, 314
scrap metal 161, 163–64, 168, 174, 242, 291, 300–14
metallographic analysis 164, 168–72, 174, 230
Mevorakh, Tel 87, 95, 97, 98, 290
Michal, Tel 99
Middle Assyrian period 212
Middle Babylonian period 212
Middle Bronze Age. *See* Archaeological Periods at the end of the index
Middle Cypriot (MC) period
 Ambelikou 237
 Paphos 199
 pottery 95–98, 237
Middle Euphrates period 33–35 33 n. 1, 37
Middle Helladic period
 pottery 322, 324–25
 ruin mounds 181, 183, 184, 191
 ship imagery and models 322, 324–25
Middle Minoan period 329, 330
Middle Pleistocene 111
Miletos/Miletus 110, 112, 121, 146, 320
 archipelago 112
Milia 97
milk-bowls 85
Milkyaton (king of Kition) 199–200
miši 149, 153
MLKTQDŠT, Phoenician goddess 201
Minoan
 Cypro-Minoan signs 239, 239 n. 25
 iconography 322, 330, 331
 Minoan-type signs 330
 pottery 293, 329
 society/people 247, 290
 thalassocracy 114
Mitrou, East Lokris 324, 326
Mochlos 236
Modi, islet 147
Monte Argentario 114
Mor, Tel 93
Mozia 108 n. 1, 111, 117
Mycenae 328
Mycenaean
 architecture 179, 180, 182–83

INDEX

burials 184, 191
collapse 146
culture 201, 321
customs 145
elite 184
Greece 145, 320
iconography 292, 331
Linear B documents 145
palatial ruin mounds 185–88
piracy 145
pottery 145–46, 207, 292, 323–31
ritual 321
ships 145
society/people 146, 248, 320
Mycenaean period 183, 186, 187
Mykonos 111
Myrtou-Pigadhes 85
myths/mythology 25–28, 62, 182–83, 193, 200, 208, 216, 266

Naḥal Kishon. *See also* Kishon River 130
Naḥal Kziv 130
Naḥal Meʻarot 327
Naḥal Naʻaman 130
Naḥal Oren 327
Nami, Tel 218, 269 n. 10
 Aegean-type pottery from 278–97, 327
 Cypriot pottery from 290, 293, 294–95
 "Horizon Nami" 297
Naqada culture 37–39, 43–44
Naṣbeh, Tell en- 69–78
naval battles 146, 152–54, 318–19, 321
Nea Paphos 202
necropoli. *See also* cemeteries
 at al-Bass, Tyre 14, 269 n. 10
 at ʻEin Asawir 31
 Laurita necropolis at Almuñécar 264 n. 4
 near Mozia 117
 at Tel Nami 293–94
 at Nea Paphos, eastern necropolis 202
Neo-Assyrian period 62, 64, 213
Neo-Babylonian period 60, 62, 202
Neolithic period. *See* Archaeological Periods at the end of the index
Nesher-Ramla Quarry. *See also* Khirbe, el- 31–46
neutron activation analysis. *See* chemical analysis

Nikokles (king of Paphos) 201–202
Nile Delta 37, 43, 111, 115, 117, 120, 146
Ninevite 5 culture 35, 39, 43, 44
Niqmaddu III (king of Ugarit) 207, 210–11
"Nomads of the Sea," 142
Nonnus of Panopolis 26–28
Norşuntepe 39
Northern Levant 1–2 (ARCANE periods) 35
Nuragic society 248

Odysseus 155
Oiniadai 110, 112, 121
Olbia de Provence 114
Old Akkadian period 215
Old Assyrian period 216
Old Babylonian period 215, 255, 256
Olympia 180, 183, 188, 191, 193
Oman 234
Orbetello 110, 112, 113, 114, 121
Orontes Valley 43
Ottoman period. *See* Archaeological Periods at the end of the index
Ousoos 25

palaces 184, 255
 at Alalakh 252, 253
 burials in/under 252–55
 at Byblos 252–53
 at Ebla, Palace G 21, 251–53
 at Ebla, the Western Palace 253, 255
 at Tel Hazor 177
 at Jericho 252–53, 255
 at Kadmos 186
 at Kamid el-Loz 253, 255
 at Mari 252, 253–54, 255
 at Megiddo 253, 255
 palatial ruin mounds 185–88
 at Phaistos 329
 at Qatna 252, 255
 their role in etiological tales 193
 at Tel Taʻanach 253
 at Tiryns 185, 188, 191
 at Tuttul 252
 at Ugarit 207, 217, 255
Palaepaphos. *See also* Kouklia 147, 199, 201, 202
Palaepaphos-Evreti 202
Palaepaphos-Teratsoudhia 85–86
Palaityros/Palaetyros 22

Palastin/Walastin (kingdom in Hatay
    region) 320
Paliotaverna 304
Palm Islands, Dubai 115
Pamphylia 153
Paphos 199–202
Papyrus Harris I 152, 319, 321
Paramali S13–97 312
Paros 111, 147
Pausanias 200
Pelasgoi/Pelastoi 319, 321
Peleset 319–21, 327
Pella 37
Pelopion tumulus, Olympia 183, 188, 191
Peloponnese 179, 212
Pelops 183, 193
Penteskouphia 267, 270
Periander 264 n. 3
Persian period. See Archaeological Periods at the end of the index
petrographic analysis 75 n. 7, 293, 295
Phaistos 328
Phaistos Disc 328–30
Pharos of Alexandria 115
Philistia 76, 320–21, 323
Philistines 146, 319
Philo of Byblos 25, 27
Phoenicia/n 14, 106
    coast 77–78, 200–201
    kingdom of 251
    mask 69–77
    necropolis at al-Bass, Tyre 14, 269 n. 10
    Phoenicians and Corinth 262–72
    pottery 69, 199, 202, 263, 264 nn. 2, 4, 265, 271
    presence in Paphos 199–202
    scripts and inscriptions 28, 199, 201, 202
    ships 262, 264 n. 3, 266, 267–70, 272
    Tanit 265 n. 8
Phylakopi 323
Pillars of Herakles 28
piracy/pirates 142–56, 216
Pisaskion, Messenia 331
Pithecusa/Pithecusae (Ischia) 110, 111, 262, 263–64
Plain of Akko Regional Survey
    (PARS) 128–39
Pliny the Elder 130–31, 265
Plutarch, Life of Pompey 144

Politiko 96, 97
Politiko-Lambertis 96
Politiko-Troullia 312
Poros 147
Poseidon 267
pottery
    Abydos Ware 43, 44
    Aegean-type 278–97
    Argive monochrome 263 n. 1
    Attic 265 n. 4, 266–67
    Base Ring Ware 92–93, 99, 294
    Base Ring Ware I 92–93
    Base Ring Ware II 92–93, 290, 294–95
    Bichrome Ware 94–95, 99
    ceramic disc, 'Akko 54, 54 n. 4, 62
    comb-incised ware 18–21
    Composite Ware 98–99
    contribution of imported pottery to chronology 31–46
    Corinthian 263–65, 263–64 n. 2, 264 n. 4, 265 n. 6, 267, 270
    cylinder-seal-impressed ware 21
    Cypriot pottery from Tell Keisan 81–99
    Egyptian 31, 37–39, 43, 44–45
    Euboean 262–63 n. 2, 263, 266–67, 271
    Fine Gray Burnished/Gray Minyan Ware 324
    Greek 76–77, 264, 265 n. 4
    Greek fine ware at Tell en-Naṣbeh 69, 75–77, 76 n. 11
    "Greek style"/East Greek ware at Tell en-Naṣbeh 75–76
    Handmade Burnished Ware 145
    Late Helladic (LH) 146, 292, 323, 324, 325, 326, 327, 328, 330, 331
    Late Reserve Slip Ware (LRSW) 33–35, 37, 43–44
    Matt-Painted Ware 324, 324 n. 2
    Mesopotamian 34–37, 39–43
    Minoan 293, 328–30
    Minoan-type 290
    Monochrome Ware 93–94, 99
    Mycenaean 145–46, 207, 292, 323–31
    oval-shaped body (OSB) juglets 39, 44, 45
    Philistine Bichrome ware 326
    Phoenician 69, 199, 202, 263, 264 nn. 2, 4, 265, 271

INDEX

Plain White Wheel-made Ware 290
proto-Corinthian 265
proto-Rhodian 202
Red-on-Black ware 95, 99
Rhodian 263, 263 n. 2, 265
    Vertically-Pierced Lugged-Handle (VPLH)
        goblets 33, 36–37, 43, 44
    Warrior Vase, Mycenae 328, 331
    White Painted Ware 95–98, 99
    White Shaved Ware 290, 294, 296
    White Slip Ware 84–92, 99, 295
    White Slip Ware I 84, 85–87
    White Slip Ware II 84, 87–92, 290
    White Slip Ware III (White Slip II late) 91–92, 99 n. 7
    workshops 292–93, 295
    zoomorphic vessels 93
Prehistoric Cypriot Bronze Age (PreBA) 312
Protogeometric period 183
Protohistoric Cypriot Bronze Age (ProBA) 312
Pseudo-Scylax 265 n.4
Puduhepa (queen of Hatti) 213
pumice 290, 291, 293
Punic West 266, 268
Punta degli Stretti promontory 114
Pyla-Kokkinokremnos 147
Pylos 212
Pyrgos-Mavrorachi 312

Qashish, Tel 45
Qatna 252–53, 255
Qiryat Ata 45
Qodi 149
quarries 137–38

Raba'in, er- 134
radiocarbon dating 37, 39, 43, 237, 322
Ramesses II (pharaoh) 145, 149, 207, 213, 318–19, 321, 329, 330
Ramesses III (pharaoh) 146, 149, 152–53, 319, 320, 321, 330
Rap'anu 207
Raqā'i, Tell al- 63
Ras el-'Ayn 22
Ras en-Naqurah/Rosh ha-Niqra 130
Ras Ibn Hani 111, 115, 216
Ras Shamra, Tell. *See also* Ugarit 205

Ratiye, Wadi 234
Recent Bronze Age (Italy) 322
relative sea level, changes in 108, 111, 112, 115, 120
Rhodes 263
Rhône River 121
Rib-Adda/Rib Addi 153–54
Ridan, Tell er- 92
"ritual tumuli" 179–83, 188, 191–92
Roman period. *See* Archaeological Periods at the end of the index
ruin mounds impacting social memory 177–93
Rundbau tumulus, Tiryns 184, 185, 188, 191

sacrifices 25–27, 58, 61–62, 64, 290, 293
Safi, Tell es- 75–76
Saint Augustine 144
Sakan, Tell es- 37, 38
Samemrumos 25
San Pantaleo island 117
Sanchuniathon 25
Sanctuary of the Horned God, Enkomi 93
Sant'Imbenia, Sardinia 266
sarcophagus from Gazi 326
Sardinia 106, 234, 236, 262, 319–20
Sarepta 94, 95, 96, 97, 98
Sargon I (Assyrian king) 259
Saronic Gulf 111, 147, 264, 267
satyr 71, 75–76
scarab 71
Sea Peoples/sea peoples 142, 145, 146, 148, 149, 152, 154, 216
    identity, sociopolitical context, and antecedents 318–31
    headgear 31, 327–31
    ships 321–27
sedimentary budget (input) 108, 110, 112–15, 117, 120
Šekelesh/Shekelesh/Sikala. *See also* Šikila 153, 319–20, 321, 327–28, 330
Semele 186
Seti (pharaoh) 207
Shakkan/Sumuqan 61
Shardana. *See also* Sherden 318–20, 321, 329, 330, 331
Sharelli (queen of Ugarit) 211, 215
Shephelah 31, 76, 77, 221, 237
Sherden. *See also* Shardana 145, 319

ships   105, 117, 143–44, 145, 154–55, 264, 264 n. 3, 271–72
    Greek   267
    iconography   64, 145, 146, 155, 267–70, 321–27, 330
    mentioned in ancient texts   144, 149, 152–54, 210
    Phoenician   262, 264 n. 3, 266, 267–70, 272
    Sea People's   321–27
    ship models   145, 322–23
    warships   145, 153, 264 n. 3, 268, 270, 318, 321, 329, 331
Shipti-Baalu   207
shipwrecks   161–75, 212, 224 n. 8, 225, 228 n. 12, 234, 236, 238, 301, 303
Shiqmona, Tel   59
Shiukh Fawqani, Tell   39
Shuna, Tel es-   37
Sicily   106, 319, 320
Sidon
    in ancient texts   154, 207
    coins from   269 n. 10
    model of the Paphian kingship at   201
    pig burial at   60
    pottery in   20, 21, 96, 97, 98
Sikels   320
Šikila. *See also* Šekelesh/Shekelesh/Sikala   149, 153
Sinai, northern   37
Siptaḥ (pharaoh)   240, 240 n. 27
Skyros   323
social elites   46
social memory   177–93
southern Arabia   296
Stagnone Lagoon   117
stamp seals   76
Stavroti-Alaminos   96
Stephania   94, 95, 97
stone tools   18, 31, 222
stone vessels   19
Strabo   263
Strofilas, on Andros Island   326
Subprotogeometric period   271
Suppiluliuma   210
Ṣumur   154
Syria   57, 210, 251, 253, 330
    animal burials in   60–62

coast   120, 161
kingdoms   251, 253, 320
seafarers   290
Syros (island in the Cyclades)   326

Ta'anach, Tel   253
Tabur-Damu   251–52
Tacitus   200
Tale of Wenamun   152–54, 200
Tanagra, Boeotia   322
Tanaja (land)   320
Tanit   265 nn. 5, 6, 268, 268–69 n. 10
Tartous   106
Ta'yinat, Tell   320
Teluleth-Thalathrat   39
temples
    animal burials in   58, 60
    of Aphrodite/Aphrodite Ourania   200, 265, 265 n.8
    at Ashkelon   200, 265
    at Byblos   200
    at Corinth   265 n. 8
    Eanna temple at Uruk   60
    Fosse Temple at Lachish   296
    at Tel Hazor   177
    at Ḥorbat Ṭurit   135
    Isthmian sanctuary   264, 266
    at Kition   304
    Kura's Temple at Ebla   251, 253
    at Tel Nami, sanctuary   290–91
    at Medinet Habu   146
    at Tel Mevorakh   87, 290
    at Mozia   117
    at Paphos   200
    at Penteskouphia, sanctuary of Poseidon   267, 270
    prostitution in   265 n. 8
    their role in etiological tales   193
    Temple 50 at Tell Abu Hawam   93
    Temple of Gu-la at Isin   60
    at Tyre   21, 22, 24, 26
Tepe Gawra   34
Teresh/Tursha   319–20
The World, archipelago in Dubai   115
Thebes, Greece   180–82, 184, 185, 188–91, 193, 328
Thebes, Upper Egypt   236, 319
Theopompus   200

INDEX 351

Thucydides 144, 271
Thutmose III (pharaoh) 152, 303, 320
Tigris area 39
Timnah 93, 94, 234
tinkers 161, 163, 164
Tiryns 180, 183, 188, 193, 292, 323, 323 n. 1, 326, 327
   Building T at 185, 191
Tjeker 152–54, 319, 320, 321, 327
tomboloi 110, 112–15, 121
tombs. See also burial
   at Tell el-'Ajjul 59, 60
   at Tel 'Akko 58, 59, 60
   at Alalakh palace. 252
   at Aya Irini 85
   on Cyprus 304
   at Tell el-Dab'a 59–60
   at Ebla, Palace G 252
   at Ebla, the Western palace 253
   at 'Ein Asawir 31–32, 37, 38, 43, 44–45
   at Enkomi 92, 93, 94
   at Tell el-Far'ah (N) 44–45
   at Giv'at Tantur 137–38
   at Hassek Höyük 37
   at Tel Hazor 59
   hypogea under palaces 252–55
   at Inshas 60
   at Tell Jemmeh 59
   at Jericho 59
   at Kition 94
   at Kolonna, warrior's grave 330
   at Kourion-Bamboula 85, 94
   at Lapithos-Ayia Anastasia 94
   at Tell el-Maskhuta 60
   at Tel Megiddo 45
   at Tel Nami 293–97
   at Palaepaphos-Skales 199
   at Palaepaphos-Teratsoudhia 85, 86
   at Tel Shiqmona 59
   at Stephania 94
   at Tragana 323, 331
   at Ugarit 93, 255–56
   at Umm el-Marra 253
trade and exchange 37, 43, 45, 46, 76, 77, 99, 111, 119, 120, 128, 142, 143, 147, 154, 163, 200, 215
   of copper 165, 166, 199, 234, 236, 237, 238, 242, 296, 303
   in correlation with piracy 143, 145, 154–55
   maritime trade/transfer 43, 75–77, 81, 99, 105, 119, 128, 142, 143–44, 161, 174, 200, 213, 264, 266, 271, 296, 330
   rag-and-bone trade at Enkomi 300–14
   sailors' trade 142, 271, 291
   from southern Phoenicia to northern Judah in the late Iron Age and Persian periods 69–78
Tragana 323, 331
Transjordan 56, 69, 77
Trikardo 112
Troad 321
Troodos foothills 199
Tudhaliya IV (Hittite king) 210
Turkey 105, 110, 112, 146, 161, 212, 234, 236
Tuttul 252
Tweini, Tell 210
Twosret (pharaoh) 240, 240 n. 27
Tylissos 236
Tyre 106, 115, 121, 266, 271
   ancient island of 14–18, 21–22, 24, 26, 106, 108 n. 1, 110, 115
   continental. See also Ushu 22, 24, 25
   Cypriot pottery from 94, 95, 96, 271
   Early Bronze Age foundation 14–28
   international trade to 77
   Ladder of Tyre 130
   in legends and myths 25–28
   mentioned in ancient texts 154, 207
   "The Rock" 22, 24
Tyre Project 14
Tyrsenoi (Etruscans) 319

Ugarit. See also Ras Shamra, Tell 62, 93, 95, 96, 97, 98, 146, 153, 154, 200, 205–18, 251, 253, 255–56, 257
Ugaritic texts 61, 149, 154, 205–18
   RS 94.2406 205–18
Ullasa 154
Uluburun shipwreck 166, 168, 173, 212–13, 225, 227, 228 n. 12, 230, 234, 236, 238, 239 n. 25, 302
Umm el-Marra 253
Uni (Weni), autobiography of 145
United Arab Emirates 234
Upper Egyptian Chronology 39

Ur, Third Dynasty of   60
Urfa   236
Urnfield   264
Urtenu/Urtenu's archive   205–17
Uruk   60
Uruk culture   39, 43
Ushu/Ušu   22, 24, 25, 154

Varangians   264 n. 3
Vathy, island of Astypalaia   326, 326 n. 3
Via Maris   56
Villanovan
    society   248
    boat models   322
Venetian Lagoon   117, 119
Veneto, Italy   117
Venice   106, 110, 111, 117, 119

Wadi Selman   120
Warrior Vase from Mycenae   328, 331
Weshesh   319, 320, 321, 328, 330
winepresses   137

writing boards   212–13

Xerxes   264 n. 3
XRF analyis. *See* chemical analysis
Xylinos   201

Yabninu   207
Yarmuth, Tel   37
Yassi Ada shipwreck   212
Yehawmilk Stele   201
Yehud province   69–78, 77 n. 13
Yemen   234
Yeri   96
Yurok   247–48, 257

Zakariya, Tell (Azekah)   93
Zethus, mythical founder of Thebes   182–83, 193
Zeus   186
Zimri-Lim   61
zoomorphic figurines   308

Printed in the United States
By Bookmasters